The Golden Age of the Chinese Bourgeoisie 1911–1937

Studies in modern capitalism. Etudes sur le capitalisme moderne

This series is devoted to an attempt to comprehend capitalism as a world-system. It will include monographs, collections of essays and colloquia around specific themes, written by historians and social scientists united by a common concern for the study of large-scale, long-term social structure and social change.

The series is a joint enterprise of the Maison des Sciences de l'Homme in Paris and the Fernand Braudel Center for the Study of Economies, Historical Systems, and Civilizations at the State University of New York at Binghamton.

For other titles in the series please see the end of the book.

This book is published as part of the joint publishing agreement established in 1977 between the Fondation de la Maison des Sciences de l'Homme and the Press Syndicate of the University of Cambridge. Titles published under this arrangement may appear in any European language or, in the case of volumes of collected essays, in several languages.

New books will appear either as individual titles or in one of the series which the Maison des Sciences de l'Homme and the Cambridge University Press have jointly agreed to publish. All books published jointly by the Maison des Sciences de l'Homme and the Cambridge University Press will be distributed by the Press throughout the world.

The Golden Age of the Chinese Bourgeoisie 1911–1937

MARIE-CLAIRE BERGÈRE

Translated by JANET LLOYD

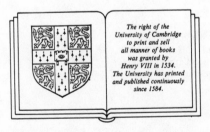

The right of the
University of Cambridge
to print and sell
all manner of books
was granted by
Henry VIII in 1534.
The University has printed
and published continuously
since 1584.

CAMBRIDGE UNIVERSITY PRESS
Cambridge
New York   Port Chester   Melbourne   Sydney

EDITIONS DE
LA MAISON DES SCIENCES DE L'HOMME
Paris

Published by the Press Syndicate of the University of Cambridge
The Pitt Building, Trumpington Street, Cambridge CB2 1RP
40 West 20th Street, New York, NY 10011, USA
10 Stamford Road, Oakleigh, Melbourne 3166, Australia
and Editions de la Maison des Sciences de l'Homme
54 Boulevard Raspail, 75270 Paris Cedex 06

Originally published in France as *L'Age d'or de la bourgeoisie chinoise*
by Flammarion 1986
and © Editions Flammarion 1986

First published in English by Editions de la Maison des Sciences de l'Homme and Cambridge
University Press 1989 as *The Golden Age of the Chinese Bourgeoisie*

English translation © Maison des Sciences de l'Homme and Cambridge University Press 1989

Printed in Great Britain

British Library cataloguing in publication data

Bergère, Marie-Claire.
The golden age of the Chinese bourgeoisie,
1911–1937. – (Studies in modern capitalism –
Etudes sur le capitalisme moderne).
1. China. Middle classes, 1911–1937.
I. Title. II. Series. III. L'âge d'or de la
bourgeoisie chinoise. *English*
305.5′5′0951.

Library of Congress cataloguing in publication data

Bergère, Marie-Claire.
[Age d'or de la bourgeoisie chinoise, 1911–1937. English]
The golden age of the Chinese bourgeoisie, 1911–1937 /
Marie-Claire Bergère; translated by Janet Lloyd.
    p.   cm. – (Studies in modern capitalism – Etudes sur le capitalisme moderne).
Translation of: L'âge d'or de la bourgeoisie chinoise, 1911–1937.
Bibliography.
Includes index.
ISBN 0 521 32054 2.
1. Middle classes – China – History – 20th century.
2. Businessmen – China – History – 20th century. 3. China – Social
conditions – 1912–1949. 4. China – Economic conditions – 1912–1949.
5. China – Politics and government – 1912–1949. 6. Shanghai (China) –
Social conditions. I. Title. II. Series: Studies in modern capitalism.
HT690.C55B4713   1989
305.5′5′0951 – dc19   88–31515 CIP.

ISBN 0 521 32054 2
ISBN 2 7351 03137 (France only)

CE

Contents

Illustrations

Acknowledgement

The maps and graphic work were produced by Madame Françoise Vergnault, of the Graphics Laboratory of the Ecole des Hautes Etudes en Sciences Sociales, Paris. I should like to express my thanks to her.

Note on the transcription of Chinese names

In this work, I have adopted the *pinyin* system, officially recognised by the People's Republic of China. However, a number of exceptions have been made in the cases of names familiar to the public in other forms, for example geographical names such as Peking, Nanking, Canton and Mukden; personal names such as Sun Yat-sen, Chiang Kai-shek, Chiang Kia-ngau, T. V. Soong, H. H. Kung and H. D. Fong; and company names such as Wing On and Sincere.

The names of Chinese authors mentioned in the notes and bibliography are transcribed in *pinyin*, except where the authors themselves use another method of transcription, in which case I have respected the form chosen by the author.

Note on Chinese weights and measurements

Mu, unit of area equivalent to 0.0667 hectares.

Picul, unit of weight equivalent to about 60 kilogrammes.

Catty, unit of weight equivalent to about 600 grammes.

Tael, traditional unit of currency corresponding to about 37–8 grammes of silver, depending on the locality and sector of activity involved. The customs tael used in the treaty ports by the Maritime Customs Administration and in statistics in general represented 38.40 grammes of pure silver and was worth 3.40 French francs in 1911, 7.11 francs in 1918 and 17.79 francs in 1920.

Dollar, a silver coin, the format and weight of which varied from one region to another. Its value, expressed in terms of the tael, fluctuated with the market. In Shanghai, it stabilised at around 0.71 of a tael for one dollar in the 1915–25 period. The term 'dollar', when not specified further, is used in this work to denote the Chinese silver dollar. When it is a matter of American money, the expression 'American dollar' is used.

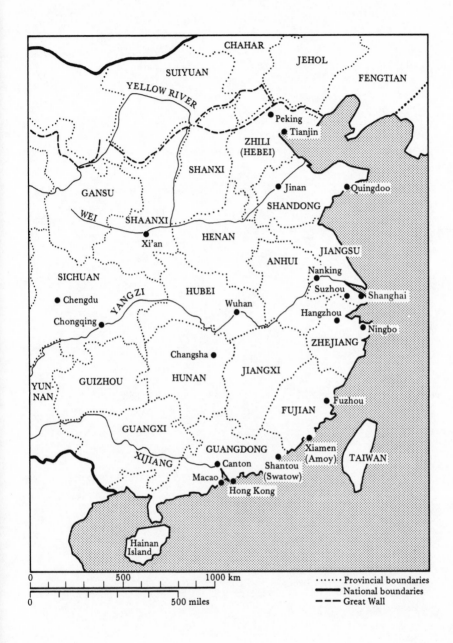

CHAHAR

JEHOL

SUIYUAN

FENGTIAN

YELLOW RIVER

Peking

Tianjin

ZHILI
(HEBEI)

SHANXI

GANSU

Jinan

Quingdoo

SHANDONG

WEI

SHAANXI

Xi'an

HENAN

JIANGSU

SICHUAN

ANHUI

Nanking

Chengdu

HUBEI

Suzhou

Shanghai

YANGZI

Wuhan

Hangzhou

Chongqing

Ningbo

ZHEJIANG

Changsha

YUN-
NAN

GUIZHOU

HUNAN

JIANGXI

GUANGXI

FUJIAN

Fuzhou

XIJIANG

GUANGDONG

Canton

Xiamen
(Amoy)

TAIWAN

Macao

Shantou
(Swatow)

Hong Kong

Hainan
Island

| 0 | 500 | 1000 km |

| 0 | 500 miles |

•••••• Provincial boundaries
——— National boundaries
– – – Great Wall

Prologue

The People's Republic and its bourgeois heritage

Peking, one September morning in 1979: the official whom I was waiting to see, on the imposing premises of the Chinese People's Consultative Political Conference, held a number of important positions. He was vice-chairman of the People's Political Consultative Conference, deputy for Shanghai to the National People's Congress and a member of the Standing Committee of that assembly. He was also chairman of the China International Trust and Investment Corporation and a director of the Bank of China. It had been no easy matter to obtain this interview.

The man who made his entrance, surrounded by about half a dozen assistants, looked younger than his official 63 years. He was dressed in the customary fashion for a Chinese cadre, in a tunic in the style of Sun Yat-sen, with a high collar and patch pockets. But his dynamic step and bearing put one more in mind of an American businessman. The gold pens in his breast pocket, the elegant watch on his wrist and his Italian-style leather shoes indicated at a glance that this was no ordinary cadre.

His name was Rong Yiren. He was the son of Rong Desheng and the nephew of Rong Zongjing, two of the wealthiest and most active industrialists of pre-communist China. The Rong family used to control the dozen or so factories of the Shenxin Cotton Mills (Shenxin fangzhi wuxian gongsi), and also the Fuxin and Maoxin Flour Mills (Fuxin mianfenchang, Maoxin mianfenchang). They were millionaires and were regarded as the Rockefellers of China. What was this Rockefeller doing in Peking? How could he be collaborating with a regime whose avowed intent had always been to wipe out capitalism? And why had the Communist Party leaders entrusted such important responsibilities to such a man?

After the death of Mao Zedong, in 1976, the new political economy introduced under the leadership of Deng Xiaoping called upon the entrepreneurs once again to play an important role in the development of China. The policy was founded upon agricultural de-collectivisation, the reform of industrial production and the reintroduction of the notions of responsibility and profit, and its aim was to reawaken private initiative. To win the cooperation of the former capitalists, in 1979 the government had decided to repay the salaries and dividends that had been suspended during the Cultural Revolution. In a single year, the equivalent of 600 million American dollars were thus spent on restoring the possessions of the former bourgeoisie.[1] 'Work and grow rich!' – Deng Xiaoping was beginning to sound like Guizot. It is true that the exhortations that Guizot used to direct at the French bourgeoisie were now addressed by Deng to the peasants. But even in the towns the private sector was developing. It expanded by 33% in 1979 and 1981, and by 1983 the number of private businesses in the trade and service sectors had risen to 3.2 million.[2]

Furthermore, the regime assigned important economic and administrative functions to a number of former leading capitalists, placing them in particular at the head of bodies that had to deal with foreigners. Rong Yiren was but one example: there were many others, such as Guo Dihuo, whose family had owned the Wing On (Yong'an) businesses before the revolution. He now headed the Guangdong Investment Company, with the mission of encouraging overseas Chinese, many of whom originally hailed from that province, to invest in the mother country.[3] Even more delicate was the task entrusted to Wang Guangying. In the aftermath of the 1949 revolution, Wang Guangyin had been nicknamed the 'red capitalist'. He was the son of a major industrialist of Tianjin and the brother of Wang Guangmei (Madame Liu Shaoqi). Rehabilitated after the grim experiences of the Cultural Revolution, he was sent in the spring of 1983 to Hong Kong to set up and direct the Guang Ming Company, the function of which was to negotiate the purchase of industrial equipment and encourage trade with countries that as yet had no diplomatic relations with China.

Many observers were surprised at this turn of events. After all, all Chinese businesses had been nationalised and their owners relieved of their responsibilities way back in 1956. Some even began to wonder whether China might not revert to capitalism! However naive such speculation may have been on the part of foreign commentators, it was certainly not disinterested when it came from the opponents of reform, survivors of Maoism or those nostalgic for orthodox Stalinism. But at least it has the merit of attracting attention to the persistence or recurrence of certain problematic aspects of modernisation and to the ambiguity of the relations obtaining between the State and the elite groups whose aid was now being enlisted – in short, to the vitality of the bourgeois heritage of which Rong Yiren, at once cadre and capitalist, may be seen as a symbol.

The course of events that led to the publication of this work

One remote effect of these post-Maoist upheavals was to reawaken my own longstanding interest in the history of the Chinese bourgeoisie. It had been strong enough to prompt me to follow a line of research which, after ten years' work, had resulted in 1975, in my *doctorat d'Etat* dissertation 'The problems of development and the role of the Chinese bourgeoisie: the economic crisis of 1920–1923'.[4] I had encountered a number of obstacles in preparing this thesis. The customary trials experienced during this kind of university work had been compounded by the particular difficulties involved in collecting and interpreting the documentary evidence and also by the cumbersome adoption of the monographic form to explore an area – that of contemporary Chinese economics and society – then (and still today) relatively unknown, even in its most general features.

But the principal difficulty lay elsewhere. My research had originally been inspired by Jean Chesneaux, one of the pioneers of Chinese twentieth-century studies in France. It was one panel in a triptych that also included the study of the other 'founding' classes of modern China – the proletariat and the peasants. From the Marxist point of view that was held by our teachers and that dominated the 1960s, the study of the proletariat needed no justification. It was regarded as not only legitimate but indispensable.[5] As for the peasantry, everyone knew – until, that is, Lucien Bianco's work cast doubt upon the matter [6] – that it was the source from which the Chinese revolution had sprung. The case of the bourgeoisie was more ambiguous. Distinctions were made between various groups within it: 'the comprador bourgeoisie' under foreign influence, the 'bureaucratic bourgeoisie' linked to a reactionary political apparatus and, finally, the 'national bourgeoisie', the only group that had worked for the progress and modernisation of the

country. Even this national bourgeoisie was subject to violent contradictions and spectacular reversals of policy: after all, on two occasions
(1911 and 1927), it had stood by and watched while revolutions that it
had itself actively helped to prepare were crushed. However, the major
characteristic of this bourgeoisie was its weakness; it was this that had
prevented it from accomplishing its historical mission of facilitating a
transition from the *ancien régime* to the proletarian revolution.

However, as my research proceeded, its subject began to dissolve:
the economic criteria used to distinguish between the various categories of the bourgeoisie seemed increasingly illusory; the contradictions between the 'revolutionary essence' of the (national) bourgeoisie, on the one hand, and its political practices on the other,
became more and more irreconcilable. I began to get the feeling that
from the (then predominant) point of view of the history of the
revolution, the study of the bourgeoisie was of very limited interest. Its
emergence in Chinese society during the 1910–20 period was no more
than a marginal episode, just a historical hiccough. Having defended
my thesis, I gave up the idea of publishing it.

Revolution and modernity

The priority now granted to modernisation over revolution in China
prompts one to reconsider the bourgeoisie's contribution to twentieth-
century Chinese history. It suggests that we should dissociate the two
elements of that revolution–modernity pair for so long welded
together by dogma. The success of Japan and of other new industrial
countries (Singapore, Hong Kong, Taiwan, South Korea) has already
demonstrated that the path that leads to economic progress is not
necessarily that of social and political revolution (even if, in the long
run, such progress may lead to revolutionary upheavals in the societies
and political systems involved). The phenomenon of the Chinese
bourgeoisie played no more than a minor role in the revolutionary
process. Nevertheless, that bourgeoisie was the first to identify its own
destiny and that of China as a whole with economic modernisation. In
the space of a few decades it explored many of the problems of
development and suggested and tried out a wide variety of solutions.

More than half a century has passed and China has moved on. But
the world around it has changed even more. The problem of backwardness is as crucial in the 1980s as it was in the 1920s. Without financial

and technical support from more advanced countries, China still has little hope of closing the gap between itself and them. Yet it continues to hesitate over the strategy to adopt in order to avoid the dangers of foreign domination and acculturation that are inseparable from any foreign intervention. Thirty years after the revolution, the importance of coastal China in the development of the national economy seems as great as ever. The remedy that would do away with this blatant dualism that is such a source of grave injustices has still not been found. It is hoped that, in the new political and economic atmosphere now prevailing, the special economic zones that it was decided to create in 1979 will serve as pilot regions and as intermediary staging posts, filling the role formerly taken by the treaty ports. Finally, the repeated attempts to rehabilitate light industry testify to the difficulty of establishing priorities. The production of consumer goods, once decried as a product of colonialism and abandoned in favour of a Stalinist strategy founded upon heavy industry, is now regarded as a stimulus to growth.

The regime has changed. But the failures and, even more, the successes of Chinese capitalism which, in the 1920s, was faced with the very same dilemmas as those that confront the leaders of today, are full of useful lessons.

It is not surprising, then, if the phenomenon of the Chinese bourgeoisie continues to inspire those who destroyed it and who dream of succeeding where it failed. It is natural – or, at any rate, common – to underestimate men or movements that are overcome by history. But the progressive and cosmopolitan force produced by the bourgeois phenomenon has survived. It may no longer dominate the course of history but it animates and fuels it. It is a force that the leaders of today are, in their turn, trying to exploit. That is why it eventually seemed to me worthwhile revising and publishing a piece of university research which had been put aside for close on ten years.

The bourgeoisie in all its different dimensions

The present work only partially reproduces the text of the 1975 thesis, however. Chapter 1 and the Epilogue have been added to give the study greater chronological depth and to highlight both continuities and discontinuities. On the other hand, in Chapter 2, 'The economic miracle', many passages on the economy have been omitted, while others have been condensed. Chapter 3, 'The new entrepreneurs in the city', and Chapter 4, 'The social structures of the new bourgeoisie', set out the results of research pursued over the past three years, making use of recent Chinese publications devoted to the history of big business. Chapters 5 and 6, which consider the role of the bourgeoisie in political life and its relations with foreigners, are in the main based upon material prepared for the manuscript of the original thesis.

Thus rearranged, the work presents a composite structure. The first part, which is of a general nature, fills in the background and indicates important factors some of whose roots reach back one or more centuries. The second part studies the growth of the bourgeois class in the brief but crucial period of its golden age, which lasted barely one decade, from the mid-1910s to the mid-1920s. It was then that, favoured by exceptional economic circumstances, namely the 'economic miracle' of the First World War and the immediate post-war years, the Chinese entrepreneurs made their mark by modernising and set themselves up as a business bourgeoisie.

The reader may be surprised at the extent to which the case of Shanghai dominates the pages devoted to the social structures of this bourgeoisie. If the emphasis is thus laid on the entrepreneurs of Shanghai, the reason is not just that they are the easiest to find out about; it is also because, of all the entrepreneurs, they were both the most active and the most numerous. Furthermore, although the activities in the various treaty ports and in the principal economic centres of the interior were sufficiently concerted to warrant the notion of a 'Chinese bourgeoisie', most of the entrepreneurs, in their ordinary activities, always appear to function as a group at an essentially local or regional level. To disregard their geographical anchorage would be to reduce the present study to a series of abstractions and to the empty categorisations characteristic of a familiar kind of Marxist analysis.

Finally, the third part of this work considers the new entrepreneurs as an integrated class with their own ideology and their own type of political action, and attempts to analyse the relations between this class and the State, the revolution and the West.

State involvement and State inertia

The problem of the State dominates the history of contemporary China, both the history of its revolutions and that of its attempts at modernisation. The State's crushing weight inevitably affected the bourgeoisie, as it did everthing else. The rising or falling star of the brief destiny of that bourgeoisie must be set against the background of either intervention or non-intervention on the part of the public authorities.

The first decade of the republican era (1915–27), which was when the bourgeoisie reached the peak of its success, coincided with the almost total eclipse not just of governmental authority but also of the very concept of a State. This was the period when China, abandoned to the anarchic rule of the warlords, was, as Sun Yat-sen put it, no more than 'scattered sand'. At first glance, it is tempting to explain the triumph of the bourgeoisie, and the social forces that it embodied, by this disappearance of public authority, generally considered to have been oppressive. Left to its own devices, one section of urban society now proved itself capable of organising the representative associations and of setting up the procedures of deliberation and cooperation, and the institutions of self-government, that are the basis of any 'autonomous' society.* The large measure of general agreement that prevailed on the objectives of economic modernisation made these spontaneous processes dynamic and to some extent effective. On the evidence of how it operated in an urban context, this Chinese society is ill-served by the adjective 'amorphous' that is sometimes applied to it.

However, the failures which brought the golden age of the bourgeoisie to an end testify to the incapacity of structures set up in this way to ensure development on a national scale in the total absence of State intervention. One may certainly point to the fragility, immaturity and incompleteness of this emergent civic society. In this connection, we should not be misled by apparent analogies with certain European precedents. The first wave of modernisation initiated by the imperial bureaucracy at the end of the nineteenth century was founded upon the preponderance of heavy industry and an appeal to public investment and foreign credit; the golden age of the 1920s, in contrast, chiefly encouraged the development of light industry, the role of capital and private entrepreneurs, and it called for investment motivated by patriotic sentiments. But the fact that the one stage was followed by the next need not imply that it was a logical succession. It was not the case

---

* Translator's note: *société civile* in the French text. The expression, borrowed from German philosophy, means autonomous, organised, social forces (as opposed to the state, with its public powers).

that the progress achieved during the first wave of modernisation led to a new strategy of development, as happened in Russia, where the industrialisation imposed by Witte led to more spontaneous growth after 1906.

In the China of the golden age of the bourgeoisie, the decline of public initiative and investment was not the outcome of any deliberate political policy. The eclipse of the State was simply a reflection of the profound weakening of political power. It was not accompanied by any strengthening of merchant banks. The dynamism of the private sector stemmed not so much from any impetus afforded by the decline of State power, but rather from the opportunities presented by the First World War. And, far from reflecting a more mature industrial system, the predominance of light industry betrayed the need for adaptation, given the inadequacy of capital and technology in a China that the world conflict had isolated from the West and cut off from the international market. In other words, it was not a matter of the bourgeoisie taking over from State initiatives so as to continue with developments that were already under way, but one of the bourgeoisie substituting its own, for State, initiatives, in order to get such developments going. In a situation of economic underdevelopment, political change and international dependence such as China found itself in, a task of such magnitude could not be successfully accomplished by society on its own, and could not have been even by a society much stronger than the one then emerging in China. In China, as in all countries which are latecomers to industrialisation, the State needed to play a determining role in the strategies of development, including those of capitalist development. It is the State's job to set up the necessary institutional framework and to enforce public law and order.

Furthermore, as in all Third-World countries, vulnerable as they are to the many forms of foreign domination, economic development in China depended upon first creating a nation. Now, while the structures set up by the Chinese entrepreneurial elite turned this group into a bourgeoisie, they were not of a kind to ensure the integration, independence and economic development of a whole nation, a nation with a population that included millions of peasants and that covered the area of an entire continent. Chinese society, of which the business bourgeoisie constituted the most resolute avant-garde, could develop neither in opposition to the State nor outside it and unaided by it.

However, the setbacks suffered by governmental policies of

economic modernisation (whether during the last decades of the Empire (1860–1911), under the Guomindang (1927–49), or under the Communist Party, (since 1949)) demonstrate all too clearly how very difficult it is for the State itself to introduce change in hierarchical bureaucratic systems which continue to manifest an unchanging inertia and inflexibility from one century to another and from one regime to another. That is why all these regimes, despite their basically authoritarian, if not totalitarian, character, have felt a need to lean upon various social intermediaries which they believed would help them to circumvent bureaucratic obstacles and to put their development plans into operation. When these intermediary partners did not exist, the State created them. The Qing court decreed that chambers of commerce should be created, Chiang Kai-shek recruited administrators for his economic policies from amongst the entrepreneurs, and Deng Xiaoping has re-instated the former disgraced capitalists. The imperatives of modernisation and the constraints of organisation to which the destiny of China is subject thus tend to palliate the oppositions between society and the Chinese State. In the midst of many fluctuations – in the shape of successive revolutions and counter-revolutions, dictatorships and civil war – a continuing dialectic has developed between the State power, its agents, who tend to become its partners if not its proprietors, and other, more or less autonomous, partners whom it would like to turn into its agents.

My enquiry into Chinese society thus finally brought me back to the problem of the State. If the bourgeoisie had been 'missing' – to borrow the expression Richard Pipes uses in connection with the history of Russia – with regard to the revolution, when it came to modernisation it was the State that was 'missing' or that failed, either in the sense that, all too present, it was too heavy-handed and missed its vocation to assist and encourage, as States had done in the rise of Western capitalism, or because, by default, it allowed the country to slip into the sterile evils of militarism.

Approached from the point of view of State power, the process of modernisation presents a new field of study that takes in official initiatives and spontaneous social actions, public institutions and 'popular'* organisations, and all the cooperation, compromise and conflict that obtains between the two sides.

I have devoted particular attention to problems of this kind by

* In the Chinese sense of the word, the opposite of which is not 'elitist' but 'State-dominated'.

reason of the developing orientation of my own interests and also in reaction to the degree of misunderstanding of these aspects of modernisation that I have detected in France, but clearly this does not justify our neglecting to study the social phenomena as well. The dialectic between State power and society remains central to the entire process of modernisation.

The phenomenon of the Chinese bourgeoisie in its golden age incorporates aspects that are quite exceptional and of particular interest. It represents an extreme advance of autonomous social forces *vis-à-vis* the State. The ground that the Chinese bourgeoisie first won, and then lost, in those years has never been regained. After 1927 the bourgeoisie was gradually smothered or swallowed up, first by the bureaucracy of the Guomindang and then by that of the communist regime. We find exactly the same thing happening first before the revolution, and then again after it. In that respect the revolutionary break of 1949 made less difference than the restoration of the State in 1927. But when it did take control, the State took over many of the ideas and procedures that had characterised the triumphant bourgeoisie. The bourgeois heritage lived on in both its hesitations and its reforms, and also in all the adjustments that it made to its development projects. The phenomenon of the golden age of the bourgeoisie still provides a useful term of reference; indeed, it even turns out to be one of the essential bases of modern China.

Part 1   Preludes

Part I Preludes

1 ❧ Tradition, opening-up and modernity

In the mid-nineteenth century, before Westerners flooded in, China was not the stagnant empire and immobile society so often described. On the contrary, for several centuries it had been experiencing a period of exceptionally rapid growth. However, that growth never led to any industrial revolution, nor did the rise of merchant communities lead to the creation of a bourgeoisie capable of converting its economic strength into political power. That being the case, whatever view one takes of the circumstances in which it came about, the opening-up of China by Westerners remains fundamental to the development of China. It is in relation to that opening-up – in its wake or as a reaction to it – that the various elements of Chinese modernity gradually emerged during the second half of the nineteenth century and, even more, at the beginning of the twentieth century.

1 Pre-modern growth and the rise of the merchant communities

The centuries that preceded the enforced opening-up of China by Westerners during the Opium War (1840–2) were centuries of growth. Between 1400 and 1850, the population increased from 60–80 million to 430 million and overall production expanded proportionately. This conclusion, derived from a series of recent economic studies,[1] is at variance with Western historiography, which for the past half-century has been dominated by the diagnosis that Max Weber produced in 1921 of an authoritarian, parochial and stagnant society.[2]

The gradual demographic increase which began in the fourteenth century and speeded up in the second half of the eighteenth century was probably connected with the state of relative peace which prevailed at that time. Between 1400 and 1770, regular migrations of people towards southern China increased the cultivated area of the country from about 370 million *mu* (25 million hectares) to 950 million *mu* (63 million hectares).[3] From the sixteenth century onwards, the diffusion of cotton and new plants imported from America – maize, ground nuts and sweet potatoes – made it possible to cultivate sandy alluvial valleys and mountain foothills. More and more, however, an increase in production depended upon an increase in productivity. In 1850 a Chinese peasant was, on average, harvesting 243 catties of cereals per *mu* (that is, about 18 hundredweight per hectare), considerably more than his European counterpart on the eve of the industrial revolution.[4] However, from the eighteenth century on, when demographic growth began to speed up, it became increasingly difficult to maintain the balance between population and resources, and more and more workers switched to cottage industries for a living. The growth of agriculture recorded during the two preceding centuries was reflected in the secondary sector, stimulating trade and commercial relations. The improvement of techniques and the growth of trade in their turn produced profound repercussions in the rural world. In the countryside, the processing of agricultural products and of metals developed, as did the manufacture of textiles, paper and porcelain. Cottage industries were far and away the most widespread.

The coordination and functioning of the craftsman system of production depended upon a commercial network. The progress of household handicrafts during the seventeenth and eighteenth centuries was closely linked with an expansion of local markets, and in the richest regions the rate of growth of those markets exceeded that of the population.[5] The presence of these thousands of local markets – William Skinner estimates there to have been as many as 63,000 at the beginning of the twentieth century[6] – turned Chinese rural society into a highly commercialised one in which handicrafts and trading were as important as agriculture.

Despite the low proportion of urban dwellers (reckoned to be 5.1% of the total population in 1843),[7] the towns played an important role in the process of rural industrialisation and commercialisation. The networks of local markets were an integral part of regional systems structured by a hierarchy of intermediate markets and large commercial centres. The most dynamic urban networks were those of the lower Yangzi, the Lingnan (the Cantonese coast and hinterland) and the coastal provinces of the South-East.

But within every large economic region, considerable variations were also to be found between a relatively highly populated and urbanised core and a periphery, usually of a hilly nature, where towns were few and far between and smaller. The connection between the hierarchy of the large cities and regional centres, on the one hand, and the multitude of units responsible for agricultural and handicraft production, on the other, was provided by the network of markets. Far from being self-sufficient within a framework of cellular units, the Chinese economy, dominated as it was by the rural sector, seems to have been activated by a kind of nervous system of dense and ramified trading relations which established the necessary communications between the mass of small-scale producers. The daily life of this highly commercialised rural society depended upon markets and merchants.

The expansion of trade brought in its train an increasing demand for coin, which increases in imports of foreign silver and in the production of Chinese copper were not altogether capable of satisfying. When private banks began to produce an abundant supply of paper money, they brought a badly needed flexibility to this system hitherto based on a rather rigid currency of silver and copper. It was in the lower Yangzi region, in the eighteenth century, that private banks and private credit made the most remarkable progress. The private bank (*qianzhuang*) was born from the system of credit practised by the merchants of Ningbo during the second half of the eighteenth century.[8] Supported by family and local solidarities, the system developed outside all governmental intervention and, in the early nineteenth century, it spread to Shanghai, where it was later to play a role of primary importance in the industrialisation of the city.

How are we to reconcile this image of a densely populated, active China, capable of feeding a rapidly expanding population, with the theories which have for so long sought to account for its stagnation? Should we give up ascribing to Confucianism all the obstacles that are so regularly diagnosed – a moral system founded upon respect for hierarchy, acceptance of the physical environment as well as of the social order,[9] 'the uncontested, absolute and despotic power of a mandarin class that tolerated no form of private enterprise',[10] and the shackles of a system of imperial institutions ill-adapted to economic progress?[11]

The fact is that Confucianism, in the form of the neo-Confucian philosophy that triumphed after the twelfth century, probably nurtured about as much anxiety and autonomous moral questing as the Puritan ethic in Europe, and incited men to moral and political action to about the same degree.[12] Such action as was taken – essentially by the bureaucracy and the local elites – was probably neither as all-embracing nor as harmful as has sometimes been suggested.[13] The degree of direct State intervention into economic life that was possible and the contribution made to the national revenue by the public sector were limited by the low level of taxation (which can be calculated, very approximately, to have been about 7% of the national product).

When the bureaucracy did intervene – as, for example, in the case of the production and sale of salt, which were public monopolies in imperial China – it exercised its control with flexibility and realism and, when necessary, teamed up with a number of large-scale private entrepeneurs.[14] But the essential factors of growth were probably the promotion of peace and internal order and, up until the end of the eighteenth century, the policy of restoring the irrigation system, which stimulated the private sector. The dynamism of this sector, which provided more than 90% of the national revenue,[15] was a reflection of the growing autonomy of the economic sphere in relation to the political. The evolution of the economic and social structures that accompanied this growth – the privatisation and commerialisation of cultivatable land, the decline of privilege, the contractualisation of leasehold farming, and the progress of literacy[17] – resulted essentially from the pressures exerted by a number of social groups. The official ideology and the imperial bureaucracy may not have positively promoted these changes but neither did they do anything to prevent them; in fact they probably even encouraged them by the policy of fiscal unification intitiated in the sixteenth century and by the measures introduced to simplify transfers of funds in the eighteenth century. The role played by the public authorities thus appears to have been weak, generally neutral and occasionally favourable.

The success of the Chinese economy under the Ming and the Qing dynasties not only makes it necessary for us to re-evaluate Confucian ideology and bureaucracy, it also poses the problem of the industrial non-development of China in new terms. Marxist analysts, who blame nineteenth-century imperialist aggression for the miscarriage of Chinese capitalism, might find new arguments here. They might draw a contrast between the autonomous growth of the sixteenth to eighteenth centuries and the stagnation and crises supposed to have been caused by foreign intervention in the nineteenth and twentieth centuries. The sequence of growth followed by stagnation is certainly clear to see and the interim period, during which the growth curves of population, prices and production all took a downward turn, certainly did coincide with the early days of European penetration between 1820 and 1860. Nevertheless, to establish the economically paralysing effect of that penetration it would be necessary to show that at the end of the eighteenth century China had truly been embarked along the path to industrial revolution.

However, there is no evidence of any market economy at that period, nor of any accumulation of capital, nor of any technological or institutional innovations of a kind to encourage industry to take off. The intensification of trade, the creation of thousands of markets and the progress made in monetary transactions were not enough to impose the laws of competition and profit upon the Chinese economy as a whole. The marketed fraction of agricultural produce (about one-third of the harvests) for the most part found outlets within a radius of a few dozen kilometres.[18] Trade further afield remained limited both in volume and in value. In between the local markets, serving particular village or urban communities, and foreign trade in commodities of an essentially exotic nature, one finds no internal, national market, only regional systems revolving around the more fertile, more highly populated, more urbanised cores which usually coincided with river deltas or alluvial valleys.[19]

The vastness of the Chinese Empire was not the only factor at work here. 'The ambiguity of growth', to borrow Michel Morineau's expression, is now a notion that is well established, and studies such as those by Karl Polanyi and Simon Kuznets have shown that a market economy, that is to say capitalism, does not spring from a multiplication of markets nor even from their more or less organised integration, but from the introduction of mechanisation into a highly commercialised society, from, in Kuznet's words, 'The extended application of science to problems of economic production'.[20]

In the absence of any technological revolution, eighteenth-century Chinese prosperity resulted from a quantitative growth, brought about by a population increase and founded upon the expansion of the agricultural sector. It corresponded to the formation of a 'full world' (*monde plein*), to borrow the expression that Pierre Chaunu has applied to the prosperous Europe of the twelfth and thirteenth centuries. While this type of growth represents a prelude that is necessary to trigger economic expansion and industrial revolution, it does not necessarily lead to such transformations. The expansion of a traditional economy may lead to one of any number of different results: in most cases, to stagnation and decline.

The difficulties that multiplied in China at the beginning of the nineteenth century certainly seem to point to such a decline. Seen from this point of view, the crisis of the years 1850–60, which compounded the tribulations caused by major rebellions with those stemming from foreign invasion, does not look like the reaction of an economy struck down in the midst of full expansion; rather, it appears as an aggravation, brought about by external factors, of a malfunctioning already manifest over the past decades.

The first symptoms of *malaise* started to manifest themselves in the 1820s. The loss of silver connected with the clandestine opium trade, and a decline in the production of the Yunnan copper mines, diminished the stock of metals and also the volume of paper currency guaranteed by that stock. The violent deflation that followed provoked a contraction of trade, particularly in the most highly developed regions of the South and East. The return of disastrous famines, bringing epidemics in their wake, the decline of food surpluses in border regions where the demographic increase had just 'peaked', and even the widespread popular unrest that provoked, as a reaction, a progressive militarisation of local society, all are signs that, after a century and a half of growth, there were now imbalances between the size of the population and agricultural production.

The Taiping Rebellion, which ravaged southern and eastern China from 1850 to 1860, turned the depression of the previous decades into a major crisis: the rebellions and the repression that followed them claimed millions of victims and it was more than half a century before the demographic deficit was restored and the devastated area of the lower Yangzi was recolonised.

The explanation for the size of this crisis must be linked to the way that the economic system itself functioned. Mark Elvin has used the expression 'high-level equilibrium trap' to describe the two phenomena of (a) the increasing absorption of surpluses by the demographic expansion and (b) the blockage of a system which should, thanks to the exceptional refinement of the technology in use, have been capable of supporting a vast population. In practice though, once it achieved its maximum output, which was limited by the traditional character of those techniques, it became progressively paralysed by the size and poverty of the population, the lack of arable land and the scarcity of raw materials.[21] Elvin's thesis, essentially a neo-Malthusian one, seems to me to give a better account of both the rapidity and the limits of Chinese growth than does the Marxist theory of a transition to capitalism thwarted by foreign aggression, for that foreign intervention was then of too recent date and too marginal to be considered responsible for the difficulties of the Chinese economy. The Nanking treaty had been signed in 1842: the concessions had barely begun to be organised, the ports had only just been opened. Besides, there is no need to invoke imperialism to explain the withering of the first buds of Chinese capitalism. Europe provides other examples of proto-industrialisation followed by stagnation and decline. The logic of the proto-industrial system sometimes results in a surge of development, but is just as likely to lead to pauperisation.[22]

Even if it had not brought about industrial capitalism, this period of growth clearly influenced the way in which China tackled the problem of modernisation at the end of the nineteenth century and the beginning of the twentieth. In this respect, the social diversification prompted by the pre-modern growth is particularly important. The traditional quadripartite division of society (into scholars, peasants, craftsmen and merchants) does not account for the complex evolutions which, in towns and countryside alike, changed the relations between the various classes and caused new groups to appear. While the status of the common people – small landowners, farmers, merchants – improved and their social and geographical mobility increased, the power of the elite groups, who were progressively deprived of their privileges as landowners, came to depend entirely upon their public functions, the wealth they possessed and the extent of their local prestige. The greatly increased numbers of intermediaries in every domain – subordinate employees, commercial agents, representatives of local communities – and, to a lesser degree, the proliferation of 'rebels', enrolled in secret societies or holed up in the mountains, increased the complexity of social relations and tended to upset the balance between the State and the social body. In this emergence of new middle strata, an important role fell to the numerous, well-structured merchant communities, which fulfilled specialised economic functions and entered into dialogue with the public authorities.

The merchant tradition, which accounted for twentieth-century Chinese capitalism's most original features, dated back to the beginning of the Empire.[23] The legal restrictions which were decreed by successive dynasties to limit the activities and luxurious life-style of the merchants, but which were never rigorously applied, were gradually withdrawn. A vigorous rise of merchant communities accompanied the development of markets in the eighteenth century. We possess no more than indirect evidence for that rise but such indications as there are all point in the same direction. The indications include an increase in the number of guilds, the expansion of commercial networks, urban dynamism and an increased cooperation between the merchants and the imperial bureaucracy. We can arrive at a very approximate estimate of the size of the merchant class on the basis of the size of the urban populations as a whole. William Skinner estimates town populations in 1843 at about 20 million. But let us discount the fraction of the urban population that lived in small centres animated solely by local markets and take into account only the inhabitants of towns with a population of more than 10,000 (where the important merchants lived). According to Gilbert Rozman's calculations, this leaves us with about 12 million people in about 1800. According to the same calculations, about two-fifths of the inhabitants of these large centres lived by handicraft or trade.[24] If we deduct the salaried employees and the little ambulant hawkers and peddlers, the affluent entrepreneurs might come to $1-1\frac{1}{2}$ million people, that is to say 0.2–0.3% of the total population. Relatively small though that figure may be, it certainly equalled those applicable to other dominant groups. For example, on the eve of the Taiping Rebellion, the gentry,* which included those holding official diplomas at every level, is calculated to have numbered about 1.1 million people.[25]

To the extent that the urban system was not integrated on a national scale, the merchant communities remained fragmented and can only be analysed within their particular regional frameworks. Their hierarchy of intermediaries was modelled on those of the commercial centres and included travelling agents responsible for prospecting local

---

* The term 'gentry', as it is generally used by historians of modern China, denotes the dominant class in traditional society. The members of this class usually combined official degrees (together with the prerogatives and advantages that went with them) with their functions as landowners.

outlets, peddlers and shopkeepers, wholesalers and retailers in the regional larger cities, and exporters, who operated mainly through Canton. At the summit of this hierarchy were the big merchants, whose activities took many forms.

These merchants, who guaranteed the cohesion of the various regional economies, also played an essential role in linking those economies together. The links, fragile and of quite a loose nature, depended upon relations of solidarity within the communities which organised inter-regional trade, that is to say the communities of merchants from Huizhou (Anhui), Shanxi and Fujian. These merchants were to be found in all the major towns of China in the eighteenth century and other groups, from Guangdong and Zhejiang, subsequently appeared. Finding themselves far from their native provinces, these merchants joined regional guilds (*huiguan*) in the towns in which they resided. At first these guilds recruited their members on the basis of their all coming from the same province and they thus included representatives from a number of social categories. But soon the merchants became predominant. The *huiguan* began to resemble professional guilds (*gongsuo*) and to reflect the particular activities of the entrepreneurs of whichever region was involved. In Shanghai, for example, the Ningbo Guild (Siming gongsuo) was controlled by bankers who were natives of that town. The number of *huiguan* established in a town was a reliable indication of its commercial importance: large regional cities sometimes boasted several dozen.[26]

Like the professional guilds, the regional guilds were organisations of local elites and they were financed by high subscription fees. They maintained temples dedicated to their respective patrons, schools and cemeteries and engaged in philanthropy and mutual social aid, as well as ensuring the smooth running of operations relating to their own particular economic sectors. They thus came to control the professional activities of their members and to arbitrate between them when disagreements arose. However, the tendency of the *huiguan* was to move away from the monopolistic and parochial preoccupations which limited the scope and influence of the traditional guilds. They lowered the barriers between entrepreneurs with different professional specialities but common geographical origins, facilitated regional emigration and developed the 'cosmopolitan' character of their cities of adoption. Finally, many of them extended to the local community as a whole services that were originally reserved for their menbers alone:

fire-fighting, protection afforded by merchant militia and public health projects. So as to run these services more efficiently, they sometimes formed federations. Such was the case in Chongqing, where the Eight Regional Guilds (Ba sheng huiguan), in cooperation with the local administration, performed as a veritable municipality. The merchants of the *huiguan* thus ran institutions whose social bases extended beyond their own community and whose objectives related to preoccupations that were not just corporatist but administrative too and, in extreme cases, even political.[27] In circumstances such as these, it may seem surprising that in China the towns did not become autonomous seats of merchant power, the cradle of a triumphant bourgeoisie, in the same way as they did in the West.

Many descriptions have been given of the classic Chinese town, the capital of a sub-prefecture (*xian*), a prefecture (*fu*) or a province (*sheng*). It would typically be an administrative city, set out in a regular street plan and defended by a rampart (symbolising public order); it would serve as a place of residence for the mandarins and remain under their bureaucratic power. In contrast to the countryside of the periphery, where various forms of autonomy or rebellion continued to exist, it constituted an outpost of imperial authority.[28] The main commercial centres would naturally also be the capitals of sub-prefectures, prefectures and provinces. In the administrative capitals, the merchants and local elites, who were informal agents of the bureaucracy at a local level, acted as if they were auxiliaries to the mandarins. Despite the importance of the economic and parapolitical networks that they controlled, the pressure that they could bring to bear upon the local administration was limited, presenting no threat to the authority of the State. Despite its numerical weakness, the bureaucracy was able to use the systems of local power for its own ends, at the same time limiting the influence of the local elites and blocking any Western-type rise of the bourgeoisie.[29]

The fact that the bureaucracy retained a firm hold over such powerful social forces can be explained first and foremost by the monopoly that the State reserved for itself in the allocation of official degrees. It was in relation to these qualifications– the symbols of social status – that the various dominant groups were defined and structured into hierarchies. However wealthy they may have been, the merchant's position remained inferior to that of scholars, whether the latter performed some official function or managed their own properties and the affairs of the community, having remained in, or returned to, their birthplaces. The inferiority attached to the status of merchant certainly contributed to a movement of upward social mobility which robbed the business communities of their leading lights and checked the formation of a bourgeoisie.[30] Nevertheless, we should not attach undue importance to the anathemas of tradition. In the eighteenth and nineteenth centuries, the merchants, as such, belonged to the local elites. The movement of upward social mobility which led the sons of merchants to seek imperial diplomas and official functions was neither invariable nor unilateral. Within a single family, different members would choose different careers depending on their own particular talents and the particular circumstances that obtained.[31]

This interchange between the dominant groups made for relative social fluidity; differences of status tended to become blurred. The families of the salt merchants of Yangzhou (Jiangsu), which produced a number of China's most prestigious eighteenth-century scholars, styled themselves *guan-shang* (mandarin-merchants). In Shanghai, in the early nineteenth century, many of the leading merchants possessed official degrees, which they had acquired either by competing for them or by purchasing them, or else as a mark of gratitude for making some generous donation to the public exchequer.

But this social fluidity, the relatively interchangeable nature of the roles of members of the dominant groups, did not lead to the birth of a specifically merchant culture comparable to those of the bourgeoisies of Europe in the fifteenth and sixteenth centuries, or the Japanese urban class in the Togukawa period. The constant incorporation of merchants into an elite which was becoming increasingly urban during the eighteenth century certainly affected the style of cultural activities: art collectors sprang up and in many towns a wide variety of sub-cultures developed. But these mechanisms through which the local forms of culture were refined and incorporated into the literary tradition continued to be governed by Confucian norms and values.[32] The evolution that began to take shape in the eighteenth century led not to the formation of a bourgeoisie but to the consolidation of a new urban elite group, transcending the distinction between scholars, or gentry, and merchants.

The imperial power, at all events, appears to have been keenly sensitive to the threat to its own authority that the formation of a united front of local elites might constitute and seems to have countered it by obliging merchants and scholars to keep apart, both geographically and in their activities.

To the extent that the hierarchy of the administrative capitals overlapped with that of the commercial centres, the merchants and the degree-holders certainly lived in the same towns. But the areas where administration and commerce operated did not coincide. The officials were involved in the hierarchical rules and regulations that provided the context for their examinations, their appointments and the advancement of their careers. The merchants organised their activities within the framework of the natural economic region as determined by the local resources and means of transport upon which the unity of the region was based. Thus the zone of the lower Yangzi, where the most powerful merchants and gentry were concentrated, was divided into the three provinces of Zhejiang, Jiangsu and Anhui, each of which incorporated territories that belonged to the neighbouring economic regions. Within the framework of a single province, scholars and merchants were thus not oriented towards the same spheres of action and decision. And within the framework of the economic region, the scholars formed rival provincial elite groups.

Thus, although the State exercised no more than partial control over economic growth, for which the rise of the private sector was responsible, it did manage to control the social transformations connected with that growth. The middle strata that developed at this time were not able either to turn themselves into a bourgeoisie or truly to set themselves up as a unified urban elite. They did not pursue any autonomous political action in opposition to the State, nor did they constitute an autonomous society. Following the opening-up of China, modern capitalism was to develop from the starting point of a twofold and paradoxical heritage. It incorporated a relative economic autonomy, on the one hand, and the absorption of society by the State, on the other. For a late-developing and dependent capitalism, the State's incapacity to take control of economic growth was to prove an obstacle just as redoubtable as its dominance over social life.

2   The opening-up of China and the birth of the modern sector

In the mid-nineteenth century, the Opium Wars opened up the Chinese Empire to Western trade. This Empire was to find itself, against its will, confronted with, and partially integrated into, a

worldwide economic system with which it had until then had no more
than limited dealings. As a result, the Chinese economy acquired a
new stimulus. Its absorbtion of capital and technology made it possible
to introduce mechanised industry and transport, stimulated the development of a modern sector and transformed the organisation of the
Chinese economy, which was now turned into a dual economy (with
two sectors, one modern, one traditional). But the manner of China's
integration into the worldwide capitalist system (what Fernand
Braudel and Immanuel Wallerstein have called the 'world
economy')[33] turned China into what would henceforth be regarded as
an underdeveloped country.

Chinese underdevelopment was progressively established in the
course of the decades that followed the opening-up of the country and
was a consequence of it. It is not the case that the 'development of
underdevelopment' is inevitably the price that must be paid for late
and 'marginal' integration into worldwide capitalism.[34] The examples
of Sweden and Prussia in the seventeenth and eighteenth centuries and
that of Japan in the nineteenth show, on the contrary, that a strong
State with firm agricultural foundations may succeed in transforming
its economy. China, for its part, did not. To the extent that the
economic modernisation of countries belatedly integrated into the
world capitalist system is first and foremost a political problem,
China's failure in this respect must be laid at the door of the Chinese
State. What is the explanation? It was in part a natural consequence of
the violent military and diplomatic pressures exerted upon it by the
foreign powers. But not exclusively: the opening-up of China was a
gradual affair. It took over half a century, from 1842 to 1895, during
which time the cohesion of China's traditional society imposed an
effective break upon foreign penetration. But the very nature of its
relation to society prevented the Chinese State from using that
historical breathing space to mobilise, under its own control and to its
own advantage, forces both old and new which could have brought
about the economic transformation of the country.

Western intervention and the introduction of a new stimulus for the economy

When the English took the course of forcibly opening up the Chinese
market, their purpose was to consolidate the interests that they had
acquired over the past few decades, The privileges that they obtained

at the treaties and agreements of Nanking in 1842, Tianjin in 1858 and Peking in 1860 (privileges soon extended to other powers as well) formed a coherent whole, a system of treaties which was to provide the legal framework for foreign penetration of China for an entire century.[35]

A number of cities were now opened up to foreigners, who were granted the right to reside there, to buy buildings and to engage in trade. In 1895, the treaty of Shimonoseki gave them the further right to set up industrial businesses. In these treaty ports, the foreigners benefited from extraterritoriality. Import dues on their merchandise were limited to 5% of the value, and if an additional transit tax of 2.5% was paid the merchandise was exempted from internal customs dues (*lijin*). Given the system set up by these treaties, it was inevitable that the foreigners would play a role of the first importance in the economic modernisation of China. The modern sector, which began to take shape in the second half of the nineteenth century, came into being as a result of their initiatives and mostly remained under their control.

Although the opening-up of China began in the mid-nineteenth century, up until 1895 foreign business developed slowly. It was only at the very end of the nineteenth century and during the first decade of the twentieth that the rate of foreign investment speeded up. The Japanese joined the Westerners, their respective fields of intervention all expanded and, with the Russo-Japanese War over, the years 1905 to 1908 marked the climax of this economic offensive. Under the domination of foreigners, the modern sector made greater progress during the last ten years of imperial rule than it had during the whole preceding half-century.[36]

Foreign business, dominant in some branches – import–export, banking, coal mining, modern transport – and rather less so in others (cotton mills and light industry), played an essential role in the generation of a modern sector. This identification of economic modernisation and foreign penetration nevertheless does not mean that China now simply became a 'satellite' of the capitalist powers, their colony or even – given that it was politically subject to no foreign metropolis – a semi-colony that the foreign powers exploited in common. Of course, many of the relations of domination that the imperialist powers imposed upon their far-flung colonies certainly existed in China. At an economic level, they were reflected in the deficit in the trade figures, the types of trade commodities, and the decline of certain handicraft activities such as cotton spinning, which came into competition, first from foreign imports and then through the home manufacture of industrial yarns. But at the beginning of the twentieth century, these phenomena were of secondary importance since the modern sector itself still played an extremely marginal role.

In the context of China as a whole and the multitudinous Chinese population, the modern sector was of little importance. Agricultural production, in which the foreigners took no part, continued to represent over 65% of the national product. In 1913, the per capita value of external trade in relation to the number of inhabitants came to no more than 1.61 American dollars. The very nature of the trade commodities manifests how little China was integrated into the world market. Although exports of exotica were soon followed by those of raw materials, China did not constitute an essential source of supplies for the West. Nor did it provide the limitless outlets that might have been expected, given its vast area and population. Apart from industrial yarns, no imported products found a large-scale market in China. Yet, despite the marginal interest that the Chinese market represented to them, the great powers worked hard to penetrate it. A persistent myth spurred them on to the conquest of what they imagined to be some Eldorado.[37] But China was resistant. It was not just its mass, the size of its population and its poverty that impeded its integration: it was the Chinese people themselves.

Later we shall return to consider the weakness of the State and its failure to take up the challenge of modernisation. All the same, the Chinese authorities did engage in negative, but on occasion powerful, action to block developments that they increasingly regarded as dangerous.[38] Furthermore, in the interior, popular resistance promoted a climate of insecurity unfavourable to the development of foreign business. However, such resistance, whether official or popular, was perhaps limited by the inequality of forces involved and, in the last analysis, came up against the military superiority of powers that practised gun-boat diplomacy.

The Chinese market's best defences against foreign imperialism remained the cohesion and flexibility of the traditional economic system. The permanence of its commercial structures and the systems of credit connected with them rested upon the stability of its market networks. The development of modern means of transport was much too limited to make any perceptible difference to the geography of distribution and the collection of products over the territory as a whole. Commercial communications, including those linking the treaty ports with the interior, were still under the control of Chinese merchants. Within this network of commercialisation in the interior, finance remained the principal mode of intervention for the foreigners. But the granting of credit was meditated by the traditional Chinese banks (*qianzhuang*), the only ones to do business with Chinese merchants.

The commercial system thus operated through two separate circuits: one (between overseas markets and the Chinese ports) was controlled by the foreigners, the other (between the treaty ports and the interior) remained in the hands of the Chinese. And although it may seem paradoxical to conclude that at the end of the Qing dynasty 'the foreign merchants served Chinese trade much more than they controlled it',[39] it is clear that to a large extent the Chinese did use them for their own ends.

Foreign influence thus directly penetrated only a very limited portion of Chinese territory – the large coastal cities of the East and the South-East. Although far distant from one another, Tianjin, Shanghai, Canton and Hong Kong shared analogous and specific cultures and economies. Open to the sea, trade-oriented and dominated by the 'bourgeois' values of their business communities, they were not simply foreign enclaves: they also perpetuated the tradition of a seafaring China, the China of pirates, merchants and adventurers who, as early as the sixteenth and seventeenth centuries, began to act as intermediaries between the Confucian empire and the foreigners – Portuguese, Japanese and Dutch – who were pressing against its southern shores.[40]

In the nineteenth century, this coastal civilisation assumed renewed vigour and acquired a wider sphere of influence. Until then, its phases of expansion, which coincided with temporary setbacks to Confucian and rural power, had always been shortlived. Faced with inland China, maritime China had on several occasions attempted to assert its own individuality, but had never managed to emancipate itself from the bureaucracy for long enough to set up solid political structures and constitute itself as an autonomous force capable of influencing imperial politics and ideology. The establishment of concessions which in practice, if not legally, eluded Chinese sovereignty, created islands of relative security and order in the treaty ports. It was in this 'refuge of concessions' that, through contact with the foreigners, but not by imitating them exclusively, a cosmopolitan and entrepreneurial

China, which had always been held in check by mandarin powers, at last took off. The development of the treaty ports was not only a triumph for the West. At the same time it gave this marginal and minority section of Chinese society, for whom modernisation was probably but the most recent of a long line of heresies, a chance to get its own back.[41]

The vastness of China was becoming organised in relation to these new poles of development. Not only was it divided into the large economic regions mentioned above, but further fundamental opposition was being established between the coast and inland China. The relations of interdependence that obtained between the various macroregions and between the core and the periphery of each of these regions were without doubt based upon the uneven development of production, commercialisation and population expansion. From one region to another and from one zone to another, it was, however, the intensity rather than the nature of the economic processes that varied. From the end of the nineteenth century on, a radical contrast developed between the coast and the interior. There were now two different worlds – the world of tradition and the world of modernism – and even the Chinese themselves were unable to reconcile the two facets.

The coastal zones, now to a large extent supplied by imports of foreign cereals and raw materials, acquired a new autonomy, being able to disengage themselves from inland China all the more effectively given that the coastal industries were in many cases working for an overseas clientele and for a restricted, local, urban market. All the same, the treaty ports did not become the enclaves living off themselves, as if quite separate from the rest of China, that are described by some authors.[42] Every famine, every civil war that ravaged the countryside was accompanied by an inflow of capital to the coastal cities and increased activity there. The poverty of the interior contributed to the upsurge of the treaty ports.

But the polarising effect exerted by the coast was not entirely negative. The problem we have – and it is still in large measure unexplored – lies in discovering to what extent and in what forms economic modernisation was diffused and new technological expertise relayed. The fact that the inland regions resisted foreign business does not mean that they scorned Western technology and Western products. The traditional commercial networks were closed to foreigners but not to some of their wares. At first, industrial yarns were purchased

by regions which did not produce their own cotton as a raw material –
northern China, Manchuria and the basin of the upper and middle
Yangzi. When cheap yarns arrived on the Chinese market from India
during the 1870s, followed by Japanese yarns in the 1890s, even the
areas that did produce cotton began to buy imported yarns. This
spelled ruin for the cottage spinning industry in many regions. At the
same time, though, the hand-weaving industry took on a new lease of
life. In social terms, the cost of such changes was high: not all the
spinners reduced to unemployment became prosperous weavers. But
in the midst of all the crises provoked by pressures exerted from outside
and transmitted initially from the treaty ports, some progress was
made. Hybrid techniques and structures appeared. With the use of
industrial yarns, the system of 'putting out' work became general
throughout the countryside and also in the towns, as cottage industries
working for the export trade, such as wickerwork, embroidery and the
making of hairnets, developed. The merchants were extending their
control over the processes of production and helping them to evolve. It
was, for example, in this way that metal-framed weaving looms, of
Japanese origin, were introduced, making it possible to increase
handicraft production several times over.[43]

Inland China was thus not unaware of the challenge of modernisation, but the terms of its response were usually those of a traditional
economy. What progress was made has scarcely been analysed at all.
No doubt it appeared negligible insofar as it took place within a system
that was judged as a whole to be antiquated. The expression 'false
modernisation' has sometimes been used to refer to the intensification
and partial improvement of the processes of production and transport,
in the absence of a true technological revolution.[44] The term 'transitional modernisation' seems to me a better description of the
elaboration of this traditional system, an elaboration that signifies the
reality and the limits of foreign influence in inland China.

The dualist structures that appeared in China at the end of the
nineteenth century were a consequence not of imperial aggression itself
but of the process of modernisation that was triggered by that
aggression. They can be explained by the progress of the modern sector
in the treaty ports, the only localities where productive transfers of
capital and Western technology took place. The foreign presence in the
ports simply made the process, in itself inevitable, all the more
humiliating and painful. It would be pointless to venture onto the

slippery slopes of counterfactual history at this point, and to wonder whether developments would have been more harmonious if China had been better protected against foreign intervention. We should do better simply to consider the difficulties encountered by the People's Republic of China today, as it struggles to avert the formation of just such a gap between the poles of development, on the one hand (still represented by the coastal zone), and the countryside, on the other.

Seen from this point of view, it seems more profitable not to ponder whether imperialism weakened the Chinese economy as a whole, but to try to understand why the Chinese modern sector created in response to foreign intervention did not develop more successfully. Here the responsibility of the Chinese State seems to be the crucial factor.

State intervention

Alexander Gerschenkron has demonstrated the importance of the role played by the State in countries that are late to be industrialised.[45] When the poverty of the rural market sets a limit on consumer demand and the supply of capital alike, development can either be financed directly by the public exchequer, as in Russia at the end of the nineteenth century, or else through industrial banks, as in Germany during the same period. Although the experience of some modern developments – in Taiwan, for example – now bring into question the necessity for the State to assume an entrepreneurial role,[46] State intervention remains essential to establish investment priorities and to create an institutional framework adapted to the new needs of economic activity.

To these economic and institutional constraints Chinese civilisation added some more of its own. The acculturation of the treaty ports, which made their modernisation possible, at the same time prevented this process of change from becoming more general. It was impossible for the experience of the treaty ports to be relayed to other parts of the country without the sanction and mediation of the imperial power.

Why did the Peking government not assume this doubly modernising role during the half-century breathing space that the hesitations of Western imperialism afforded it between 1842 and 1895? And why did it fail after 1900, when, in a pre-revolutionary situation, it tried to bring about reform 'from above', choosing what Martin Malia has called the 'Prussian option'?[47]

In Marxist and neo-Marxist analyses – in particular those of Wallerstein – the weakness of the State structures in peripheral countries is presented as an inevitable consequence of their reinforcement in the core. The suggestion is that it is explained by the subordinate role that these countries play in the world capitalist economy.[48] Such an analysis hardly accounts for the Chinese State's failure to meet the challenge of modernisation in the second half of the nineteenth century. As we have seen, China at that time was of scant importance to the world economy and its vulnerability stemmed more from the armed forces of the foreigners than from economic exploitation on their part. Meanwhile, so long as military conflict remained limited, China continued to live out its history according to its own rhythm. The threats of imperialism and the need for economic modernisation were perceived and analysed as part of a much more general crisis, characteristic of any dynasty's declining phases, when the effects of popular revolts were compounded by the militarisation of regional powers and the alienation of the gentry and local elite groups. Not only did this internal crisis absorb the financial and military strength of the Empire, it also dominated the attention of many leaders, whose solution was to meet classic evils with classic remedies. Now, while the disorder created by foreigners on the fringes of the Empire did not constitute a new evil, economic modernisation did, for its part, represent a new remedy. To impose it, its partisans would have to overcome ideological inertia as well as many socio-cultural obstacles.

As we have seen, the Confucian tradition did not encourage active intervention by the State in the economic sphere. Nevertheless, during the second half of the ninteenth century, it became accepted that the development of industry was an essential factor of survival for the State, and hence for the dynasty. But it took time for that idea to become established. Not that China lacked clear-sighted observers capable of immediately evaluating the implications of foreign penetration and suggesting reforms of a kind to avert the dangers by promoting Chinese development.[49] These early 'reformers' were for the most part educated in the treaty ports or abroad. From their direct contacts with the West, they concluded that if China was to survive, it would have to change: it would have to become initiated into modern technology and science, reform its teaching system, institute new juridical codes and perhaps even adopt representative political institutions. But unlike the Indian or Vietnamese bourgeoisies, which acquired political power and social prestige as a result of their association with the colonial administrations that dominated their countries, in China the coastal reformers did not manage either to trigger off or to control the developments that they declared to be necessary, nor did they manage to convert their expertise into power.[50]

The power still lay with the imperial bureaucracy. And even if that bureaucracy failed to provide the drive for change, it was still the only possible instrument of its legitimation. That is why the reformers of the coastal regions strove to get their ideas adopted by high officials, who had the authority to recommend them at court and possibly even to get them implemented. The ideology and policies of modernisation were thus advanced through the personal relations established between high officials and the reformers, who were now promoted to advisory positions, given special responsibilities and sometimes even absorbed by the bureaucratic apparatus, on a more or less temporary basis. But progress was slow. The 'Western Affairs' Movement (Yangwu yundong) was impeded on the one hand by resistance on the part of the conservatives, and on the other by rivalry between its own promoters.

What with bureaucratic reticence followed by bureaucratic compromise, the impetus for reform flagged. Such measures as were introduced became subject to qualification and modification. Up until 1895 there simply was no institution capable of organising and coordinating modernisation efforts. Even if it had wished to implement a policy of modernisation, the State did not possess the means to do so. Without fiscal reform, its resources were too weak for it to adopt a strategy of direct industrial investment: land taxes had not been raised since the eighteenth century, so State revenues could not be increased much. Furthermore, those revenues were divided out in such a way as to favour the provinces at the expense of the central government. Apart from the growing revenue provided by Maritime Customs dues, the resources at the disposal of the government were limited and inflexible, barely sufficient to cover administrative and military expenses. Consequently, with very few exceptions, publicly owned enterprises (guanban) could not be developed.

However, the investment of public funds in official enterprises and managerial interference on the part of government officials were not the only, or even the predominant, forms taken by bureaucratic and

State action in economic life. The Chinese government was remarkably adept at coopting private investors and adminstrators, delegating some of its powers to them and even integrating them into the administrative apparatus. The imperial government officials consti- tuted no more than the kernel of the Chinese bureaucracy. They were surrounded by networks of collaborators, advisers, secretaries, dele- gates and partners. It was not so much a bureaucracy, more a flexibly structured 'bureaucratic complex', which enabled the State to exercise a measure of control over the producers (or merchants), without itself shouldering responsibility for the processes of production (and com- mercialisation).

It was essentially upon this 'bureaucratic complex' that the pro- moters of the 'Western Affairs' Movement depended. Not only did they gather the reformers of the coastal regions around them, as it were as 'brains trusts', they also strove to mobilise private skills and capital to promote modern industries which they planned to keep under their own control. This mixed system of merchant management and official supervision (*guandu shangban*) made it possible to channel Chinese capital from the treaty ports into industrialisation. But the inefficient organisation of these mixed undertakings and the preferential treatment given to official credit in cases of bankruptcy made for growing reticence on the part of the officials.

The failure of the mixed companies has often been blamed on the system itself, reckoned to be incompatible with the true spirit of enterprise. It is suggested that the Chinese government, being unable – for ideological and financial reasons – to adopt State capitalism, opted instead for a bureacratic capitalism the very terms of which – private management and finance along with official supervision – were contradictory. But such a view may well be largely dictated by *a priori* ideological assumptions made by liberal historians themselves. Given the organisation of Chinese society and the nature of its relations with the State, it is not necessarily the case that the *guandu shangban* system was by definition incapable of bringing about modernisation. Perhaps it was really the conditions in which the system was applied in the nineteenth centuary that were responsible for the failure of the mixed companies. Weakened by the absence of any consensus and by the rise of the regional powers, the government was no longer in a position either to define or to impose the terms of collaboration acceptable to both officials and merchants. Emboldened by their experience in the treaty ports, the merchants now desired not only to control economic processes but also to benefit from the social and political advantages which normally stem from such control. The combination of dynastic decline, on the one hand, and the expansion of the merchant communities, on the other, called for a renegotiation of the terms of cooperation between the State and the private sector. However, that renegotiation never took place. At the end of the nineteenth century, the achievements of the strictly Chinese modern sector (as opposed to the modern sector developed by foreigners in China) consequently appear to have been both limited and disparate.

The serious military and diplomatic setbacks suffered by the Chinese government during the Sino-Japanese War (1894–5) and the Boxer Rebellion (1898–1901) brought about a radical change in their modernisation policies. In the face of such dangers, a consensus emerged on the need for such policies. The imperial court now embarked upon a series of reforms aimed, on the one hand, at encouraging the development of the private sector and, on the other, at reinforcing State collaboration with the new modernising strata of society, to benefit which many new concessions were introduced.

Three sectors were particularly affected by the imperial policy of reform: education, the army and the administration. The objective was to restore the imperial power by creating a modern State served by a centralised, specialised and well-informed bureaucracy. To rally the progressive forces whose cooperation was indispensable to its success, such a policy of reform had to make them some political concessions. From 1906 on, the introduction of a number of elements of parliamentarism was intended to strengthen national cohesion around the central power and, in particular, to tighten links between the government and the urban elites. A similar strategy had been adopted by Bismarck when he came to power in 1862, by Witte after the 1905 revolution, and even by the reformers of the Meiji period, who now directly inspired the Chinese leaders. Why was it not successful in China?

Such a strategy of reform may be conservative in conception, but it is revolutionary in its effects and is likely to be resisted by vested interests. Its success is thus entirely dependent upon the authority of the government. If that authority falters, as it did in China after the death of the Empress Ci-xi in 1908, a number of opponents are likely to take concerted action against the regime. But the failure of Chinese reformism may more generally be explained by the fact that it came too late. The central government's attempt to break with the passive role that it had for so long adopted in economic life came just when it was emerging, much weakened both financially and politically, from the crises of the 1895–1901 period. It was those crises that had prompted the reforms, by revealing the urgent need for them. But their consequences for the State exchequer were so dire that the success of the reform policy was compromised right from the start.

The withering of central government coincided with the decline of its political control over its own bureaucracy. Resistance to the reforms stemmed from the inertia of the hierarchical system and from rivalries between officials in Peking itself. But the gravest obstacle to government policy was the autonomy and non-cooperation of the provincial power-holders. The latter did not accept the imperial government's new doctrine. The initiatives of the modernising State seemed to them to compromise the local consensus upon which the Confucian philosophy and their own authority rested. Finding its prerogatives threatened, the local bureaucracy did not come out in open revolt, but its submission was purely formal; in practice, imperial directives were sabotaged and rendered ineffective.

To get round the resistance of the provincial bureaucracies, the government then made an attempt to gain direct control over the local business communities by encouraging them, through the law of 1904, to organise themselves into chambers of commerce. In China, chambers of commerce were not spontaneous and autonomous organisations whose function was to represent the economic interests of their members. They were created, between 1904 and 1911, in response to government directives and in conformity with precise and uniform rules dictated by Peking. The government sought, through the chambers of commerce, to circumvent the local bureaucracy, which was refusing to mediate on its behalf, and to set up a direct alliance with social forces that were capable of contributing to modernisation. But in the principal economic centres – in Shanghai and above all in Canton – the government could only persuade the merchants to create these chambers of commerce by dint of granting them concessions which dangerously strengthened the autonomy of the chambers and the power of the guilds that controlled them.[51] While seeking to gain control of the merchant communities, the government in fact increased their power and independence. Furthermore, the new chambers in general opted for collaboration with the local authorities, from whom they claimed immediate protection and whose day-to-day preoccupations they shared; they thereby strengthened the position of those authorities in their confrontations with Peking. The isolation and impotence of the central government stemmed from its alienation not only from the local bureaucracy but also from the bureaucratic complex, in which the actions and interests of the local officials coincided with those of the local elites and the entrepreneurs.

A policy of modernisation pursued 'from above' implies the granting of limited political concessions and more considerable social and economic advantages, in return for which the new urban strata capable of overseeing the work of transformation agree to subordinate their own activities to directives from the government. Such a policy needs an administration on the spot that can promote and apply those directives. More fundamentally, it depends upon the modernising social strata recognising the State's essential role in the maintenance of national cohesion and independence. In China, none of these conditions applied. The State was impoverished, its political control limited and Chinese patriots rejected the Manchu dynasty, underlining its foreign origin to portray its weakness as a betrayal. It thus proved impossible for direct collaboration between the government and the new modernising social strata to take the place of the bureaucratic capitalism of the 1870–1900 period. The explanation for the failure of the modernisation policy adopted by the Manchu dynasty and the Confucian bureaucracy does not lie solely in the heavy drain on public finances that resulted from the repayment of the foreign debt from the beginning of the twentieth century onwards. It also, and perhaps above all, stems from the government's intrinsic weakness, its political hesitations, its extremely limited control over its own bureaucracy, and the growing alienation from it felt by the dominant classes, in particular the new urban elite groups of the treaty ports.

3 The new urban elites of the treaty ports

The appearance of a modern economic sector and the development of the large coastal cities speeded up the social evolution that had begun to get going over previous centuries. The urban elite expanded, prospered and became increasingly distinct from the old leading social

strata. Its composition also changed. The opening-up of China introduced many new opportunities for making a fortune and led to a
diversification of skills and careers. New social groups appeared upon
the scene as the old groups became increasingly isolated from Western-
style activities.

The cohesion of this new elite, usually referred to in contemporary
texts as *shenshang* (scholars and merchants) was based on a new set of
values – those of pragmatism, modernism and nationalism. The
expansion of new urban institutions reflected this cohesion and also
promoted it. The institutions themselves were modelled on a combination of Confucian administrative practice and the example of the
West, and so retained a composite character. But it was within the
framework that they provided that a new social and political
consciousness soon developed.

The emergence of new social groups

The great revolts that shook the Chinese Empire in the mid-nineteenth
century checked demographic growth. But although it was estimated
that, at the end of the century, the figure for the total population had
dropped, the urban population, for its part, had increased: between
1840 and 1893 it is estimated to have swelled from 20 to 23.5 million; in
other words, the proportion represented by the urban population had
risen from 5.1% to 6%.[52]

The coastal cities, which were expanding rapidly, offered many
opportunities for making a quick fortune. Like the various foreign communities in contact with which it lived, the Chinese business community of the treaty ports comprised a high proportion of pioneers, self-
made men and adventurers. For this Chinese society, as for the Western
societies which produced expatriates in search of as rapid and profitable
a career as possible in China, a treaty port represented a 'frontier'. Huge
fortunes could be made and lost there. The tone was set by the *nouveaux
riches*. Commercial vigour often turned into frenzied speculation. The
euphoria of growth was punctuated by huge waves of financial panic
which would paralyse economic activity for a while, ruining a number
of magnates. The 1883 crash did not bring development to a halt but
nevertheless gave it a feverish and somewhat chaotic character.

It was the compradores who were best placed to seize the new
opportunities, and they did so with alacrity. The Portuguese word

compradores originally denoted the Chinese servants of the earliest foreign merchants in Canton and Macao, who went to market to barter their masters' wares in exchange for provisions of various kinds. As trade developed, the role of these people became increasingly important. The foreigners, ignorant of the local language, customs and monetary systems, entrusted their compradores with all transactions engaged with the Chinese public. Their role thus varied according to the nature of the businesses that employed them. Those who worked for export companies acquired their supplies from tea or silk wholesalers. Others, working for import companies brought cotton fabrics and yarns onto the market. The most important were the compradores who worked for foreign banks; they were responsible for the trustworthiness of the Chinese employees placed in their charge and for the reliability of dealings with Chinese banks.

At the end of the nineteenth century, the importance acquired by the compradores could be measured by their personal fortunes, which ranked among the largest not only in the treaty ports but in China as a whole. Their annual salaries (between 1,000 and 2,000 taels) were supplemented by commissions paid by their foreign employers, by the interest which they secretly charged their Chinese clientele, by the benefits that accrued from their roles as treasurers and from the management of deposited funds and, finally, by the profits from the businesses that they themselves owned. Overall, the sums amassed by the compradores between 1842 and 1894 have been estimated to be as high as 530 million taels. That is considerably less than the collective income of the gentry (reckoned at 645 million taels per annum),[53] but in assessing its importance we should bear in mind that it was divided between fewer beneficiaries – a few hundred people, rising to a few thousand by the end of the century – and we should remember that these sums were deployed in the modern economic sector that had generated them and were for the most part ploughed back into it. With wealth such as this, the compradores were highly respected people. The lowly origin of their profession was forgotten. They played a highly active role in the local business community. In Shanghai, they were to be found at the head of the principal professional and regional guilds. In 1911 the Shanghai General Chamber of Commerce numbered 7 compradores among its directors (out of the 16 individuals whose professions it is possible to identify).[54]

The group of compradores expanded along with overseas trade and foreign businesses. It is estimated to have numbered 250 individuals in 1854, 700 in 1870 and about 20,000 at the beginning of the twentieth century.[55] Most came from a handful of specific regions – Canton, Shanghai and Ningbo. The pledge demanded by the foreign employer from a new comprador whom he engaged would usually be paid by those already in his employ in the case of a native of their own region. It was through the payment of such pledges that the Cantonese ensured their pre-eminence in the comprador group up until the 1870s. After that, they were faced with competition in Shanghai, in the shape of compradores from Jiangsu and Zhejiang, who were more familiar than they with financial and banking affairs. As always in China, family connections reinforced the cohesion of the group: comprador posts were often hereditary and were considered as family possessions.

Although the compradores constituted the most easily identifiable group, plenty of other Chinese entrepreneurs were also profiting directly from the opening-up of the ports. Some merchants specialised in the import – export trade. Resident as they were in the treaty ports, they had at their disposal collection and distribution networks and could control the movement of merchandise in the interior. Some were true wholesalers, buying up products which they then tried to resell. But most were simply intermediaries, or brokers, who did not invest much capital of their own but passed stocks on directly to merchants in the interior with whom they were in communication. As with the compradores, their activities depended upon foreign business.

The development of the import–export trade gave rise to new forms of credit. The bankers of Shanxi province, whose wealth had in the past been based upon the management of public funds and the financing of inter-provincial trade, did not find it easy to adapt to the conditions created by the opening-up. Their decline coincided with the rise of the *qianzhuang* banks. Although these had originated back in the eighteenth century, they reached the peak of their activity around the beginning of the twentieth, when they acted as intermediaries between the Chinese merchants and entrepreneurs, on the one hand, and the foreign banks established in China, on the other. One of their essential functions was to apportion the credits forthcoming from these foreign banks among the Chinese entrepreneurs. Despite the financial crises which periodically caused the least firmly established of the banks to disappear, the number of *qianzhuang* in Shanghai increased steadily: there were 56 in 1886, 82 in 1903 and 113 in 1906. A handful of large families, such as the Li and the Fang, originally from Zhenhai near Ningbo, dominated this banking sector.[56]

Less directly concerned with the new economic activities, some officials who were responsible for negotiating on the spot with foreign consuls worked to consolidate Sino-foreign cooperation based upon the defence of the most immediate interests common to both sides. The local and pragmatic nature of their intervention distinguishes these officials from the 'reformers of the coastal regions' mentioned above. The latter were usually obliged to set their projects before high-ranking imperial officials and to exercise their own talents within the latters' sphere of influence and in their shadow. In contrast, the local officials enjoyed considerable powers of initiative, favoured by the decentralisation of the imperial administration and the novelty and complexity of diplomatic relations with the Westerners. In this respect they resembled Western diplomats and administrators, whose independence increased the further they were from their homeland and who, in the light of the prevailing circumstances, would improvise policies that were in keeping with what they judged to be in the interest of their own countries and, above all, with their own spirit of adventure.

The new intelligentsia that emerged in the treaty ports at the end of the nineteenth century maintained fewer links with both the country-side and the bureaucratic apparatus than the scholars had had in the past. The marginal individuals that it included had not had the chance to pursue careers as scholar-officials. Many had been educated by foreign missionaries, in some cases completing their studies at American or European universities. Others had picked up an edu-cation in the technical schools associated with the earliest shipyards or in military academies. Their knowledge of foreign languages had been acquired in the lower echelons of the Maritime Customs Service. Their numbers increased after 1905, when imperial examinations were discontinued and integration into the public services was more officially dissociated from the acquisition of diplomas.

For those emerging with their diplomas from the new education system, prospects for the future were limited. The education that they had received led them to break with the Confucian ideology and order. In many cases, however, it had been an education of mediocre quality which ill prepared them to assume the responsibilities of modern management. Furthermore, Chinese modernisation was not progressing fast enough to open up a wide spectrum of careers for them. The most gifted and the best connected of them obtained administrative posts as specialists in foreign relations. A few became journalists, doctors, lawyers or publishers. Many were employed, on temporary contracts, by the new schools.

The relatively marginal social position of the new intelligentsia afforded it a kind of political and ideological autonomy. The intelligentsia found it more difficult than the other groups that had emerged in the treaty ports to establish its position in between the two worlds between which it mediated. It had turned its back on traditional society, which did not recognise it anyway, or hardly, but could not yet find its place in the newly emerging order. It was thus a non-integrated intelligentsia, receptive to all kinds of counter-ideologies and open to the influence of any movement advocating reform or revolution. At the beginning of the twentieth century, it was this intelligentsia, without any real support from any other particular class, that was responsible for the diffusion of new, imported ideologies, relaying to the elites of the treaty ports slogans which were not always in harmony with their political prudence and social moderation.

Finally, the China of the treaty ports created new links with China overseas. Chinese emigration to the countries of South-East Asia (known in China as the Southern Seas countries – Nanyang) had been going on for many years. The constitution of European colonial empires in the nineteenth century created new possibilities for employment and wealth in these regions, and many Chinese – particularly from the southern provinces – were keen to take advantage of them. At the beginning of the twentieth century, 7.6 million Chinese were estimated to be living abroad, essentially in the Southern Seas (Nanyang). Not all made their fortunes. However, many were successful in carving out an important role for themselves in the economic life of their host countries, where they acted as intermediaries between the European colonisers and the local population. The Sincere Trading Company (Xianshe gongsi) and its rival, the Wing On Company (Yong'an gongsi), as well as the Nanyang Brothers' Tobacco Company (Nanyang xiongdi yancao gongsi), were set up in Hong Kong at the turn of the century by entrepreneurs or the sons of entrepreneurs who had made their fortunes overseas. These businesses, which later transferred to Shanghai, where they ranked among the largest concerns in China, were thus originally developed abroad, without either help or interference from the imperial administration.[57]

Most of the Chinese who emigrated preserved family and religious links with the mother country. But the Peking government, which suspected them of favouring a return of the Ming dynasty, for a long time held them at a distance. As the treaty ports developed and the Chinese seaboard became increasingly important to the life of the nation, links between the metropolis and the overseas communities grew closer. As the idea of economic modernisation gained ground, the wealth and skills of the overseas Chinese came to be regarded as trump cards. China now felt inclined to identify with these expatriates who, on their own, had achieved a veritable conversion to the modern world: in 1880, as in 1980, it was hoped that they would agree to act as advisers and bankers. From 1895 on, the Peking government thus tried to involve the Nanyang businessmen in its policies of reform and economic development. Zhang Bishi, a Cantonese who, at the age of 18, had set off to seek his fortune in the Dutch East Indies and Malaysia and had subsequently become one of the richest merchants in South-East Asia, was in 1903 appointed vice-president of the new Ministry of Trade. His principal function was to encourage the repatriation of overseas capital.[58]

In addition to traditional family and clan links of solidarity, various factors combined to strengthen the unity between overseas China and coastal China and to create between these two peripheral parts of China a veritable symbiosis that overrode geographical and political differences. Among these factors were a common desire to increase production and trade, the importance attached to material profit and the vigour of a nationalism stimulated by constant contact with the non-Chinese world. Chinese society in Shanghai and Canton was closer to that of the overseas communities of Singapore and Hong Kong than to the rural world of the inland provinces. Now, just as the Empire, in one of those huge oscillations by which its destiny was marked, was beginning to turn away from its agrarian–bureaucratic, internally oriented tradition and to open up to the peripheral maritime influences, Chinese emigration assumed a historical role. It was within the framework of the treaty ports and through them, that the *émigrés*, newly reintegrated into national life, made their influence felt, provided models of behaviour and brought in capital.

The social rise of the *nouveaux riches* who, within the space of a few

years or decades, made a place for themselves in the ranks of the local
elites, testifies to the mobility of a society in which the law of profit was
beginning to compete with Confucian values. And it was not simply a
matter of upward social mobility – there were virtually no barriers
between one group and the next. Every boundary could be crossed,
and was.

The integration of the new urban elite groups

The integration of the urban elite groups was officially encouraged by
the re-evaluation of the status of merchants. An imperial edict
promulgated in April 1903 declared the State's concern for the
entrepreneurs: 'We must abandon all feelings of superiority where they
are concerned . . . and tolerate no separation [between mandarins and
merchants]'. Between 1903 and 1907, the new Ministry of Trade
introduced a number of systems of awards designed to honour
investors, technicians and entrepreneurs in the industrial sphere. The
measures were more or less symbolic, for they did not bring about the
evolution of customs and conditions so much as recognise that it was
taking place. Ever since the second half of the nineteenth century, the
imperial government had been replenishing its exchequer by the sale of
more and more official titles and posts. By 1900, it is estimated that
most civil servants had acquired their status by buying it rather than
by qualifying for it by examination. Merchants of any importance,
with contacts in the administration, thus had no difficulty in obtaining
suitable qualifications and functions, most of them with the title of
expectant *doatai* (circuit supervisor).

In 1897, by which time the importance of industrial and commercial
development was recognised, the legal restrictions affecting investment by officials were lifted by edict. Here again, the official measures
simply recognised the *de facto* situation: ever since the 1870s, officials
had ceased to consider themselves bound by the legal regulations. So
the liberalisation of the legal prescriptions did not have the effect of
increasing their participation in the business sphere, for they were
already active there. The major factor unifying the various urban
groups remained their common participation in the growth of the
modern sector and the profits from it and, more generally, their
commitment to the opening-up process and their involvement in it.

The economic atmosphere of the treaty ports not only favoured the emergence of new social types but also encouraged the traditional merchants to reorientate their activities. For example, in 1901, the brothers Rong Zongjing (1873–1938) and Rong Desheng (1875-1952) reinvested their profits from a little *qianzhuang* bank in the Maoxin Flour Mills, thereby laying the foundations of one of the largest Chinese capitalist businesses of the twentieth century.[59]

The officials and the gentry were also seeking to profit from the new opportunities for making money. Their intervention in trade, money-lending and finance continued for the most part to be indirect; they would become shareholders, appoint others to manage their companies or run them themselves under assumed names. But they were less reticent about being openly involved in industrial concerns (*shiye*), which the contemporary political philosophy regarded as the most prestigious sector of economic activity and the basis of State power. Between the mandarin who combined his business activities with his official functions (sometimes even merging the two) and the one who abandoned his official functions to devote himself to the management of his business affairs, many compromises were possible. The best-known example is that of the cotton mill proprietor Zhang Jian (1853-1926), a successful candidate in the competitive Imperial Palace examinations (*jinshi*), who entered the business world without abandoning that of the scholar and whose outstanding talents enabled him to remain a full member of both the old and the new elites.

His case was exceptional. Transition from the traditional gentry to the industrial capitalist class was usually a more protracted and uncertain process. Slotted between the nineteenth-century governor-generals and the twentieth-century captains of industry, some of whom were grandsons of the former, was a generation of men of multiple activities and uncertain vocations. One example is Nie Qigui (1850–1911). Thanks to the protection of his father-in-law, Zeng Guofan (1811–72) – the victor over the Taiping Rebellion – he pursued an official career in Shanghai and in the provinces of the lower Yangzi, exploiting this to lay the foundations of business concerns which his sons – in particular Nie Yuntai (1880–1953), who became one of the leading capitalists of Shanghai–were later to develop with great success.[60]

The social basis of the new elite groups was thus a complex one. Within their ranks members of the local elite from the great gentry families rubbed shoulders with newcomers who had emerged from the

popular strata. The common feature of all these men was an exceptional ability to exploit the opportunities for making money and for
social advancement that the treaty ports afforded. Even when they had
no direct contacts with the foreigners, their activities revolved around
Western concerns. The lack of differentiation between their various
activities made for a measure of osmosis between the different groups.
A comprador was also a merchant, a banker was an entrepreneur, and
both of them might also hold official posts. Nevertheless, the interpenetration between the groups did not result in complete fusion and the
term *shenshang*, denoting the urban elite in general, still covered plenty
of distinctions.

However, at the beginning of the twentieth century, the balance
between the constituent elements of this urban elite was tending to
shift. Until that time, the officials and the gentry had played the
leading role in its evolution. Their dominance was based upon their
administrative experience, their initiative, the preferential treatment
that they received from the authorities, and their access to public
funds. But the discontinuation of the official examinations, in 1905,
and the decline and withering of central government, deprived the
gentry of its principal marks of social differentiation and weakened its
power. In the treaty ports, the merchants took advantage of these
changes to confirm their own new importance both on a general
political level and as leaders of the urban community. As a result of all
this, relations between the two groups altered.

The new values of urban society

Hitherto, cooperation between the various urban elite groups had been
based upon the merchants' acceptance of terms laid down by the
gentry and the scholar-officials. The merchants bought themselves
official titles, made donations to the public exchequer and steered their
children into mandarin careers. They were thus integrated into an
established system that was not of their making but to which they
could belong and which accepted them. That relative flexibility had
ensured the durability of the system of social organisation.[61] From the
late nineteenth century on, it was the merchants who increasingly
came to impose their values on the urban society of the treaty ports.
These values included pragmatism, which, in the name of profit,
sanctioned every kind of collaboration with the foreigners; modernism,

which justified borrowing from the West; and nationalism, which provided a defence against slurs of acculturation and legitimised all economic activities pursued in the name of overriding national interests.

The merchants were primarily concerned to improve their working and living conditions. They moved into the foreign settlements to escape from the endless disturbances in the provinces and from unfair interference on the part of the imperial administration as well as to improve their relations with their foreign employers or partners. They committed their fortunes to banks which could not be raided by the Peking government, and they invested in European and American companies which could not be taken over by the Chinese officials. The Chinese entrepreneurs were also keen to make the most of the modern facilities of the foreign settlements – a cheap supply of running water and of domestic and industrial electricity, and an urban telephone network. Despite the fact that they were treated as second-class citizens there, liable to taxation yet excluded from municipal responsibilities, Chinese merchants went to live in the settlements because it was in their interests to do so.

The Westernisation that stemmed from their collaboration with the foreigners took forms that were dictated by the immediate prevailing circumstances. The compradores installed themselves in houses that were built and furnished in the European style, since these were as a rule provided by their European employers. They abandoned their long blue silk robes for jackets and trousers whenever the latter, which were symbols of their extraterritorial status, could enhance their prestige or afford them protection, particularly when their business travels took them inland. To facilitate communication with their foreign employers or partners, they spoke in pidgin English (*pidgin* being a corruption of the word '*business*'), which uses Anglo-Indian and Portuguese words in sentences with a Chinese construction. Some became Christian converts, but usually only so as to consolidate their positions in the professional business world: Zhu Zhiyao (1863–1955), the comprador for the Banque de l'Indochine, came from a Catholic family; the compradores working for English or American businesses opted for Protestantism.[62]

It was a hybrid kind of culture that emerged from this superficial Westernisation, but it nevertheless constituted a starting point for the modernisation of Chinese society. Society could no more 'be changed by decree' in China than it could in Europe. The imperial edicts that in

1902 prohibited the binding of feet, in 1904 made precise recommendations for the organisation and syllabuses of the new schools, and in
1907 authorised girls to travel abroad to pursue their studies, were
simply sanctioning developments that had got going several decades
earlier, in the business circles of the treaty ports, the first places to
experiment with feminism, modern education and democracy.

Traditional Chinese society provided some basis for all these
innovations. But at the beginning of the century, the new social values
became established chiefly through imitation; reproduction of Western
ideas and practices remained the most important factor in this
evolution. Modernism was equated with Westernism. Yet, even as
they imitated the foreigners, the merchant communities and, more
generally, the modernised elite groups of the treaty ports were also
trying to check their advance. The treaty ports, where every kind of
acculturation took place, were also the cradles of Chinese nationalism.
The political philosophy of the Empire discouraged nationalistic
reactions to the Westerners, as it did to other barbarians. Foreigners,
who were tolerated and so far as possible kept on the margins of the
Empire, were allowed to participate in Chinese civilisation in a
secondary fashion and even to cooperate with Chinese officials. Those
were the attitudes that, on the basis of a fundamental misunderstanding, gave rise to the treaty-port system. But once established, the
system produced unexpected consequences, 'perverse effects'. The fact
was that in the clash of economic and cultural systems, the processes of
assimilation worked not to China's advantage but to the West's.

The Chinese residents of the treaty ports were probably the first to
realise this, as they were the first to be affected. A certain degree of
acculturation and relative subordination to foreign business constituted the price that they paid for their economic success. During the
last decades of the nineteenth century, the purchase of official titles was
still able to convert that economic success into a social one. But as the
mandarin system declined it became necessary to seek other means of
legitimation. Through a kind of dialectical reversal, initiation into the
Western way of life, which used to make for exclusion from Chinese
society, now came to be seen as a means of salvation for that same
society. The elites and merchants of the treaty ports realised that the
presence of foreigners was a challenge that had to be met in the same
terms – that is, with economic development and social and political
progress – and they concluded that their mission was to take up that

challenge. Unlike the European and Protestant entrepreneurs of Europe in the seventeenth century, who looked upon their profits as a divine blessing, these twentieth-century Chinese entrepreneurs saw their successes as a possible means of national salvation. The precocious and vigorous nationalism of the elite groups of the treaty ports was part and parcel of their relative cultural and economic alienation.

If that seems a paradoxical statement, it is only because it runs counter to analyses that set up an opposition between, on the one hand, a 'national bourgeoisie' (*minzu zibenjia*), working with purely Chinese capital and manifesting a spirited hostility towards the foreign competitors with all their privileges and, on the other, a comprador bourgeoisie (*maiban zibenjia*), subject both politically and economically to those same foreigners.Such a clear-cut opposition is completely artificial. Even if we limit ourselves to the purely economic criteria used by those analyses, we are bound to note that, strictly speaking, there were no Chinese businesses independent of the foreigners in the treaty ports in the early years of the twentieth century. All Chinese concerns of any importance were either subordinated to, or closely connected with, foreign business: the latter financed them, supplied them, or provided either equipment for them or an outlet for their products. In 1910, when the big foreign banks of Shanghai decided to discontinue the credit for the *qianzhuang* and refused to honour their 'native orders' as valid currency, the financial market collapsed and all economic activity in the town found itself threatened.[63]

Relations between Chinese entrepreneurs and foreigners were based upon a position of dependence or interdependence. The descriptions 'comprador bourgeoisie' and 'national bourgeoisie' were no more than political labels and did not come into use until later when, between 1920 and 1930, the Chinese Communist Party resorted to them to justify its successive alliances and breaks with the social forces of moderation. The term 'national bourgeoisie' then came to mean those who were willing to collaborate with the Communist Party. Those who rejected it were dubbed 'compradores'. Roles varied according to political fluctuations.

In truth, if a contradiction did exist, it was more apparent than real and it was not between a 'national bourgeoisie' and a 'comprador bourgeoisie' but between the relative economic and cultural alienation of the modernised urban elite groups and their more or less unanimous nationalistic aspirations.

From the 1900s on, the resentment that developed in the treaty ports against the foreign presence in all its aspects became permanent. The authority of the Shanghai Mixed Court, the territorial extension of the foreign settlements and their management, the administration of the Maritime Customs and the fixing of customs tariffs, the foreigners' seizure of the mines and railways – all these were the sorts of problem which mobilised opinion among the elite groups that took part in large demonstrations and formed activist committees.

But the merchants were by no means the only fervent nationalists. The students were often its most ardent propagandists. The urban gentry also played a crucial role in the Movement for the Return of Sovereign Rights, which, from 1905, strove to bring the mining and railway companies created by the foreigners under Chinese control and to forestall any new foreign initiatives. But foreign intervention usually took the form of economic expansion which, while it threatened China's general interests, also immediately affected particular fields of action in the business world, that is to say trade, industry and finance. The Chinese merchants thus found themselves doubly involved: as citizens anxious to save their country (*jiuguo*) and as entrepreneurs faced with competition. That double involvement of the business world in imperialism heightened their self-awareness and made their reactions particularly specific and effective. The increasing number of boycotts organised during the first decade of the twentieth century testifies to the importance of the role played by what could already be called bourgeois nationalism in the creation and development of Chinese nationalism.

Boycotting was a means of exerting pressure that the Chinese guilds had already long employed to bring recalcitrant merchants and corrupt officials into line. It was an effective weapon, which had got the better of more than a few uncooperative merchants and had often put a check on imperial power. Traditionally, however, its use had been limited to precise cases concerning the running of particular businesses or trades within a single town or town quarter. With the 1905 anti-American boycott, boycotting took on a new character. It spread to all the merchant communities of the treaty ports and assumed a political form. The merchants were keen to protest against the racial discrimination against the Chinese that had been introduced by the American immigration laws. The defence of national interests and honour was now organised on the basis of the Chinese coastal regions as a whole. Over the years that followed, boycotting increased. It became an economic weapon used for political ends which proved relatively effective in the short term and to the extent that the Chinese merchants were auxiliaries and collaborators who were indispensable to foreign businesses.[64]

Unlike the xenophobia that predominated inland and that characterised peasant revolts such as the Boxer Rebellion, the modernist and nationalist ideology of the treaty ports constituted not a rejection of the West but, on the contrary, an attempt to come to terms with it both as a model and as a threat. The realism implicit in such behaviour, which was based both on compromise and protest, was particularly characteristic of the business world. The merchants' and entrepreneurs' desire for immediate profits made them collaborate with the foreigners. Their rather limited understanding of Chinese civilisation and history probably made it less painful for them to accept the inevitable process of acculturisation; on the other hand, their ambitions for themselves rendered them hostile to the privileges and encroachments of the Westerners.

In many respects, that ideology coincided with or even inspired the policies of reform adopted by the Manchu government after 1900. So the fact that this government did not succeed in mobilising these new urban elite groups in its support may seem somewhat surprising. However, we have already drawn attention to the intrinsic weakness of the Chinese State at this time. Its failure was also connected with the evolution of urban society itself. The integration of its various constituent groups into specific institutions had the effect of transforming its political role, or rather of creating a political role for it. Hitherto, the government and its bureaucracy had controlled all the parallel local networks of power – those of the gentry, the merchants and the secret societies. But now, the new urban institutions constituted a force of opposition which, despite its elitist nature, soon acted as a pole of attraction for the discontent that was felt on all sides. It thus came to express the claims of the secret societies and the frustrations of the peasants as well as those of the urban rebels.

The gradual institutionalisation of the political power of the urban elite groups

The increasing importance of urban institutions at the end of the nineteenth century and the beginning of the twentieth was part of a more general trend towards local autonomy (*difang zizhi*). This term, borrowed from the Japanese, did not make its appearance in Chinese political literature until the very end of the nineteenth century. However, the conflict between the partisans of bureaucratic centralisation (*junxian*) and those who favoured a devolution (*fengjian*) of public powers to the natural social groups (villages, clans) and the local elite groups had been going on for over a thousand years. By the nineteenth century, increasingly serious drawbacks were presented by the brutal separation between the State and society, a separation symbolised by the ruling which prohibited officials from being employed in their own native provinces. What with demographic pressure, the bureaucratic system, which had not expanded proportionately, slackened its grip and the officials' control over the population became increasingly tenuous. The lower level of the imperial administration was the sub-prefecture (*xian*), in which the population might number as many as 200,000 to 300,000 inhabitants. No officials employed and paid by the State operated below the *xian* level. Consequently, local government inevitably passed into the hands of the local elites and other natural social groups. But in the *fengjian* tradition, local autonomy denoted far more than a residual field abandoned to the spontaneous initiatives of the communities concerned. It was seen as an instrument of bureaucratic control. For even if the social groups were left free to manage their affairs in their own way, their actions were nevertheless in the last analysis expected to contribute to the realisation of the State's objectives, namely the maintenance of order and the collection of a proportion of the society's wealth, in the form of public taxes. This subordination of local management to the interests of the State was implemented by the so-called decimal hierarchies, organised on the basis of units composed of ten homes. Through a system of collective responsibility, taxes were collected, policing was maintained and records were kept. Furthermore, this subordination depended upon the collaboration of the local elite groups, whose loyalty was guaranteed by their Confucian education and by their sense of belonging to a dominant class whose prerogatives stemmed from an ideological and political system that transcended local interests.[65]

The civil wars of the second half of the nineteenth century upset that delicate balance between State control and local autonomy. The decimal hierarchies went into a steep decline, while the role of the elite groups became more important as many new powers – both military and fiscal – devolved upon them. Generally speaking, it was the urban elite groups who benefited from this devolution, this opening-up of the bureaucratic apparatus. From the mid-nineteenth century onwards, the exodus of the high-class rural gentry from the countryside speeded up. The big absentee landlords now lived in the towns where, as we have already noted, their economic interests and social behaviour were often very similar to those of the leading merchants. From the late nineteenth century onwards, both these groups became increasingly preoccupied with the question of modernisation, which, at this point and for many years to come, remained an essentially urban problem. The trend favouring modernisation underlined the gap developing between, on the one hand, the lower gentry who had remained in the countryside and, on the other, the upper gentry and the big merchants of the treaty ports and the coastal cities. The countryside, suffering from inadequate administration and deserted by the traditional gentry, fell into the hands of an extremely corrupt infra-bureaucratic class. Within it, the petty personnel of the official bureaux (*yamen*), who were directly recruited and paid by the magistrate, rubbed shoulders with local leaders whose functions had survived the disappearance of the decimal hierarchies and who now held their posts by personal right instead of being elected by the community.[66]

In contrast, in the towns, the new elites – gentry and merchants (*shenshang*) – were extremely active. On an informal level, their functions and responsibilities tended to spill over into areas hitherto reserved for the orthodox apparatus of the imperial administration. Not only were members of these urban gentry assuming more and more public responsibilities at a local level, but these tasks were becoming increasingly diversified. They included philanthropy, the maintenance of order, the upkeep of canals and dykes, and frequently even involved problems of town planning and port organisation. Meanwhile, the promotion of trade and industry became one of their major concerns. The absorbtion of most of the upper gentry into the new urban elite, during the second half of the nineteenth century, hastened the disintegration of the traditional Chinese political system and at the same time encouraged the emergence of a new, modernising and cosmopolitan China. The predominant role assumed by the elite groups in this minority China stands in stark contrast to the state of vast areas of rural China, abandoned as they were first to local petty tyrants and subsequently, under the warlords' regime (1917–27), to *condottieri* of all kinds.

The local elites' promotion of community interests took place in a spirit of social openness and modernity. We have already noted[67] how the professional guilds (*gongsuo*) and regional associations (*huiguan*) freed themselves from their corporatist and geographical limitations and came more and more frequently to act as representatives and agents of the urban communities. The scholarly societies (*xuehui*), which had been multiplying since 1895, and the education associations (*jiaoyu hui*), the first of which took shape in Jiangsu in 1905, developed preoccupations of a far less academic nature than those of the literati circles from which they had emerged: they now proposed administrative reforms and produced plans to improve the training of officials. The agricultural societies (*nonghui*), which made their appearance at about the same time (the Shanghai one was created in 1897), took an interest in Japanese agronomic experiments and reported on their results in their magazines.[68] In terms of modernity, these local associations and organisations clearly owed much to the model provided by the institutions of the treaty ports. In Shanghai, in particular, the municipal management of the Chinese districts in the city was inspired by projects realised in the International Settlement and the French Concession. Foreign influence was also discernible in the introduction of a number of democratic procedures into local institutions. Even traditional institutions presented a number of forms of limited democracy: their directors were usually selected by public vote (*gongju*), in general assemblies. The latter were also expected to pronounce on major problems and projects. However, the rigorous criteria for the selection of the members of those assemblies, and the need for a preliminary consensus of opinion, limited the scope of such practices. Although the power of the old guard and the 'bigwigs' was subject to certain controls, it remained dominant. The principal innovation of the early years of the twentieth century was the introduction of quantitative procedures in voting and majority rule. They first appeared in the regulations of the Shanghai General Chamber of Commerce in 1903 and were also adopted when a municipal council for the Chinese City of Shanghai (Shanghai zonggongju) was created in 1905. Even if the limited size of the elecorate reduced the importance of this innovation in real terms, it nevertheless testified to the urban elite's ability to evolve towards both democracy and administrative efficiency.[69]

As early as the second half of the nineteenth century, the urban elites had constituted a technocratic class which included both technological experts and experts in Western activities in general. Now they were tending to become a political class. In the early years of the twentieth century, the integration of their institutions into the bureaucratic apparatus and the formalisation of their power speeded up this evolution.

The devolution of local administration to the urban institutions was sanctioned by the *fengjian* tradition and made necessary by the numerical inadequacy and frequent incompetence of a bureaucracy confronted with the totally new problems of modernisation. It was thus beset by fundamental misunderstandings. The court regarded it as a means of mobilising the energies of society in the service of a policy of economic reform and development, the necessity for which was becoming increasingly obvious to it. However, it had no intention of forfeiting the control that the bureaucratic apparatus enabled it to wield over that society. For the urban elites, the mobilisation of social energies that they were attempting to bring about through the local institutions was an end in itself. It was not the case that they were out to do away with or even to weaken the unifying framework represented by the imperial regime. But influenced as they were by a mixture of *fengjian* ideology and Western liberalism, they reckoned that such a mobilisation could not fail to be in the general interest.

At the beginning of the twentieth century, the government, which had encouraged the development of the urban institutions, began to feel some alarm at their success. The entire functioning of the bureaucratic apparatus depended upon the existence of exclusive channels of communication conveying information in the form of memoranda upwards to the Throne and imperial directives downwards from it. There seemed to be no way of preventing the increasingly close relations between the local magistrates and the urban elites, at sub-prefectorial and provincial levels, from entering into competition with regular hierarchic relations and giving rise to collusions and rivalries which would be harmful to the smooth functioning of the administration and the central government's control over the bureaucratic apparatus as a whole. The court thus ran into the classic dilemma that eventually faces all regimes bent on imposing policies of economic development and social change from above: the problem was how to ensure that change took place without compromising, in the more or less long term, the existence of the structures that had initiated it.

The danger for the imperial power was all the greater given that the activities of the urban elite groups that were supposed to provide the administration with technical collaborators extended considerably beyond the fragmentary and limited framework originally assigned to their activities. The problem of modernisation which faced all the various urban associations, each in its own sphere, could not be resolved by each sector pursuing its activities in isolation: at least a minimum of coordination, whether spontaneous or imposed, was needed.

That coordination between the various organisations was ensured by a small group of elite members – scholars, merchants and officials – all of whom were endowed with wealth, social prestige and an interest in public affairs. In Jiangsu, for example, they included Zhang Jian, Huang Yanpei (1878–1965), Ma Liang (1840–1939), Luo Zhenyu (1866–1940) and Xu Dinglin (1857–1915).[70] The fact that the same figures headed the various organisations clearly facilitated the development of direct contacts between those organisations at a local level and increased their influence over the administration. At the same time, this situation helped the elites to become politically aware. This class of experts and managers thus acquired a political identity – as reformers, modernisers and liberals.

To ward off the threat that they represented, the Peking government, in 1905 and 1906, launched a whole series of reforms designed to integrate most of the urban organisations into the orthodox administrative structure. Its purpose was to provide a formal framework for the power of the elite groups, the better both to use it and to control it. Imperial decrees thus officially recognised and extended throughout the territory the networks of the chambers of commerce (January 1904), education societies (July 1906), agricultural societies (1907) and local autonomy information offices (*zizhi yanjiusuo*) (August 1908).[71]

These organisations were brought under the control of the central power by supervisory ministries, also newly created – the Ministry of Trade, set up in 1903 and reorganised as the Ministry of Agriculture, Industry and Trade (Nonggongshangbu) in 1906,and the Ministry of Instruction (Jiaoyubu), also set up in 1906. The programme of constitutional reform was announced in August 1908. It aimed to set up a whole hierarchy of local and provincial assemblies, only partially elective, the entire pyramid to be topped by a national assembly half of whose members were to be nominated by the government. The immediate consequence of this institutionalisation was to speed up the development of local organisations. By the end of the Empire there were as many as 794 chambers of commerce[72] and 723 education societies,[73] not to mention the new local assemblies located in the sub-prefectures (*xian*) and the provincial assemblies (*ziyiju*)

The impetus for the invasion of a domain hitherto the preserve of the State and its bureaucracy by new socio-economic forces linked with the processes of modernisation came from two quarters – from the elites themselves and, equally importantly, from the court. However, the government measures designed to preserve its own control soon proved ineffective. The new political class whose emergence had been encouraged by Peking rejected the subsidiary role intended for it and became an increasingly rebarbative critic of the imperial power and the regime. The local elites made the most of the new structures, which provided them with a means of expression and intervention to consolidate their own political power, while at the same time preserving their autonomy and their leading role. In this connection, the role of the provincial assemblies elected in 1909 seems to have been extremely important.[74]

Even more alarming for the government was the competition that the spontaneous movements of regrouping and federation represented for the orthodox hierarchies and supervisory authorities. It was not merely at a local level that the effects of concerted action were making themselves felt. Links were being established across provincial boundaries between similar associations, and these launched general nationwide programmes. In May 1911, delegates from the education societies met in Shanghai to work out such a general programme. In the following August, they set up a permanent coordinating body, the Chinese Education Society (Zhongguo jiaoyuhui).[75] It was also in Shanghai that in November 1909, deputies, representing 16 different provincial assemblies, met, at the suggestion of Zhang Jian, to launch a campaign petitioning for the creation of a real parliament. In the summer of 1910, the movement made progress, establishing a Federation of Provincial Assemblies (Ziyiju lianhehui), on the basis of which a veritable opposition party was organised during the following spring; it called itself the Friends of the Constitution (Xianyouhui).[76] The idea of a Federation of Chambers of Commerce emerged from a convention of provincial delegates held in Shanghai in 1907.

The legitimacy that the government had conferred upon the social organisations by integrating them into the orthodox administrative apparatus thus developed a distinctive character that the regime had not bargained for. The official recognition granted to these organisations simply had the effect of sanctioning the legitimacy that in fact sprang from their representative character. Of course, this did not amount to popular representation. The members and directors of the local associations and assemblies only represented a limited urban elite: they were selected according to traditional consensus procedures or elected by limited suffrage that represented no more then 0.42% of the population.[77] This small urban elite had already been associated with the exercise of power in the past, but it had remained under the direction of the officials. By the beginning of the twentieth century, the foundation for its power was the modernising movement and it was taking advantage of the decline of central power to break the imperial monopoly over legitimacy. As a result of the mobilisation of economic and social forces, dictated by the needs of modernisation, the ancient practices of imposing control through delegation rebounded against the government. Although the degree to which they were representative was very limited, the local organisations became their own sources of legitimacy and, between 1906 and 1909, they were greatly strengthened by the political and administrative reorganisation of the regime.

In 1909, the imperial power began to resist these developments that it had neither foreseen nor desired and this stimulated rivalry between the old sources of legitimacy and the new. The conflicts that ensued projected the elites into the opposition and turned reformists into revolutionaries. The local institutions and assemblies now became the focus of a mass movement expressing a wide range of dissatisfactions. The campaign petitioning for a parliament was organised during the first three months of 1910 by the provincial deputies of the National Assembly and was supported by the chambers of commerce, the education and agricultural societies and by various civic associations. It collected 25 million signatures, a total far greater than could be accounted for by the membership of the local organisations alone.[78]

Behind the specifically Chinese nature of the institutions and mentalities that affected these developments, we find the classic revolutionary processes of the eighteenth century at work – an opposition of elite members which placed itself at the head of popular opposition, and a reformist movement which became a vehicle of revolution and in 1911–12 led to the overthrow of imperial power and the establishment of a sovereign parliament.

The resemblances to the English and French revolutions underline the modernity of the 1911 revolution as compared to the earlier agrarian uprisings – the Taiping and Boxer Rebellions – which had more in common with the Russian *bunt*. But does that mean it is legitimate to speak of a bourgeois revolution and a Chinese bourgeoisie?

If, by bourgeoisie, we mean a class which devotes itself to industrial development on the basis of free enterprise and in accordance with the laws of economic rationality, the answer must be no. Clearly, no such class existed in China at the end of the Manchu Empire. On the other hand, we should also recognise that the French revolution of 1789, the prototype always cited, was not a bourgeois revolution either.[79] So perhaps we should simply abandon this unlocatable bourgeoisie to the history of ideas.

The evolution of Chinese society at the beginning of the twentieth century was governed not by industrialisation (for that had hardly even begun), but by the idea of necessary and beneficial change, the idea of modernisation. The social diversification produced by modernisation policies, the disintegration of the gentry, the emergence of a veritable urban elite class and the development of a non-integrated intelligentsia all contributed to undermine the foundations of an *ancien régime* which, in direct confrontation with the peasant masses, relied on the support of a restricted bureaucratic elite. As social structures became more diversified, the society which began to take shape accommodated the rise of intermediary bodies – chambers of commerce and educational and agricultural societies – all of which provided a basis for the creation of representative institutions.

This society was dominated by the urban elite groups that had emerged from the old gentry and the merchant class. The capitalists who embarked upon the path of industrial development represented no more than a small fraction of those elite groups. A flexible coalition existed between them and the rest of the elite class, a coalition that drew upon the spirit of openness and innovation of the former and the social stability of the latter. As the years of the first half of the century passed, the capitalist avant-garde grew, establishing its specific character more firmly, yet still maintaining its solidarity with the elite body as a whole, to which it remained linked by common sentiments of social conservatism, nationalism and mistrust of the central State power. Far from slowing down the formation of a capitalist class, the presence of that elite body provided this still very minority group with a powerful social basis. It was the fact that they belonged to this urban elite that enabled the Chinese capitalists to wield an influence quite out of proportion to their limited numbers and their relative economic and social weakness.

Part II The emergence of a bourgeois class

2 ❧ The economic miracle

Between 1910 and 1920, Chinese capitalism expanded rapidly. This was the golden age (*huangjin shiqi*) of the national industries, a spontaneous capitalism that had begun to prosper in the aftermath of the 1911 revolution. But far from promoting the accession of a bourgeois power capable of encouraging the development of productive forces, and anxious to do so, this revolution instead ushered in an era of profound decline for the State. The rise of Chinese capitalism at this time was the result of spontaneous growth stimulated essentially by external factors – the world situation during the war and its immediate aftermath – but then taken over and controlled by society itself.

With most of the foreign powers absorbed by the war effort, the Chinese entrepreneurs found themselves called upon to provide for the needs created by the import of industrial products over the past decades. Industrialisation developed, based on import substitution and stimulated by demands that could no longer be satisfied by foreign products.

The economic miracle did not disappear when the war came to an end. The world reconversion crisis (1920–2) affected, but did not paralyse, the activities of the principal treaty ports. However, the modern sector of the Chinese economy was soon faced with other difficulties: it ran up against, on the one hand, a renewed offensive on the part of imperialism and, on the other, imbalances between the various sectors that resulted from economic growth itself. The stagnation of agricultural production put a drastic break on industrial development. The 1923–4 crisis in the cotton mills was just the first in a succession of initially agricultural blockages which for half a century accompanied every increase in the rate of industrial growth in China.

The fact that a golden age materialised just at the point when the

State, suffering a sharp decline, had virtually ceased to intervene is evidence that economic life was independent of institutional frameworks. And the persistence of the golden age throughout the world reconversion crisis shows how unaffected by the mechanisms of colonial domination this economic growth was, for it continued even within the framework of purely national resources and constraints. However, the fragile and short-lived nature of this economic miracle, which lasted for barely a decade, clearly indicates the limits of the twofold autonomy that it enjoyed.

1.   The First World War: a magnificent opportunity

The First World War provided a unique opportunity for expansion for the modern sector of the Chinese economy. The decline of imports and foreign competition led to the development of substitute industries; the increased demand for raw materials and foodstuffs stimulated exports, and meanwhile the rise of silver on the world market reinforced the buying power of Chinese currency. Yet this expansion was slowed down by a number of handicaps connected with the state of war and aggravated by the underdevelopment of China itself. After the Armistice, the need for reconstruction in Europe perpetuated and even reinforced the favourable wartime situation, while the handicaps that had resulted from the hostilities gradually faded away. It was in the immediate aftermath of the war that the modern sector found itself able to take full advantage of the exceptional opportunities that had been opened up.

As soon as the First World War broke out, most of the great powers involved in it diverted their energies away from China to devote them to the armed struggle. The extent of their eclipse from China varied from one case to another. In Germany's case it was virtually total: she lost her territorial bases following the Japanese operations in Shandong in 1914–15 and the possessions and interests of her nationals there were confiscated by the Chinese government when it went over to the Allied camp in 1917. For England, the reverse suffered was essentially commercial: in 1917–19, her exports of cotton fabrics for the Chinese market dropped 48% as compared to the pre-war period.[1] France, Italy and Belgium also slackened their economic links with China. Only Japan and the United States maintained or improved their positions.

At the outbreak of the war, a large proportion of the staff of foreign businesses were called up for active service and left China. The large banks sent home their reserves. Many companies were forced either to close down or to reduce their activities. The Chinese market now benefited from a *de facto* protection which it had hitherto been deprived of through the unequal treaties of the nineteenth century. The decline of foreign influence was reflected by a sharp drop in imports, particularly in cotton products: in 1913, China had purchased from abroad 19 million bales of cloth and 2.5 million piculs of yarns. By the end of the war, those figures had fallen respectively to 14 million bales and 1.3 million piculs.[2]

At the same time, the war caused a heavy increase in the world demand for raw materials and foodstuffs. At the beginning of the war, the production and stockpiles of non-ferrous ores used in the composition of alloys destined for the armament industry, such as tungsten and antimony, were far too low to meet demand. Their value rose rapidly, in the case of tungsten increasing from 7.42 (American) dollars per (English) pound (in weight) in 1913 to 25.33 dollars in 1916.[3] There were similar increases in the prices of vegetable oils used for making varnish, and those of leather and wool, which were needed for equipping the troops. Other prices also rose: those of flour, eggs and meat, all indispensable for feeding the troops, and that of black tea, large quantities of which were consumed by the Russian army. China, which was a large producer of raw materials, found itself well placed to satisfy the new demands of the world market.

The increase in purchases made by Western powers from the countries producing raw materials, such as China and India, reinforced the rise in the price of silver on the international market. The disturbances in Mexico following the 1913 revolution caused a net deficit in world production just when the countries that were at war needed to mint more silver coins for the upkeep and payment of their troops. Great Britain, which before the war had each year assigned about 3 million pounds sterling to the mint, spent 14 millions on minting coins between 1914 and 1916. Despite the Pittman Act of 1918, authorising the American Treasury to melt down or sell some of its reserves, the price of silver continued to rise, increasing from 0.563 American dollars per ounce in 1914 to 1.121 dollars in 1919.[4]

The higher value of silver led to a rise for the Chinese tael (see Table 2.1).

Table 2.1. *Average value of the Chinese tael (average rate of exchange on the markets of London and New York) from 1914 to 1919*

Years	US dollars	Pounds sterling
1914	0.67	2s. 8¾d.
1915	0.62	2s. 7¼d.
1916	0.79	3s. 3$\frac{13}{16}$d.
1917	1.03	4s. 3$\frac{13}{16}$d.
1918	1.26	5s. 3$\frac{7}{16}$d.
1919	1.39	6s. 4d.

Source: C. F. Remer, *The Foreign Trade of China*, p. 250.

This rise of the tael operated like a revaluation, increasing the buying power of Chinese currency in the world market. It also made it easier to pay off the foreign debt, which was payable in foreign currencies, all of which were connected with the gold standard. In 1917, 70 million Chinese dollars sufficed to cover payments which would have required 100 million the previous year.[5]

The war thus diminished foreign competition, opened up new export markets and strengthened the buying power of Chinese currency in the world market. But it was a favourable opportunity that the Chinese could only seize and exploit within the limiting framework of an underdeveloped economy and in accordance with the possibilities offered by a partially colonial system deeply affected by certain handicaps which also stemmed from the world conflict – the unpredictability of international exchange rates, the scarcity and high cost of freight, the difficulties involved in financing overseas trade, and the lack of machinery and equipment.

As the war dragged on, the main powers involved each adopted a war economy subject to ever stricter State controls. Many restrictions were introduced to control and limit the movement of capital and merchandise. Merchant fleets worldwide were hit by military operations and requisitioning and declined as a result, while the cost of maritime shipping increased proportionately. In 1913, the cost of freight travelling from Shanghai to London was £2 sterling per metric ton; by 1918, it had risen to £50. Costs for the Shanghai to San Francisco run increased at a similar rate, rising from 5 American dollars per metric ton to 60–70 dollars.[6] The sharp increase in the price of raw materials on the European market did not always compensate

for the rise in freight costs and, as a result, the scarcity of tonnage and
the prohibitive cost of shipping continued, throughout the war, to limit
the development of Chinese imports and exports. As a result, at the
very moment when the decline of foreign competition was stimulating
national industry, it was becoming more and more difficult for Chinese
entrepreneurs to obtain supplies of indispensable machinery and
equipment. The priority given to war materials by the European
countries further aggravated these supply difficulties. As soon as war
broke out, imports of machinery fell, dropping from 4 million taels
worth in 1914 to 2.2 million in 1915.[7] England stopped delivering steel
and the price of Australian steel, sales of which slowed down but
continued, doubled between the beginning and the end of 1915. In its
report to its tenth general assembly, the Hanyeping Mining and Iron
Company deplored the fact that, because of the impossibility of
improving its equipment, the company had not been able to make the
most of the advantageous situation created by the war.[8] The handicraft sector then made an effort to cater for demands that the national
industries were unable to satisfy. In the northern provinces, weaving
was developed both as a cottage industry and on the level of small
workshops. The progress of these weaving crafts depended upon the
diffusion of industrial yarns and was accompanied by an unpreceden-
ted upsurge of commercial capitalism. It did not constitute a revival of
archaic methods, but on the contrary testified to the irreversible nature
of the opening-up of China. This is a particularly clear example of
transitional modernisation.

Nevertheless, even the combined efforts of the modern and the
traditional sectors could not make up for the withdrawal of the
European powers. While it favoured national Chinese business, that
withdrawal simultaneously encouraged the expansion of Japanese and
American interests, sowing the seeds of new difficulties and future
conflicts. American penetration took an essentially financial form. In
line with this, the Asia Banking Corporation was set up to organise the
combined interests of a whole collection of trusts which set out to gain
control of Chinese businesses and took part in the expanding trade
relations between China and America. By 1917, the United States
share of Chinese overseas trade had risen to 11% for imports and 20%
for exports.[9] Japan made even more rapid progress. By 1915, the
Japanese government was seeking to extend the territorial and political
bases of its economic penetration. In its Twenty-one Demands, put

forward in 1915, it presented itself as heir to the former German possessions in Shandong and claimed the right to 'advise' the Peking government. Over the following years, the negotiations for the Nishihara loans provided the opportunity for a new diplomatic offensive. Japanese capital was introduced into China through the intermediary of large companies such as the Eastern Colonisation Company (Tōyō takushoku kaisha), the Far-Eastern Prosperity Company (Tōa kōgyō kaisha) and the Sino-Japanese Industrial Company (Chū-Nichi jitsu-gyō kaisha).[10] Unlike the Americans, the Japanese were not content simply to acquire shares. They also made many direct industrial investments in cotton mills, heavy industry and a number of modernisation operations. The number of Japanese spindles operating in China tripled between 1913 and 1919, increasing from 110,000 to 332,000.[11] Imports of merchandise kept pace with those of capital. On the eve of the outbreak of war, Japan had supplied China with 15.5% of its imports; by 1919, she supplied 29.9%.[12] By 1917, Japan had supplanted Great Britain as a supplier of cotton fabrics and also became a major vendor of industrial equipment.

In the modern sector, the difficulties provoked by the war led to a failure to make profits rather than to genuine losses. They showed how limited the effects of external favourable circumstances can be for a dependent economy. It was only when the state of war came to an end that Chinese industry truly entered upon its golden age.

The favourable circumstances survived the war that gave rise to them. Far from falling off, the demand for raw materials and foodstuffs increased. The needs of war were replaced by those of reconstruction. Even more supplies were needed to feed the undernourished civilian population than for the armies. Chinese exports increased in response to this apparently 'insatiable' demand. The customs inspectors stationed in the various treaty ports were all in agreement that 1919 was an 'exceptionally prosperous' year (Chongqing and Shanghai), 'an excellent year' (Hankou), 'a record year' (Wenzhou, Wuhu).[13]

The increase in exports was all the more remarkable given that the value of silver continued to rise and with it the exchange rate of the Chinese tael. But the needs of the European buyers were so pressing that, undaunted by this unfavourable exchange rate, they were prepared to pay top prices for Chinese merchandise. To give some idea of the profits made by the exporters, it is enough to note that by

Table 2.2. *Increases in imports of industrial materials in 1919 (values expressed in customs taels)*

Category of materials	1918	1919
Railway engines	732,424	10,426,470
Coaches	2,011,998	4,844,302
Electrical apparatus	4,808,355	6,110,028
Textile equipment	1,808,887	3,905,821

Source: The China Yearbook, 1921–1922, pp. 1004–6.

February 1920 the Chinese tael, having risen steadily for four years, had an exchange rate of 1.48 American dollars.

The increasing strength of the Chinese tael, which did nothing to arrest the growth of exports, naturally provided direct encouragement for imports. Its full effect came to be felt just as the handicaps caused by the war were disappearing. The moment the Armistice was signed, transportation costs to America fell from 60 to 40 dollars per metric ton. Shipyards resumed work and by 1920 freight costs were more or less back at their pre-war level.

The return to a normal shipping situation coincided with the reconversion of the war industries: Chinese entrepreneurs could at last order and take delivery of the equipment that their expanding outlets on the domestic market made necessary. 'So far as textile machinery was concerned, demand was so high that potential buyers attached more importance to fast delivery than to the matter of cost.' By the first months of 1919, Anderson, Meyer and Company alone had received over twenty orders amounting to millions of taels.[14] Other industrial branches, such as railways, flour mills and oil works, were soon buying heavily too (see Table 2.2).

1919 thus found China enjoying a combination of favourable circumstances: exports were stimulated by the exceptionally heavy American and European demand and imports continued to be encouraged by the falling value of gold, which operated, for Chinese buyers, as a devaluation of Western currencies would. Chinese businesses benefited at once from the demand created earlier by Western imports, the relative protection afforded by the decline of foreign competition, and the improved supplies of machinery and equipment from the European and American markets. Such a combination of circumstances was bound to lead to expansion in a modern sector that was by now more directly sensitive to the kinds of stimulus that stemmed from fluctuations in world politics.

2   The upsurge of the modern sector and the second wave of Chinese industrialisation

The second wave of Chinese industrialisation, which took place between 1914 and 1924, was quite unlike the earlier experience of the 'Western Affairs' Movement in the late nineteenth century. Industrialisation imposed from above, as attempted by the imperial regime in the years of its decline, was now superseded by a 'horizontal' industrialisation, borne along by the current of popular nationalism that mobilised the energies not only of the entrepreneurs but also of a proportion of the intelligentsia and the bureaucracy. These social strata initiated all kinds of moves that gave this process its own specific character. The earlier industrialisation, which had reflected the military preoccupations of the ruling classes, had concentrated chiefly upon heavy industry, and resulted in the setting-up of large businesses financed, either partly or totally, by public funds. In contrast, in this new period of industrialisation actions were deliberately tailored to needs: those involved sought to cater for the existing demands of the market and were prompted in so doing by a desire for immediate profits. They consequently favoured the production of consumer goods. The movement of industrialisation thus proceeded with the expansion of light industry and small or medium-sized businesses: the average level of investment in modern businesses of every kind registered by the Ministry of Agriculture and Trade in 1920 was 140,000 dollars.[15]

Between 1912 and 1920 Chinese industry achieved an annual rate of growth of 13.8%, whereas over the 1912–49 period as a whole it amounted to no more than 5.5%. And even if one excludes the period of economic dislocation represented by the Sino-Japanese War, the rate between 1912 and 1936 amounts to only 9.2%.[16] A rate of growth comparable to that of the 1912–20 period was only achieved during the first five-year plan, between 1953 and 1957.

The expansion was particularly remarkable in the cotton industry, the pilot sector among the national industries (see Table 2.3). The creation of new cotton mills, hampered at the beginning of the war by the lack of equipment, speeded up in 1919. Between 1914 and 1918,

Table 2.3. *The increases in the number of Chinese spindles and looms provided by national capital between 1913 and 1920*

Years	Spindles	Looms
1913	484,192	2,016
1914	544,780	2,300
1918	647,570	3,502
1919	658,748	2,650
1920	842,894	4,310

Source: Yan Zhongping, *Tongli ziliao*, p. 134.

Table 2.4. *The progress of the Dasheng Cotton Mills*

Years	Spindles	Total capital (in millions of taels)
1914	66,700	1.9
1920	100,000	2.9
1921	135,040	3.2

Source: Zhon Xiuluan, *Zhonggue minzugongyede fazhan*, chapter 2.

eight factories had been set up; 1919 saw the establishment of four, followed by nine more in 1920. In 1922, the number of new cotton mills rose to 49. This expansion was due to the efforts of a handful of big businessmen. The doyen of the group, Zhang Jian, had created the Dasheng Cotton Mills (Dasheng shachang), setting up his first factory in Nantong (Jiangsu) in 1899. In 1907, he opened another factory in Chongming (Jiangsu). During the war he established a new branch in Haimen, which started production in 1921. At the same time, he was completing the equipment of his already existing factories and extending their range of operations (see Table 2.4).

Nie Yuntai also made the most of the situation created by the war and reorganised the Hengfeng Cotton Mill (Hengfeng shachang), a factory comprising 15,000 spindles, which had been making heavy losses and which he had acquired before the 1911 revolution. He now set up a company with capital of over one million taels.[17] Mu Ouchu, a younger man (1876–1942), returned from the United States at the beginning of the war. Within five years he had founded three large cotton mills: Deda (Deda shachang) in 1915, Housheng (Housheng shachang) in 1918 and Yufeng (Yufeng shachang) in 1919. Over one

Table 2.5. *The expansion of the Shenxin Cotton Mills*

Name of factory	Date of creation	Number of spindles	Capital in millions of dollars
Shenxin no. 1	1915	38,800	3.0
Shenxin no. 2	Factory bought by the Rongs in 1917	35,400	1.9
Shenxin no. 3	1921	51,000	2.0
Shenxin no. 4	1920	17,600	1.7

Source: Maoxin Fuxin Shenxin zonggonsi sazhounian jiniance.

million dollars of capital was sunk in each of these concerns, through which Mu Ouchu controlled a total of over 100,000 spindles.[18]

The Shenxin Cotton Mills,[19] which belonged to the Rong family also expanded during the war (see Table 2.5).

Most of the new cotton mills were set up in Shanghai, about 15 of them according to Yan Zhongping's census, which was based on 40 establishments. Even so, it is clear that many factories tended to cluster around areas where cotton was produced. They were set up in Jinan (one), Tianjin (six), Zhengzhou, near the cotton fields of Shandong and Hebei, and also in the middle Yangzi region.[20]

In the absence of any statistics relating to production, the rapid acquisition of new equipment is a clear indication of the expansion of the national cotton industries. And that expansion is confirmed by a number of indications showing an increasing diffusion of Chinese cotton fabrics and yarns on the domestic market. As early as 1916, for instance, the Hankou customs inspector noted an increase in transit certificates issued in this port by the Chinese government to the products of national industries exempted from *lijin* dues. The increase was connected with the expanding market for Chinese cotton fabrics and yarns, which replaced Japanese products in the western provinces, in particular in Sichuan, traditionally a large buyer of cotton goods.[21]

Another leading sector of national industry was flour milling, which had been introduced and developed during the war. Before 1914, in the whole of China there had existed no more than a dozen modern mills, most owned by foreigners. Flour supplies for large urban centres such as Shanghai and Tianjin had been imported from abroad. From 1914 on, these imports were gradually discontinued and the Western powers themselves began to try to purchase flour on the world market. China

Table 2.6. *The progress of the Maoxin and Fuxin Mills*

Names of the mills	Location	Date of creation	Capital in dollars
Maoxin no. 1	Wuxi	1901	
Maoxin no. 2	Wuxi	1916	
Maoxin no. 3	Jinan	1919	250,000
Fuxin no. 1	Shanghai	1913	500,000
Fuxin no. 2	Shanghai	1914	1,900,000
Fuxin no. 3	Shanghai	1926	
Fuxin no. 4	Shanghai	1913	
Fuxin no. 5	Hankou	1918	1,500,000
Fuxin no. 6	Shanghai	1919	400,000
Fuxin no. 7	Shanghai	1920	1,500,000
Fuxin no. 8	Shanghai	1919	

Sources: Maoxin Fuxin Shenxin zonggongsu sazhounian jiniance; CWR, 27 August 1921, pp. 654–6.

was by now developing its own flour mills: 26 were set up between 1917 and 1922 and in 1920 exports in flour were worth as much as 20 million taels. It was essentially Shanghai and the lower Yangzi region that were affected by this boom, and to a large extent it coincided with the success of the businesses of the Rong brothers, who owned the Maoxin and the Fuxin Mills (see Table 2.6).

Oil mills followed a similar, if more restricted, course of development. Apart from Manchuria, which had been colonised by Japanese interests, the main manufacturing centre was Shanghai. But the effect of the war seems to have been to provoke a general takeover of foreign factories by Chinese capital, rather than a wave of newly created establishments. For example, the Hengyu Company, one of the largest in Shanghai, founded by the Germans in about 1910, was bought up at the beginning of the war by Li Jingxi (a relative of Li Hongzhang).[22]

If Shanghai thus appears as the main centre of the textile and food industries, it was around Canton that factories producing cigarettes, paper and matches were set up. The customs records for 1919 note that the Guangdong Tobacco Company (Guangdong tuzhi yancao gongsi) and the Patriotic Company of Southern China (Nanfang aiguo yancao gongsi) were growing 'like mushrooms'. But the growth in production in particular reflected the successes of the Nanyang Brothers' Tobacco Company.[23] Established in Hong Kong originally, this company had until 1912 been content to sell its products on the spot or in Singapore. The war provided it with a chance to develop markets in China itself –

Table 2.7. *The developing production of the Nanyang Brothers' Tobacco Company (1912–17) (quantities expressed in cases of 50,000 cigarettes)*

Years	Cases	Index of Growth
1912	4,758	100
1915	18,609	391
1917	33,825	710

Source: *Nanyang xiongdi yancao gongsi shiliao*, p. 19.

in Canton, which in 1919 took about a quarter of its production, in Shantou (Swatow), in Xiamen (Amoy) and in Yunnan province. In 1916, the Nanyang brothers opened a branch in Shanghai, but in the lower Yangzi region they ran into competition from the British American Tobacco Company and also from Japanese imports. In establishing a grip on this market, the Nanyang Brothers' Tobacco Company employed every trick in the modern advertising book: posters, banknotes offered as prizes in a certain number of cigarette packets, and so on. Their campaign was successful: in 1917, two new branches opened in Ningbo and Shanghai. In 1919, the company was reorganised: it increased its capital and transferred its headquarters to Shanghai. Increasing production had kept up with widening markets (see Table 2.7).

Another feature of this period of expansion was the appearance of new kinds of industry. Ma Yushan (1878–1929), a rich entrepreneur who had made a fortune from confectionery in the Philippines, tried to create a modern sugar industry. China was at this time importing over half the sugar that it used: 450,000 out of 800,000 metric tons. The war had upset relations between the industrial powers and the colonial cane producers. This gave China a chance to enter the market. But the Chinese capitalists failed to seize that chance and, instead, the large English refineries of Hong Kong profited from the situation. However, at the end of the war their huge profits stimulated Chinese initiatives. With the aid of the biggest industrialists of Shanghai (Zhang Jian and Nie Yuntai), Ma Yushan in 1921 organised the National Company of the Refineries of China (Zhonghua guomin zhitang gongsi) with capital of 5 million dollars and set about encouraging the cultivation of sugar beet in the northern provinces.[24] It was rare for such large amounts of capital to be invested in new manufacturing sectors. They usually sprang up simply as a result of the general multiplication of already existing small businesses: hat-making workshops, soap factories, paperworks, glassworks, factories producing napkins, carpets and sewing machines, breweries, and wine- and lemonade-producing plants. Of the 200 small manufacturing plants set up during the war in Peking, very few employed over 100 workers.[25]

Expansion in heavy industry was much less widespread than in light industry: where it occurred, it was chiefly with the backing of foreign capital, Japanese in particular. Between 1913 and 1921, production in modern coal mines rose from 12 million to 20 million metric tons, but barely one quarter of it was controlled by Chinese capital. The production of iron mines, which tripled in the space of a few years, reaching 1.3 million tons in 1920, was, for its part, completely controlled by Japanese capital.[26]

The most remarkable progress made by industries producing machinery and equipment was made by the mechanical engineering works, which were multiplying rapidly in Shanghai. Between 1912 and 1924, 202 new workshops of this kind are recorded as being set up, over 50% of them between 1918 and 1921. Many of these new workshops (29%) were devoted to the maintenance and repair of equipment of various kinds. Next in importance came the manufacture of knitting machines, hand-weaving looms, and equipment designed for processing agricultural products and for the production of wood-turning lathes and small motors used in small semi-industrial workshops. Most of these mechanical engineering works were modest concerns. A 1920 enquiry relating to 114 of them shows that they employed on average no more than 25 workers and that 25% of them used no form of mechanical power (46% were equipped with electric motors and 25% with motors that ran on other types of fuel). The largest concerns were the shipyards and the workshops that manufactured modern textile equipment, such as the Qiuxin and Dalong Companies (Qiuxin zhizao jiqi lunchuanchang and Dalong jiqichang). But it was difficult for them to expand fast enough to keep up with demand and in most cases these businesses limited themselves to the repair and maintenance of equipment imported from abroad.[27]

The imbalance between the development of light industry and that of heavy industry, between the production of consumer goods and that of machinery is still condemned by Chinese historians as a feature of colonial underdevelopment and a fundamental cause for the fragility of the system. Both conclusions call for qualifications and reservations. A predominance of light industry is characteristic not only of a colonial economy but equally of a delayed movement of industrialisation taking place solely within the private sector and seeking to make profits by supplying consumer demands. A dearth of long-term investment may not stem from a lack of capital (for in this case, as we shall presently see, it was relatively abundant), but may be caused by the absence of any *political will* for development. The eclipse of State power made economic expansion a strictly haphazard affair that reflected the existing market forces. It was a pragmatic operation which was furthermore conditioned by the level of technology in the Chinese modern sector, which now, with the foreigners gone, was left dependent upon its own resources. These were limited. The changes that had taken place since the end of the nineteenth century had made, on balance, for, on the one hand, a transitional wave of modernisation and, on the other, the establishment of large-scale industries based on simple technology, such as cotton mills. Recent examples of industrialisation – in Taiwan, Hong Kong, Singapore or South Korea – show that an initial predominance of light industry with a basis of low-level technology does not, in itself, constitute an obstacle to further development. It is all a matter of the international context, for this type of industrialisation depends to a large extent upon the growth and tendencies of external trade. In this respect the second Chinese movement of industrialisation was no exception.

Following a period of moderate expansion up until 1917, the development of external trade kept up with that of the industrial sector. The total value of imports and exports rose from 1,040 million taels in 1918 to 1,676 million in 1923 (see Table 2.8). This growth was determined in the first place by that of exports, which increased by 34.5% between 1918 and 1919. China's chief exports continued to be raw materials, but these were diversifying and in some cases processed merchandise was taking the place of primary products. Commercial transactions were assuming a less colonial character.

From 1918 onwards, the collapse of the Russian market, following hard upon the closure of the English outlet, dealt a severe blow to the sale of Chinese teas, but, stimulated by American demand, exports of silk rose rapidly, increasing from 87,517 piculs in 1914 to 131,000 in 1919.[28] Overall, however, the increase in exports was due above all to the introduction of new types of merchandise. Sales of foodstuffs and

Table 2.8. *The development of the value of external Chinese trade between 1911 and 1937 (value expressed in taels before 1933 and Chinese dollars after 1933)*

Years	Imports	Exports	Overall value of external mode	Commercial balance
1911	471,504	377,388	848,842	− 94,166
1912	473,097	370,520	843,617	−102,577
1913	570,163	403,306	973,468	−166,857
1914	569,241	356,227	925,468	−213,015
1915	454,476	418,861	873,337	− 35,615
1916	516,407	481,797	988,204	− 34,610
1917	549,519	462,932	1,012,450	− 86,587
1918	554,893	485,883	1,040,776	− 69,010
1919	646,998	630,809	1,277,807	− 16,188
1920	762,250	541,631	1,303,882	−220,619
1921	906,122	601,256	1,507,378	−304,867
1922	945,050	654,892	1,599,942	−290,158
1923	923,403	752,917	1,676,320	−170,485
1924	1,018,211	771,784	1,789,995	−246,426
1925	947,865	776,353	1,724,218	−171,512
1926	1,124,221	864,295	1,998,516	−259,926
1927	1,012,932	918,620	1,931,551	− 94,312
1928	1,195,969	991,335	2,187,324	−204,614
1929	1,265,779	1,015,687	2,281,466	−250,092
1930	1,309,756	894,844	2,204,599	−414,912
1931	1,433,489	909,476	2,342,965	−524,014
1932	1,049,247	492,989	1,542,236	−556,258
1933	1,345,567	612,293	1,957,860	−733,274
1934	1,029,665	535,733	1,565,399	−493,932
1935	919,211	576,298	1,495,510	−342,913
1936	941,545	706,791	1,648,336	−234,754
1937	953,386	838,770	1,792,156	−114,616

Source: Hsiao Liang-Lin, *China's Foreign Trade Statistics 1864–1949*, table 1, pp. 22–4.

oil products increased after the Armistice. China also began exporting more leather and even raw cotton: Japanese cotton mills, expanding rapidly, were willing to pay high prices for Chinese cotton. There was a short-lived export boom in non-ferrous ores, in particular antimony and tungsten. In 1916, China sold 12 million taels worth of antimony, that is to say over 40% of the needs of the world market. Within a few months, ore prices doubled at Changsha, the outlet for the greater part of what was produced,[29] but the boom soon collapsed under pressure from Bolivian competition. Meanwhile, the pattern of imports was undergoing a fundamental change: the proportion of consumer goods,

Table 2.9. *The pattern of investment in modern Chinese banks between 1912 and 1920*

Years	Capital (in millions of dollars)	Index
1912	36.0	100
1916	37.0	105
1920	51.9	144

Source: Zhang Yulan, *Zhongguo yinhangye fazhanshi*, p. 41.

particularly cotton fabrics, dropped while that of machinery and equipment rose. In 1920, the latter accounted for 28.5% of the total value of Chinese foreign purchases.[30]

The divergence between the evolution of imports and that of exports helped to improve the trade figures, which had been showing an increasing deficit ever since the 1880s. Over the 1899–1913 period, it had on average been as high as 115 million taels per year; between 1915 and 1919 it dropped to 48.4 millions and for the year 1919 the figure was as low as 16 million. By the end of the war, the trade figures had thus evened out, thanks to the growth of exports and an overall drop in imports, achieved at the expense of consumer goods rather than machinery and equipment. Such a trade balance may well be characteristic of an underdeveloped economy, but in this case it was no longer that of a dependent one. It corresponded, rather, to the first phase of growth in a modern national economy.

Throughout the boom period, the growth of trade and production was supported by an increasing availability of credit and stimulated by rising prices and profits. The decline of the foreign banks undermined external trade but did not affect the domestic market, where the Chinese had always controlled finance. Indeed, that decline made large sums available to national businessmen, in the shape of the capital of the elite groups and compradores, which, for reasons of security or self-interest, had hitherto chiefly been invested in foreign activities.

The rise of modern Chinese banks dates from the First World War. (see Table 2.9). Between 1918 and 1919 alone 96 new banks were set up! Admittedly, most retained close links with the public authorities. That is true of the extremely official Bank of China (Zhongguo yinhang) and the Communications Bank (Jiaotong yinhang), a dozen

Table 2.10. *Increase in the deposits of the National Commercial Bank from 1913 to 1918 (in millions of dollars)*

Years	Deposits
1913	2.6
1914	3.9
1915	4.3
1916	5.0
1917	8.2
1918	10.0

Source: 'The Development of Modern Banking in China', *CWR*, 20 September, 1919.

or so provincial banks and many 'political' banks, whose founders either came from government circles or maintained close links with high officials. The activities of all these establishments were limited to the manipulation of State funds and loans. In contrast, a dozen or so modern banks, mostly established in Shanghai, were managed on a purely commercial basis.

In 1915, the National Commercial Bank (Zhejiang xingye yinhang), created in 1906 in Hangzhou, moved its headquarters to Shanghai. During the war it extended its network of branches into the central and northern provinces and the rapid increase in the sums deposited with it testifies to its success (see Table 2.10).

The Shanghai Bank of Trade and Savings (Shanghai shangye chuxu yinhang), generally known as the Shanghai Bank, was set up in 1915 by Zhang Jian in partnership with Chen Guangfu (1881–1976), along with a number of other entrepreneurs. It enjoyed immediate prosperity: its initial capital of 100,000 dollars rose to 1 million in 1919, while its deposits rose to 5 million dollars. The Industrial Bank of Zhejiang (Zhejiang difang shiye yinhang) was created in 1915, following the reorganisation, on a purely commercial basis, of the former Provincial Bank of Zhejiang, which now gave up handling public funds, since a branch of the Bank of China had seen set up in Hangzhou. We should also mention the Salt Gabelle Bank (Yanye yinhang), set up in Peking in 1915, the Ningbo Bank (Siming yinhang), created that same year in Shanghai, and the Zhongfu Bank (Zhongfu yinhang), established in Tianjin in 1916.

The part played by these banks in the financing of national undertakings was nevertheless limited by the antiquated structures of

Table 2.11. *The increase in the number of* qianzhuang *in Shanghai from 1913 to 1920*

Years	Creations	Closures	Banks in existence
1913	3	–	31
1914	9	–	40
1915	2	–	42
1916	10	3	49
1917	–	–	49
1918	19	6	62
1919	7	2	67
1920	4	2	71

Source: *Shanghai qianzhuang shiliao*, p. 188.

the market. Before the war, no Chinese stock exchange had existed, nor had any produce exchange. The stock exchange of Shanghai, in the International Settlement, only dealt in foreign securities. The creation of a Shanghai Stock and Commodity Exchange (Shanghai zhenquan wupinjiaosuo), in February 1920, set the style for a whole string of imitations. By the end of 1921, Shanghai possessed 140 establishments most of which dealt exclusively in their own shares. But a few months later a general crash put an end to this 'stock exchange storm' (*xinjiao fengchao*).

In order to finance business, the modern banks thus had to resort to direct loans, in exactly the same fashion as the traditional *qianzhuang* banks. But the fact that the modern banks were obliged to demand guarantees from their clients, in the form of property mortgages or the deposit of merchandise, set them at a disadvantage to the *qianzhuang*, which operated according to the old traditional rules and on the basis of personal connections, and were prepared to offer unsecured, so-called confidential loans on trust (*xinyong*). As a result, despite the spectacular but essentially speculative success of the modern banking sector, the *qianzhuang* continued to operate as the real business banks. By 1920, Shanghai could boast 71 of them (as compared with 31 in 1913) and the capital that they controlled – 7.7 million dollars – had increased fivefold since just before the war (see Table 2.11).

Within the short space of a few years, the number of *qianzhuang* thus increased by roughly 130%. Concurrently, the mass of capital that they controlled increased by over 500% (see Table 2.12).

Table 2.12. *The increase in the capital of the Shanghai* qianzhuang *between 1913 and 1920 (capital in dollars)*

Years	Banks	Total capital	Index 100 = 1912	Average capital per bank
1913	31	1,600,000	113.1	54,300
1914	40	2,000,000	137.7	51,200
1915	42	2,100,000	145.2	51,500
1916	49	2,800,000	190.0	57,700
1917	49	2,800,000	190.0	57,000
1918	62	4,300,000	295.0	71,000
1919	67	5,200,000	355.0	79,000
1920	71	7,700,000	522.0	109,000

Source: Shanghai qianzhuang shiliao, p. 191.

The capital invested in the *qianzhuang* came from a number of quarters. The compradores, who until 1914 had entrusted their funds to the foreign banks, turned to the *qianzhuang* during the war years. But it was above all the traditional investors of funds, the opium merchants and the owners of dyeing businesses, who addressed themselves to the *qianzhuang* when it came to investing their fortunes, now swollen by their wartime speculations. The opium merchants had long had dealings with the *qianzhuang*. With very little capital at their command initially, these merchants had needed a series of short-term loans to launch the sale of their merchandise. Once they had made their fortunes (and after prohibition the illegal traffic in opium increased these more and more rapidly), they themselves quite naturally branched out into banking. For example, at the time of its creation, in 1915, the Xingyu Bank (Xingyu qianzhuang) was financed by three opium businesses and was managed by a former comprador for a foreign import firm which used to give preferential treatment to the orders of these particular businesses. Businessmen in the dye trade, who had made huge profits at the beginning of the war by speculating on the increasing scarcity of foreign chemical products, now seized the opportunity to finance credit banks, setting up even more of these than the opium merchants, and usually on a more solid and reputable basis.[31]

The increase in the capital of the *qianzhuang* gives no more than a partial idea of the way in which their financial means grew. The operations of these banks had always depended upon the deposits that they received from their clients, first and foremost from the business-men who had founded them. The accounting records left by these *qianzhuang* are by no means complete, but a few isolated cases will help to give some idea of how they operated.

The Hengxing Bank (Hengxing qianzhuang), founded in 1905 by a Ningbo financier, possessed capital to the tune of 100,000 taels on the eve of the war. In the years that followed, that capital fluctuated not at all, but deposits, which had amounted to 582,000 taels in 1913, were in excess of 800,000 taels by 1919. As a result, more loans were made: 407,748 taels in 1913, 931,031 taels in 1919. Most were short-term loans of fairly modest sums (ranging from 5,000 to 30,000 taels) and were chiefly designed to ease the cash flow of the businesses that received them. In most cases the banks asked for no guarantees: in 1919, loans on trust of this kind accounted for two-thirds of the advances agreed. The beneficiaries were merchants and industrialists. The Shanghai *qianzhuang* played a particularly important role in the financing of local silk factories. But the accounts of the Hengxing Bank show that the *qianzhuang* also made loans to large modern cotton spinning mills such as the Dasheng and Hengfeng Cotton Mills.[32] So the *qianzhuang* could be described as business banks financing the expansion of both the modern and the traditional sectors. But the personal nature of the banks' relations with their clients, which ensured the continuing popularity of the *qianzhuang* banks, at the same time limited the scope of their activities. The *qianzhuang* were essen-tially local establishments. Although the major ones had branches in the various treaty ports, they did not constitute a sufficiently coherent network to guarantee reliable financial backing for an expansion that was taking place on a national scale and within a worldwide frame-work. On several occasions – October 1916, May 1917, October 1918, November 1919 – the financial market of Shanghai was struck by severe squeezes, the effect of which was to put a break on business expansion.

In the absence of a stock exchange market and a national bank rate to refer to, let us consult, as a barometer of economic and financial development, the rate of interest on inter-bank loans (*yinzhe*) in the Shanghai market place. The monthly average rate rose from 0.06 cadareen (or 1/100th of a tael) per day in 1919 to 0.17 in 1922.[33] Although this rise in the value of silver may be explained by purely financial reasons (the return to the metropolis of metal reserves from foreign banks and the speculative buying of gold on the world market), the particular needs of an expanding economy no doubt played their part: for instance, the sale of harvests for export led to a growing run on silver in the financial markets of the large towns.

The price records at our disposal are constructed by a variety of methods and on the basis of a range of heterogeneous data and do not provide evidence reliable enough for accurate analyses. Nevertheless it is possible to detect a rise of between 20% and 44% in wholesale prices during the First World War. This evolution, which is quite moderate compared to that which affected Western countries during the same period, can be explained by the fact that agricultural prices remained stable while industrial prices soared. Within the framework of a traditional rural economy, this stability of agricultural prices (which did not affect the prices of certain export products) is not really the sign of a stagnant market. Rather, it indicates the favourable nature of climatic conditions, in other words the relative equilibrium of the rural world. The stability of agricultural prices and the rise in industrial ones may both be regarded as signs of prosperity.[34]

It was above all in the business world that this prosperity paid off. Between 1914 and 1919, the average profit made by cotton mills per bale of yarn rose by 267%,[35] while the profits of the *qianzhuang* rose on average by 80%.[36] Major companies increased their profits by 20% or even 50%. Dividends rose from 30% to 40% or even 90%. The profits made by entrepreneurs were all the greater given that they were scarcely shared among their employees at all: the wages of craftsmen and workers rose by no more than about 7% in Canton and between 10% and 20% in Shanghai.[37]

3   The modern sector and the national economy: resistance to the world reconversion crisis

The expansion of the modern sector accentuated the dualism of the Chinese economy. A gap was developing between the large coastal cities oriented towards international trade, on the one hand, and inland China, still living according to the rhythm of its harvests, on the other. All the same, Shanghai, Tianjin and Canton could not be regarded as enclaves of the colonial type, completely alien to the country surrounding them and developing along totally independent lines.

In the early 1920s, the agrarian crises and famines which assailed inland China affected the economy of the treaty ports with consequences both direct and indirect that I have attempted to analyse elsewhere.[38] But one may also wonder to what extent the modern sector, which developed thanks to the circumstances of the international situation, remained dependent upon those circumstances and governed by their fluctuations. The reactions of the treaty ports to the severe 1920–2 reconversion crisis in the West and in Japan highlight the relative Chinese autonomy – an autonomy which was not simply a consequence of China's underdevelopment. Within the framework of regional solidarities, the abundance of natural resources and the vitality of the domestic market tended to mitigate the consequences of the crisis and made it possible for the national industries to continue to expand.

The reconversion crisis which struck the major economic powers did not arise until 18 months after the end of the war. In England and France, the need for reconstruction and the recovery of the consumer market had stimulated demand. But in these deeply war-torn countries, the runaway rise in prices was turning into inflation. In the United States, where the liquid funds accumulated during the war maintained a high level of internal demand, the speculation which accompanied the replenishment of stocks was emphasising the inflationist nature of the expansion. It was in Japan, with the silk crash of March 1920, that the crisis exploded. Repercussions from the Japanese crisis were immediately felt on the New York stock exchange and gradually all industrialised countries found themselves involved in the depression. Everywhere, credit became harder to find, industrial production fell off, firms went out of business and unemployment spread. International trade was also severely hit. The markets of the industrialised countries were closed to luxury products and to imports of certain raw materials. The crisis thus soon spread beyond the circle of industrialised countries where it originated, reaching Latin America, Australia, India and finally China, whose exports now found fewer outlets in Western markets.

Furthermore, China now had to cope with the fluctuating value of silver on the international market. After the sharp rise in its value during the war and immediately after, in March 1920 silver began to fall, when the European countries sold heavily, and it continued to fall until the end of 1921, when it stabilised at more or less its pre-war value. The sudden fall of silver carried with it the Chinese tael, which dropped from 1.48 (American) dollars in February 1920 to 0.74 dollars in December 1921.[39] The weakening of the tael in relation to foreign currencies linked to the gold standard inflicted repercussions upon the price of Chinese imports, which now shot up. Such a situation was not in itself unfavourable to the national economy, to the extent that the prohibitive rates for imports constituted a sort of protection for a market with no customs barriers, particularly at a time when the depreciation of the tael was stimulating exports. But in 1920, Chinese exports also became affected: '... the conditions abroad are a stone wall against any activity.'[40] The world reconversion crisis was short-lived but severe, striking all the major economic powers simultaneously. Even a dramatic devaluation of the tael could not keep exports going when they were being refused by Western markets right across the board.

The turn for the worse in the international situation was thus immediately reflected in the brake put upon the growth of external trade. Its overall value, which had reached the record figure of 1,276 million taels in 1919, peaked at 1,302 millions the following year. Then exports dropped by about 16%. Despite the diversification introduced over recent years, luxury or semi-luxury goods, such as silk or tea, were still playing a major role and their decline determined that of other commodities generally.

France and the United States were the principal buyers of Chinese silk, between them absorbing virtually all exports from Shanghai and Canton. Now, in the spring of 1920, demand from the American market ceased and a kilo of silk, which had fetched 36 American dollars in 1919, was a few months later worth no more than 10.[41] The Lyons market also suffered an abrupt depreciation, with prices falling from 500 to 200 francs per kilo between the beginning and the end of 1920.[42] Furthermore, the market was flooded by Japanese stocks which the Tokyo government was trying hard to get off its hands. The tea crisis was even more serious: the new difficulties of the situation now compounded the profound unease produced in 1918 when Russia, hitherto China's major client, stopped buying tea.

The closure of foreign markets directly affected activity in the major export ports, namely (in decreasing order of magnitude) Shanghai (handling 41.4% of exports in the 1919–20 period), Dairen, Tianjin and Hankou. By the end of 1920, trade was virtually at a standstill.

Activity remained no more than sporadic in 1921 and 1922. Only in 1923 did foreign demand begin to pick up again.

Chinese producers and intermediaries working for the major export companies were badly hit by the crisis. Many faced the possibility of going out of business in the winter of 1920. The Shanghai Guild for Silks and Cocoons appealed in vain to the Peking government for financial aid. The Hankou albumen and egg merchants for their part appealed to the Chinese Chamber of Commerce. But it was probably some of the tea merchants and producers who were most lastingly affected. They suffered heavy losses betwee 1918 and 1921 and a number of plantations were converted or abandoned.[43]

However, contrary to what might have been expected, the prices of Chinese exports did not collapse entirely. The fall in prices that accompanied the beginning of the crisis was less drastic in China than in Western countries: for example, the price of sesame seeds in London fell from 70 to 30 shillings per hundredweight, a drop of about 56%, whereas in China the same product depreciated barely 20% (from 8 to 6.5 taels). In the autumn of 1920, 'Chinese new season products for export are being offered at prices either the same or slightly lower than those of last year.'[44] By 1921, when Western rates were still extremely low, Chinese prices were rising to recover or even exceed their earlier level. One case in point was that of raw silk and cotton, the price of which rose from 24 to 37 taels per picul between January and September 1921.[45] Thus, while the difficulties of Western markets affected the volume of transactions, they had few repercussions on the prices of the products that China was seeking to export.

How can these differences be explained? Contemporary observers pointed to the ignorance of the Chinese merchants and their inexperience of the world market; 'Long isolation from the outside world ... [has] not prepared the Chinese merchant to look to other countries and to general financial and commercial undercurrents ... This unpreparedness is to be found in present market prices in China of raw materials, which are still at high levels when prices in other parts of the world are declining.'[46] But to understand the buoyancy of Chinese prices, we should also bear in mind that a number of shortages were occasioned by the partial failure of the cotton crops in 1920 and of the silk cocoons in 1921. The importance of these agricultural circumstances, which in this case counterbalanced the international situation, is but one aspect of the all-important role that the domestic market played in the evolution of the Chinese economy. It was the immensity and vitality of this market that provided a bulwark against the spread of the world depression. The very mass of Chinese consumers offered the country as a whole a relative measure of protection against the fluctuations of foreign demand: 'Merchandise destined for export, that foreigners were unable to buy, were used in China itself.'[47] In Shandong and southern Manchuria, the development of local silk mills – in a handicraft or semi-modern format – made it possible to process on the spot cocoons that had previously been sent off to the treaty ports. As for raw cotton, Chinese factories were absorbing increasing quantities and, as purchasers, were taking the place of the Japanese cotton mills.[48] The effects of the export crisis were thus cushioned by the vitality of the Chinese market and its ability to adapt to the situation. Meanwhile imports, unlike exports, continued to grow steadily, without wavering even when the international situation was reversed.[49] Stimulated by the rise in Western prices and encouraged by an increasingly favourable rate of exchange, many Chinese merchants had placed large orders at the beginning of 1920. But a few months later, when the merchandise ordered began to arrive in China, many of these businessmen found themselves unable to take delivery. The trouble was that the stability of export prices was not repeated in import prices. From April 1920 onwards, the sudden depreciation of silver and the consequent weakening of the tael led to an immediate and proportionate rise in the prices of Western goods; and import contracts invariably stipulated that these be paid for in gold-standard currency. By May 1921, the prices of goods on the Tianjin market were thus three times higher than in the previous year.[50] We must remember that in China all import operations were partly, if not first and foremost, speculative. The element of speculation involved related to the fortunes of the value of silver, and hence of the tael, during the interval of time (sometimes as long as several months or a year) that elapsed between the signing of the order contract and taking delivery of the goods. The price in gold-standard currency (francs, pounds sterling and American dollars) indicated in the contract remained unchanged, but its equivalent in taels fluctuated according to how much silver in the meantime rose or fell on the world market. Of course, the Chinese merchants could have insured against this element of uncertainty by using an indent system of payment, that is to say by agreeing upon a rate of exchange at the moment of signing the contract, or else by immediately buying foreign currencies. But Chinese importers had been favoured ever since 1915 by the rapid rise of silver, the spin-off from which had gone to swell their normal commercial profits, and they were consequently not inclined to adopt a policy of prudence.

In December 1920, when the tael was only worth 0.71 (American) dollars, there arrived on the market products ordered in February and March, when the tael had been worth over 1.40 dollars. To take delivery, the Chinese merchants were thus obliged to pay out twice as much as they had expected. The situation was the more critical given that more orders than usual had been placed (in response to the temptations of speculation more than to the needs of the market), and at a time when Western prices were at their highest. In Shanghai and Tianjin, stocks were piling up in the foreign warehouses. This blockage of merchandise was inconvenient to the Western and Japanese importers and presented acute financial problems for the Chinese businessmen, most of whom operated with very little capital, counting upon a rapid turnover of stocks. Many Chinese buyers at this point tried to extricate themselves from commitments that they could no longer fulfil. Dissatisfaction with the quality of the merchandise was claimed as a pretext for refusing to accept delivery. Some merchants declared that they had been forced out of business; others elected to disappear without warning or, as the Chinese saying goes, 'to leave for Ningbo'. At all events, in all these cases the losses were borne by the foreign import companies, who thereupon condemned 'the crisis of morality in Chinese business'.[51]

But what was brought into question even more than the 'proverbial honesty of the Chinese merchant' was the efficiency of a traditional trading system when it came to coping with the exigencies of international business transactions. While the Westerners accused the Chinese of duplicity or inexperience, the Chinese claimed to be the victims of circumstances beyond their control. The sectors hardest hit were cotton fabrics and metals. Other sectors of imports, such as equipment for the textile industry, electrical apparatus and building materials, stimulated by the continuing prosperity of the national industries, went on expanding. The profits of the past and the promise held out by the future were of more account than the present unfortunate turn of events. Thus it was that the overall value of imports increased despite the diminishing trade in cotton fabrics and

metals. In the light of these general developments, the partial import
crisis appears to have been of a financial and speculative nature rather
than purely commercial. It could even be suggested that the difficulties
encountered by the Chinese importers were to a large extent due to the
fact that 'there is no cooperation among the banking institutions,
foreign or Chinese, that can be utilised to ease the situation gradually'.[52]

The lack of unity in the Chinese financial market, the absence of any
central bank, and the weakness and instability of the central power,
made it impossible for the government to intervene either to revive or
to restrict credit. Nor was there any way of launching an effective
spontaneous movement of solidarity within a community divided
between Chinese banks and foreign banks, particularly as the latter
were themselves more or less directly dependent upon governments
with divergent interests.

The banks most directly affected by the external trade crisis were the
qianzhuang which financed the movement of merchandise between the
treaty ports and inland China. Given that they lacked large reserves of
capital, their success was essentially dependent upon a rapid turnover
of stocks. Meanwhile the solvency of their business clientele, who also
operated without much initial capital, also depended upon rapid sales.
By the end of 1920 and in 1921, the falling-off of trade was having
repercussions on the activities of the *qianzhuang*. The banks were
regretting the advances that they had made to Chinese merchants
involved in exports and were furthermore suffering from the bankruptcy or insolvency of many cotton-cloth wholesalers who had been
taken by surprise by the falling exchange rate. To recoup their funds,
the *qianzhuang* pushed such wholesalers into forced liquidation, thereby
swamping the market with an excess of goods. Only at this price could
most of the traditional banks recoup their outlay. But their behaviour
during the crisis once again underlined their dependent position.
Indispensable intermediaries between the Chinese world and the
foreign businessmen though they were, they lacked all powers of
decision and so aggravated the movements of the market instead of
taking steps to counterbalance them.

The crisis also hit the foreign banks: it brought to a head the rivalries
that set them one against another and it highlighted the impossibility
of any true collaboration between them and the Chinese financiers.
The foreign banks seldom insured against the exchange risks involved

in import–export contracts and so they too were not unaffected by the crisis which had assailed the Chinese importers. These banks financed the movement of merchandise between the foreign markets and the treaty ports. Refusals to accept delivery of many consignments of goods forced them to extend their periods of credit. The problem of obtaining the extra payments of interest on these loans soon became the subject of extremely tricky negotiations between the Chinese and the foreign communities. In most cases the banks were obliged to give up their hopes of satisfaction.[53] The resounding crash of the French Industrial Bank of China, which declared itself bankrupt on 30 June 1921, testified to all these difficulties and aggravated the disorganisation of the Chinese financial market, at the same time creating a serious political incident in France. The crisis also put pressure on the *de facto* collaboration established in the Shanghai market between Chinese and foreign financiers. The attempts of the Hong Kong and Shanghai Bank to maintain the local exchange rate of the tael, whatever the fluctuations in the value of silver, were thwarted by the massive sales of silver organised by the Chinese speculators of Jiujianglu.*[54]

The modern Chinese banks, which played a much less important role in the financing of imports and exports than either the *qianzhuang* or the foreign establishments, were less affected by the external trade crisis. But their relatively protected position, given that they were underwritten by State funds, was threatened by the seemingly imminent bankruptcy of the Peking government. In these difficult circumstances, many banks were refusing even to manage deposits, as they could find no way of usefully investing them either in the business world or in government loans. Money accumulated during the boom was thus lying unused. It was this situation that gave rise to one of the most extraordinary waves of speculation in Shanghai, which had already seen its fair share of them. This one has been dubbed 'the stock exchange storm' (*xinjiao fengchao*) by Chinese historians.[55]

From Shanghai, where in 1921 140 stock exchanges were set up, the movement spread to the other large treaty ports. Several hundreds of millions of dollars are estimated to have been mobilised by these establishments and audited without any real transactions of merchandise ever taking place. These speculations distorted prices by creating a fictitious demand. And with all available capital tied up in this way,

* In Chinese, *lu* means 'street'. Jiujianglu thus means Jiujiang Street.

regular trade found itself without any means of finance. Credit dwindled as speculation raged; Chinese banks became extremely cautious, safeguarding their capital by imposing prohibitive interest rates. These were as high as 25% per year in Shanghai at the end of 1921.[56] As a result, in 1922 speculation calmed down. But security was bought at the price of a certain passivity. The cohesion of the financial market had sufficed to ward off the immediate danger of the crisis. But the Chinese banks failed to perform the functions that were assumed by the banking world elsewhere: they failed to mitigate fortuitous difficulties and did not ensure that solid and lasting connections existed between available capital and industrial and commercial business concerns. The antiquated nature of the structures that prevented the crisis from spreading on a national scale aggravated it, in contrast, in the treaty ports.

But there was one advantage to this world crisis which disrupted external trade and the financial market: it delayed the foreign powers' aggressive return to the Chinese market, affording Chinese industries a further respite. Between 1920 and 1922 industry continued to expand as rapidly as during the boom years of 1919–20. In 1921 alone, 42 new factories opened in Shanghai, 16 of them textile works.[57] The development of already existing firms was to a large extent responsible for this expansion. In Nantong, Zhang Jian, the proprietor of the Dasheng Cotton Mills, proceeded to acquire all the new equipment that his factories needed. In the spring of 1921, he was awaiting delivery of 4,000 English spindles and 3,000 looms and preparing to open a seventh subsidiary branch and to set up a large weaving factory. In Ningbo, the Hefeng Cotton Mills (Hefeng shachang), which in 1921 showed a profit of 700,000 dollars (almost as much as their total capital of 900,000 dollars), were also planning to expand.[58] The cost of new equipment could be recovered by the reinvestment of their profits, which continued to be very high.

All this Chinese industrial activity, during a period of world depression, highlights the peculiarly national character of Chinese business. With very few exceptions – one being that of non-ferrous ores, production of which declined along with the decline of world demand after 1919 – Chinese industries found within China itself both their raw materials and their clientele. Thus, although the effects of the world reconversion crisis were felt in China, they were limited. The check to expansion came a little later, with the 1923–4 crisis of the cotton mills, which coincided with the end of the world depression. These divergences of development and phasing underline the difference between the modern sector of the Chinese economy, on the one hand, and the colonial systems, on the other, for the latter were directly shaped by the world market and circumstances obtaining in the home countries of the colonial powers. All the same, the national character of the modern Chinese sector afforded it no more than a relative measure of protection. Fledgling Chinese industry had proved capable of riding out the changing fortunes of the world situation, but would it be able to resist being returned to a partially colonial status? Furthermore, would not the links of solidarity that tied the modern sector to the national economy as a whole engender uneven rates of development and risks of blockages caused, in particular, by agricultural stagnation? Considering the record of the decade in which the industrial basis of pre-communist China was established, the growth of these war and post-war years was not so much a mirage as a fragile miracle threatened not only by an aggressive return of imperialism but also by profound structural imbalances.

4   A fragile miracle: the cotton mills crisis, 1923–4[59]

The crisis of the Chinese cotton mills in 1923–4 was as matter both of the impossibility of further growth and of the growth that had already been achieved. From 1923 on, the development of Chinese industry came up against, on the one hand, the diplomatic and political moves of the foreign powers and, on the other, blockages that resulted from earlier bursts of progress.

Following the end of hostilities and the brief period of respite afforded by the reconversion crisis, imperialism returned to its aggressive offensive in China. The direct clash between unequally developed economies was no doubt important but did not constitute the sole cause and framework for the confrontation which now developed. This took place at the level of international diplomacy and it embraced political, cultural and military spheres alike. Many protagonists flocked to the banner of imperialism. Their interests were often divergent and their methods discordant. It was not easy for them to see which, of all the possible forms of intervention, would make it easiest for them to balance the costs and advantages of domination, for, although theoretically possible, this domination was not necessarily either profitable or desirable.

Conscious of their growing power and concerned by the territorial ambitions of Japan, the United States returned to press for an Open Door policy.[60] They were anxious to use the Washington Conference (1921–2) to re-establish equal opportunities for rival powers and to forge new links between China and the rest of the world. But their policies were not followed by the other powers.

The failure of the Western powers to 'disengage' from China during this period underlines the crucial role that already established interests played in the perpetuation of colonial or semi-colonial systems. It was these interests that, in the name of realism, called for and obtained the support of the politico-military apparatus upon which the economic exploitation of China had until now depended. Under their influence, the aggressive return of imperialism after the war tended to take the form of a 'restoration' of rights and privileges.

We are as yet – and perhaps always will be – unable to evaluate the overall effect of foreign intervention on the Chinese economy, but in the particular situation of the 1922–3 period the conflict that arose over the raw cotton embargo presents an example of the dangers that imperialism introduced into the development of the modern sector.

In 1922, the price of raw cotton began to rise. This was to be a determining factor in the cotton mills crisis. There were multiple reasons for the rise but the Chinese press principally blamed increasing exports to Japan. Japan, whose cotton mills were supplied almost exclusively by imported raw materials, absorbed the greater part of the Chinese cotton that was sold abroad: 803,000 piculs out of 974,000 in 1923. This Chinese cotton represented no more than a fraction (about 5–10%) of the total needs of the Japanese spindles, as the United States and India were Japan's principal suppliers. However, Chinese cotton presented two advantages to the Japanese: prices were usually lower and the supplier's market was relatively close at hand. So, as soon as the price of American or Indian cotton began to rise, Japanese demand for Chinese cotton increased, as was the case in 1922.

These exports represented no more than 10–13% of the total Chinese production of raw cotton, but they were taken from the commercialised fraction – almost half – of the harvest. They thus deprived Chinese cotton mills of about one-quarter of the supplies still available after the traditional spinning and padding of clothes had been catered for. Besides, the fluctuations in Japanese demand intro-duced an extra factor of uncertainty and speculation into the Chinese market, already ill-organised at the best of times. Superior financial resources and more up-to-date information enabled the Japanese buyers to steal a march on the Chinese cotton mill proprietors and to buy up large quantities of raw cotton either for export or to supply Japanese factories established in China or else as a speculation, for resale. Their extensive operations certainly constituted an artificial factor which pushed prices up. Finally, as the statistics show clearly, the success of the Chinese cotton mills constituted a threat to the sale of Japanese products in China. Whereas in 1916, the Japanese had sold 1,320 million piculs of industrial yarns, their sales fell to 364,000 in 1923. It seems legitimate, in these circumstances, to suppose that Japan's increased purchases of raw cotton were in part dictated by a strategy designed to destroy Chinese competition: the creation of 24 new Japanese cotton mills in China between 1920 and 1923 can only have aggravated the threat.

Chinese industrialists therefore considered a cotton embargo to be a measure of economic preservation, and as the 'central problem' (*xiao-jian*) of expansion. They were anxious to staunch the outward flow of raw materials, to restore the advantage of their national resources to their own businesses and to halt priority supplies to the rival Japanese factories whose products were flooding the Chinese market. A request for the prohibition of exports submitted at the end of 1922 by the Chinese Cotton Mill Owners' Association (Huashang shachang lian-hehui) was approved by the Peking government and an official decree was published. But the Japanese press made a fuss, the diplomatic corps invoked a number of treaties and, in May 1923, faced with unanimous opposition from the 'nations interested', the Chinese government was forced to lift the embargo. Exports of raw cotton thus continued to increase. In 1924 they reached 1.08 million piculs as compared to 1919 when, with a larger harvest, they had amounted to 1.07 million piculs.

The failure of the embargo was not the only or even the main cause of the crisis in the cotton mills. The embargo, which could have been applied easily and rapidly, would certainly have attenuated the diffi-cult situation. But the Chinese entrepreneurs themselves regarded it as a 'temporary measure', a 'negative remedy' which would not resolve the fundamental problem of maintaining a balance between the speed of industrial development and that of agricultural development.

Of all the imbalances created by a decade of rapid industrial expansion, the most serious was the fact that the booming textile industries, with their need for raw materials, were increasingly out of step with Chinese agriculture, which was incapable of keeping the factories supplied and at the time feeding the population.

It was not in China alone that agriculture played an essential role during the early phases of industrialisation. But in China the nature of agricultural production and the style of industrialisation conferred a particular importance upon the relationship between agriculture and industry. In the first place, the heavy demographic pressure left no more than a minimal agricultural surplus, which climatic conditions the slightest bit unfavourable soon turned into a deficit. Secondly, with light industry predominating, agriculture was required to fulfil a double function: (a) to provide a direct supply of most of the raw materials indispensable to keep the factories running; and (b), by means of agricultural exports, to finance the purchase of foreign machinery and equipment. Industrial expansion was thus immediately dependent upon agricultural prosperity. At first the post-war boom had benefited from the excellent 1919 harvest. But from 1921 onwards, agricultural production – hit by drought in the provinces of the north and north-west and then by flooding in the Yangzi region – turned out to be incapable of satisfying the needs of Chinese industry engaged, as it was, in a 'great leap forward'. The tension in the market for raw materials and the scarcity of raw cotton, which were features of the period beginning in 1922, were consequences of a blockage that industry suffered as a result of the inelastic nature of agricultural production.

The number of Chinese spindles had more than doubled between 1919, when they numbered 1,781,972, and 1923, by which time they totalled 3,749,288. It was in 1920–1 that imports of equipment for textile factories peaked. The imports of those two years represented 42.6% of all purchases made between 1911 and 1930. The acquisition of all this new equipment was reflected in an increased demand for raw materials. There are no firm statistics, but one may make a calculation based upon the number of spindles installed and the production of yarns. This gives a demand figure of 5.4 million piculs of raw cotton in 1923 (as compared to 2.7 million in 1918) for Chinese industries, and roughly the same amount for foreign industries established in China.

Chinese agriculture was quite incapable of satisfying that demand since at the very point when the demand for raw cotton began to rise, cotton production began to decline. The 1918 harvest had been particularly good. The 1919 harvest did not benefit from such favourable climatic conditions but nevertheless remained satisfactory. However, 1920 saw the beginning of a decline that coincided with famine in the northern and central provinces. In 1921, production in the Yangzi region (Jiangsu and Hubei provinces) was hit. In the months following the climatic catastrophe, the need to replenish food supplies was so pressing that the peasants turned to grains, neglecting their commercial crops. When climatic conditions improved, food production rose but cotton production, in contrast, did not achieve its former levels. The continuing stagnation is all the more difficult to understand in view of the fact that the price of cotton on the major Chinese markets increased dramatically in 1923–4. That fact notwithstanding, until 1926–7 the area of land under cotton cultivation was still smaller than in 1919, except in a few zones, such as Jiangsu province, well served by the railways and waterways, close to the coastal industrial centres and at the same time traditionally oriented towards commercial crops.

Should we blame the inflexibility of the cotton supply upon the inertia of the 'lamentably ignorant' Chinese race, as some foreign observers have done? Or should we argue that in the domains of transport and monetary transactions insufficient progress had as yet been made to allow the market laws to exert their full effect, except in a few favoured regions? The fact is that in some cases difficulties of commercialisation, however real, were overcome. For example, in Shanxi province, remote and isolated though it was, the area devoted to cotton cultivation increased steadily from 1919 to 1923. Here the high quality of the cotton, famous for its whiteness and its heavy yield, played a more determining role than the poor transport conditions and the remoteness from industrial centres. In contrast, in Zhili province, situated advantageously close to the capital, the size of the area devoted to cotton cultivation shrank perceptibly over the same period.

The poor conditions of commercialisation certainly increased the risks for the peasant who turned to the production of industrial raw materials, but those risks stemmed essentially from Chinese agri-

culture's failure to progress and expand. Since the end of the nineteenth century, very little land had been cleared, and that only in
marginal and relatively infertile zones. Whatever land was cultivable
was already under cultivation, so cotton cultivation could in general be
extended only at the cost of grain production. Since that production
ensured no more than a minimal level of supply, such an extension
threatened the very existence of the peasants. Their conservatism in
this respect was a survival reflex. The natural bases of the Chinese
agricultural economy made the massive extension of cultivated areas
and higher productivity impossibilities until such time as a technological and social revolution took place. For the time being, the cotton-
spinning industry could expect no overall increase in the production of
raw cotton.

The 1923–4 crisis in Chinese industry stemmed to a large extent
from these supply difficulties. Between October 1922 and June 1924,
the average monthly price of cotton on the Shanghai stock exchange
rose by 73%, increasing from 28.25 to 49 taels per picul. In 1923, most
Chinese cotton mills were running at a loss. The Chinese Cotton Mill
Owners' Association in Shanghai suggested that the factories cut their
production by a half. While new spindles, ordered one or two years
earlier (in the days of prosperity) continued to increase production
capacity, the older spindles lay idle: during the second three months of
1923, 985,000 Chinese spindles out of a total of 2,639,000 ceased
operation or operated at a reduced rate. Faced with serious financial
difficulties and with insufficient support forthcoming from the
qianzhuang, many Chinese cotton mill owners were obliged to close
their factories: in the autumn of 1923, 25-30% of the Chinese cotton
mills in Shanghai closed down. Others were forced to turn for help to
their Japanese rivals: over 200,000 Chinese spindles were mortgaged
and takeovers multiplied. In 1923, the Huafeng Cotton Mills (Huafeng
fangzhi gongsi) changed hands, as did the Baocheng Cotton Mills nos.
1 and 2 (Baocheng diyi dier chang) in 1925.

The vulnerability of the Chinese businesses is underlined by the fact
that, during the same period, the English and Japanese cotton mills
established in China continued to work on a full-time basis, some of
them even continuing to make a profit. The British Ewo Cotton Mills
paid out 30% dividends to its shareholders during 1922 and the profits
of the Japanese Commercial Cotton Company went up 27% during
the first three months of 1923. The weakness of the Chinese businesses

in comparison to their foreign rivals stemmed from their insufficient financial resources and from mismanagement which increased running costs and cut productivity. Insufficient initial capital, too many fixed rather than liquid assets, constant cashflow crises imperfectly remedied by short-term loans from the *qianzhuang*, short-sighted management and excessive and overprompt payments to shareholders all placed Chinese businesses at the mercy of fortuitous circumstances. There was nothing new about these handicaps: prosperity had mitigated their drawbacks, but the crisis now rendered them intolerable.

The growth caused by the 'miracle' thus faltered at the first reversal. Prosperity had conjured up a dream of a definitive economic change. But perhaps it also brought the collapse of that dream closer. The crisis of 1923 brought into question not only the future of Chinese industry but also its recent past and the nature of the progress accomplished. It posed the problem of spontaneous growth – promoted solely by private efforts and interests – within an economy that was retarded and under foreign domination. It also focused attention upon the principal agents of that growth – the new Chinese entrepreneurs.

3 ✎ The new entrepreneurs in the city

The economic miracle brought a new stimulus to urban expansion. The annual rate of urban population growth was far higher than that of the population as a whole. The urban expansion reflected the attraction that the new poles of development exerted upon rural societies. Round the expanding towns, suburbs were springing up and old town walls coming down to improve communications between the new quarters and the old city centres. In the foreign concessions whose boundaries the Chinese authorities were now refusing to extend, demographic pressure was rising, but not as fast as the price of land, an area where speculation was rife.

Social structures in these expanding towns were becoming at once more complex and more sharply differentiated. A worker proletariat was emerging, while the modern intelligentsia and bourgeoisie began to draw away from the other urban elite groups. Some historians, struck by the similarities between these developments and their European precedents, have been inclined to isolate these new elite groups from the still very traditional framework within which they belong.[1] But significant though they may be, these developments remained marginal – in relation not only to Chinese society as a whole but also to its relatively modernised urban fringe. The upper echelons of the new entrepreneurial bourgeoisie still tended to merge with the older elite groups, whose influence was based on their wealth as landowners, their access to public positions and finance, and the age and respectability of their families. As for the lower strata, here the entrepreneurs were indistinguishable from the group of small merchants and craftsmen from which so many of them originated.

One way of identifying the new entrepreneurs is certainly by means of economic criteria such as the size of their businesses, the amount of their capital, the number of their employees and the volume of their production. Since it was not only the most wealthy who were drawn to modern techniques, technological criteria are also important. We may also refer to those who, with the general support of the business world, were chosen as representatives in the chambers of commerce and employers' associations. Finally, we should not forget that many entrepreneurs were recognised as such by the national or local public authorities, who conferred honours upon them or invited them to act as advisers or experts.

Yet even when identified according to these criteria, the group of entrepreneurs as a whole lacks sharp definition. It is an amorphousness that reflects the realities of the situation. At this period of highly competitive capitalism, high profits and relative amateurism, the world of business attracted a wide range of members of the older elite and adventurers, merchants and artisans. Their careers in it were generally brief, culminating either in ruin or in wealth and representing no more than a passing phase in the process of upward social mobility. Even as they strove to set themselves up as a specific elite, the new entrepreneurs maintained many links with the older urban elite and the traditional merchant class, through which, for the most part, they made their influence felt. The new entrepreneurs were capable of banding together to take certain kinds of action or for certain general purposes, but as a group they always functioned on a local or regional level. In this chapter, we shall be concentrating on the entrepreneurs of Shanghai, as they were the most numerous and most active, and are the ones we possess the most information on.

1 Businessmen in the town

Urban expansion

The growth of the great coastal cities resulted essentially from people flocking into the towns from the countryside, for the expansion of the modern economic sector attracted many country people. Shanghai as a whole, all sectors included, totalled 1.3 million inhabitants in 1910 and twice that number, 2.6 million, by 1927.[2] The number of inhabitants born outside the town fluctuated between 72% and 83%.[3] The commercial and industrial areas of the town were spreading: northwards in the direction of Zhabei, eastwards along the other bank of the Huangpu, towards Pudong, and to the south of the old walled city, at

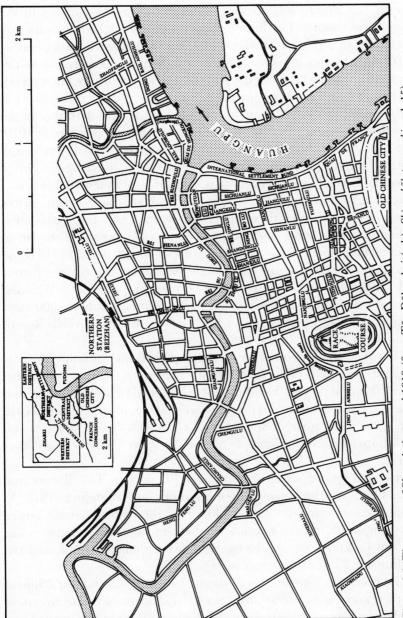

Figure 3.1 The streets of Shanghai, around 1919 (from Tōa Dōbunkai (ed.), *Shina shōbetsu zenshi*, vol. 15)

Nanshi (see Figure 3.1). Demographic pressure was growing in the foreign concessions. The French Concession, which had a population of 115,946 in 1910, had reached 297,072 by 1925, with a density of 29,076 inhabitants per square kilometre. In the International Settlement (IS), which was twice the size (covering 22.6 square kilometres), the population was also growing: it rose from 501,541 inhabitants in 1910 to 840,226 in 1925, with an even higher density than that of the French Concession – 22,192 inhabitants per square kilometre in 1910, 37,178 in 1925.[4] The price of buildings rose together with, or even more swiftly than, the population figures. In the International Settlement, a *mu* of land which, on average, had sold for 8,281 taels in 1911, was worth 16,207 25 years later.[5] Along the main shopping streets, prices did not just double; they increased tenfold. At the Nanjinglu–Sichuanlu intersection, in the central district (Zhongqu) of the International Settlement, a *mu* which had gone for 30,000 taels in 1915 could be sold for 350,000 taels in 1929! In the Settlement's northern (Beiqu) and western (Xiqu) districts, prices rose proportionately: in Bei Henanlu, the price of a *mu* of land rose from 1,500 to 10,000 taels between 1912 and 1929, while in Jing'anshilu (Bubbling Wells Road), it rose from 3,000 to 25,000 taels.[6]

The Municipal Council of the IS issued 81,903 building permits between 1910 and 1925, 47.2% more than over the previous fifteen years.[7] Most of the new buildings were designed to provide accommodation, but many industrial premises were also going up. Between 1910 and 1925, in the town of Shanghai as a whole, 816 new factories and workshops are recorded, compared to 77 built over the fifteen previous years.[8]

Most impressive were the commercial buildings. The Sincere and Wing On Companies opened their big shops on Nanjinglu in 1919. At about the same time the new building for the IS Municipal Council was completed and the famous view of the Bund took shape as the modern buildings for the Hong Kong and Shanghai Bank and the Jardine and Matheson Company went up.

The polycentric structures of the treaty ports – with their Chinese quarters and their concessions – made for disparities in the growth of the different sectors of the town. Such disparities are a feature of any process of urban development, but in China they were greater than elsewhere because of the foreign presence. In Shanghai, for example, right up until 1943, when the concessions were ceded back to China,

Table 3.1. *Population growth in the various sectors of Shanghai between 1910 and 1927*

	Total population	Chinese quarters	International Settlement	French Concession
1910	1,289,353	671,866	501,541	115,946
1927	2,641,220	1,503,922	840,226[a]	297,072[a]
Increase	1,361,867	832,056	338,685	181,126
	(104.8%)	(123.8%)	(67.5%)	(156.2%)

[a]These are in fact the figures for 1925.
Source: Zou Yiren, *Jiu Shanghai renkou bianqian*, p. 90, table 1.

the average rate of demographic growth there remained higher than in the Chinese quarters. Between 1910 and 1942, the population increased in the French Concession by 20% each year, in the International Settlement by 5.79% and in the Chinese quarters by 4%. From 1930 onwards, the waves of refugees seeking the protection of some foreign power, to escape from the Japanese invaders, account for this disparity.[9] However, in the relatively calm years of the economic miracle, the rate of demographic growth in the Chinese quarters was considerably higher than in the IS (see Table 3.1).

What gave rise to this (temporary) reversal? One reason could be lack of space. The boundaries of the International Settlement were redefined for the last time in 1899. Its area, fixed at 22.60 square kilometres at that date, was henceforth to remain unchanged. On the other hand, the French Concession was significantly expanded, for the last time, in 1914, when it spread to cover 10.22 square kilometres. The availability of land encouraged the rapid demographic growth of the years that followed: it was during this period that the French Concession became the residential sector favoured by both the Chinese and the foreign bourgeoisie of Shanghai.

Meanwhile, the average demographic growth rate of 67.5% in the International Settlement does not reflect the real expansion that took place in particular areas. In some – in the eastern (Dongqu) and the western (Xiqu) districts – it was even more rapid than in the French Concession and in the Chinese quarters during the period of the economic miracle (see Table 3.2 and Figure 3.2).

The contrast between the central (Zhongqu) and the northern (Beiqu) districts, where the population declined or barely increased at

Table 3.2. *Population growth in the various districts of the International Settlement of Shanghai from 1910 to 1925*

	Central district (Zhongqu)	Northern district (Beiqu)	Eastern district (Dongqu)	Western district (Xiqu)
Area	2,820 *mu*	3,040 *mu*	16,193 *mu*	11,450 *mu*
Population in 1910	124,353	139,040	90,390	71,581
Population in 1925	122,776	166,442	265,849	189,571
Evolution of the population between 1910 and 1925	−1,577	+27,402 (+19.7%)	+175,459 (+194%)	+117,900 +164.8%)

Source: Luo Zhiru, *Tongjibiazhong zhi Shanghai*, tables 37 and 38.

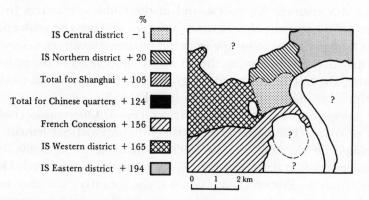

Figure 3.2 The evolution of the populations of the foreign concessions in Shanghai, 1910–25/27 (from Tables 3.1 and 3.2)

all, and the eastern and western districts, where it doubled or almost tripled within fifteen or so years, can be explained by a number of historical and economic factors. The central and northern districts were the oldest. They corresponded respectively to the English and the American Concessions, which in 1863 merged to form the International Settlement. In the central district, the commercial heart of Shanghai, the population density was already as high as 60,000–70,000 inhabitants per square kilometre in 1900. The development of the eastern and western sectors came later, with the rise of light industries in Shanghai, which began between 1910 and 1920 and continued right up to the eve of the Sino-Japanese War in 1937. As we shall see later, it was along the eastern and western borders of the settlement that most of the industries set up during the boom years of the First World War established themselves. By the time that this phase of development had come to an end, the demographic balance of the various sectors was reversed. The population of the eastern (Dongqu) and western (Xiqu) sectors, which in 1910 accounted for only 37.3% of the total population of the Settlement, represented over 61% by 1925. During the 1930s, they were to account for 70%.

Up until 1927, the town of Shanghai could be identified with the old imperial administrative area of the *xian*. Its territory extended over 557 square kilometres and included many rural zones as well as fifteen or so villages. Within this loosely structured complex, a number of urban centres emerged. To the south of the concessions, the Chinese City, the old capital of the *xian* (*xiancheng*), had been founded in the mid-sixteenth century, under the Ming dynasty; it continued to be known as the 'walled town' (*chengnei*) despite the fact that the walls had been destroyed following the 1911 revolution. The southern suburbs of Nanshi, which developed as activity on the Huangpu grew, represented a kind of Chinese *bund*. To the north of the Soochow Creek, Zhabei derived its name from Laozha, a little town that had appeared two hundred years earlier. Finally, on the eastern bank of the Huangpu, the Pudong quarter revolved around the presence of the shipyards, warehouses and docks, for the most part foreign-owned. Nanshi, Zhabei and Pudong were the outlying areas that the economic miracle turned into industrial suburbs (see Figure 3.3).

The complexity of this urban structure naturally affected the composition and hierarchy of the Shanghai elite groups. The Shanghai Municipal Council for the International Settlement and that of the French Concession were composed of members of the foreign elites and foreign advisers. They also included Chinese councillors. The walled town, Zhabei and Pudong depended upon local Chinese administrative offices which remained more or less autonomous and were never truly unified until the municipal reform of 1927.[10] Furthermore, the Chinese residents in the foreign concessions had their own representative organisations, such as the Chinese Ratepayers Association of the International Settlement, which, though not officially recognised by the Shanghai Municipal Council, was nevertheless influential and heeded. There were many chambers of commerce, the foreigners

NANJING-SHANGHAI-WUSONG LINE

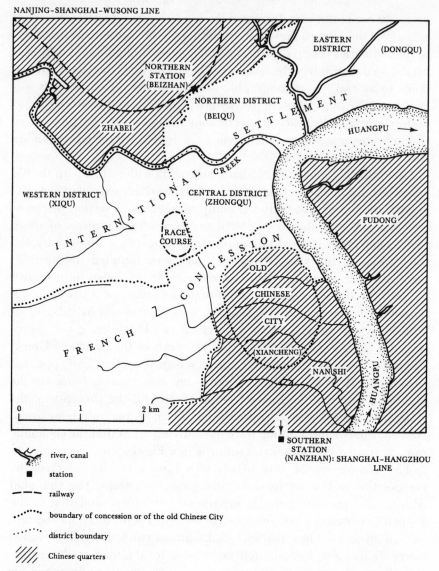

Figure 3.3 Structure of Shanghai, around 1919: the foreign concessions and the Chinese quarter

running their own inside the concessions. The largest Chinese chamber of commerce was also to be found in the northern (Beiqu) sector of the International Settlement: this was the Shanghai General Chamber of Commerce (Shanghai zongshanghui). But there also existed another chamber, in the old southern walled city, which was recruited and organised on a quite different basis from the General Chamber. Alongside these institutions, there were dozens of professional organisations recruited on a regional or purely professional basis,[11] not to mention secret societies, the Green Gang (Qingbang) in particular.

This welter of power networks to a large extent reflected the interaction of the various urban sectors, which provided the framework for the economic activities and social existence of the elite groups of Shanghai. What was the position of the entrepreneurs within this rapidly expanding town? Where did they set up their offices, shops and factories?

The Shanghai business quarter

No political will or government presided over the growth of Shanghai. The town developed with the expansion of first trade, then industry, and essentially thanks to the efforts of its own residents. Natural factors certainly contributed towards its growth: Shanghai was a seaport and along the banks of the Huangpu it provided a base for all activities associated with shipping. The Soochow Creek, in the past of more importance than the Huangpu, served as a route for internal shipping and represented a second major axis for trade and industry. Being a town of concessions, Shanghai was also regarded as a place of refuge. When first instituted in the mid-nineteenth century, the concessions had been regarded as zones reserved for foreign residences and businesses, but it was not long before they were attracting Chinese investors and entrepreneurs anxious to avoid the exactions of the imperial administration and to make the most of the opportunities afforded by the Western presence. Both fashion and a desire for security led to a concentration of firms in the concessions. The structure of the business quarters was in some respects organised along traditional lines: for instance, all Chinese entrepreneurs practising similar activities and, for the most part, sharing common geographical origins tended to be found together, in particular streets. The relative importance of all

Table 3.3. The distribution of businesses in Shanghai in about 1919

		International Settlement				French Concession	Chinese City	Nanshi	Zhabei	Pudong	Total	Number of establishments
		Centre %	N %	E %	W %	%	%	%	%	%	%	
Financial establishments	Modern banks	96	2			2					100% =	54
	Qianzhuang	72	1			1		26				96
	Traditional banks	100										26
	Pawnbrokers making loans against security	23	18	13	17	5	13	8	3			112
	Total of financial establishments	59.7	7.6	5.2	6.6	2.7	5.2	11.8	1	0		288
Services	Insurance companies	94	2			4						82
	Auctioneers	100										9
	Building societies	83		4	9	4						23
	Shipping companies	20	20	4		32		24				25
	Customs offices	47				36		17				66
	Transport companies	31	44					23	2			48
	Warehouses	19	37	22	4	10			1	7		82
	Total number of services	51	17	6	1	13	0	8	1	2		335
Trading companies	Luxury products and foreign products	79.7	5.7	0.9	1.1	6.4	4.3	1.6				434
	Textiles	66.9	4.3	0.6	1.85	6.8	11.4	8.0				324
	Health	54.8	9.6	0.8	7.4	7.4	7.0	10.5	2.1			228
	Agricultural products	62.3	6.7	4.1	4.2	8.7	11.3	6.7				194
	Timber and furniture	42.5	11.1	5.8	5.8	3.7	13.2	5.8				188
	Foodstuffs	27.0	11.4	5.1	5.1	14.9	8.6	25.1	2.5			429
	Total number of trading companies	56	8	2	4	9	9	11	2	0		1,797

Industry group	Subcategory								Total
Mechanical engineering industries	Shipyards	6	15	47		15	23	—	13
	Mechanical engineering workshops		34	47		9	2	—	47
	Total number of mechanical engineering industries	5	30	47	3	10	5	—	60
Textile industries	Silk mills	4	28	20	3	38		—	68
	Cotton carding works		25	42		8		—	12
	Cotton mills		48	44	10		4	—	27
	Weaving		17	23		23	10	—	30
	Hat factories	18	10	10		14		—	21
	Total number of textile industries	3	16	25	3	23	2	—	158
Food-processing industries	Flour mills	17	17	34		17	5	—	18
	Rice factories	25	30	4	8	17		—	24
	Oil mills		12	38		38	2	—	8
	Total number of food-processing industries	18	20	20	4	20		—	50

(Totals bracketed: 13 + 47 = 60; 158; 50 — overall total 268.)

Note: In calculating percentages, decimal values have been rounded out; as a result, the real sums that should have appeared in the 'Total' column are in some cases slightly over, in others slightly under 100. These variations have been disregarded.

Sources: Shanghai zhinan, part 6, pp. 33b–34 (for the financial establishments), pp. 34–5 (for the services), pp. 6–32b (for the trading companies), pp. 1–6 (for the mechanical engineering, textile and food-processing industries); *ZSIIYB,* vol. 1, no. 4 (July 1921) for the textile industries.

these geographical, political and social factors varied from one sector of activities to another (see Table 3.3).

Finances and services

The 1919 edition of the *Shanghai Guide* (*Shanghai zhinan*) mentions 54 modern, foreign and Chinese banks.[12] Without exception, all these establishments were situated on concession territory. The financial heart of Shanghai was the central (Zhongqu) district of the IS, where 52 banks were located. The major foreign ones were to be found on the Bund, along the Huangpu. Only two Chinese banks managed to install themselves on this important thoroughfare; the rest were located before the Bund, towards the north of the central distict, particularly in Ningbolu (called after the town from which many of the Shanghai bankers originated) and Beijinglu (see Figure 3.1).

The traditional banks, of which there were many more, were concentrated in the same quarter (see Figure 3.4). Most traditional finance took the form of the *qianzhuang*. The *Shanghai Guide* lists 96 of these, 69 of which were located in the central district of the IS and 25 in the Nanshi suburbs. These banks made their first appearance at the end of the nineteenth century in Ningbo, along with the development of provincial and inter-regional trade, a fact which accounts for their relatively massive presence in the old port quarter of Nanshi. But it was in the second half of the nineteenth century that they really took off, as import–export trade grew and thanks to the financial backing (in the form of short-term, unsecured loans) from foreign banking establishments. The IS *qianzhuang* thus became established in Shanghai at about the same time as the Western Banks, acting as intermediaries between the latter and Chinese wholesalers. The fact that they are all to be found in the same neighbourhood reflects the organic solidarity (or dependence) that obtained between them.

Pawnbrokers specialising in loans against security, 112 in all, seem in contrast to have been much more widely distributed. 71% of them installed themselves on IS territory, dispersed more or less evenly over its various districts. Many were located in the Chinese City and in Nanshi. It is true that their role was very different from that of the *qianzhuang*. The advances that they made were for the most part short-term consumer loans and they strove to establish close ties with the humble urban folk who constituted their clientele.

A number of service industries, closely linked with financial activity, also clustered together in the central IS district. 94% of Shanghai's insurance companies were to be found here. Eleven were situated along the Bund, the remainder scattered along the major thoroughfares – Jiangxilu, Guangdonglu and Sichuanlu. The central district could also claim 82% of the building societies and nine auctioneers. The latter played an extremely important role in the sale of imports – cotton fabrics in particular – to Chinese wholesalers (see Figure 3.5).[13]

A number of other service industries established themselves mainly in the foreign concessions. For reasons of a geographical nature, their locations were more varied. The 25 shipping companies and the 66 customs offices (whose task was to complete customs formalities for their clients) were naturally installed close to the Huangpu wharfs, some in the Bund quarter (in the central district of the IS) but some in the French Concession, around the Quai de France, and in Nanshi, the Chinese port quarter.

The 48 transport companies responsible for sending on merchandise, essentially by rail, established themselves close to the railway stations. The Northern Station (Beizhan), on the Nanking–Shanghai–Wusong line, was situated in Chinese territory, on the outskirts of Zhabei, but transport companies preferred the northern district of the IS. There were twelve in Jielu alone, right next to the station. Transport companies were also concentrated (although in smaller numbers) in the southern suburbs of Nanshi around the Southern Station (Nanzhan), which was the terminus of the Hangzhou–Shanghai line.

The construction of warehouses clearly demanded large tracts of land. That is why some large companies, both foreign (Jardine and Matheson, Butterfield and Swire) and Chinese (The Chinese Merchants' Steam Navigation Company (Lunchuan zhaoshangju)) chose to build about half a dozen on the Pudong wastelands. However, the majority (91%) of these warehouses were distributed between the various IS districts and the French Concession. This choice of position can be explained by the role played by stocks of merchandise held as security in the financing of the import–export trade. The Chinese wholesalers, who controlled most of the trade circuits between Shanghai and inland China, generally operated with very limited working capital. So when the port was opened, the large foreign transport and

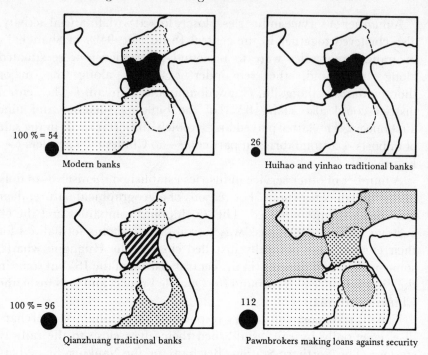

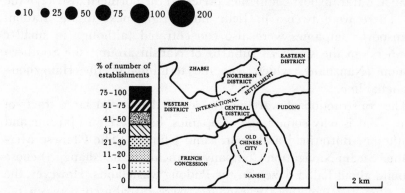

Figure 3.4 The distribution of financial establishments in Shanghai, around 1919 (from Table 3.3)

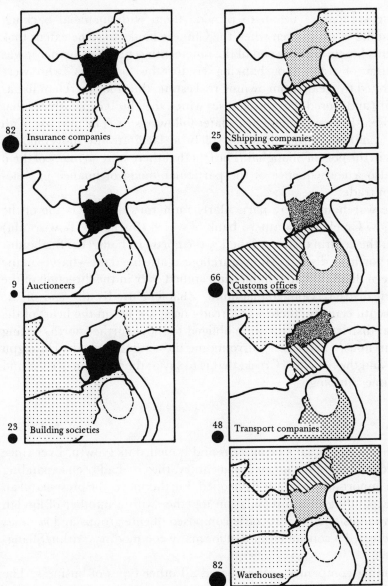

Figure 3.5 The distribution of service industries in Shanghai, around 1919 (from Table 3.3)

trading companies began to provide them with financial backing, continuing to do so even when the Chinese banks to some extent took over this function at the end of the nineteenth century. Whether it was a matter of trading or banking credit, the foreigners, who were prohibited by treaty from owning real estate, thus took merchandise as security and stored it in warehouses which they built expressly for that purpose. Modern Chinese firms later followed suit. The purpose of all these warehouses was thus not solely to facilitate the movement of goods in the port of Shanghai. The fact that there were so many of them was also a consequence of the particular mode of finance in Sino-foreign trade.

The warehouses were particularly numerous on either side of the Soochow Creek, the southern bank of which (Suzhoulu, Bowuyanlu) was in the central district of the IS, the northern bank (Bei Suzhoulu) in the northern district. Many warehouses also lined the wharves in the northern district (Bailaohuilu) and spilled over in the direction of the eastern district (Dong Bailaohuilu, Zhaofenglu). By the end of the nineteenth century, there was already no space left in the heart of the central district and firms were obliged to move further north, setting up warehouses in the zone surrounding the confluence of the Huangpu River and the Soochow Creek, that is to say at the junction of river and maritime shipping.

Trade

Trade was Shanghai's *raison d'être* and it fuelled its growth. Ever since the second half of the nineteenth century, the city had been expanding as the import–export trade developed. Furthermore, the presence of an ever expanding urban population together with a number of foreign communities and a bourgeoisie composed of elite groups and *nouveaux riches* created a consumer market for many commodities within Shanghai itelf.

Trading companies outnumbered all other types of business. The *Shanghai Guide* classifies them into 85 categories.[14] The system of classification that it adopts reflects corporatist traditions of extreme differentiation between the various activities: hat factories selling hats for men are distinct from shops selling fashions which include hats for women; shops selling socks are not to be confused with shops selling other kinds of clothes. It also seems likely that some of the estab-

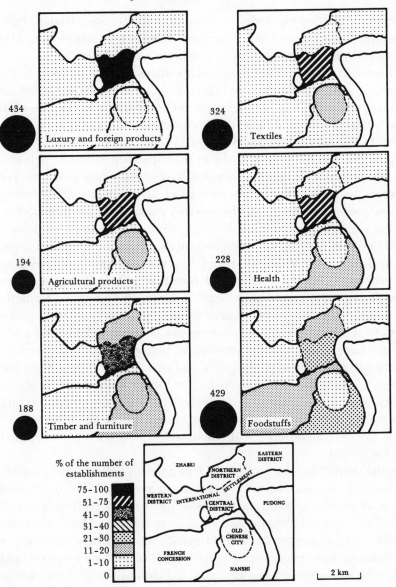

Figure 3.6 The distribution of commercial establishments in Shanghai, around 1919 (from Table 3.3)

lishments classified as 'trade' involved activities of an artisan nature: furniture dealers were also carpenters, fabrics merchants were also tailors and dressmakers, and jewellers were also goldsmiths.

The trade map of Shanghai reveals an extremely uneven distribution of trading concerns (see Figure 3.6). To illustrate the point, let us consider a sample of 31 different branches of trade. In the case of 20 of these, half or more of the firms are concentrated in the central sector of the IS. Their positioning is understandable in the cases of shops designed to cater for the needs of a wealthy, cosmopolitan clientele or a Chinese bourgeoisie quick to adopt Western consumer patterns. We discover the central district to contain virtually all the shops selling foreign goods (*yanghang*), all the modern chemist shops of Shanghai, most of the shops selling silks, foreign fabrics, antiques and furniture – whether foreign or Chinese – and most of the bookshops and stationers.

The distribution of shops did not follow the population overflow into other districts. There are a few food, furniture and textile stores, shops selling foreign goods, and bookshops, in the northern district (formerly the American Concession), where foreign residents installed themselves in the second half of the nineteenth century, to be joined a few decades later by the Chinese intellectual bourgeoisie. But the western residential quarters and the more industrial eastern zones of the district are very badly served. As for the French Concession, it boasts quite a wide range of shops but in every sector its role is of secondary importance. The central district thus profited most from the preference given to the concessions, with their well-do-do clientele and their relative security.

In the central district, trade, which had begun to be developed early – in the mid-nineteenth century – continued to expand. The traditional system of confining similar activities to particular streets or quarters further encouraged the concentration of businesses. How could one possibly open a hat shop anywhere but in Shanxilu, where all twenty of the Shanghai hat designers plied their trade? What book vendor would wish to establish himself anywhere but in Fuzhoulu or Henanlu, where 36 bookshops (almost a third of all Shanghai bookshops) were already located? Nanjinglu, with its 203 shops (almost a fifth of all the shops included in our sample) remained the city's most bustling and prosperous commercial thoroughfare. Nevertheless, some activities were unaffected by the tendency to gravitate to the central district. There was, for instance, no room in the central district for the wholesalers of bulky products. The grain trade was therefore concentrated in the old port suburb of Nanshi, where over half (54%) the shops specialising in grain were located and where sea-going junks and small coasters came to unload cargoes purchased in Manchuria. The organisation of the grain trade, already busy by the early nineteenth century, resisted the geographical and economic pressures for change introduced by the opening of the port of Shanghai. It continued to be controlled by the traditional guilds, and Nanshi, with its Bean Street (Doushijie), remained its major centre. A similar phenomenon may be observed in the case of the timber trade, which was also concentrated principally in Nanshi (34% of timber firms) but also along the Soochow Creek in the northern district of the IS (18%).

Historical factors were also operative. The old Chinese City incorporated many trades associated with the traditional small-scale crafts: lacemaking, the production of paintbrushes, fans, lacquer-work, furniture in the Chinese style and the collection of antiques. And it seems probable that the reasons why 78% of the shops selling fruit and local products were concentrated in Nanshi and in the French Concession was that, in the nineteenth century, the market gardeners of the region had been accustomed to bring their produce to town by way of the network of canals and moats that surrounded the old walled town.

Finally, there were the concerns dealing in basic necessities, serving the needs of the general mass of consumers. These were distributed fairly evenly over all the various quarters: grocers supplying the countless indispensable condiments for seasoning daily meals, fishmongers, herb vendors, whose wares were preferred to modern medicaments and were at the same time less expensive than the remedies prescribed by the traditional Chinese pharmacies. However, these establishments represented only a tiny fraction of the trade of Shanghai. And their relatively wide dispersion did not offset the general imbalance of a network that was based upon the pre-eminence of the central sector of the IS.

Industry

In Shanghai, where light industry predominated, factories, manufacturing plants and workshops merged with the urban fabric. In contrast to the concentration of financial and commercial concerns inside the central sector of the IS, industrial firms were distributed relatively

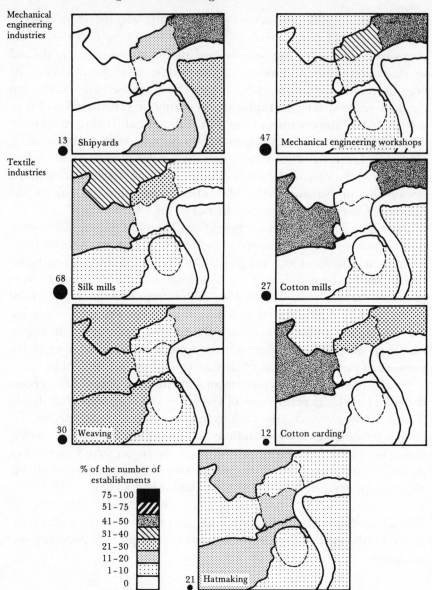

Figure 3.7 The distribution of mechanical engineering and textile industries in Shanghai, around 1919 (from Table 3.3)

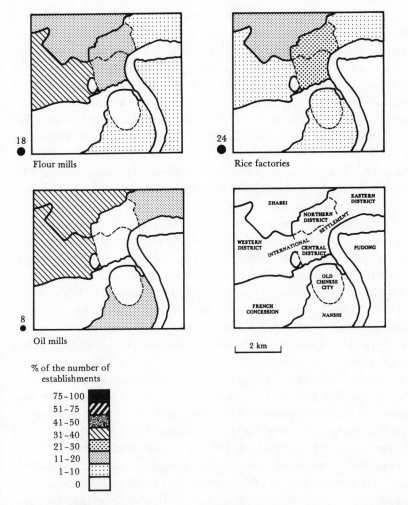

Figure 3.8 The distribution of foodstuff industries in Shanghai, around 1919 (from Table 3.3)

widely over the northern quarters of the town (the western, northern and eastern sectors of the International Settlement and the Chinese Zhabei quarter) and the peripheral complexes of Nanshi and Pudong (see Figures 3.7 and 3.8).[15]

The positioning of factories, like that of banks and commercial businesses was governed by security consciousness. Of the 14 cotton mills set up with Chinese capital in Shanghai itself, 12 were to be found in the International Settlement territory. However, industrial establishments require considerable space and, by 1900, industrialists were turning away from the overcrowded quarters of Hongkou (in the northern sector of the IS) and electing to set up premises on the wasteland of Yangshupu (in the eastern sector of the IS) or in Xiaoshadu (in the western sector of the IS) or in Zhabei. The history of industrialisation in Shanghai can be read in the stratification of its manufacturing quarters. In the western sector of the IS and Zhabei, we find silk mills, cotton-weaving factories, engineering workshops and printing works – small businesses, set up during the second half of the nineteenth century, many still run on semi-traditional lines. The modern industries – cotton mills, flour mills and oil mills, established in the twentieth century – were situated in Yangshupu or in Xiaoshadu, along the western borders of Zhabei, or even further afield to the west in the suburbs of Jessfield Park or Caojiadu. All these industrial areas were served and linked by the Soochow Creek, which supplied them with water and facilitated transport.

Two other, peripheral, industrial centres developed beyond the attractions afforded by this waterway. One, at Nanshi, revolved around a number of large Chinese concerns, some public, some privately owned; the other, at Pudong, was in the vicinity of the foreign shipyards.

The origin of the engineering industries in Shanghai dates back to the opening of the port and the creation, during the 1860s, of the first naval repair yards, which were soon followed by shipyards. These were situated in Pudong (where the International Dock Company, Boyd and Company and the Pudong Dock Company all installed themselves) or else to the north-east of the mouth of the Soochow Creek on the as yet deserted wharves of the former American Concession, where Farnham and Company set up its yards. It was here that Chinese mechanical engineering workshops began to spring up from the 1870s onwards. Initially, most of them worked as sub-contractors for the foreign shipyards. Most operated in a semi-traditional fashion and with very little capital. The earliest made their appearance in the north of the central sector and in the northern sector of the IS; the *Shanghai Guide* notes that 19 were still in operation here in 1919. However, after 1900, many of these establishments moved to the new quarters of Yangshupu, where other new businesses were also establishing themselves. In 1919, this area contained 22 workshops. With 38 workshops and 8 shipyards, the borders of the northern and eastern sectors represented the zone with the greatest concentration of mechanical engineering works in Shanghai. However, two large concerns financed by national capital were to be found in Nanshi – the Jiangnan Arsenal (first set up in Wusong, to the north of Shanghai, then in 1865 transferred to Gaochangmiao) and the Qiuxin Works, established in 1906.

The first textile industries to modernise were the foreign silk mills, soon followed by the Chinese ones. From 1878 onwards, these installed themselves along the two banks of the Soochow Creek, some (28%) in the territory of the International Settlement, in the northern district, on Bei Suzhoulu, Bei Zhejianglu and Alabaisituolu, others (20%) on the southern bank, in the western distict, on Chengdulu, Xinzhalu and Maigenlu. But the largest concentrations (38%) were up river, in the Chinese suburb of Zhabei, in Guangfulu, Chang'anlu and Hengfenglu.

The development of the cotton mills came later. It began at the very end of the nineteenth century and continued through the first two decades of the twentieth. By this time, industrial land was hard to come by both in the heart of the concessions and in Zhabei. So the new factories were set up on the margins of the International Settlement: 48% in the eastern district, 44% in the port suburbs of Yangshupu and in the furthermost quarters of the western district near Xiaoshadu, where the northernmost of them were bordered by the loops of the Soochow Creek. Some were even situated beyond the Settlement limits, out towards the Jessfield Park district.

A few weaving workshops were connected with the large cotton mills. They were modern concerns (*gongsi, gongchang*) and were situated, as were the spinning mills, in the eastern (17%) and western (23%) districts of the International Settlement. But many of the weaving workshops were no more than artisan concerns manufacturing traditional fabrics, known as 'patriotic fabrics' (*aiguobu*) following the eruptions of xenophobic boycotts in 1915 and 1919. These workshops (*buchang, aiguobuchang*) were concentrated in Zhabei (23%) or on the western margins of the French Concession, on the fringes of Nanshi (23%). Workshops producing hats and socks, which were compact and needed no heavy equipment, were to be found in every quarter of the city.

Industries connected with foodstuffs were concentrated along the Soochow Creek, where rice, oil products and wheat from the interior were unloaded. A particularly high proportion of flour mills was located

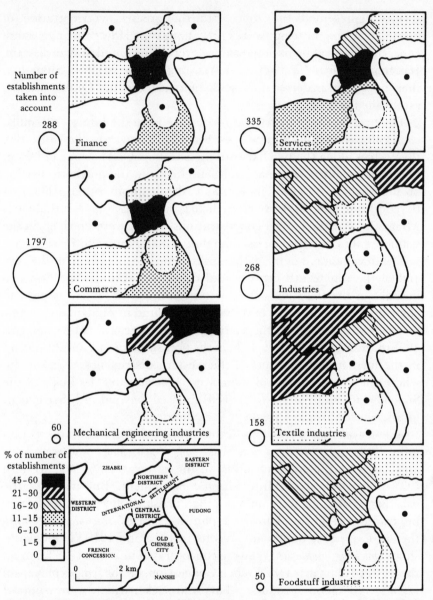

Figure 3.9 The distribution of the different sectors of economic activity in Shanghai, around 1919: a recapitulation of the preceding figures

here. These were modern works, which had made their appearance at the beginning of the twentieth century. They were strung out along the south bank between Jessfield Park and Suzhoulu (in the central district of the IS), to the north of the river along Bei Suzhoulu (in the northern district of the IS) and also in Zhabei. Mechanised or semi-mechanised oil works, which had been introduced slightly earlier – at the end of the nineteenth century – clustered together upstream, in the Chinese suburbs of Caojiadu and in the part of the western district that was contained by the twisting course of the Xiaoshadu. Rice factories were more widely distributed: a third of them were grouped together along the Soochow Creek, but some were located in the heart of the central district and even as far afield as Nanjinglu, in the old Chinese City and in Nanshi. In most of these establishments, the production side of the business was still to a large extent run on traditional lines and was more or less indistinguishable from the commercial side.

Nor was this exceptional. While certain quarters do seem to have been more particularly industrial zones, small factories were dotted all over Shanghai. Thus virtually half (48%) of Shanghai's 72 printing works were established in the central sector of the International Settlement, where they were in close communication with the book-shops in Fuzhoulu, Shandonglu and Henanlu. Brick works, tile factories and dye works were also an integral part of the urban fabric.

Industry was still by no means specialised and far from segregated. But even as it stood, it gave Shanghai its character of a great modern metropolis.

2   Businessmen in urban society

The entrepreneurial group, which emerged at the time of the First World War, made its initial impact through its material wealth. In the absence of any documentation on the basis of which to assess their fortunes, the chance records of loans, bankruptcies and family share-outs nevertheless provide us with some information of a fragmentary nature. During the first two decades of the century, the fortune of some merchants and industrialists could be counted in millions of dollars. That of the industrialist Zhu Zhiyao, the founder of the Qiuxin Works, was established at 2.16 million dollars in 1918.[16] Song Weichen (1866–?), who was one of the first industrialists to set up match factories in China but who also invested in the mining, chemical and engineering industries, owned over three million dollars' worth of shares of various kinds.[17] As a result of the commercial and industrial prosperity of the 1920s, these fortunes increased. When the Nanyang Brothers' Tobacco Company was reorganised in 1919, its proprietors put 10 million dollars into the new company.[18] By the end of the 1920s, the Guo family, which, among other businesses, owned a number of large shops and cotton mills, was reckoned to be worth 40 million dollars.[19]

We know even less about the structure of these fortunes than about their size. However, the general impression given is that real estate was of no more than secondary importance here. In this respect, the case of the Nie family is rather exceptional. The Nies came from a family of large-scale cotton mill owners, with origins, admittedly, amongst the upper gentry. At the time of the First World War, they reinvested the huge profits from their Hengfeng Cotton Mills in the purchase of 48,000 *mu* (about 3,000 hectares) of arable land. The cultivation of this land was entrusted to tenant farmers, its management to a company that was also delegated with policing powers. By the early 1920s, the high income produced by the land made it possible for the Nies to expand and modernise their cotton mills.[20] Such a combination of agriculture and urban business (whether industrial or commercial) does not appear to have been the general rule. Usually, entrepreneurs preferred to reinvest their capital either in expanding or creating businesses or in the purchase (speculative for the most part) of urban land or buildings. In 1918, when the Qiuxin Works went broke and were bought up by French capital, an inventory of the assets of Zhu Zhiyao was drawn up. It underlines the urban nature of these industrial fortunes. Out of an overall total estimated at 2.16 million dollars, factories (spinning mills, oil mills and engineering works) represented 1.15 million dollars' worth and the remainder was made up by land and buildings situated in various quarters of Shanghai – Nanshi, the French Concession and the Chinese City.[21] The buildings owned by the Zhu family in the Chinese quarters of Shanghai were part of the family heritage. For reasons of security and profit, the modern entrepreneurs preferred to invest in the concessions. For instance, of the 3 million dollars invested by the Guo family between 1919 and 1922 in the purchase of land and buildings in Shanghai, 2.95 millions (95%) financed the acquisition of buildings situated in the central and northern sectors of the International Settlement.[22] A number of possibly not altogether trustworthy sources indicate that, in the early 1930s, the Guo family owned over 300 buildings in Shanghai.[23]

The urban nature of the fortunes of the new entrepreneurs of the treaty ports marked them out from the European entrepreneurs of the early industrial period, most of whom retained the standing of the landed gentry and the income that went with it. The essential problem for Chinese modernisation in the early days was not so much one of innovation or even of the accumulation of capital, but rather how to acquire technological expertise. Direct or indirect exposure to Western material civilisation was the determining factor in the setting-up of business concerns. Merchants and compradores, and even artisans, were in this respect better placed than landowners. When the first phase of Chinese industrialisation was taking place, at the end of the Manchu dynasty, the landowners had played at least some kind of role. The entrepreneurs of the golden age pulled away from that urban elite class, whose members, even though they pursued economic, social and political activities of a very different nature from those of the rural gentry, remained for all that closely linked with the structures of the *ancien régime* through the land that they owned and through their close ties with the public authorities. At the time of the First World War, there appeared on the margins of this class a narrow social fringe committed to the ideology of industrial growth and economic rationality – a truly modern bourgeoisie. This shift, which came about under the influence of the economic boom, also coincided with the spread of Western influence. Most of the new entrepreneurs who represented this modern bourgeoisie had been educated abroad. They were both more up to date with the realities of the contemporary world and less bound by traditional constraints. All the same, they retained close links with the landed gentry from which they themselves had sprung and with which they still shared many common interests.

After the 1911 revolution, the balance between the social groups included in this elite class shifted considerably. The role of the qualified men of letters had declined. In Zhejiang, for example, they constituted no more than 2.6% of the members of the new provincial assembly elected in 1921, in contrast to their 68.7% membership on the eve of the revolution.[24] Their ranks were further thinned out as they died off, for after the abolition of the imperial examinations systems in 1905 they were not replaced. In their traditional activities as the financers and managers of urban philanthropic organisations, the scholars and the members of the gentry were increasingly frequently replaced by public authorities and experts specially trained in health and public works. A case in point was Jinan (Shandong), where, in 1917, the Benevolence Bureau (Guangren shanju) was supplanted by a Public Office of Philanthropy.[25]

The urban elite, which was recruited from amongst the merchants, entrepreneurs, landowners, and graduates from the modern schools, now stole a march on the gentry and consolidated their influence over the local administrative authorities. After the 1911 revolution, the dispossession of the bureaucratic institutions in favour of bodies representing local interests – provincial assemblies, chambers of commerce and societies for the promotion of agriculture and education – clashed, on a national level, with the unifying, authoritarian and centralist reactionary policies of Yuan Shikai and, on a regional level, with the rival ambitions of the militarists. Despite this, the power of the urban elite continued to grow. Even if they were not successful in preserving the administrative and fiscal prerogatives that their local organisations had seized in 1912–14, the local elites managed to exert a much greater influence over the bureaucracy than they ever had before the revolution. Essentially, the reason for this was that the principle according to which it had been forbidden under the imperial regime to select magistrates from amongst the local scholars had lapsed. Now the bureaucracy was recruited on the spot. The local elites tended to act in such a way as to safeguard their interests against intervention from public authorities, foreign encroachment and popular dissatisfaction. This basis of social conservatism, nationalism, and distrust of the State power, favoured the formation of many ties of solidarity between the local elite class and its pioneering, entrepreneurial bourgeois fringe. The formation of this entente was made easier by the fact that a number of the leaders of the pre-revolutionary urban and reformist elite were still extremely prominent on the Shanghai political and economic scene. One was Zhang Jian, Minister for Industry under Yuan Shikai, in whose Dasheng Cotton Mills in Nantong (Jiangsu) the number of spindles doubled between 1914 and 1921.[26] Another was Yu Xiaqing (1867–1945), the director of the General Chamber of Commerce and of the Ningbo Guild, who, during the war, invested 2 million taels in steam shipping companies – the Sanbei (Sanbei gongsi) in 1914, the Ningshao (Ningshao gongsi) in 1917, and the Hong'an (Hong'an gongsi) in 1917.[27] The personal careers of these prominent individuals strengthened a trend of evolution that led the treaty ports from urban revolution to industrial revolution.

The entrepreneurs of the new generation, which included the brothers Mu, Nie, Guo, Rong and Jian, distanced themselves much more than their elders had both from the old society and from the bureaucratic authorities, and their desire for emancipation and autonomy led to conflict. In general, however, the pioneers of economic modernisation received considerable support, in many forms, from the urban elites, and this facilitated their operations, ensuring them of far-reaching success. Mu Ouchu could never have amassed sufficient capital to set up his first cotton mill in 1917 without the help of a group of merchants who entrusted him with the huge profits they had made from speculations on the dye market after German imports had been stopped at the beginning of the war. The bourgeois avant-garde found a useful platform and a sympathetic audience in the chambers of commerce and guilds, still in almost all cases controlled by the urban elites. Thanks to their encouragement, the new economic ideas and experiments commanded the interest and support of much wider groups than the circles in which they had originated.

Another reason why the modern bourgeoisie managed to establish itself so swiftly in relation to the local elites was that its rise was supported by the parallel emergence of an intelligentsia which shared a similar experience of the contemporary world. Like the new entrepreneurs, the new intellectuals who prepared the way for and led the May Fourth Movement of 1919 – Cai Yuanpei, Hu Shi, Jiang Menglin, Guo Bingwen – were for the most part educated abroad and had returned to China armed with new ideas and expertise. They too distanced themselves from the old society, dismantling the links which, under the Empire, had turned the scholars into officials and had equated *zheng* (politics) with *jiao* (orthodoxy). They were in favour of a new education (xin jiaoyu), based upon respect for individuality (*gexingzhuvi*).[28] They too received from the urban elites assistance which enabled them to move on to the implementation of their ideas. Jiang Menglin's Movement for the New Education would probably never have existed without the support of the powerful and respected Jiangsu Education Association (Jiangsusheng jiaoyuhui).

Quite apart from the many links which respectively bound the group of new entrepreneurs and that of the modern intelligentsia to the class of the local elites, the modernist avant-garde of the treaty ports also benefited from the alliance between its intellectuals and its business proprietors. All this is a far cry from the picture painted by a certain kind of Western literature inspired by sentiments favourable to the Third World, which makes use of the vague and disparaging label 'comprador' to describe a bourgeoisie cut off from the society from which it emerged, bent on imitating – if not serving – its foreign models, yet envied by all other social groups. The relations that the new Chinese bourgeoisie entertained simultaneously with both the traditional elite groups and the upwardly mobile classes of urban society were both numerous and close. They were developed on a family and friendly level, were manifest in the diverse careers pursued by the various members of a single family, sometimes within a single lifetime, and were an integral part of the structure of Chinese society.

Take the example of Chang Kia-ngau (1889–1979), who began his career in the Bank of China in 1913 and in the early 1920s became one of the principal organisers and spokesmen of modern Chinese banking circles. Through his elder brother, Carson Chang, a jurist, philosopher, writer and journalist, he was linked with the world of publishing, journalism and further education. Through his sister, Zhang Yuyi, by her first marriage the wife of the poet Xu Zhimo, he had connections with the world of literature and art. The industrialist Zhu Zhiyao was similarly connected, by family ties and their common membership of the old Catholic community[29] in Shanghai, with the Ma family, which included Ma Jianzhong, the famous grammarian who initiated the bureaucratic drive towards modernisation at the end of the nineteenth century, and Ma Liang, former Secretary of Foreign Affairs under Li Hongzhang and the founder of Fudan University, a scholar as expert in Latin as in Chinese.[30] The close collaboration between the cotton mill owner Nie Yuntai and the educationist Huang Yanpei, a graduate of the *ancien régime*, seems to have been based upon personal ties of friendship and a shared conviction of the urgent need to reform the system of professional training for Chinese youth. In 1919, the two men worked together to set up the Chinese Society for Vocational Training (Zhonghua zhiyejiaoyushe).

The range of professions followed within a single family, from one generation to the next or among the members of a single generation, illustrates how few barriers there were between modern entrepreneurial circles and other urban elite groups. Li Ruxiong (1891–?), grandson of a well-known Ningbo poet, who launched himself into the business world in 1912 and a few years later became director of the Hwafoo Commercial Bank of China in Shanghai, was the younger brother of Li Ruyin, one of the first Chinese pilots, who was educated in England.[31] It is by no means rare to find a successful entrepreneur diverging into a political career. The interpenetration of business and government was a widespread phenomenon which had already accounted for a number of the peculiar features of the earlier wave of Chinese modernisation. During the 1920s, the forms taken by this interpenetration underwent a change. It was no longer a matter of the entrepreneurs seeking social prestige and protection from the administrative authorities. Now they were bent upon expressing in a new form the power that was already theirs in the economic sphere. After the First World War, Rong Desheng, who was the son of a minor customs official, found himself, with his brother, at the head of a veritable industrial empire in the shape of the Maoxin–Fuxin–Shenxin General Company (Maoxin Fuxin Shenxin zonggonsi). It was at this point that he embarked upon a political career; he was elected to the Jiangsu provincial assembly in 1918 and to the Peking parliament in 1921.[32]

In contrast to the entrepreneurs of the preceding generation, the great bankers and industrialists of the 1920s for the most part no longer regarded business simply as a source of income and a step-up in the direction of other, more prestigious activities. They approached business as a profession and when they sent their children abroad for costly further education, it was not so as to enable them to escape from the world of their origins but, on the contrary, to prepare them to manage the family business better.

It may be objected that there were plenty of large-scale industrialists and, above all, big bankers from the 1920s who were to be found as ministers or high-ranking officials under the Nanking government during the 1930s. The banker Wu Dingchang (1884–1950) became Minister of Industry; Chang Kia-ngau was appointed Minister of Communications in 1935. In 1928, the industrialist Mu Ouchu became vice-president of a short-lived Ministry of Industry and Trade.[33] But in these instances the changes of career reflect not so much the inclinations of the entrepreneurs themselves, but rather a change in the political and economic situation of the country. As we shall see in Chapter 5, the establishment of the Guomindang regime in

1927 marked a return in force for bureaucratic control over the business world and paralysed the progress of business concerns. The only option for bankers and industrialists was to revert to administrative management – when they got the chance to do so.

The bureaucratisation of the entrepreneurial class from 1930 on thus appears to have been conditioned by historical circumstances in general. During the 1920s, it never occurred to businessmen to abandon their businesses in order to devote themselves to affairs of State. There was no reason for them to do so. Their political importance as entrepreneurs was already well and truly recognised by both the provincial and the national public authorities, who turned to them to provide management or advice for technical ministerial departments (of finance, industry, agriculture and trade) and to sit upon *ad hoc* consultative committees (on customs tariffs, monetary reform and the paying-off of public debts), and who sent them off on official missions abroad and, in some cases, showered them with honours.

For instance, one of the pioneers of the chemical industry, Song Weichen, who started his career in Shanghai in 1899, pursuing it until 1922 in Hankou, was in 1914 appointed Councillor of the Senate (Canzhengyuan canzhong). He subsequently also served as a councillor to the President of the Republic, Li Yuanhong, and as military governor of Hubei province.[34] Usually, however, it was to bankers that the government appealed – no doubt in the hope of also obtaining their financial collaboration. Ministerial advisers included Sun Yuanfang (1883–?) from the Zhongfu Bank (Zhongfu yinhang) at the Ministry of Agriculture and Trade and Fu Xiao'an (1870–1940) at the Ministry of Finance. Li Ming (1887–1966), from the Zhejiang Industrial Bank, was in 1923 appointed as a member of the Commission for the Reorganisation of Finance; and in 1925, Duan Qirui, the provisional leader of the government, appealed to Chen Guangfu, co-founder in 1915 of the Shanghai Bank, to chair the Rehabilitation Conference (Shanhou huiyi) called to prepare a plan to salvage the State and its institutions.[35]

In most cases such administrative appointments were essentially symbolic in nature. Not many of these bankers and industrialists actually performed their duties: their functions were honorific as were the decorations of the national Jiahe (Excellent Harvest) order, which were generously distributed to at least the upper echelons of the entrepreneurs. The recorded recipients of this order include the bankers Song Hangzhang (1872–1968), first decorated in 1919 and then again in 1923, Sun Yuanfang, Zhao Xi'en (1883–?), Fu Xiao'an, Li Ming (decorated three times between 1920 and 1921) and Xu Enyuan (1884–?), who received a first-class Jiahe at the same time as a French *légion d'honneur*. Others mentioned in the records are industrialists such as Song Weichen and the cotton mill owner Nie Yuntai and – more rarely – we find the names of merchants and compradores such as, for example, the Cantonese Chan Lin-pak, decorated in 1921 and again in 1923, and his brother Chan Lin-chung.[36]

These honours reflect the social prestige that was by now attached to the activities of the entrepreneurs. However, the real power of the new bourgeoisie found expression through the professional organisations that initially enabled it to break through into the ruling classes.

3   Breaking-through to the ruling classes: the organisations of the new bourgeoisie

To safeguard their power and protect their particular interests, the new entrepreneurs both set up their own organisations and also further developed the role that they played within existing merchant institutions.

The formation of employers' federations, at the end of the First World War, stemmed from action that was both united and spontaneous. The Shanghai Bankers' Association (Shanghai yinhang gonghui) was organised around the publication of the *Bankers' Weekly* (*Yinhang zhoubao*), the first issue of which appeared on 29 May 1917. The small group of its promoters included the elite of the young bankers of Shanghai. They were led by Song Hangzhang and Chang Kia-ngau, respectively director and assistant director of the Shanghai branch of the Bank of China. Song and Chang were determined to manage their bank free from governmental intervention and along the lines of international financial rules. Song Hangzhang, the elder of the two, had been educated in Shanghai itself, at the Anglo-Chinese Academy, but Chang Kia-ngau had graduated from the University Waseda in 1909, with an economics degree.[37] They were surrounded by a group of young entrepreneurs – the majority born in the 1880s and still in their thirties – who were all educated abroad, for the most part in Japan, and were anxious to introduce modern banking practices into China. One case in point was Li Ming, who had graduated in 1910 from the Yamaguchi College of Commercial Studies. Appointed manager of the Zhejiang Bank (Zhejiang yinhang) in Hangzhou, he rebelled against interference from officials and turned the bank into a private establishment, the Zhejiang Industrial Bank (Zhejiang difang shiye yinhang), transferring its headquarters to Shanghai.[38] Like Li Ming and at about the same time, Xu Jijin (1881–) studied at the Yamaguchi College of Commercial Studies, graduating in 1910. On his return to China, he became director of the local branches of the Bank of China, then entered the Zhejiang Commercial Bank (Zhejiang xingye yinhang) in Shanghai, where he worked in collaboration with Xu Xinliu (1890–?), who, for his part, had studied from 1908 to 1913 at the Universities of Birmingham and Manchester, and then at the University of Paris in 1914.[39]

Chen Guangfu reacted similarly against the bureaucratic system of banking management which confronted him on his return from the United States, and in 1915 he founded the Shanghai Bank. He had graduated in 1909 from the Wharton School of Finance of the University of Pennsylvania and was first appointed as director of the Jiangsu Provincial Bank (Jiangsusheng yinhang). In an effort to escape from official pressures, he transferred the bank's headquarters from Nanking (the provincial capital) to Shanghai. However, the opposition that he encountered from the bureaucracy led him to resign his position. With the aid of Zhang Jian and Chang Kia-ngau, he then founded the Shanghai Bank, which was to become one of the most prosperous private banks in China, representing a point of reference and a model for the new type of management.[40] Another member of the group that launched the *Bankers' Weekly* was Sun Yuanfang. Born in 1883, Sun had pursued his further education in the United States, first at the Wesleyan Academy, then at the Massachusetts Institute of Technology, then at Brown University. In 1916, he took over the direction of the Shanghai branch of the Zhongfu Bank, which he had just helped to found.[41]

Such were the men that Song Hangzhang gathered around him in the spring of 1917, on the premises of the Bank of China, to launch the *Bankers' Weekly*. In the following year, Song suggested that the same group should set up the Shanghai Bankers' Association. Five new Shanghai banks joined the already existing group, bringing to twelve the total number of establishments represented at the official inauguration of the Association, on 8 July 1918. By 1925, seven years after its founding, the number of associated banks had doubled, to 24. Its rapid growth was a sign of the dynamism of the modern banking sector in Shanghai.[42]

The composition of the governing body of the Association remained relatively stable from 1918 to 1926, taking into account the fact that its membership was increased from seven to nine in 1922. Sun Yuanfang and Ni Yuanfu, of the Salt Gabelle Bank, who were elected and re-elected four times, served on it continuously; Song Hangzhang, Chen Guangfu and Li Ming each served on it for three terms, Qian Yongming (1885–1958) twice.[43] Most of the directors of the Association represented the Shanghai branches of large official or semi-official banks with headquarters in Peking – the Bank of China, the Communications Bank and the Salt Gabelle Bank. However, these Shanghai establishments retained a large measure of autonomy in relation to the general management of their banks and disapproved of Peking banking practices that were too open to governmental and administrative influences.

Some financial and personal connections nevertheless did exist between the headquarters of the banks and their branches. For example, soon after having helped to found the *Bankers' Weekly* in 1917, Chang Kia-ngau left Shanghai for Peking, where he assumed the position of assistant governor-general of the Bank of China.[44] Similarly, Qian Yongming, appointed vice-president of the Communications Bank in 1922, also moved to Peking.[45] The presence of these men in Peking, and their important positions there, immediately conferred a national importance upon the initiatives taken in Shanghai. On the basis of the lead given by Shanghai in 1916 and 1917, banking associations now began to be set up in many large cities – in Hankou, Suzhou and Hangzhou, as well as in the north in Peking, Tianjin and Harbin. In December 1920, at the suggestion of Chang Kia-ngau, these associations amalgamated to form a national federation, the Chinese Bankers' Association (Quanguo yinhang zonghui), which promptly became one of the main instruments for the politics of governmental reform advocated by the new entrepreneurs of Shanghai.

A spontaneous initiative, this time on the part of the industrialists, was also responsible for the creation, in 1918, of the Chinese Cotton Mill Owners' Association. This gave institutional form to a group that had been organised the previous year to fight for the retention of the

export tax on raw cotton that Japanese buyers wished to see suppressed.[46] Although this association was from the outset organised on a
national scale, the cotton mill owners of Shanghai played a predominant role in it, particularly Nie Yuntai, its founder and first president,
and Mu Ouchu, its indefatigable organiser.

The employers' federations were modern in the way that they
perceived their role. Their attitudes were those of international
capitalism, dominated by the notions of growth, progress and competition. They were also concerned to diffuse economic information
and published professional magazines to which the foremost specialists
of the time contributed. The short space of a few years thus saw the
launching of not only the *Bankers' Weekly* in 1917 in Shanghai, but also
the *Quarterly Review of the Chinese Cotton Mill Owners' Association*
(*Huashang shachang lianhehui jikan*) in 1919, the *Monthly Banking Review*
(*Yinhang yuekan*) in Peking in 1921 and the *Banking Review* (*Yinhang
zazhi*) in Hankou in 1923. These magazines provide exceptionally full
and accurate information on the activities of the modern sector during
this period and on the obstacles to its further development. The
importance that they ascribe to the study of external markets testifies
to their efforts to situate that development within the framework of
worldwide economic forces. Their defence of class interests also
assumes a modern dimension. Solidarity is no longer centred on
already established interests, as it was in the guilds; instead, it focuses
upon interests of the future. The monopoly tradition was being
superseded by the ideology of growth: 'The fact is that our internal
trade has become international ... The traditional banks and
exchange establishments ... can no longer answer the needs of today; it
is now the (modern) banks that provide financial aid for the government, businesses and other concerns. But in order to continue these
banking activities, certain measures must be taken, certain policies
adopted. Bankers must be kept well informed. This cannot be done
without the framework of the activities and information of individual
banks ... It is essential to set up a banking association.'[47]

Despite their proclaimed ambitions, the new employers' federations
did not manage to supersede the traditional organisations. In Shanghai, for instance, the Bankers' Association never acquired the power of
the Native Bankers' Guild (Shanghai qianyehui), which continued to
control financial life in the market place as it fixed the exchange rate
(*yangli*) between the currency unit (the tael) and the silver dollar, as

well as the inter-bank interest rate (*yinzhe*). It also retained a monopoly over compensation operations.

Creating their own organisations was therefore not enough for the new entrepreneurs. They would also have to storm the traditional institutions. So in Shanghai the entrepreneurs were to be found at the head of the most influential regional associations. For example, the banker Song Hangzhang was president of the Shaoxing Association. Sun Yuanfang, who held shares in a number of Shanghai flour milling concerns, was a member of the governing body of the Guild of Flour Merchants.[48] Finally, they were also active in the General Chamber of Commerce, where their influence had been increasing ever since the end of the First World War.

In 1918, the Shanghai General Chamber of Commerce, which brought together the Chinese businessmen from the foreign concessions, still had the air of a federation of guilds, dominated as it was by the powerful Ningbo Clique (Ningbo bang). The extremely high annual subscriptions, amounting to hundreds of taels, restricted its membership to a total of about 300. Thus, apart from the guilds, only the major business concerns were represented there. Powers of decision were held by a bureau which had slightly expanded since 1911: it now included 35 directors instead of 21, but its composition had changed hardly at all.[49] Of the 35 directors elected in 1918, 8 had been serving since 1911. Most were compradores (Wang Yiting, Xi Ligong, Yang Xinzhi and Zhu Lanfang) whose commercial activities had prospered as foreign trade developed and who were, on occasion, ready enough to invest in modern industrial ventures: for example, Wang Yiting had provided financial backing for the Lida Mills (Lida mianfenchang) in 1907, the Shenda Mills (Shenda mianfenchang) in 1910, and also for an electric light-bulb factory.[50]

Most of the new directors elected in 1918 were cast in much the same mould as their predecessors. They were still what might be described as the 'transitional' type of entrepreneurs, whose interest in the modern sector by no means excluded activities of a traditional nature and whose industrial operations amounted to no more than a general diversification of their investments to include more trade and finance. One such was Gu Xingyi, a rice and bean merchant who had initially (1907–10) been principally interested in the food-production industries, investing along with Wang Yiting in the Lida and Shenda Flour Mills. But he had widened his outlook during the war years, helping to finance the creation of the Chinese shipyards at Hexing.[51] However, the 1918 elections did bring on to the board of directors of the Chamber of Commerce three figures who represented the new bourgeoisie: the banker Song Hangzhang, the cotton mill owner Mu Ouchu and another modern banker by the name of Fu Xiao'an. It was, as yet, no more than a limited invasion of the General Chamber of Commerce. The modernist avant-garde represented less than 10% of the board of directors and, in the cases of Song and Mu, it brought to power men who were, relatively speaking, both older and more eminent than the young businessmen for whom they acted as leaders: Song was at this time 46 years old, Mu 42.

The real breakthrough of the new entrepreneurs in the Chamber came about at the next elections, held in 1920.[52] The structures and methods of the Chamber had been severely upset by the crisis of 4 May 1919, when it replaced almost all the members of its board of directors; only two members of the 1918 board were re-elected, one being the cotton mill owner, Mu Ouchu. The most striking feature of the new team elected to head the Chamber was its youth. One-quarter of the directors were under 40. Among these young directors we come across the names of bankers for the first time (Fang Jiaobo (1881–?) and Qian Yongming), industrialists (Jian Yujie (1875–1957)), and entrepreneurs (Sun Meitang (1884–?)), who were to play a dominant role in the business world over the next two or three decades. Symbolic of the Chamber's rejuvenation was the election of Nie Yuntai, who, at 41 years old, took over as chairman from the 73-year-old Zhu Baosan.

The board, which comprised 33 directors, was still dominated by wholesale merchants, of whom there were 16. But entrepreneurs from the domains of industry and modern transport had 11 representatives, and 6 bankers, some modern, others traditional, completed the membership. The modern sector had always been represented on the Shanghai Chamber of Commerce but never before so emphatically or so specifically. The merchant investors had been replaced by professional entrepreneurs. Cotton spinning, the foremost sector of national industry, was represented by Mu Ouchu, the owner of the Housheng and Deda Cotton Mills in Shanghai and of the Yufeng Cotton Mills in Zhengzhou (Hebei); Nie Yuntai, the proprietor of the Hengfeng works; and Rong Zongjing, the co-founder (with his brother) and general manager of the Shenxin Cotton Mills. Rong, the proprietor of the Maoxin and Fuxin Flour Mills together with another flour mill owner, Lu Weiyong, was spokesman for the agricultural food-production industries. The brothers Jian Zhaonan (1870–1923) and Jian Yujie from Hong Kong, both members of the board of directors of the Chamber, had recently moved the headquarters of their business to Shanghai: this was the Nanyang Brothers' Tobacco Company, the five factories of which were at that time employing over 10,000 workers. Another of the industrialists on the board of directors was Sun Meitang, then aged 37, who was one of the pioneers of the clock-making industry.[53]

Traditional banking was represented by Fang Jiaobo, a native of Ningbo, who was also contributing to the advancement of modern banking methods in his capacity as manager of the Donglu Bank (Donglu yinhang).[54] Two other directors of the Chamber of Commerce were Qian Yongming, whom we have already encountered playing an active role in the Shanghai Bankers' Association, and Zhuang Dezhe of the Shanghai Bank. Yuan Liguo (1880–?) was spokesman for the leaders of maritime transport. Yuan was a native of Zhejiang and was 41 years old in 1921 when he became the general manager of the Ningbo–Shaoxin Company (Ningshao gongsi).[55] Finally, among the new directors elected in 1920 we should also note the presence of Feng Shaoshan, a 36-year-old Cantonese who was to become one of the principal and most radical editors of the *Shanghai General Chamber of Commerce Monthly Review (Shanghai zongshanghui yuebao)*.[56]

But this invasion of the younger employers into the top circles of the Shanghai General Chamber of Commerce was only partially confirmed by the 1922 elections, which brought back onto the board a number of the old-style entrepreneurs: men such as the compradores Yu Xiaqing (aged 54) and Lao Jingxiu (aged 59); also the rice merchant Gu Xingyi and the silk wholesaler Shen Liangfang (aged 55), a participant in the 1911 revolution in Shanghai who later, in 1918, became vice-president of the Chamber of Commerce and was much criticised during the May Fourth Movement.[57]

The conflicts that broke out in the Chamber of Commerce during the 1920s reflected many other tensions apart from possible divergences between the moderns and the semi-moderns: rivalries between regional groups and relations with the local authorities and also with foreigners were issues that involved more than the problem of modernity. All the same, the presence of the new entrepreneurs on the board

of directors of the Chamber did bring about certain changes in the
Chamber itself; its structures became more open and, relatively
speaking, more democratic. By 1928, the membership of the Chamber
had increased by 62%, reaching a total of 488, while that of its board of
directors had increased by 37%, bringing the number of directors to
58. The presidency now devolved upon a triumvirate flanked by four
vice-presidents. Guild-based representation was no longer predominant; only about a quarter (23.4%) of the Chamber, that is to say 114
members, now represented guilds. The list of directors still included
some of the young avant-garde of 1920: Mu Ouchu and the Rong
brothers, Nie Lusheng (the brother and successor of Nie Yuntai), Sun
Yuanfang, Fang Jiaobo and Feng Shaoshan. These were flanked by
wholesale compradores of the earlier generation: Yu Xiaqing, Lao
Jingxiu and Wang Yiting.[58] Apart from during the 1919 crisis, the
accession of the new entrepreneurs to the elite leadership of the
Shanghai business world thus took place without encountering any
major difficulties. Under their influence, the Chamber, with considerable prudence, did move forward, modernising its organisation and –
as we shall presently see – attempting to free its economic and political
strategy from the constraints of officialdom, even if its position often
appeared less advanced than those of the business, banking and
industrial associations.

The power that the new entrepreneurs had acquired at the head of
the Shanghai General Chamber of Commerce still did not allow them
to direct the policies of that august institution in the directions that
they would have chosen, but it set the seal upon the importance of their
role in Shanghai business circles and in the city society more generally.
As the gentry declined, the dominant position in this society was filled
by the bourgeoisie. It brought together the mass of *ancien régime* elites
and the fringe element of new entrepreneurs in a flexible coalition
which derived its social stability from the one group and its taste for
progress from the other. There are many reasons to explain why this
integration came about so rapidly and proved so effective: a tradition
of consensus politics which led the elites to adopt flexible attitudes and
a real openness of mind which led them to extend an interested
welcome to innovation, even if they did not themselves initiate it; the
existence of complex and intricate networks of interest that eroded the
boundaries between the modern and the traditional sectors; and, even

more crucial, the very structures of the new group of business leaders whose geographical, family and professional connections reflected the traditional principles upon which Chinese society as a whole was organised.

4 ❧ The social structures of the new bourgeoisie

During the 1920s, the bourgeoisie, whose importance, as such, was increasingly recognised by urban society, was gradually constituting itself as a specific and coherent social class. Now that it was no longer necessary for members of economic elites to enter the bureaucracy in order to break into the ruling class, social mobility seemed less desirable. Gone were the days when millionaires would buy themselves titles and responsibilities in order to enter into dialogue with the authorities. Although the prestige of graduates and scholars persisted, there were fewer temptations for this bourgeoisie to move into the public bureaucracy or to return to the life of a landowner. Proud of its wealth, skill and economic success, which tended to be regarded as so many moral virtues, the new bourgeoisie began to set itself up as a group of employers.

The structures of this group of employers are as difficult to pin down as are its limits. Large-scale banking, commercial business and modern industry, from which its members came, did not constitute well defined sub-groups. Most entrepreneurs pursued a number of activities either simultaneously or in succession. It is often difficult to determine a dominant pursuit in careers that are so varied.

It is nevertheless worth trying to sketch in a typology for these entrepreneurial leaders based upon the nature of their activities, for a study of their collective careers will allow us to make out the various paths which led them to become employers. The history of individuals is less important than that of families, however. The rise of Chinese capitalism cannot be understood without studying Chinese family structures. Plenty of authors have condemned these structures and the nepotism that they encouraged as major causes of the failure of capitalism in China.[1] Such an interpretation is contradicted not only by the phenomenon of the nineteenth-century European industrial bourgeoisie (particularly in France),[2] but also by the success of the overseas Chinese during the twentieth century. Family solidarities gave the emergent capitalism flexibility, dynamism and buoyancy when faced with crises. It is impossible to grasp the development of these businesses without taking into account, on the one hand, the roles played by sons and sons-in-law and the partnerships between cousins or uncles and nephews, and, on the other, the relations forged with other families through marriage. The family itself, conceived in the widest sense, was part of a vaster network of kinship and clientship hinging on a common ancestor, similar geographical roots, or occasionally, the profession of a common religious faith (as in the case of certain Catholic clans in Shanghai).

Regional links were also fundamental to the structure of the new bourgeoisie. These often overlapped with the networks of family relationships, but they extended further, making it possible to set up vast systems of interests and loyalties.

The family relations and provincial or local loyalties upon which the development of the new bourgeoisie was founded were also the very bases of Chinese social organisation as a whole. They represented values that were by no means limited to the modern economic elite groups, but these groups managed to get traditional values to serve the new ends of growth.

1   Regional solidarities: the geographic structures of the Shanghai business community

In Chapter 1, we examined the role played by regional guilds (*huiguan*) in the traditional towns. Although the big merchants always extended their influence by working within these associations during the eighteenth and nineteenth centuries, the *huiguan* generally recruited rich and poor alike, on the basis of their common geographical origin (*tongxiang*). That is no doubt why, paradoxically, these traditional and particularist associations played an essential role in the development of Chinese capitalism. By helping their members to find employment and financial backing, the *huiguan* favoured the rise of a host of small-scale entrepreneurs, for they strove to help each one to seize his chance and remained easily accessible to all members of the communities that they controlled. Who knows how many of the magnates who, years or decades earlier, had arrived barefoot in Shanghai and whose success their biographers ascribe solely to hard work and intelligence, in fact received crucial help from their already established compatriots? In 1872, Yu Xiaqing was a little 15-year-old apprentice fresh from his native Zhenhai (near Ningbo). Throughout the long career which made him one of the main merchant shipping entrepreneurs of Shanghai and president of its Chamber of Commerce, he enjoyed the financial and political backing of the powerful Ningbo Clique, of which he himself eventually became a leader.[3] The great comprador and tobacco wholesaler Zheng Bozhao, whose opulent life-style dazzled Shanghai society in the 1920s, began his career in 1902 in a marketing company working for the British American Tobacco Company, whose employees and shareholders were all natives of Guangdong province, as was Zheng himself.[4]

Far from rendering the structure of the market place more rigid, regional solidarities such as these increased its dynamism. They were exclusive, of course, to the extent that each one provided aid only for the members of one particular community. But every entrepreneur who came from one of those particular communities could benefit from the system.

However, the benefits offered varied in relation to the particular regional guilds concerned. In Shanghai, where 23 of these guilds operated, the most important, in terms of quality if not numbers, was that of Zhejiang province.[5] It incorporated several guilds. The old Ningbo Guild (Siming gongsuo), with its 60,000 members, had been joined by the Association of Natives of Ningbo in Shanghai (Ningbo lü Hu tongxianghui) and a number of other groups connected with various localities in the Ningbo prefecture. The various groups thus reflected the particular characteristics of geographical localities far smaller than the provincial unit. But that did not prevent the power of decision from being concentrated in the hands of a small number of leaders, each of whom combined several roles of an economic, political, socio-cultural or philanthropic nature. The power of the Ningbo Guild stemmed from its control over the banking sector. Traditional bankers had been making their way from Zhejiang province to Shanghai ever since the eighteenth century. Most came from Zhenhai (in the Ningbo prefecture) and from Shaoxing. Some, such as the Fangs, founded powerful dynasties. This family's origins went back to Fang Jietang, who had settled in Shanghai at the beginning of the nineteenth century and whose descendants had continued his work there over four generations.[6]

Despite the crashes provoked by the crisis of the Franco-Chinese War in 1884 and that of the 1910 wave of rubber speculation, and despite growing competition from the bankers of Jiangsu, the Ningbo entrepreneurs continued to control the traditional banks (*qianzhuang*) of Shanghai. In 1921, 78% of these establishments (54 out of the 69 traced) were affiliated to the Shaoxing or Ningbo regional guilds. By 1932, the bankers of Zhejiang controlled 73% of the capital invested in the *qianzhuang* of Shanghai.[7] However, in the meantime they had diversified their activities. As compradores for the large foreign banks, they were initiated into modern finance. One example was Xu Chunrong (1839–1910). He arrived in Shanghai from Ningbo during the 1870s and founded seven *qianzhuang*, all of which went into liquidation during the 1884 crisis. After this, he moved into partnership with the industrialist Ye Chengzhong (1840–1900) to finance the creation of four new *qianzhuang*, but at the same time he also became a comprador for the Deutsche Asiatische Bank. His eldest son, Xu Baochu, also pursued a career with the foreign banks (working as a comprador for the Park Union Bank in 1920 and 1921 and also for the American Express Company). Meanwhile, his younger son, Xu Xingquan, took over from his father at the Deutsche Asiatische Bank.[8]

Without abandoning either their *qianzhuang* or their positions as compradores, the Ningbo financiers were soon launching themselves into the creation of modern banks. One of the first to do so was Yu Xiaqing. He was a comprador for the Russo-Asiatic Bank in 1907 and later worked in that capacity for the Nederlandsche Handle Maatschappij Bank. In 1915, he called upon the capital of his compatriots from Zhejiang to found the Ningbo Bank, the management of which was entrusted to the owner of a *qianzhuang*, Sun Hengfu, who was, naturally, also a native of Ningbo.[9]

The Ningbo bankers thus adapted their traditions to the needs of modern times. While the *qianzhuang* continued to provide a solid basis of operations for the financiers already established in Shanghai, more recent immigrants went straight into modern banking, in many cases after a period of training abroad. Li Ming, born in Shaoxing in 1887, studied in Japan, then in 1915 took over the directorship of the Zhejiang Industrial Bank, which he converted into a private establishment in 1918.[10]

The rise of the natives of Ningbo in the banking sector cannot be disassociated from the leading role that they played in inter-regional and international trade. The first founders of the *qianzhuang* in Shanghai had also been merchants, established in the Chinese city (Nanshi), where they owned bazaars (*baihuo*) and dealt in cereals and fabrics. After the 1880s, when silk exports began to take over from the export of tea, the skills of the Ningbo merchants (who came from a cocoon-producing area) became indispensable to the foreign companies. It was at this point that compradores of Zhejiang origin began to supplant those of Cantonese stock in the export companies. By 1920, out of 90 major compradores recorded as operating for foreign banks and trading companies in Shanghai, 43 were natives of Zhejiang.[11]

The comprador wholesalers and bankers of Zhejiang were also among the first to invest in modern industry. Ye Chengzhong, the pioneer of the silk spinning mills, engineering industries and match manufacturing in Shanghai, was born in Zhenhai close to Ningbo, as was his partner, Song Weichen.[12] Ye Chengzhong's son-in-law Liu Hongsheng (1891–1956), who was known as the 'match king' in the 1920s and was the owner of many trading and industrial companies, was also born close to Ningbo, at Dinghai.[13] The founder of the Chinese clock-manufacturing industry, Sun Meitang, also came from Ningbo, and it was Yu Xiaqing, a native of Zhenhai who, with the backing of his compatriots, chief among them the Fang family, launched, during the First World War, the first private Chinese shipping companies.

The heads (*dongshi*) of the regional guilds of Zhejiang were recruited from amongst these entrepreneurs. The banking Fang family dominated the Ningbo Guild throughout the nineteenth century until, at the end of the century, it was forced to share power with the newly arrived Zhu Baosan and Yu Xiaqing families. The oligarchic structure of the Guild now took concrete form with the creation of a board of directors (*dongshihui*) coopted from the descendants of the founding members and former directors. The informal power of this board was far greater than that of the representatives regularly elected by the members of the guild as a whole. An attempt to make the system more democratic was made in 1909, with the creation of the Shanghai Association of the Natives of Ningbo, but it proved unsuccessful, for the new association, which was organised on the Western elective model, soon fell under the control of the leaders of the Ningbo Guild. The role played by the Ningbo entrepreneurs in the economic life of Shanghai, particularly in developing the modern sector, ensured that they were overwhelmingly represented in the General Chamber of Commerce. At the 1918 elections, 12 directors (out of a total of the 21 whose geographical origins are known) came from the province of Zhejiang. In 1924, that figure rose to 26 (out of 35).[14] Small wonder the Chamber of Commerce sometimes looked more like a sub-branch of the Ningbo Guild!

To succeed in business in Shanghai, find capital there and make useful contacts, it was thus best to be a native of Zhejiang. But Cantonese connections could also be useful. The 60,000 Cantonese of Shanghai were distributed among associations connected with various sub-prefectures, the most active being those of Xiangshan and Nanhai. These associations were federated to form the regional guilds of Eastern Guangdong and Western Guangdong, under the direction of the Canton Guild.[15] Gone, however, were the days when the word 'Cantonese' was synonymous with 'comprador' in Shanghai. Since the 1880s, the decline in exports of tea had put an end to the pre-eminence of the Cantonese, who had been the experts in the wholesale tea trade. By 1920, the number of major Shanghai compradores of Cantonese origin had fallen to 7 out of a total of 90.[16] The tradition was carried on only by a few isolated, if brilliant, men. Zheng Bozhao provides one example. Born in 1861, in the sub-prefecture of Xiangshan, Zheng soon established himself in Shanghai, where he set up a trading company specialising in tobacco and cigarettes. In 1902, the British American Tobacco Company hired his services to market a number of their brands. He was so successful that in 1922 it decided to make its agent into a partner and in 1930 he was appointed as the exclusive representative for all its brands in the crucial geographic area of Shanghai and Zhejiang. The loyalty with which Zheng Bozhao served the interests of his foreign partners and employers – camouflaging trade marks so that the sale of the company's cigarettes would not be affected by various anti-English and anti-American boycotts – was reminiscent of that of his nineteenth-century predecessors. His foreign employers recognised the value of his services by assigning him 49% of all the profits that he made. By 1937, on the eve of the Sino-Japanese War, Zheng Bozhao had amassed one of the largest fortunes in Shanghai. Calculated at 3,000 million dollars, this fortune was mostly reinvested in property speculations.[17]

The other great Cantonese compradores of the twentieth century – Lao Jingxiu, from 1905 an employee of the British-owned Reiss and

Company, and Chen Bingqian, who worked for Burkill and Son, another British company – came from a different mould. They were much closer to the Shanghai community of Cantonese entrepreneurs, for they engaged in economic and financial operations of a widely diverse nature and were involved in many business concerns set up by their compatriots. For example, in 1919 Lao Jingxiu and Chen Bingqian played an essential role in the refloating of the Nanyang Brothers' Tobacco Company, whose proprietors, the Jian brothers, also of Cantonese origin, were suffering from competition from the British American Tobacco Company.[18]

The Cantonese were almost completely excluded from the banking sector (monopolised by the Zhejiang entrepreneurs and, to a lesser estent, by those of Jiangsu), but on the other hand they dominated the field of large modern shops. It was they who founded the department stores of Nanjinglu during the First World War: the Wing On establishments created in 1915 by the Guo brothers from Xiangshan, the Sincere Company, whose proprietor, Ma Yingbiao, was also a native of Xiangshan and, finally, in 1924–25, the shops of the Sun Sun Company (Xinxin gongsi), opened by Li Yutang, another Cantonese, from Taishan.[19]

One of the principal strengths of the Cantonese entrepreneurs in Shanghai lay in the close financial ties that they maintained with overseas Chinese communities in the Southern Seas (Nanyang), where many of them had embarked on their own careers, and with Hong Kong, where most of them had set up their first businesses. Thus the list of shareholders in the Nanyang Brothers' Tobacco Company included the names of Chinese merchants established in Vietnam (where the Jian brothers had an uncle and where they had themselves worked at the start of their careers).[20] By virtue of both the careers of their promoters and the origin of their capital, the Cantonese businesses of Shanghai often have the air of an extension, in the motherland, of the activities of the overseas Chinese. Many of the Cantonese entrepreneurs in Shanghai originally hailed from the sub-prefectures of Xiangshan and Nanhai, both of which produced large contingents of overseas immigrants. These immigrants were only too glad to use their maintained Cantonese connections and provide financial backing for their compatriots operating in Shanghai. The Shanghai entrepreneurs themselves sometimes still considered themselves as immigrants: Jian Zhaonan, the founder of the Nanyang

Brothers' Tobacco Company, was a director of the Shanghai Federation of Overseas Chinese (Shanghai huaqiao lianhehui).[21]

Apart from large-scale commerce, the activities of the Cantonese also extended to certain industrial sectors such as the cigarette industry, dominated by the Jian brothers' company, and cotton mills, which the Guo brothers helped to develop. In the early 1980s, the Wing On group that the latter controlled was one of the largest in Shanghai and in China.[22] The Cantonese were kept well informed about developments in the world outside (no doubt through their many contacts with overseas communities) and they were quick to exploit new techniques and ideas. In 1924, one of their number, Chang Huantang, set up the Chinese Cinema Company (Zhonghua dianying gongsi), the first Chinese company to import and produce cinema films.[23]

The most numerous group in the Shanghai business community was composed of entrepreneurs born in the city itself or in the neighbouring province of Jiangsu: the Jiangsu guild could boast 100,000 members, although most came from the small-scale merchant class.[24] In the second half of the nineteenth century, however, when the troubles of the Taiping Rebellion had caused a large influx of refugees into Shanghai, a number of entrepreneurs from Jiangsu province began to enter into competition with the bankers from Zhejiang, setting up their own *qianzhuang* and taking over the functions of compradores in the large foreign banks.

The Xi were natives of Suzhou, from an old family of shopkeepers in the town. Ejected by the Taiping, the four Xi brothers found employment and became investors in the Shanghai *qianzhuang* until, in 1874, the youngest, Xi Zhengfu, obtained the post of comprador to the Hong Kong and Shanghai Bank. Through the ramified interactions of recommendations and cooptions, the whole family soon found itself embarked on compradorial careers. Members of the Xi family and kin were to be found in all the large foreign banks of Shanghai, in the Russo-Asiatic Bank, the National City Bank and the Yokohama Specie Bank. Over three generations, the family produced a direct line of eleven compradores and also managed to place its sons-in-law as compradores (see Figure 4.1).

But unlike the Zhejiang entrepreneurs, the Xi never moved on to private modern banking. By the end of the nineteenth century, Xi Zhengfu had, however, himself invested large sums in the Imperial

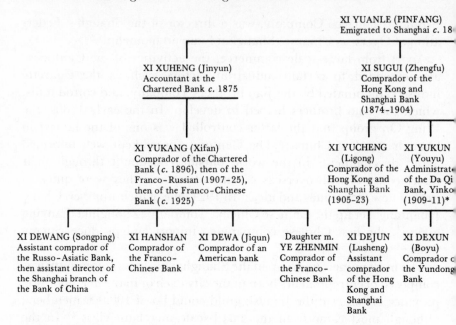

*Created by the government in 1904, the Hubu Bank was reorganised as the Da Qing Bank in 1908; after 1911 it became the Bank of China.

Figure 4.1 Four generations of Shanghai bankers and compradores: the Xi family (from Wu Peichu, 'Jiu Shanghai waishang yinhang maiban')

Bank (Da Qing yinhang): his 1,320 shares credited him with 6% of the bank's private capital. But only two of his grandsons took up careers in modern national finance, and then not as entrepreneurs but as managers for the State capitalism practised by the Guomindang in the 1930s. One became the manager of the Central Bank (Zhongyang yinhang), the other the director of the Shanghai Mint.[25]

However, we do find an important and dynamic group of men from Jiangsu among the modern bankers of Shanghai. In contrast to the Zhejiang bankers, they had acquired neither their experience nor their wealth from a previous career in the *qianzhuang* or the foreign banks. Born into the families of minor elites in circumstances of moderate ease, Chen Guangfu, Chang Kia-ngau and Qian Yongming studied abroad, and then, on their return to China, assumed positions of responsibility in official banks; the Shanghai branch of the Provincial bank of Jiangsu for Cheng Guangfu, that of the Bank of China for Chang Kia-ngau and that of the Communications Bank for Qian Yong-

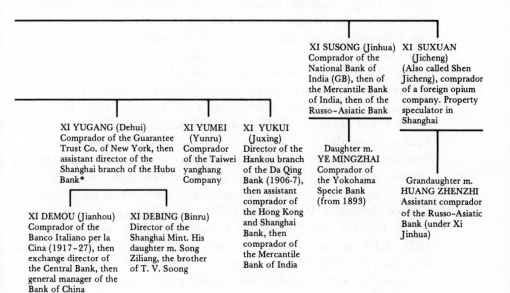

XI SUSONG (Jinhua)
Comprador of the
National Bank of
India (GB), then of
the Mercantile Bank
of India, then of the
Russo-Asiatic Bank

XI SUXUAN
(Jicheng)
(Also called Shen
Jicheng), comprador
of a foreign opium
company. Property
speculator in
Shanghai

XI YUGANG (Dehui)
Comprador of the Guarantee
Trust Co. of New York, then
assistant director of the
Shanghai branch of the Hubu
Bank*

XI YUMEI
(Yunru)
Comprador
of the Taiwei
yanghang
Company

XI YUKUI
(Juxing)
Director of the
Hankou branch
of the Da Qing
Bank (1906-7),
then assistant
comprador of
the Hong Kong
and Shanghai
Bank, then
comprador of
the Mercantile
Bank of India

Daughter m.
YE MINGZHAI
Comprador of
the Yokohama
Specie Bank
(from 1893)

Grandaughter m.
HUANG ZHENZHI
Assistant comprador
of the Russo-Asiatic
Bank (under Xi
Jinhua)

XI DEMOU (Jianhou)
Comprador of the
Banco Italiano per la
Cina (1917-27), then
exchange director of
the Central Bank, then
general manager of the
Bank of China

XI DEBING (Binru)
Director of the
Shanghai Mint. His
daughter m. Song
Ziliang, the brother
of T. V. Soong

ming. It was as managers of these establishments that they helped to
encourage modern banking techniques in Shanghai. Their influence in
the town's business circles stemmed more from their personalities and
the size of the funds that they managed than from their individual
fortunes. They were more managers than investors. And provincial
connections seem to have played a less determining role in their careers
than in those of the Zhejiang bankers.

The entrepreneurs from Jiangsu province included among their
number a few of Shanghai's major cotton mill owners: the brothers
Rong Zongjing and Rong Desheng, natives of Wuxi and the owners of
the Shenxin Company; the Mu brothers, the sons of a cotton merchant
of Shanghai itself, who found financial backers for their Deda and
Yufeng Cotton Mills among their father's friends; Bei Runsheng and
Xue Baorun, both from Suzhou, who founded the Housheng Cotton
Mill together; and Wu Linshu (1878–?), who first launched himself
into the cotton trade and then, in 1920, founded the Tongyi Cotton

Mills (Tongyi fangzhi gongsi).²⁶ The cotton trade, in which the merchants from Jiangsu province were extremely active, often constituted the launching pad from which to embark on the creation of cotton mills and it was no doubt in this way that the Jiangsu group acquired a certain pre-eminence in this industrial sector.

But there were also many entrepreneurs of local origin in the mechanical engineering industries: Yan Yutang (1880–1958), the founder and organiser of the Dalong Works, and Zhu Zhiyao, whose family, originally from Zhejiang, had emigrated to Shanghai over a century earlier and who revived his ancestors' interest in shipping (junks, in their case) by creating the Qiuxin shipyards and workshops. Jiangsu province also gave Shanghai industry one of its pioneers of applied chemistry, Wu Yunchu (1891–1953). Wu, a native of Jiaxing, set up the Tianchu Seasonings Factory (Tianchu weijingchang) in 1923. Its huge profits later enabled him to finance several establishments for the production of industrial chemicals.²⁷

Shanghai, with a total of 23 regional guilds, also contained many entrepreneurs from other provinces such as Sichuan, Hunan and Anhui. But their influence – as regional cliques – cannot be compared with that of the Zhejiang, Guangdong and Jiangsu Guilds. The links of solidarity formed within these three regional groups counted for much in the structuring of the business community.

In business life, links of regional solidarity operated mainly at two levels – in the recruitment of personnel and in the raising of capital – but the two often tended to overlap to the extent that the principal individuals responsible for running the business were recruited from amongst the major shareholders. In cases where the proprietors of the *qianzhuang* and other traditional establishments did not themselves assume the responsibility of running the business, they would for preference systematically appoint administrators who came from their own native regions. Despite the increased scale of these businesses and the professionalism of their methods of organisation, these links of solidarity still counted for much in the twentieth century, even in the modern sector. Employers did not seek to free themselves from the constraints that such links represented, for they afforded them an extra guarantee of loyalty on the part of their employees, since they shielded them from the temptations that surrounded them and turned the business itself into the only point of anchorage in the lives of all these provincial exiles. The Wing Tao Wo Tobacco Company (Yongtaihe yanhang), which the comprador Zheng Bozhao set up in 1919, to market the products of the British American Tobacco Company, employed 200 people in Shanghai itself and its lower Yangzi branches. All were of Cantonese origin, as was Zheng Bozhao himself, and they mixed very little in local society.[28] In the larger industrial companies, technological constraints – the recruitment of qualified engineers, for instance – somewhat tempered the practice of regionalist recruitment. Nevertheless, the bonds of local solidarity persisted. The Maoxin–Fuxin–Shenxin General Company, which in the 1920s comprised eleven flour mills and nine cotton mills, employed a total of 957 managers, of whom 617 (that is, 64.5%) were natives of Wuxi, even though no more than four factories in the group were actually situated in Wuxi. Whether they worked in Jinan (Shandong), Hankou or, as most did, in Shanghai, most of the managers in the Rong brothers' factories came from Wuxi, as did the proprietors themselves.[29]

The same regionalist principles dictated the raising of capital. When an entrepreneur needed funds, he would turn to his own compatriots. Between 1916 and 1919, the Guo brothers decided to extend their operations from Hong Kong to Shanghai, where they set up the big Wing On Company shops. The capital of the new company amounted to 2.5 million Hong Kong dollars, 0.5 million of which came from the Wing On establishments in Hong Kong and 0.14 million from the Guo family, while 1.8 million were invested by shareholders who were for the most part overseas Chinese. The close ties that the Guo brothers had established with the overseas communities of the Nanyang, in the early years of their careers when they set up their first businesses in Sydney, Fiji and the Philippines, explain the massive financial support later forthcoming from these same communities.[30]

In business communities governed by custom, as society itself was, and in which written contracts were as yet of negligible importance, it was vital for all entrepreneurs and investors to be able to identify their partners, to be acquainted with their families and guarantors, and to know where to find them if the business failed. The persistence of regionalism coincided with that of personal liability in business companies. Although general partnerships (or private companies) (*hehuo*), the predominant form of partnership at the beginning of the century, were later gradually replaced by joint-stock companies, even the latter continued to be organised in a fairly idiosyncratic manner. The Shenxin Cotton Mill was created in 1915 by the Rong brothers as a company of unlimited liability (*wuxian gongsi*). Its shareholders were few in number and they possessed no powers of decision, no shareholders' meetings were held, and the directors (that is, the Rong brothers themselves) wielded a virtually sovereign authority. Although the industrial empire of the Rongs expanded during the 1920–30 period, its style of organisation remained unchanged.[31]

The Wing On Company of Hong Kong was created in 1907 on the basis of a collective partnership involving a dozen or so partners recruited from amongst the members of the Guo family, their friends and their colleagues. In 1916, this association changed its form in order to absorb capital from outside and became a 'public limited company' (*gonggong youxian gongsi*), but its organisation remained virtually unchanged. And although it was with the aid of many small shareholders that the Wing On Company of Shanghai was set up in 1919, the company rules contained a number of clauses designed to safeguard the power of the Guo brothers.[32]

The fact is that, even when known as 'limited companies' (*youxian gongsi*), the Chinese companies of the golden age retained many characteristics of private companies. Their shares were not put on the market (where no establishment existed for their sale) but were made available within the social circle, of varying dimensions, of their promoter or promoters. Furthermore, acquisition of such shares afforded the holders very little control over the running of the business. In circumstances such as these, relations of personal trust between investors and promoters were indispensable in the launching and development of a business. Regionalism provided one of the bases of that reciprocal trust, but it was also strongly dependent upon the family spirit.

2   The family structures of Chinese capitalism

Family relations in the world of business were organised on the basis of a number of different axes and formed networks as vast as they were complex. The father–son combination was, naturally, common. Although some of the entrepreneurs of the golden age were self-made men, in every branch we come across employers who started off by following in their fathers' footsteps. The cotton mill owner Nie Yuntai picked up his knowledge of the cotton industry in the Hengfeng factory acquired by his father Nie Qigui, who made him responsible for its management in 1904.[33] On a much more modest scale, Rong Xitai, who at the turn of the century founded several *qianzhuang* and flour mills, making his two sons partners in the businesses, laid the foundations for the future empire of Rong Zongjing and Rong Desheng.[34] When Yang Cansan (1887–1962), who was to become one of the principal bankers in China, entered the world of business in 1910 at the age of 23, he started off by working in his father's commercial business in Chongqing.[35]

But the development of the economic life of the major Chinese ports was so rapid that it became difficult to maintain partnerships between two generations. Many fathers would turn over to their sons the management, if not the direction, of the businesses that they themselves had set up or that father and son had set up together. Partnerships between brothers seemed to work out better. In many cases these involved only two brothers, either because there were no others in the family, as in the Rong and Jian families, or (as was more frequently the case) because two of a number of brothers shared personal affinities and complementary talents and decided to pursue their ambitions together. In some fraternal couples, renown and authority were equally distributed, as in the case of Jian Zhaonan and Jian Yujie, the founders of the Nanyang Brothers' Tobacco Company. Although the elder brother assumed responsibility for public relations and political contacts right up to his death in 1923, Jian Yujie then proved himself perfectly capable of taking his place. The Rong brothers, Rong Zongjing and Rong Desheng, the one born in 1873, the other in 1875, also appear to have been extremely close in temperament as well as age and they worked in close association in all their ventures, although the first place went to Rong Zongjing, no doubt by reason of his seniority (see Figure 4.2). Of the five Guo brothers, it was the two eldest, Guo Le (1874–1956) and Guo Quan (1876–1966) who set up the Wing On group (see Figure 4.3).[36]

On the other hand, it sometimes happened that one of the two brothers in a pair became better known than the other, with the result that it is his name that is more often – or even exclusively – mentioned. Thus the renown of Zhang Jian, a liberal reformer and distinguished scholar as well as an entrepreneur, tended to obscure the personality of his brother Zhang Cha, who made few public statements but managed the Dasheng Cotton Mills with flair.[37] The same applies to the Mu brothers. The better-known was Mu Ouchu, who in the early 1920s

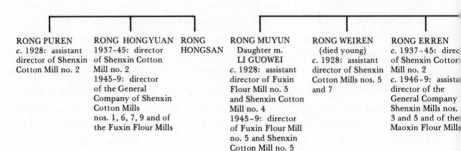

Figure 4.2 Flour mill and cotton mill proprietors: the Rong brothers (from *MGRWZ*, vol. 1, pp. 278–84; and *Rongjia qiye shiliap*, vols. 1 and 2)

laboured tirelessly at the head of the Chinese Cotton Mill Owners Association to improve national production. But it was his brother, Mu Shuzhai, a cotton merchant much respected in the Shanghai market place, who raised the capital necessary to set up the Housheng Cotton Mills in 1915 and the Deda Cotton Mills in 1916 and who was largely responsible for running them.[38]

The presence of two or more brothers in a business concern made for the establishment of relations between uncle and nephew similar to those between father and son. Thus in the Rong family, following the death of the elder brother, Rong Zongjing, close collaboration was maintained between Rong Desheng and his nephews.

Although Chinese families were organised on the patrilinear principle, women played a by no means negligible role in business strategy. Marriages helped to seal financial alliances and to acquire collaborators of substance. The links between Rong Zongjing and Wang Yuqing, who in 1912 pooled their capital to set up the Fuxin Mills, were reinforced thanks to several of Rong's children marrying into the

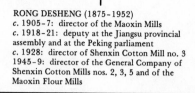

RONG DESHENG (1875-1952)
c. 1905-7: director of the Maoxin Mills
c. 1918-21: deputy at the Jiangsu provincial
assembly and at the Peking parliament
c. 1928: director of Shenxin Cotton Mill no. 3
1945-9: director of the General Company of
Shenxin Cotton Mills nos. 2, 3, 5 and of the
Maoxin Flour Mills

RONG YIXIN	RONG SHUREN	RONG YIREN	RONG YANREN	RONG JIREN	RONG HONGREN
c. 1946: director of Shenxin Cotton Mill no. 3	Daughter m. YANG TONGYI son of YANG SHOUNAN, a Wuxi Cotton Mill proprietor	(1916-) c. 1946: manager of the Maoxin Flour Mills 1957-66: assistant mayor of Shanghai 1959-66: vice-minister of Textile Industries 1979: president of the China International Trust and Investment Corporation	c. 1946: aide to Rong Erren	c. 1946: manager in the Maoxin Flour Mills	c. 1946: manager in the Maoxin Flour Mills

Wang family.[39] Sons-in-law, brothers-in-law, uncles, nephews and cousins by marriage invariably played a useful part in the business. After the second generation, such links between cousins would still persist, becoming more fragile, however, strained by the conflicts which would multiply in proportion to the number of descendants. But in the case of the great families with which we are concerned such conflicts were not a feature of the golden age. They arose later on, in the 1930–40 period, with the appearance of the third generation and the dramatic choices that faced the entrepreneurs with first the Japanese invasion and then the communist victory.

Family relations in the business world served many purposes. To a large extent they provided the basis for finance, management and technological progress; they also facilitated relations with the public authorities. I need not repeat my earlier remarks concerning the importance of personal trust in the financing of business ventures. In this sphere, family connections were of more account than either ties of friendship or professional or regional links of solidarity, for family

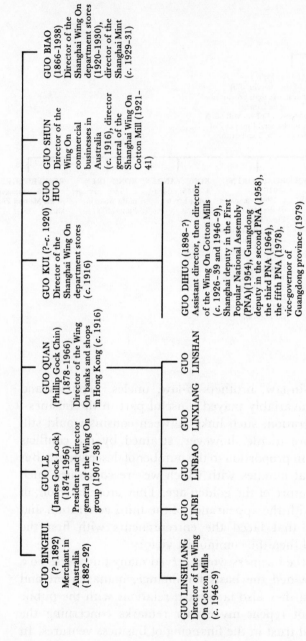

Figure 4.3 A family of wholesalers and industrialists: the Guo family (from *MGRWZ*, vol. 1, pp. 285–90; *Shanghai Yong'an gongside chansheng fazhan he gaizao*; and *Yong'an fangzhiyinran gongsi*)

relations provided the most reliable guarantees. When the brothers Guo Le and Guo Quan decided to extend their operations in Shanghai, they turned to their cousin, Guo Biao (1868–1938). He had extended a welcome to Guo Le when he had first arrived in Australia and had given him employment in the fruiterer's that he had opened there, in partnership with another Cantonese from Xiangshan, Ma Yingbiao. In 1900, Ma Yingbiao had returned to Hong Kong, where he had founded the Sincere department stores and, following their success, he too was thinking of opening a new branch in Shanghai. The rich Guo Biao found himself solicited at once by his cousin Guo Le and by his former partner and compatriot Ma Yingbiao; in the end he chose to help Guo Le. Guo Biao thus became one of the major shareholders in the Wing On department stores of Shanghai and worked as a director of the company alongside Guo Le.[40]

Often the family would provide most of the upper management in the businesses that it helped to finance. According to an enquiry undertaken in 1928, in the group controlled by the Rong brothers (that is, the twelve flour mills of the Maoxin and Fuxin Companies and the seven cotton mills of the Shenxin Company) there were a total of 54 posts of director generals, directors and assistant directors (see Table 4.1). Of these posts 19 were filled by Rong Zongjing himself, who was the director general (*zong jingli*) of every factory in the group. Of the 35 remaining posts, 3 fell to Rong Zongjing's brother, Rong Desheng, who was the director (*jingli*) of the Fuxin Mills nos. 1 and 3 and of the Shenxin Cotton Mill no. 3. Three of Rong Zongjing's and Rong Desheng's sons shared between them the four posts of assistant director (*fuchangzhang*) or director's assistant (*zhuli*) in the Shenxin Cotton Mills nos. 2, 3 and 5. Other members of the Rong clan (Rong Yuequan, Rong Eshen and Rong Jiren) filled another five posts. In all, the Rongs occupied 31 posts of responsibility in the factories of the group, that is to say they accounted for 57.5% of the upper management. Most of the remaining posts were filled by members of families related to the Rongs by marriage. Rong Desheng's son-in-law, Li Guowei, held director's responsibilities in the Fuxin Mill no. 5 and the Shenxin Cotton Mill no. 4; in both of these posts he was assisted by one of his cousins. Wang Yuqing, co-founder of the Fuxin Mills in 1912, retained the post of director in factory no 7. His brother, Wang Yaochen, who was related by marriage to the Rong family, held a total of five posts of director or assistant director (mostly in mills belonging

Table 4.1. *The upper management of the Maoxin–Fuxin–Shenxin General Company*

	Number of posts occupied	% of the upper management
Rong family	31	57.5 } 83.5
Families related by marriage	14	26.0 }
Trusted friends and shareholders	6	11.0
Experts with technical skills	3	5.5
Total	54	100

Source: Rongjia qiye shiliao, vol. 1, pp. 287–8.

to the Rong group) and had also placed his eldest son as a sub-director in the no. 2 Shenxin Cotton Mill. The sub-directorships of Fuxin Mills nos. 2, 3 and 8 were also held by a relative by marriage. Relatives to the Rongs by marriage thus held 14 directorial posts – 26% of the upper management. Of the posts concerned with directing the business 83.5% were thus controlled by the Rongs and their relations. The rest were held by five trusted family friends, most of them natives of Wuxi and shareholders in the group, one co-founder of the Fuxin Mills, and one engineer, Zhu Xianfang, who was in charge of Fuxin Cotton Mills nos. 2, 5 and 7.

Although the Maoxin–Fuxin–Shenxin group was organised as a joint-stock company, it operated as a family business. As the senior member of the family, Rong Zongjing played the predominant role right up to his death in 1938. The Rong sons were initiated into the responsibilities of management in one or other of the businesses belonging to the group. Posts of responsibility were filled essentially by members of the clan or, rather less frequently, by those families related by marriage. The few directors recruited from outside the extended family circle were almost invariably long-standing associates and natives of the same sub-prefecture as the Rongs. The circle of directors and managers thus remained relatively restricted, with many of them performing several functions at once, since 54 directorial posts were shared between 21 people. It is striking to note that in these textile and foodstuff industries, which led the industrial field, the largest group of companies included only one engineer among its directors. Does this mean that the family structures of the business world inhibited the process of professionalisation that was necessary, and blocked the transfer of technological expertise?

Many entrepreneurs appear, on the contrary, to have preferred those family structures precisely because they facilitated such a transfer. They might arrange marriages for their daughters in such a way as to introduce modern technological and managerial experts into the family circle, or it might be a case of sending off some of their children to acquire their further education in Chinese or foreign universities. It was generally in the second generation that technological expertise was brought into the business through the education received by certain members of the family clan. In 1902, Yan Yutang founded, under the name of Dalong, a workshop which was to become the leading mechanical engineering works in China in the 1920–30 period. Yan Yutang was the son of a minor comprador and himself worked as a go-between in a foreign company. He was perfectly capable of choosing the right branch of business (shipbuilding and repairs) and of winning orders, but he had no technical training. He was therefore obliged to leave the management of the workshop to a professional, Chu Xiaomao, whom he had made his business partner – for five years. By 1907, Yan Yutang reckoned himself sufficiently knowledgeable about technical problems and himself took on the directorship of his workshops. But from 1910 on, it was his sons who took over these responsibilities and it was the sixth of them, Yan Qinglin, who after his return from Germany, in 1932, was responsible for the decisive technological progress made by the Dalong workshops.[41]

Similarly, the Guo brothers had virtually no training when they entered upon their commercial apprenticeships as young men. When they diversified into the textile industry in 1920, they were forced to rely on the expertise of a Chinese engineer from overseas, Luo Ganbo. Luo, who came from a Cantonese family, had acquired his technical education first in Manchester and then in New Bedford, Massachusetts. His technical management proved efficient. But the Gou brothers 'did not trust this foreigner'. They sent off two of their children to be educated, one (Guo Linbao) in Manchester, the other (Guo Dihuo) in New Bedford! When Guo Dihuo returned to China in 1926, he became the technical director of the family cotton mills.[42] The social rise of the merchants' sons through the acquisition of diplomas was no new phenomenon in China. But now the purpose of the young people's education was seldom to allow them to escape from the business world; rather, it was to make sure they could help to expand it.

Finally, family connections were useful in relations with the public powers and in predisposing high-ranking officials in favour of one's business interests. The entrepreneurs who came from mandarin families, such as Zhang Jian and Nie Yuntai, were not the only ones to cultivate political contacts that were useful to their businesses. Merchants, such as the Guo brothers, were also capable of finding such support. But they tended to turn towards the revolutionaries of the South rather than to the Peking government. In doing so, they were probably prompted by their regional loyalties as much as or more than by any political convictions. The Guos, who came from the same sub-prefecture as Sun Yat-sen (Xiangshan, in Guangdong province) had long-standing connections with the Sun family. As early as the beginning of the century, the Guo brothers' cousin, Guo Biao, joined the Revolutionary Alliance (Tongmenghui) created by Sun, and became one of its principal leaders in the Chinese overseas community of Australia. In 1923, the younger brother, Guo Quan, was made a financial adviser to the revolutionary government of Canton. Thereafter, the Guos remained closely linked with the Cantonese clique of the Guomindang, which did not fail to secure protection for their interests from Chiang Kai-shek's government: it is, for example, significant that the preferential fiscal treatment meted out to the Guos in the autumn of 1927 coincided with the arrival of Sun Fo (Sun Yat-sen's son) in the Ministry of Finance of the Nanking government.[43]

But the family system has often been condemned for weighing so heavily upon business life. It is certainly true that the inevitable family quarrels had a harmful effect on business. For example, in 1918 the businesses of the Nie family seemed for a time threatened by difficulties arising from the succession to Nie Qigui. Family squabbling led to a division of the Nie concerns. The Hengfeng Cotton Mills were split into nine and the family business became a general partnership (or private company), with Nie Qigui's eight sons and widow as partners (see Figure 4.4). Nie Yuntai was successful in keeping control of the management, however.[44] It is also a fact that the business coffers were often drawn upon to finance the expenses of various members of the family, either to cover personal spending or to float another new company as a consequence of fluctuating family circumstances. In all these cases, loans were agreed without any guarantees and were subject to minimal rates of interest. In the year 1931 alone, when credit was hard and expensive to come by on the Shanghai market, which had been hit by the world crisis, loans contracted in this fashion from the Wing On group by members of the Guo family amounted to 1.6 million dollars.[45]

However, there were advantages to the family system too. In times of crisis, the flexibility of financial management made it possible to assist the industrial concerns that were in difficulty by drawing on the profits from more lucrative sectors – property speculation, for example. In the early 1920s, by selling properties situated in the new industrial quarter of Yangshupu and by using the high rents from his other Shanghai properties, Yan Yutang was able to save his Dalong engineering works during the 1923 crisis and even to launch them into the manufacture of equipment for the textile industry, in competition with foreign companies.[46]

Capital shifted constantly between the various family businesses, even outside periods of crisis. At the beginning of the First World War, the Nie family used 600,000 dollars from the large profits coming at this time from its Hengfeng Cotton Mill to reinvest in the purchase of land at Zhongfuyuan, near Lake Dongting in Hunan province. After clearing and preparing this area, which extended over more than 48,000 *mu*, it was leased out to 3,000 peasant families. In 1916, when this agricultural property was bringing in a substantial profit to the Nies, they used it to expand and modernise the Hengfeng Cotton Mill and to set up a new factory which they called Hengfeng no. 2.[47]

Equally, the running of a business might be made easier by the presence at its head of a number of to some extent interchangeable directors. The hierarchy of brothers, sons and nephews was by no means rigid. It resulted from a family consensus which could vary in accordance with the prevailing circumstances. In this respect, the Nie brothers' changes of position, at the head of the Hengfeng Cotton Mills, is revealing. In 1924, after a series of setbacks, Nie Yuntai was obliged to step down in favour of his brother Nie Lusheng. But after the Sino-Japanese War, when the Nie family was attempting to regain possession of its factories, which had been placed under the control of the Ministry of Economic Affairs by the Nanking government, Nie Lusheng remained out of the limelight, compromised by his collaboration with the Japanese occupying forces and with the puppet government of Wang Jingwei. Nie Yuntai was now given the task of making the necessary approaches and resumed his position of prominence

ZENG GUOFAN (1811–72)
Governor general of Jiangxi–Jiangsu–Anhui provinces
Member of the Imperial Grand Secretariat

↓

ZENG JIFEN (Nie Chongde)(F) (?–1942)
m. NIE QIGUI (c. 1850–1911)
1884: director of the Shanghai Arsenal
c. 1899–1904: governor of Jiangsu and Zhejiang provinces

NIE YUNTAI (Qijie) (C.C. Nieh)
1880–1953 (3rd son)
c. 1909: director general of the
Hengfeng Cotton Mills
c. 1919: director general of the
Hengfeng Cotton Mills Company
1920: president of the General
Chamber of Commerce
1922: director general of the
Da Zonghua Cotton Mills
1946: president of the Associated
Hengfeng Cotton Mills

NIE GUANCHEN (4th son)
c. 1909: assistant director
of the Hengfeng Cotton Mills

NIE LUSHENG (6th son)
c. 1919: assistant director of the
Hengfeng Cotton Mills Company
after 1924: de facto director of
the Hengfeng Cotton Mills Company
1943: member of the executive
committee for the administration of
the mixed (Sino–Japanese) Hengfeng
Cotton Mills

NIE LIUKANG (Hangzhang)
c. 1918: assistant director of
the Hengfeng Cotton Mills
c. 1946: director general of
the Associated Hengfeng
Cotton Mills
1954: manager in the mixed
company of Hengfeng Cotton
Mills

*It has not been possible to determine the position of these sons in the family, in terms of seniority.

Figure 4.4 From officialdom to the cotton industry: the Nie family (from *MGRWZ*, vol. 2 pp. 249–55; and *Hengfeng shachangde fasheng fazhan yu gaizao*, pp. 3–5, 43–4, 74, 97–9, 134–7)

after successfully restoring the Nie possessions to the family.[48] Through such switches of leadership dictated by circumstance, it proved possible to continue to run the business so as to serve family interests.

The manifest need to make sure that the business survived and prospered acted as a brake on the system based on family solidarity, and limited the risks involved. While membership of the clan may have conferred the right to live off the family business, it did not automatically confer the right to direct it. In the vast warren of brothers and brothers-in-law of the first generation, and sons, sons-in-law, nephews and cousins of those that followed, it was perfectly possible to pick out individuals according to their personal qualities and skills. The 'dead

NIE JUANWEI*	NIE GUANGYAO*	NIE SHENYU*	NIE SHAOXUAN*	NIE GUANGJIAN*
1919: receives a share in the division of the Hengfeng Cotton Mills	1919: receives a share in the division of the Hengfeng Cotton Mills	1919: receives a share in the division of the Hengfeng Cotton Mills	1919: receives a half-share in the division of the Hengfeng Cotton Mills	died young

wood' may have continued to draw salaries and receive dividends, but they appear to have been steered firmly away from any responsibilities.[49]

Thus the family system, as such, does not appear to have been detrimental to these businesses. It was a style of administration that afforded Chinese businessmen real possibilities of adapting to the modern economic environment without breaking with social traditions. The persistence of these ties of regional and family solidarity in the Chinese capitalism of the golden age should not be regarded either as archaic or as peculiarly Chinese features. For example, in the early nineteenth century, at the point when the French bourgeoisie was establishing itself as a business class, it presented a number of similar characteristics. It too depended upon family structures in its progress towards modern capitalism. In the Poupard family, studied by Louis Bergeron, wives, sons and sons-in-law all played a determining role in the success of the family business. In the Saint family we find the same partnerships between brothers, nephews and cousins continuing throughout four generations. And such families themselves fitted into a wider network of solidarities, such as international Protestantism.[50]

Nevertheless, the business bourgeoisie of the treaty ports cannot be defined solely by these links of solidarity. The eruption of modern technology and the diffusion of new management methods introduced their own kinds of constraint, which varied from one sector to another. For that reason, we must try to sketch in, albeit briefly, a typology of entrepreneurs according to their various branches of activity.

3   A rough typology of Chinese entrepreneurs

It is difficult to classify the entrepreneurs according to the nature of their economic activities as these could be both multiple and diverse. Our method, arbitrary though it may be, must be to try to distinguish a dominant activity. Let us take two types of entrepreneur as examples: employers in the mechanical engineering industry and cotton mill owners. Quite apart from (imperative) reasons of documentation, this choice may be justified on the combination of two counts: (a) these branches of activity constituted the most prominent sectors in modern industry and (b) they were subject to different constraints where the indivisibility of capital was concerned. Whereas mechanical engineering works could be set up with a very modest outlay on equipment and then expand gradually, the cotton mill owners, who were obliged to acquire large quantities of technical equipment at the outset, had to start off with a considerable amount of capital. The technological input was gradual in the one case, massive in the other, and the disparity of the initial financial constraints in the two cases affected the social recruitment of these entrepreneurs, the way they financed themselves, their management methods, and also the nature of their achievements and the extent to which they themselves infiltrated the ruling classes.

The entrepreneurs in the mechanical engineering industry

The development of the mechanical engineering industry began in the second half of the nineteenth century, with Shanghai as its centre. After the Jiangnan Arsenal (Jiangnan zaochuanchang) had been set up by the public authorities in 1862, a dozen or so private works sprang up between 1866 and 1894, the majority specialising in repairs to foreign shipping and maintenance for the machinery of silk spinning mills and cotton carding workshops. From 1894 onwards, the rate at which such works were established speeded up. By the eve of the First World War, there were 91 mechanical engineering workshops in Shanghai, more and more of them specialising in the maintenance of machinery for the textile industry, printing presses and the light equipment used for the processing of agricultural products. A rapid expansion took place during and immediately after the war. By 1924, the number of workshops in Shanghai had risen from 91 to 284, more and more turning out lathes and small motors (very useful in the semi-traditional hat-making industry and the processing of agri-cultural products). Many workshops specialised in the manufacture of spare parts. But the production of equipment for modern industry – cotton mills, flour mills and cigarette factories – only began to get going at the very end of this period and really took off in the years following.[51] Who were the men responsible for developing this sector?

The overwhelming majority came from the traditional handicraft sector – men with their own small businesses, or workers employed in the shipyards. Most had started out as blacksmiths or carpenters. By 1913, the entrepreneurs recruited from these strata of technicians of relatively modest means accounted for 80% of the employers in the mechanical engineering industry.[52] In this branch of industry, which was particularly dependent on technology, it was men already engaged in the mechanical engineering profession who were responsible for the introduction of new technology. They had picked up their skills from the foreigners, either at the head of a small traditional workshop (*shougongye zuofangzhu*), trying to cater for the demands of the modern shipyards, or else directly employed by one of those yards as a workshop supervisor (*tounao*) or a foreman (*lingban*). By the very end of the nineteenth century, the foreign shipyards of Shanghai were employing 4,900 Chinese workers. The largest, the English yards of Boyd and Company and S. C. Farnham, each employed a workforce

2,200 strong. The Jiangnan Arsenal, a Chinese concern, meanwhile employed 2,821 men.[53]

Of course it was extremely difficult for these craftsmen and workers to find the funds necessary to set up their own undertakings, and the sums invested were usually quite modest – 300 dollars on average, in the nineteenth century, and not much more than 1,000 between 1895 and 1913. To assemble such a sum, the modest craftsman or worker would put aside savings from his income or salary and appeal to family and friends for assistance. Most of the workshops set up in this way were individual firms (*duzi*). In 1913, no more than 21% of them ranked as general partnerships. However, as the level of initial investment outlay rose, the proportion of small independent craftsmen who were successful as firm owners began to decline.[54]

On the other hand, the foremen, workshop supervisors and team leaders were becoming more prominent. These technicians seem to have found it easier to raise the necessary capital. In the Chinese factories where they worked they were paid good wages, often twice as much as ordinary workers, and large bonuses on top of them. In the foreign shipyards, the Chinese managers, who were generally responsible for the hiring of labour (*baogong*) and the supply of raw materials (*baoliao*), could supplement their wages with many extras that accrued from their role as intermediaries. Furthermore, when they decided to set up on their own, these managers could in many cases count on the financial support of their erstwhile employer, for whom they became regular sub-contractors and for whom they provided various services as well as spare parts. Often, it was even the case that, for the first few years after setting up for himself, the small-firm owner continued to work for his old employer.[55]

The existence of these small-scale innovative capitalists, who remained deeply involved in the process of production, was characteristic of the sector of mechanical engineering. Concentrated as they were in Shanghai, these entrepreneurs who had started out as mechanics, managed, over the decades and successive generations, to create a veritable tradition of modern technology which underpinned the industrial expansion in the town throughout the twentieth century, conferring upon it a pre-eminence (still recognised today) in leading sectors.

The capitalism of these engineers, sprung directly from the craftsmen class, seldom led to the establishment of big firms. And in social terms the small-scale employers that it threw up remained in the upper echelons of the working class. The technical success of these small workshops capable of reproducing foreign machinery such as lathes, motors, printing presses and small-scale textile and agricultural equipment was not rewarded by an equivalent economic and social success. The financial resources of these employers were too limited for them to ensure either rapid expansion for their businesses or integration into the upper bourgeoisie of the business world for themselves. Circumstances permitting, as during the golden age, the most they could expect was to diversify their production and clientele a little and to set up their sons at the head of workshops similar to their own.

Through the relatively obscure careers of these workers who were both able and eager to adapt their craftsmanlike traditions to the needs of modern production, modern technological expertise was spontaneously absorbed, with no interventions on the part of the public authorities. The many setbacks encountered by industrialisation projects in Third World countries have often been attributed to the absence of 'intermediate' management and of techniques of a kind to facilitate the transaction from traditional practices and societies to the constraints of advanced technology. The life stories of these modest pioneers illustrate the importance of their role in the development of the modern sector in China.

Ying Baoxing was the son of a Hangzhou silk manufacturer. In 1904, at the age of 14, he arrived in Shanghai and embarked upon an apprenticeship in a boilermaking works; he then entered a craftsman's workshop as a journeyman. In 1915, he set up a small spare-parts factory which, among other things, produced parts for motor cars. During the 1920s, the increasing number of cars in Shanghai brought prosperity to Ying Baoxing, who now took on about a dozen workers and modernised his workshop equipment.[56] The career of Chen Rongbao followed a parallel course. He was the son of a carpenter-joiner of Wuxi (Jiangsu province), who started out working with wood, specialising in producing the kind of moulds used in bronze casting. Abandoning carpentry for metalwork, he then completed an apprenticeship as a blacksmith and rose through the various ranks in the profession, becoming first an assistant journeyman, then a journeyman specialising in the manufacture of spare parts for ships. In 1915, he set up his own forge, which he equipped five years later with two lathes, turning it into a mechanical engineering works with a workforce of five.[57]

In the case of the workshop supervisors, foremen and team leaders who seized the chance provided by the economic boom produced by the First World War to set up on their own, fewer came from Shanghai's foreign firms than in the cases of their predecessors. However, a few small-scale businessmen were still emerging from those firms. The management of the Arnhold, Karberg and Company Workshops – set up in 1900 by the Germans and subsequently taken over by British interests – within the space of a few years provided the national engineering industry with half a dozen entrepreneurs with a variety of special skills.[58] Nevertheless, during this period, most of the engineers who set up for themselves had had their training in Chinese works. In this respect, the Jiangnan Arsenal continued to play an important role. A number of its foremen turned themselves into knitting machine manufacturers. But by this time, there were plenty of other establishments, apart from the Arsenal, that provided a technical training for such men: the railway workshops, the maintenance departments of the large cotton mills and a number of mechanical engineering works set up with Chinese capital during the nineteenth century or the early years of the twentieth.

The foremen employed in these Chinese concerns could probably not count on so much financial support from their employers as could the technicians employed by certain foreign entrepreneurs. All the same, they appear to have been prepared to turn to other associates in order to raise the necessary capital and they thus set up numerous general partnerships (hehuo), some of them with an unusually large number of partners. In 1918, when Zhang Weilun, an ordinary worker in the Susong Railway Company depot, founded the Fengtai Workshop (Fengtai jiqichang) for the manufacture of motors and equipment for processing agricultural produce, he possessed no more than 200 dollars of his own. However, thanks to the cooperation of his workshop mates and technicians from other works, both Chinese and foreign, he managed to raise capital to the tune of 5,000 dollars. There were 22 shareholders, most contributing no more than 100–200 dollars, very few putting up as much as 400 dollars. Virtually all the shareholders were themselves in the trade – skilled workers, foremen or workshop supervisors. A few brief indications suggest that the principle governing the assembly of these associates stemmed from their common membership of the Red Circle (Hongbang), an organisation of a part-secret, part-regionalist nature whose influence was strong among the joiners of Ningbo origin, who constituted a large proportion of the skilled workers of the foreign shipyards. Although none of the documentation refers, either by name or by implication, to a 'workers' cooperative' this type of capitalism does appear to have come very close to just that.[59]

The Chinese firm from which the largest number of leading technicians flocked to set up their own businesses was the Qiuxin Company, founded in 1906. Its very name, meaning 'search for novelty', indicated its orientation. The resounding crash of the company in 1918–19 was no reflection on the excellence of the technical training that it provided, but rather brought into question its methods of financial management. The difficulties that assailed it from 1915 onwards, as well as the relatively high standard of its technology, no doubt explains the fact that a number of its leading technicians were soon to be found at the head of quite a range of concerns, for example workshops producing equipment for processing agricultural produce and for naval construction and repair yards.[60]

Once in a while, the space of a single lifetime sufficed to progress from a man's apprenticeship in modern technology to the creation of a capitalist business of major standing, but it was rare for such a technological and financial leap forward to take place within a single generation. Thus most of the major Chinese mechanical engineering companies were not set up by the technicians themselves but by entrepreneurs with access to the traditional sources of wealth and expertise, that is to say men from families with merchant or civil service backgrounds.

By the mid-nineteenth century, there may have been fewer workshops set up by merchants and officials than by technicians, but those that existed were much better financed. Two firms founded in the early years of the twentieth century – Qiuxin and Dalong – between them accounted for over 60% of the capital invested in mechanical engineering in Shanghai between 1895 and 1913 (50,000 dollars out of 80,000).[61] The profile of the big entrepreneurs in the mechanical engineering industry falls into a more classic mould than that of the technician-entrepreneurs. On the strength of their family connections and political contacts, they were able to obtain plenty of loans (even from foreign banks). Their deep interest in technology prompted them to seek the necessary training either in China or abroad. And this was matched by the equal attention that they paid to the commercial situation and the state of the market. Their skills were less specialised than those of the technician-entrepreneurs, but they kept themselves well informed regarding the business world and, like all the great Shanghai entrepreneurs, they kept a number of different activities going simultaneously. A measure of vertical integration was sometimes the purpose of this diversification, which enabled them to protect their various businesses by exploiting the integrated network of their interests. Some were more, some less, successful at this game, as is illustrated by the contrasting destinies of two businessmen, Zhu Zhiyao and Yan Yutang, both of whom founded large firms between 1902 and 1904. Fifteen years later, one of them, Qiuxin, suffered a resounding crash while the other, Dalong, went on to become the principal Chinese mechanical engineering business of the 1920s. By the eve of the Sino-Japanese War, its production was modern, diversified and competitive.

Zhu Zhiyao (known in the French circles of Shanghai as Nicholas Tsu) was the scion of a great Catholic family of Zhejiang province which, to extricate itself from the confiscations which accompanied the prohibition of Catholicism at the beginning of the eighteenth century, sold its land and turned to the fishing and shipping industries.[62] The family settled in Shanghai at the beginning of the nineteenth century. By 1863, when Zhu Zhiyao was born, his father was a wealthy entrepreneur owning three *qianzhuang*, seven large sea-going junks (*shachuan*) and numerous buildings in the Chinese city (Nanshi). He had also set up a thriving service of barges on the Huangpu, in the Dongjiadu quarter. As a child, Zhu Zhiyao would often visit his father's yards to watch the carpenters and blacksmiths building junks. Although Zhu Zhiyao's interest in mechanical engineering may initially have been aroused by his father's activities, it was neither easy nor straightforward to make the transition from a traditional shipbuilding yard to a modern business. As a result of growing competition from steamships, coupled with the loss of several large junks in a typhoon off the coast of Shandong, the business of Zhu Zhiyao's father collapsed. Zhu Zhiyao was now taken on as a comprador on board the fleet of the Chinese Merchants' Steam Navigation Company. He owed this engagement to the patronage of his maternal uncle, Ma Jianzhong, a great scholar and reformer and a member of the Company's board of directors, and a friend of its director Sheng Xuanhuai (1844–1916). It was around this time that Zhu became interested in foreign technology. He accompanied his uncle Ma Jianzhong on a mission to Europe and took the opportunity to visit a number of major French factories along with him. Back in China, he worked hard to diffuse Western expertise and, with the help of his brother, produced a *Journal of Natural Sciences* (*Gezhi bao*), which continued to appear until 1898. Zhu greatly consolidated his position in the business world in 1897 when he succeeded one of his relations in the post of comprador for the Banque de l'Indochine. His entry to this bank was smoothed by several factors: the family precedent, his connections with Ma Jianzhong and his brother Ma Liang and with the Society of Jesus and the French missionaries, the financial backing that the two brothers gave him, and the fact that he belonged to the Catholic faith. The position that he acquired in this bank later enabled him to contract many substantial loans.[63]

One of the first, arranged in 1904, involved 10,000 taels, which Zhu Zhiyao added to his savings from his earnings as a comprador, and was thus able to invest capital to the tune of 40,000 taels in the Qiuxin Works that he was planning to create. In the following year, these workshops were set up in Nanmatou, in the Chinese suburbs to the south of Shanghai, along the banks of the Huangpu (at this date still wasteland). One hundred workers were employed there under the technical direction of a former foreman from Arnhold, Karberg and Company. Qiuxin repaired and manufactured equipment for oil mills and also for the construction of small steamships. Thanks to the Ma brothers' connections in official circles, the firm also obtained maintenance contracts and orders from public services – the railways, the tramways, and so on. By well before the First World War, the Qiuxin Works could boast a production that was both modern and diversified and that included metal bridges, engines of 300 horsepower or more, railway carriages, and even a chimney stack 70 metres high and weighing 55 metric tons! But a combination of factors were to bring Zhu Zhiyao to the point of collapse: the scarcity of iron and steel during the First World War and the rising cost of these commodities, Zhi Zhiyao's ill-starred attempts at vertical integration, namely his ambitious plans to set up steel works, which led him to buy into several mining companies, and finally his heavy borrowing, to the tune of 1 million taels, from the Banque de l'Indo-Chine, to finance these schemes. In 1918, he found himself forced to sell Qiuxin to a number of French interests (Messageries maritimes, Schneider and the Banque de l'Indochine). Yet, at the beginning, Zhu Zhiyao had held a number of trump cards. He was a true pioneer, drawn on by an ambitious vision of Chinese industrialisation, which he wanted to support by providing it with the equipment that it needed. His undoing – like that of the cotton mill owners a few years later[64] – proved to be the absence of a national, structured and coherent banking system. This alone could have helped him to overcome specific and extremely localised difficulties in a number of sectors of a situation which, overall, ought to have favoured the success of his business ventures.

With less ambitious projects and a more cunning approach in adapting to fortuitous circumstances, Yan Yutang was successful where Zhu Zhiyao failed.[65] When Yan founded the Dalong Works in 1902, the capital at his disposal amounted to no more than 7,500 taels, amassed with the help of two partners whom he soon bought out of the business. Yan was the son and nephew of compradores and himself worked as a go-between for a foreign company. He had no technical training but had a knack for choosing the right branch of business. Quickly rejecting the notion of competing with the foreign shipyards, in 1906 he branched out into a maintenance service for textile equipment, for which he also manufactured spare parts. He won the custom of the Japanese cotton mills, in particular those of the Nagawaita group. The expansion of his workshops thereafter kept pace with that of the cotton industry. In 1922, Dalong began to manufacture machinery; and, in 1925, to ensure himself of an outlet for this new line of production, Yan Yutang began first to rent, and then to buy up, cotton mills. By the eve of the Sino-Japanese War, he had acquired seven of these. With the market expanding, the Dalong Workshops increased and diversified their production. By 1937, they were manufacturing 40,000 spindles per year, of English, Japanese and Swiss design.

From the First World War onwards, new types of entrepreneur emerged to develop and diversify the mechanical engineering industry. Some came from other branches of the modern industrial sector. At the instigation of Nie Yuntai, the leading Shanghai cotton mill owners in 1921 combined to form the Chinese Mechanical Engineering Company (Zhongguo tiegongchang). Their aim was to produce on the spot all the equipment they needed and could no longer import in sufficient quantities from a Europe and an America involved first in the war, and then in the reconversion crisis. The Chinese Mechanical Engineering Company, which was set up as a joint-stock company, started out with capital of 350,000 dollars. The list of its shareholders included the names of the leading cotton mill owners of Shanghai, Wuxi and Tianjin. Nie Yuntai, the son of the former director of the Jiangnan Arsenal, himself took an interest in mechanical engineering. But he entrusted the promotion and management of the new company to an engineer from one of his cotton mills. However, despite all the capital and expertise at its disposal, the new company soon ran into insurmountable difficulties. By 1923, the cotton mill crisis was already compromising the resouces of its financial backers and closing down its outlets.[66]

Not all Chinese engineers, most of whom were trained abroad, were content to put their skills at the service of the big investors. Some tried to set up their own firms and, during the 1920s, ten or so were successful despite considerable financial difficulties. One of the most successful was a graduate of the Peking Institute for Advanced Industrial Studies (Beijing gaodeng shiye xuetang), Hu Juewen, the owner of the Xinmin Workshop (Xinmin jiqichang), which he set up in 1921 with capital of 24,000 dollars. Admittedly, Hu Juewen's father-in-law was a friend of the cotton mill owners Mu Ouchu and Mu Shuzhai and, thanks to him, Hu Juewen obtained many orders for textile equipment. When the crisis hit the cotton mills, he managed to convert his business, switching to the maintenance of kilns for firing tiles, thus assuring it of a future of regular expansion.[67]

Closely linked with the expansion of the shipyards in the nineteenth century and that of the cotton spinning mills and other processing industries in the twentieth, the development of mechanical engineering produced a diverse range of entrepreneurs. Most came from the upper strata of the working class – highly skilled craftsmen, foremen and team leaders. But the handful of big businessmen who dominated the sector came from the elite groups, either traditional (merchants and officials) or modern (industrialists, engineers). These businessmen played an essential role in the transfer of technology, a process which began in the second half of the nineteenth century and speeded up in the first decades of the twentieth. On the other hand, there is little sign of these entrepreneurs in the chambers of commerce and the pro-

Table 4.2. *The social origins of the Shanghai cotton mill owners*

Names of the spinning mill proprietors	Names of their businesses	Social status[a]
Chen Yuting	Weitong	Merchant
Liu Bosen	Baocheng no.1 and no.2	Unknown
(Sheng Enyi)[b]	Sanxin	Mandarin
Mu Ouchu	Housheng and Deda	Merchant
Mu Shuzhai	Deda	Merchant
Nie Yuntai	Henfeng and Da Zhonghua	Mandarin
Rong Zongjing	Shenxin	Modern industrialist
Sheng Enyi	Sanxin	Mandarin
Wang Qiyu	Zhentai	Merchant
Wu Linshu	Tongyi	Merchant
Wu Jingen	Puyi	Mandarin
Xu Songchun	Yongyu	Merchant
Xue Wentai	Zhenhua	Merchant
Zheng Peizhi	Hongchang	Merchant
Zhu Zhiyao	Tongchang	Modern industrialist

[a] The social status considered is that of the parents and grandparents, except in the cases of Wu Linshu, whose career is known to us but whose origins are not, and Rong Zongjing and Zhu Zhiyao, who launched into their investments in the spinning mills from other sectors of modern industry.
[b] Although the Sanxin Cotton Mill was run by a general manager, the real boss of the cotton mill was Sheng Enyi, who had inherited the factory from his father, Sheng Xuanhuai.
Sources: Boorman and Howard, *Biographical Dictionary*, vol. 3, pp. 38–40; Bush, *The Politics of Cotton Textiles*, pp. 28–30, 54–5, 56, 63–4; *Hengfeng shachangde fasheng fazhan yu gaizao: MGRWZ*, vol. 1, pp. 270–3, 278–84, vol. 2, pp. 249–55; Mu Ouchu, *Ouchu wushi zishu; Rongjia qiyu shiliao*, vol. 1, chapter 1; *Shanghai minzu jiqi gongye*, pp. 136–64; *WWC 1925*, pp. 610–12; *WWC 1931*, p. 345; *ZGJDMR*, pp. 245, 249.

fessional associations, and their social and political impact – as a specific group – seems to have been limited.

The cotton mill owners

The size of the initial sums required limited the recruitment of cotton mill owners to the most well-to-do strata of society. By way of example, let us examine the recruitment and organisation of two groups of entrepreneurs – those of Shanghai and those of Tianjin. In 1920, Shanghai was the major centre for the cotton industry, with 19 cotton mills (founded with Chinese capital), investments in excess of 20 million dollars and equipment that included 400,000 spindles in operation (and another 185,000 in the process of being installed).[68] The names of 18 of the owners of the 19 cotton mills recorded are known to us. Taking into account the fact that some owned more than one establishment, and if we eliminate Liu Bosen, whose social origin has proved untraceable, our sample of identified business proprietors is reduced to 13 names (see Table 4.2).

The majority of these cotton mill owners (8 out of 13) came from merchant families. The father of Mu Ouchu and Mu Shuzhai was a large-scale wholesaler who was already involved in the Shanghai cotton trade at the beginning of the twentieth century. Less than a quarter (3 out of 13) of the Shanghai cotton mill owners came from mandarin families. Nie Yuntai's (maternal) grandfather was the general, Zeng Guofan. And Sheng Enyi was the son of a very high-ranking official at the end of the Manchu dynasty by the name of Sheng Xuanhuai. You might say that, in a sense, Nie Yuntai and Sheng Enyi were continuing the tradition of mandarin enterprise embodied by their forebears, but these scions of famous families had acquired a new style of behaviour which made them seem more like merchant entrepreneurs than the former mandarin ones. They did not seek to combine important official functions with their economic activities. Few of them attempted to run businesses in their native home towns, as good Confucian gentry anxious to further local prosperity would have done. For them, business was not a means but an end and for that reason they preferred to operate in the security of the Shanghai concessions. Nearly all their many activities were pursued within the framework of the modern economic sector. These sons of mandarins had opted for the business world and seemed perfectly at home in the society of the treaty ports.

Finally, the cotton mill owners of Shanghai also included two employers who had moved in from other branches of the modern sector: Rong, 'the flour king' (*mianfen dawang*), and the shipbuilder, Zhu Zhiyao.[69] Rong Zongjing was keen to find a profitable way of investing the huge profits realised by the Maoxin and Fuxin Flour Mills that he had set up in Wuxi and Shanghai just before the First World War. He and his brother, Rong Desheng, already had some experience of the textile industry: in 1905–7 they, along with a Wuxi comprador, had taken a hand in setting up the Shenxin Cotton Mill (Shenxin shachang) in that town; Rong Desheng had even been responsible for its management for several years. But in 1915, following a disagreement with the other shareholders, the Rong brothers had pulled out of the business and had proceeded to set up their own factory, known as the Shenxin Cotton Mill (Shenxin shachang), this time in Shanghai. The Shenxin group soon became one of the largest in Shanghai and hence in China. By 1920, the capital invested amounted to 4 million dollars (about one-sixth of the total capital invested in the Chinese cotton mills of Shanghai) and the 80,000 spindles of Shenxin represented about 13% of their production capacity. The Shenxin group expanded rapidly and by 1922 included two more cotton mills, controlling a total of 130,000 spindles.[70] Cotton mills now played as important a part as flour mills in the Rong industrial empire.

The aims of the shipbuilder Zhu Zhivao were different. His main purpose in founding the Tongchang Cotton Mill (Tongchang sha-chang) was to create a reliable outlet for the production of his Qiuxin mechanical engineering works. However, the collapse of these in 1918 compromised the development of the businesses associated with them.

Whatever their social origins, all the Shanghai cotton mill owners possessed a measure of either direct or indirect experience of Western economic methods. The manner in which this had been acquired varied according to the family fortune and the age of the individuals concerned.

The 'doyen' of the new cotton mill owners, Nie Yuntai, had picked up his training 'as he went along', in the course of the various stages of his career. As was customary in mandarin families, he had been educated exclusively at home, by private tutors. However, his father, who knew the treaty port society well, taught him English at an early age. As far as the mechanical and electrical sciences went, Nie Yuntai was self-taught. It was by running the little Huaxin Cotton Mill, to which his father had appointed him manager in 1904, that he learnt the ropes of the textile industry.[71] A few years later, it was more common to spend some time studying abroad. This was very expensive, however. For Sheng Enyi, Sheng Xuanhuai's fourth son, the question of financial obstacles did not arise and, after attending the Institute for Advanced Industrial Studies in Peking, the young man continued his education at London University followed by Columbia University.[72] Mu Ouchu, on the other hand, only learnt about foreign technology by dint of determined efforts pursued well into adulthood. He had entered an apprenticeship with a cotton merchant at the age of 15, returning to his studies in 1898, when he was 22. He learnt English and took an examination to enter the Maritime Customs Administration. It was while working in a subordinate capacity in these offices that he found out about Western management methods. At the age of 33, he handed in his notice and went off to the United States to learn about the techniques of growing and processing cotton in various institutes in Wisconsin, Illinois and Texas.[73]

The case of Mu Ouchu is somewhat exceptional. Most of the cotton mill owners of the golden age had to be satisfied with a 'Western-style' training in China itself. One such was Wang Qiyu (1883–?), the founder of the Zhentai Cotton Mill (Zhentai shachang), who attended the Saint-John University of Shanghai. Otherwise, it was a matter of making do with the experience afforded by their daily, extremely diverse activities, as did nearly all the heads of firms who emerged from the merchant class – Wu Linshu, the Rong brothers and, a little later, the Guo brothers.

Accustomed as they were to handling capital, the cotton mill owners of the new generation nearly always themselves took on the management of the firms that they created. Nie Yuntai, Xue Wentai, Mu Ouchu, Zheng Peizhi, Liu Bosen, Chen Yuting, Xu Songchun and Mu Shuzhai never allowed anyone else to run their firms. And while the proliferation of factories in the Shenxin group made it necessary for Rong Zongjing to appoint assistants in each of his factories, he nevertheless retained control of the key departments, the recruitment of personnel, the supply of raw materials and the marketing of the manufactured products.[74]

Conscious of the limitations of their own training, the cotton mill owners of Shanghai did, however, entrust the technical direction of their firms either to foreign engineers or to Chinese ones recruited locally. The latter came from local engineering workshops. At the time of the First World War, it was still rare to find Chinese engineers who had been trained abroad. All the same, Mu Ouchu managed to find one – Gu Weijing, a graduate of the Massachusetts Institute of Technology and of Harvard University, to whom Mu Ouchu entrusted the technical direction of the Yufeng Cotton Mills that he established in Zhengzhou (Henan) in 1919.[75]

Many of the moves made by the Shanghai cotton mill owners show that they paid considerable attention to the problems of industrial technology. We have already mentioned the attempts made by the most prominent of them to set up a mechanical engineering works capable of supplying them with the equipment that they needed. On a more modest scale, Mu Ouchu also invested in mechanical engineering, financing a small textile equipment factory called Weida.[76] Anxious to provide training for a skilled workforce, Nie Yuntai in 1920 provided financial backing to set up a Shanghai technical college with its own spinning, foundry and mechanical engineering workshops. Furthermore, Nie regularly offered training grants to his cotton mill employees to enable them to study in Europe or the United States.[77] Mu Ouchu adopted similar policies in his Housheng Cotton Mill, where he handpicked the beneficiaries: one of these, in his early twenties, was H. D. Fong, who later became one of the founders of modern economics in China.[78] That these cotton mill owners took technical problems seriously is also borne out by the professional training that some of them provided for their sons and nephews.

Despite differences of origin and education, a particular type of Shanghai cotton mill owner does emerge: a skilful manager, capable of handling a multitude of affairs and keenly aware of the effects of technical factors on the life of his businesses. All his activities revolved around the firm, as did all family and friendly relations and, in some cases, political contacts. It is the predominance of their economic objectives that gives the Shanghai cotton mill owners their air of modern entrepreneurs.

The modernity of Shanghai emerges particularly strikingly when cotton mill owners such as Nie Yuntai, Mu Ouchu and Rong Zongjing are compared with the entrepreneurs of Tianjin. The modern textile industries of Tianjin got off to a slower start than those of Shanghai. Before the First World War, the town possessed only one cotton mill, with 5,000 spindles. But during the golden age, between 1916 and 1922, six large cotton mills were established there. The total capital invested amounted to close on 19 million dollars. Tianjin, with 223,000 spindles, now became the second largest centre of the cotton industry in China.[79]

This remarkable burst of activity was connected with the massive injection of capital from the warlords of the Northern Clique (Beiyang junfa) and the politicians with whom they were linked (see Table 4.3).

The principal investors in the Tianjin cotton mills belonged to the bureaucracy that controlled the northern provinces and the Peking government. All of the 25 shareholders recorded (except Wang Zhilong and Zhang Ruiting) held or had in the past held important posts in the civil or military hierarchies. They were or had been presidents of the Republic (Li Yuanhong, Xu Shichang (1855–1939)),

Table 4.3. *The social origins of the principal shareholders of the cotton mills of Tianjin (in about 1920)*[a]

Names of shareholders	Names of businesses	Shareholders' functions	Political affiliations
Bao Guiqing	Hengyuan	Military governor of Heilongjiang (1917) Minister of War (1921–2)	Zhili Clique (connected with Anfu Club)
Bian Shouqing	Hengyuan	President of the Zhili Provincial Assembly Adviser to Cao Kun	Zhili Clique
Cao Kun	Hengyuan	Military governor of Zhili (1916)	Zhili Clique
Cao Rui	Hengyuan	Civil governor of Zhili, *Chargé d'affaires* to Cao Kun	Zhili Clique
Cao Rulin	Yuyuan	Communications Minister (1917–19) Interim Minister of Finance (1918)	New Communications Clique
Chen Guangyuan	Huaxin	Military governor of Jiangxi	Anfu Club
Duan Guxiang	Hengyuan	Salt Tax commissioner	Anfu Club
Duan Qirui	Yuyuan	Prime minister (1916–17, 1918)	Anfu Club
Duan Zhigui	Yuyuan	Peking Garrison commander	Anfu Club
Gong Xinzhan	Huaxin	Minister of Finance (1919), Prime Minister (1919)	Faction of Duan Qirui
Li Yuanhong	Huaxin	President of the Republic (1916–17, 1922–3)	–
Ni Sichong	Yuyuan	Military governor of Anhui	Anfu Club
Tian Zhongyu	Hengyuan	Military governor of Shandong	Zhili Clique (?)
Wang Kemin	Yuda	Governor of the Bank of China Minister of Finance (1917–18)	Zhili Clique
Wang Yitang	Yuyuan	Minister of the Interior (1916) President of the Chamber of Deputies (1918)	Anfu Club
Wang Zhilong	Yuyuan	Wholesaler (timber, cereals, military supplies) Collaborator with General Ni Sichong	Anfu Club

Table 4.3 (*cont.*)

Wu Dingchang	Yuyuan	President of the Gabelle Bank	Communications Clique
Xu Shichang	Huaxin	President of the Republic (1918–22)	–
Xu Shizhang	Huaxin	Vice-Minister of Communications	Communications Clique
Xu Shuzheng	Yuyuan	High Commissioner for Mongolian Affairs	Anfu Club
Yang Weijun	Huaxin	*Chargé d'affaires* to Zhou Xuexi	(?)
Zhang Ruiting	Hengyuan	Manufacturer of military uniforms	(?)
Zhang Zuolin	Hengyuan	Military governor of the provinces of Manchuria	Fengtian Clique
Zhou Xuexi	Huaxin	Former collaborator with Yuan Shikai Minister of Finance (1912–13, 1915–16) Business founder and manager	
Zhou Zuomin	Yuyuan	President of the Kincheng Bank	Communications Clique
Zhu Qiqian	Yuyuan	Minister of the Interior (1914–16) Vice-President of the Senate (1918–19)	Communications Clique

a The enquiry concerns four spinning mills: Huaxin, Yuyuan, Hengyuan, Yuda.
Sources: Shareholders' names appear in Zhu Chunfu, 'Beiyang junfa dui Tianjin jingaigongyede touzi'. The biographical information appears in Boorman and Howard, *Biographical Dictionary: WWC 1925: WWC 1931*; and Nathan, *Peking Politics 1918–1923: Factionalism and the Failure of Constitutionalism.*

heads of government (Duan Qirui, Gong Xinzhan), ministers or vice-ministers (Bao Guiqing, Cao Rulin (1876–1966), Wang Kemin (1873–1945), Wang Yitang (1878–1946), Xu Shizhang), national or provincial parliamentary leaders (Bian Shouqing, Wang Yitang, Zhu Qiqian), civil or military governors (Cao Kun (1862–1938), Chen Guangyuan, Ni Sichong, Tian Zhongyu, Zhang Zuolin (1873–1928)), and so on. Most were between 40 and 50 years of age and had embarked upon their careers under the Manchu dynasty. However, it would be mistaken to regard them simply as survivors from the old mandarin system. In many respects, they constituted a 'new bureaucracy'.

Educated under the aegis of Yuan Shikai, this 'new bureaucracy' was characterised by its relative familiarity with Western technology and culture. In the case of some of its leaders, contact with the modern world had come about through the military training that they had received in one or other of the academies or special schools created by Yuan. Duan Zhigui and Li Yuanhong were both products of such schools. At the time when they entered upon a military career, during the 1880s, it represented a new type of training in which the scions of great families rubbed shoulders with men who had risen through the ranks, such as Cao Kun. In the cases of some of these generals – Zhang Zuolin, for example – the service they had seen in semi-modern warfare had constituted their sole form of training. Others, on the other hand, had travelled abroad to complete their studies. Duan Qirui was one: in 1889, he went to study at a school of artillery in Germany.

Of the civil servants, the eldest, who were at the peak of their careers in about 1920, had for the most part received a classical education. President Xu Shichang had set the most prestigious of the imperial examinations: he both held a doctorate (*jinshi*) and was a member of the Hanlin Academy. Wang Yitang also held a doctorate. The shareholders of the Tianjin cotton mills also included several graduates from the *ancien régime* (*juren*) – Wang Kemin, Wu Dingchang, Zhou Xuexi (1866–1947), Zhu Qiqian, and one holder of a bachelor's degree (Shen Yuan). Most of these high-ranking officials had become acquainted with the realities of modern life and foreign countries relatively late in life, usually in the course of a mission or posting to Japan. Men like Wang Yitang and Wu Dingchang, who had had the chance of an education in foreign universities were few and far between among them.

On the other hand, for the younger of them – such as Xu Shizhang (born in 1886) and Xu Shuzheng (born in 1880) – periods of study abroad were more common. Among the political elite groups, a wide gap separated the generation of fifty-to-sixty-year-olds from their immediate successors, the forty-year-olds, whose education had coincided with massive student migrations in the direction of Japan, Europe and America.

The new bureaucracy's openness to the impact of the modern world made it relatively easier for it to handle military, financial, railway or diplomatic affairs than the mandarin bureaucracy of the last decades of the imperial regime. But while skills had improved, attitudes had changed hardly at all and relations with the busines world remained as ambiguous as they had been in the days of the 'Western Affairs' Movement at the end of the Manchu dynasty. Even if the need for economic modernisation was at this point uncontested, this modernisation continued to be regarded, theoretically, as a source of State power and, practically, as a means for officials to increase their fortunes.

The sums invested in modern industry were only a small fraction of those that the bureaucracy devoted to property and financial speculations.[80] It was only in about 1916 or 1917 that, at the sight of the huge profits being made by the cotton and flour mills, the warlords, ministers and high-ranking officials began to show an interest in the modern processing industries. They were all keen to exploit the favourable circumstances and to make some sound investments. However, nothing in their own experience qualified them to take direct charge of the management of the businesses that they were helping to set up. Besides, the demands of their own political or military careers would not have left them the time to do so.

Thus the essential role in the setting-up and management of the new businesses fell to relatively obscure individuals, who acted more or less as sub-contractors delivering military provisions to the warlords upon whom they depended and whose troops they supplied. Positioned in between the bureaucratic world and the merchant community, these intermediaries used the influence of both to raise capital and appoint men with the necessary skills for the new industries.

Wang Zhilong was the son of a poor Tianjin boatman. He was apprenticed at a very early age, then went into the timber trade, after which he opened a shop selling rice. A lucky meeting with General Ni Sichong decided his future. When Ni Sichong became military governor of Anhui province, he made Wang his army supplier. Wang grew rich manipulating the money that he made from the military and at the same time won the protection and friendship of the general, becoming his intimate adviser and espousing his political career. He financed and in large measure organised the Anfu Club, which dominated the political life of Peking from 1918 to 1920.[81]

However, speculating with timber, cereals and military funds was a risky business and Wang Zhilong decided that modern cotton mills would bring him greater profits. In 1916, he travelled to Shanghai to consult Rong Zongjing. On his return to Tianjin, he managed to persuade Ni Sichong to invest 1.1 million dollars and also obtained financial backing from the leading lights of the Anfu Club; he was now in a position to set up the Yuyuan Cotton Mill (Yuyuan shachang) with capital of 3.6 million dollars.[82] In this case, links of solidarity within the political cliques filled the same function as local and family links of solidarity did in the Shanghai business world.[83]

Just as Yuyuan was the Anfu Club cotton mill, Hengyuan was that of the Zhili Clique.[84] Like Yuyuan, it was created by the initiative of a merchant working as a supplier of provisions to the military. Zhang Ruiting started out by making uniforms for the troops of a group of warlords – Bao Guiqing, Tian Zhongyu and Zhang Zuolin. With the financial backing of these generals, in 1916 in Tianjin, he set up a weaving workshop specialising in the production of the heavy cloth used for military uniforms. He then tried to lay his hands on a cotton mill recently set up by the provincial authorities. The civil governor of Zhili province was Cao Rui, who was also business adviser to his brother, the general and political leader, Cao Kun. Far from allowing Zhang Ruiting to take over the provincial business, Cao Rui decided instead to make use of his experience to launch a large cotton mill financed by capital of 4 million dollars provided by the generals in the entourage of Cao Kun and Zhang Zuolin.

The shareholders of the Huaxin Cotton Mill (Huaxin shachang) formed a group that was more heterogeneous than that of the Yuyuan Cotton Mill, but was dominated by the personality of Zhou Xuexi. Zhou Xuexi, who came from a family of high-ranking Anhui officials,[85] had worked for about ten years in the entourage of Yuan Shikai. When Yuan had made him responsible for coordinating the efforts at industrialisation which were just beginning in Zhili province, Zhou Xuexi had exploited his privileged position to found a number of businesses which would profit from the monopolies and privileges granted by Yuan Shikai.

Zhou Xuexi's interest in cotton mills was also stimulated by the longstanding connections that linked his family with that of Yang Shoumei (1875–?), the great Wuxi industrialist.[86] Zhou had frequently lent him financial support and rendered him political services. He had even taken on a cousin of Yang Shoumei's, Yang Shounan, to assist him in the management of his own businesses. Zhou Xuexi displayed very real administrative talents in the tradition of the modernising mandarins of the nineteenth century and it was perhaps thanks to these, as well as to the solid capital behind it, that the Huaxin Cotton

Mill was soon prospering, and establishing new factories in Tangshan and Qingdao.

However, in many respects, the cotton mills of Tianjin seem to have been more vulnerable than those of Shanghai. In the first place, there was no local industrial tradition behind them. They were thus obliged to depend heavily upon foreign technicians, in this case Japanese. Both Yuyuan and Huaxin were placed under the technical direction of Japanese engineers. But even that was not enough and, in the total absence of any skilled workforce, at the beginning of 1916 the Yuyuan Cotton Mill took on Japanese at every technical and administrative level – as managerial advisers, workshop supervisors, heads of department, foremen and even ordinary workers. In the years that followed, the cotton mill turned to the pupils of the Professional Technical Institute of Baoding (Baoding zhigong xuexiao) and also to 2,000 workers (in particular, mechanics) brought in from Shanghai and Henan province. Thanks to these policies of importing workers and encouraging training, by the end of the First World War the Yuyuan Cotton Mill was able to dispense with the services of the Japanese, with the exception of the chief engineer.[87]

The Tianjin cotton mills suffered from other drawbacks too. Imperfect though the network of the *qianzhuang* traditional banks may have been, it did to a certain extent sustain the progress of the modern industries in Shanghai by giving many short-term loans. Nothing of the kind existed in Tianjin. Large sums of initial capital were certainly invested – even if not all the funds promised were always forthcoming. But after that, there was no source of financial support available to help the cotton mill owners to overcome whatever hazards might arise. The modern banks of Peking and Tianjin were almost exclusively devoted to speculating with public bonds. The only course open to the cotton mills was to resort to Japanese financiers. These were only too happy to oblige. Their good relations with the Anfu Club and a number of the warlords engaged in the factions in Zhili and Fengtian provinces smoothed the path for such operations. Of the four cotton mills financed by the warlords and their political friends, three ended up by falling under total Japanese control in the early 1930s.

The establishment of cotton mills in Tianjin during the First World War marked an important stage in China's industrial development: it resulted in a significant increase in the production of cotton yarns and the transfer of a new proletarian core to this big northern port. But where were the entrepreneurs? Where should one seek them? Among the military and bureaucrats who had grown rich on the funds that they were in the habit of exacting? For them, modern industry was just another means of making money, and not the most effective. Political manoeuvring and the employment of military force were more lucrative. The survival of their businesses was really not their major concern. In that area, they left things to intermediaries – sub-contractors and stewards. It was these men, positioned on the edge of the commercial and bureaucratic worlds, who took initiatives, collected capital and information, chose equipment and hired skilled workers. But their position remained dependent: they could only take action with the approval of their employers and protectors. To the extent that they were never the 'decision-makers', they cannot be regarded as true entrepreneurs.

The social structures of the new bourgeoisie appear to have been extremely intricate. The young Chinese employers' openness *vis-à-vis* the modern world, and their ability to exploit the opportunities for innovation and making money provided by the welcomed expertise of that world, both united them as a group and gave them dynamism. But as a group they remained, for all that, a part of traditional society. They maintained, on the one hand, family and regional links of solidarity and, on the other, connections with the groups from which they themselves had emerged – the mandarins, the gentry, the merchants and the craftsmen.

The modernity of this bourgeoisie was thus not based on a break with tradition but on its ability to make tradition serve new objectives. The proliferation of personal connections made it possible to recruit entrepreneurs with many different types of background and training without disrupting the coherence of the group of employers as a whole. The spirit of innovation was combined with the practice of age-old virtues such as diligence and frugality and with traditional forms of family and social discipline of a kind to encourage a movement of modernisation that improved techniques even as it respected traditional modes of behaviour. New technological expertise was spontaneously and independently sought and acquired from contacts with foreigners, without any State or public encouragement. It was Chinese (urban) society itself that rose to the challenge of modernisation and it did so according to its own terms and in the context of its own particular values. As Chang Kia-ngau, one of the pioneers of this spontaneous modernisation, remarked, the leading bankers of the golden age had the exceptional gift of 'rejecting old, worn-out ideas and welcoming new ones' and in that sense their contribution to the process of 'bringing Chinese society up to date' was just as important (if less assertive) as that of the May Fourth intellectuals. However, as Chang went on, 'most of those bankers are full of Chinese ideas and values and that is what qualifies them to take on the role of leaders'.[88] Characterised as it was by, on the one hand, openmindedness and, on the other, traditionalism, Chinese modernisation in the golden age presents one of the earliest and best examples of what can be called 'Confucian-style modernisation'.

Part III   The bourgeoisie and the quest for power and modernity

5 ⮞ The bourgeoisie, the State and the revolution, 1911–27

The political awakening of the modern elite groups, which took place at the beginning of the twentieth century under the influence of ideas imported from the West, came about earlier than their full assumption of an economic and social role. The precocious nature of this political awakening was responsible for many of the weaknesses of the new class, weaknesses that were thrown into sharp relief by the 1911 revolution. The failure of the Nanking Republic (January–February 1912) was the failure of a class still too weak and too ill-defined to impose upon China the new order founded upon trade and technology, competition, and (relatively) concerted democratic action, that had evolved in the treaty ports. In general, this emergent bourgeoisie limited itself to operating within the framework of a common front with the local elites; it was not powerful enough to set up the political structures without which it could not flourish. China's destiny continued to lie with inland China and the military and bureaucratic apparatus which alone seemed capable of governing it.

Once Yuan Shikai had placed himself at the head of this apparatus, he set about reviving the attempt to impose reform and modernisation 'from above' that had proved too much for the declining Manchu dynasty during the last decade of its reign. Without allowing the new elite groups any initiative, but nevertheless trying to cater for their needs and aspirations, Yuan for a while sought to gain their support to push through necessary reforms and to shore up his dictatorship. But it was not long before the growing militarism of the new regime and the monarchical aspirations of its leader combined to abort this latest attempt at a collaboration between the State and emergent bourgeoisie and to prevent the establishment of a Chinese Meiji.

From 1917 onwards, the decline of the central power had the effect of lifting the bureaucratic constraints which business circles had been subject to, and meanwhile the prosperity of the modern sector encouraged action on the part of autonomous social forces in the towns. Carried along by this wave of prosperity which was decreasing class opposition, the bourgeoisie was inclined to place its reliance upon the mass movement that had arisen in the wake of the demonstrations of 4 May 1919. As the State became increasingly decrepit, the large towns generated an upsurge of unifying revolutionary feeling fuelled by passionate nationalism. The bourgeoisie went along with this trend, attempting – with considerable success – to orientate it to its own advantage. It was no longer supporting a central government whose future looked uncertain.

European imperialism in its most traditional – political and military – forms seemed to be on the wane. Chinese capitalism was booming and the Chinese intelligentsia had been won over by Western ideas. These factors looked like so many trump cards that would make it possible to graft an entrepreneurial, liberal and cosmopolitan bourgeoisie onto the old mandarin and peasant civilisation of China. The political profile of this bourgeoisie was now becoming more distinct. It no longer expressed a vague reflection of foreign attitudes as it had in 1911, like a fragile mask borrowed from some theatrical store of Western historical props; now it had the features of a class in full expansion. And although Chinese liberalism, which was now given theoretical formulation and political expression, resembled Western liberalism on a number of counts, that was more a matter of coincidence than of imitation.

The early failure of that liberal graft was a consequence of the grave economic difficulties that assailed the bourgeoisie from 1923 onwards. It was also caused by the radicalisation of the revolutionary movement under the influence of the Communist Party. That radicalisation frightened the bourgeoisie, isolated it and eventually drove it into the arms of Chiang Kai-shek. When he came to power, in 1927, China reverted to a bureaucratic and authoritarian model of development.

Was it a case of the inevitable failure of a third force? I believe the political bid for power made by the Chinese bourgeoisie as it reached the zenith of its short-lived destiny to be well worth analysing on its own account. Certainly not in order to dismiss the crucial part played by foreign domination (to which we shall return in the next chapter), but the better (a) to evaluate the difficulties inherent in this attempt at modernisation, which was doomed to failure on the economic level if it did not simultaneously develop on the political level, and (b) to assess to what extent the bourgeoisie of an underdeveloped country was capable of taking on the historic task that had fallen to the bourgeoisies of the West in earlier centuries.

1   1911: the elusive bourgeois revolution

Let us start by demolishing a longstanding misapprehension: the 1911 revolution which led to the fall of a 2,000-year-old empire was not a bourgeois revolution. In the wake of their 1949 victory, the Chinese historians who were reinterpreting their history in Marxist terms turned the 'old democratic revolution' (*jiuminzhuzhuyi geming*) of 1911 into the more or less obligatory bourgeois stage that is supposed to come between feudalism and socialism.[1] According to them, the bourgeoisie organised that revolution and was also its major beneficiary. But that is not the case unless, that is, the bourgeoisie is given a very wide definition that, alongside the business world and the urban intelligentsia, includes high-ranking officials, landowners, military officers and the heads of secret societies and armed bands. It is my opinion that the specific natures of these respective groups undermine such an interpretation, which comes down to assimilating the bourgeoisie to the ruling classes in a society that was, on the whole, still agrarian and traditional.

If we adopt a more restrictive definition, that of an urban elite connected with modern business, it seems that this elite took only a limited part in the preparation and unfolding of the revolution. That was in part for inevitable geographical reasons, for this bourgeoisie was active only in the more developed parts of China, where a modern economic sector existed. The only regions where the modern elite groups played a specific part in the revolution were the provinces of the lower Yangzi, Jiangsu and Zhejiang, within Shanghai's sphere of influence, to a slightly lesser degree the delta of Canton and, further inland, the enclave of Wuhan. It was precisely as a result of focusing upon the cases of the provinces of Zhejiang and Jiangsu that historians such as Zhang Kaiyuan and Ding Richu concluded that it had been a bourgeois revolution.[2] But if we look at Canton, we can see that the role played by the urban elite groups was far less important, for here the attitudes adopted by the merchants were full of contradictions and hesitations,[3] as they were in Wuhan, where the main concern of the urban elites, working through the chambers of commerce and the merchant militia, was to maintain public order.[4]

Outside these centres of development, the absence or extreme weakness of modern elite groups meant that in most areas the revolution amounted to no more than an uprising of a traditional nature, controlled by the gentry, secret societies and local garrisons acting on their own account, or quite simply, by groups of bandits.[5]

To determine the true character of the revolution it would be necessary to understand what the parts played by the semi-modernised urban core and the periphery respéctively amounted to and also their reciprocal interactions. Given the existing state of historical research that is more or less impossible. At first sight, however, the geographic disproportion of the two zones suggests that the effect of action taken in the vast interior must have outweighed that in the few developed centres. And the very rare regional studies at our disposal confirm that hypothesis.

Let us take the example of Zhejiang province (which together with Jiangsu, constituted the heart of semi-modernised China). The picture here is one of striking contrasts. The 'central' zone, consisting of the coastal sub-prefectures of Jiaxing, Hangzhou, Shaoxing and Ningbo, presents a contrast with the poor, mountainous margins of the South and the West.[6] The urban elite groups who ensured success for the uprising in Hangzhou on 27 October 1911 were in close communication with the elite groups of Shanghai, who were also involved in the revolutionary movement. As a result, the people of Zhejiang found themselves heavily represented in the regional capital. On the other hand, these elite groups exercised no control at all over events in the southern and western margins of their own province. In these regions, where the traditional gentry predominated, the chambers of commerce, education associations and local assemblies were used not to liberate social forces but to control them. Here the uprisings of the autumn of 1911, which were not inspired by any reform projects or revolutionary ideology (or even terminology), were led by local military garrisons or even groups of bandits. They resulted in social chaos, followed by a concomitant reinforcement of the traditional oligarchies, activated by a reflex of self-preservation.

If such contrasts are striking enough on a provincial level, they are even more so in the context of the country as a whole. What disqualifies the 1911 revolution from being a bourgeois revolution is not so much the existence of these backward outlying areas but rather their relative importance in national life and the fact that the urban elite groups were incapable of making them a part of their own plans for reform.

The Shanghai business world and the radicalisation of opposition to the imperial government on the eve of the revolution

The opposition to the central government that developed over the last decade of the imperial regime was dominated by elite members who came from gentry or mandarin families or were closely connected with them. It was they who organised the constitutionalist movement, they who headed the chambers of commerce, the education or agricultural associations and the merchant militia, they who got themselves elected to the provincial and local assemblies created in 1909 and, finally, they who in 1919 launched the campaign for the convocation of a parliament.[7]

During the two or three years leading up to the revolution, this opposition became more radical. The idea of a constitutional monarchy, favoured by Liang Qichao, was overtaken by a plan for a republic, supported by Sun Yat-sen and his party, the Revolutionary Alliance. Chinese Marxist historiography attributes this radicalisation of the opposition to the influence of a 'lower and middle bourgeoisie', which they label as 'national' (*minzu zibenjia*). Emphasising (justifiably enough) the social conservatism of the constitutionalists, historians such as Zhang Kaiyuan and Lin Zengping trace its origin to the wealth of this group which, for argument's sake, they redefine as the 'upper bourgeoisie' (*zichanjieji shangceng*). I believe that in so doing they quite overlook the many links which connect this group with the old, traditional society.[8] In accordance with the same economic criteria, they also include the compradores in the 'upper bourgeoisie'. But difficulties arise when it comes to the identification of the smaller-scale wholesalers and entrepreneurs. These are classified as constituting the ranks of the 'national', lesser bourgeoisie. In present-day Chinese historical studies, the adjective 'national' in theory refers to the origin of the entrepreneurs' capital, but in fact it is applied to their political attitudes. It thus turns out that the national bourgeoisie consisted of those who supported Sun Yat-sen and the Revolutionary Alliance before and during the 1911 revolution. Yet the enquiry carried out by Ding Richu[9] shows that, of the eight Shanghai entrepreneurs known to have rallied to the Revolutionary Alliance as early as 1909–10 – Shen Manyun, Wang Yiting, Yu Xiaqing, Ye Huijun, Gu Xingyi, Li Weizhuang, Li Zhengwu and Li Houyu – all, without exception, belonged to the urban elite group, that is the 'upper bourgeoisie'. At the time of their revolutionary activities, several of them (Yu Xiaqing and Wang Yiting, for example) either had recently been or still were compradores; in the preceding years, most of them (Yu Xiaqing, Shen Manyun and Wang Yiting, for example) had played an active part in the constitutionalist movement.

It is but a step from here to the conclusion that these entrepreneurs linked with foreign interests were in fact members of the 'national' bourgeoisie, and the constitutionalist movement was already revolutionary (that is, liberal and democratic), but it is a step that Chinese historians are reluctant to take!

Clinging to Marxist orthodoxy, which sets so much store by the role of infrastructures, these historians are perhaps underestimating the influence of cultural factors in the evolution of the urban elite groups on the eve of 1911. The emergence of these elite groups coincided with the diffusion in China of a number of concepts (such as democracy and nationalism) imported from the West. Most had been formulated during the eighteenth and nineteenth centuries, when the local bourgeoisies were coming to power. As transmitted in China by the young intellectuals and some of the officers of the New Army, the new ideological teaching sometimes came over in a somewhat incomplete and incoherent form. The urban elites engaged in modern industry who were its recipients seem to have constituted the link between the imported ideology and the realities of the situation in China. Democracy, constitutionalism and nationalism were in tune with their own aspirations. But the political radicalisation produced by this ideological overdetermination did nothing to eradicate the social conservatism that they had inherited from the elitist tradition. Thus the speeded-up process of the bourgeoisie's accession to maturity was fraught with confusion. Despite the violent polemics and hostility between Liang Qichao and Sun Yat-sen, the reformist programme advocated by the one and the revolutionary plan of the other coincided on many points. At a time when people were still groping after ideologies and when vagueness in a political programme could be covered up by a charismatic personality, the attitudes of the modern urban elite groups, who were helping both the reformists and the revolutionaries, are not really surprising. Far from there being a strict division between the 'upper' and the 'lower' bourgeoisie and between the 'comprador' and the 'national' entrepreneurs, the line of separation between elites who were reformist and who were revolutionary was elastic and unpredictable. It largely depended upon the personal relations that the leaders of the various political organisations managed to develop with particular local communities. Political life was underpinned by the system of personal connections (*guanxi*) just as much as economic and social activities were.

It is well known how greatly influenced the political choices of overseas Chinese communities were by the tours of the Southern Seas (Nanyang) and America that Liang Qichao and Sun Yat-sen undertook in the early years of this century. Less well known, perhaps, is the role played by geographical links of solidarity and by the friendships that the revolutionary leader Chen Qimei (1876–1916) cultivated with a number of the major elite groups and entrepreneurs of Shanghai.[10] Chen Qimei was a native of Wuxing, in the prefecture of Huzhou (Zhejiang). Upon his return from Japan in 1909, he became director of the regional organisation of the Revolutionary Alliance in Shanghai. He was helped by the support of one of his fellow-citizens, Yang Xinzhi, a financier and comprador established in Shanghai, where he had founded a school for the children of families from Huzhou. This school provided Chen Qimei with temporary employment and a chance to meet other Shanghai entrepreneurs who were connected with the Zhejiang Clique. They included Wang Yiting[11] and also the Li brothers, the grandsons of the famous banker and builder of junks, Li Yeting (1807–48).[12] The eldest, Li Houyu, had served his apprenticeship along with Wang Yiting in a family *qianzhuang*; the second, Li Weizhuang, employed by the Jiangsu provincial finance bureau, is believed to have joined the Revolutionary Alliance during a visit to Japan in 1908; the third, Li Zhengwu, a silk wholesaler, is supposed to have rallied to the revolutionary organisation under the influence of Chen Qimei himself.

Other major partisans of the revolution on the eve of 1911 included the great comprador Yu Xiaqing, a native of Zhenhai (Zhejiang); the grain wholesalers Ye Huijun and Gu Xingyi, both natives of Shanghai; and, finally, Shen Manyun, a comprador, banker and industrialist from Wuxi (Jiangsu) and the most politically active of this group.

All these revolutionaries belonged to the Shanghai elite. They had held, and continued to hold, important posts in the local organisations: Li Houyu had been president of the General Chamber of Commerce in 1906–7 and its vice-president from 1907 to 1909. At the beginning of 1911, Yang Xinzhi, Wang Yiting and Shen Manyun all belonged to the Chamber's board of directors. Shen Manyun was also a member of the municipal Chinese government, and Yang Xinzhi had for the past ten or so years been one of the most influential leaders of the Ningbo Guild.[13]

Although most of these revolutionaries came from the merchant and comprador wing of the local elite, no deep sociological or political differences appear to have marked them out from the Shanghai elite groups and entrepreneurs who were closer to the gentry and who were active in the constitutionalist campaign. In 1910, when Shen Manyun was a member of the Revolutionary Alliance of a year's standing and was on a regular basis financing *The Rise of the People* (*Minlibao*), the organ of the revolutionary party in Shanghai, he was still actively campaigning for the constitution. In June, he even agreed to go to Peking as representative of the Chamber of Commerce in an attempt to hasten the convocation of a parliament![14]

The relative confusion of reformist and revolutionary activities is also evident in the alacrity with which members of the elite from the mandarin and constitutionalist wing rallied to Chen Qimei as soon as the uprising began. One particular case in point was Li Pingshu (1853–1922), the president of the Chinese municipal government. Others were Zhu Baosan, the vice-president of the Chamber of Commerce in 1905–6, and Zhou Jinpiao, who became its president in 1911.

Despite the important role played in the revolutionary movement by a number of individuals from the ranks of the merchants on the eve of 1911, the overwhelming impression given by the Shanghai elite groups is that of a united front. Whether they came from a mandarin or a merchant background, they were all in favour of change and many went so far as to prepare for it actively. In this consensus we should no doubt recognise the effects of an elitist tradition and social organisation which restricted responsibility to a limited circle of leaders – no more than a few dozen – who were to be found at the head of all the local associations and organisations and, pretty soon, also at the head of the town's provisional military government.

But how should we explain the discrepancies between the basic conservatism of these urban leaders who became the major agents of change in Shanghai and the revolutionary ideologies in the name of which those changes were brought about? Should we, as I have on occasion in the past, speak of 'ideological confusion' and 'political immaturity'?[15]

In the Chinese political tradition, freedom is not defined so much in terms of the individual but rather in opposition to the authoritarianism of central government.[16] So it is not surprising if the local elite groups regarded the establishment of their own power as a triumph for democracy. Seen from this point of view, reformist policies seeking to institutionalise the power of these elite groups, as opposed to the imperial bureaucracy, tended to become confused with a revolution the immediate aim of which was to bring those same elite groups to power. In short, the underlying stimuli for the 1911 revolution should be sought neither in the rise of the merchant class nor in the diffusion of imported ideologies nor in the militant and subversive actions of Sun Yat-sen. They lay in the persistent inability of the imperial power to win over the local elite groups as they evolved and its failure to gain their support so as to ensure both its own continuing existence and their continuing prosperity.

The actions of the emergent bourgeoisie, which sometimes – as in Shanghai – took undeniably original forms, must be understood within the general context of the relations between the central power and the local elite groups.

The united front of the urban elites in the revolutionary turmoil

The insurrection that burst out in Wuhan on 10 October 1911 was a military one. The merchants played no immediate part in it. However, they had not been uninvolved in the disturbances that preceded the revolutionary explosion. The campaign against the nationalisation of the railways that shook Sichuan province during the spring and summer of 1911 had been actively supported by the chambers of commerce and guilds of Chongqing and Chengdu. In October, the merchants of Wuhan were quick to come to the aid of the military insurgents.[17] They helped to maintain order and organised militia to stop looting and arson. The president of the Chamber of Commerce was even made chief of police. Furthermore, the Chamber of Commerce lost no time in advancing a loan of 200,000 taels to the insurgents.

In Shanghai, the bourgeoisie did not simply cooperate with the revolutionaries after the uprising: they did so before it, in fact they helped to prepare for it.[18] At the very beginning of 1911, Shen Manyun founded a patriotic organisation, the Association of Chinese Citizens (Zhongguo guominhui), very close in spirit to the Revolutionary Alliance. At the same time, the merchant militia, created in 1906 for the purposes of self-protection and self-defence, were reorganised and placed under the overall command of Li Pingshu. Their membership, which had already increased from 250 to 700, now rose to 2,000.

Immediately after the Wuhan insurrection, regular collaboration was set up between Chen Qimei and Li Pingshu, who met daily on the premises of the *Rise of the People*. The modern militia were in control of the town. The municipal government of the Chinese City neutralised the local police. The Chamber of Commerce promised subsidies. And when Chen Qimei dismantled the Manchu garrison and took over the Jiangnan Arsenal, on 3 November, Shanghai became republican.

But in this great burst of Chinese unity that the 1911 revolution represents, every province and every town went through its own historical experience. In Canton, at first the only effect of the news of the insurrection of 10 October was to prompt the governor general, Zhang Mingqi, to hang on to power by declaring his neutrality in the civil war and by strengthening provincial autonomy. His plan, which had the approval of the gentry, was subverted by the merchants who, at a meeting of the Ai-yu Charitable Association held on 29 October, opted for the republic and proclaimed the independence of Guangdong. But the merchants were not strong enough to enforce their decision and it was not until 9 November that Zhang Mingqi gave in to growing pressure from the revolutionary troops and fled from the town, abandoning power to the representative of the Revolutionary Alliance Hu Hanmin (1879–1936). Although Canton was an important commercial centre, the merchants of the town thus played no more than a minor role in the revolutionary events. Their weakness stemmed from their division. Here the Chamber of Commerce had not been able to get the 72 guilds and 9 charitable associations to accept it as the mouthpiece of the business community. The process of modernisation had been slower in Canton and, as a result, the urban elite was less united. The merchants were an isolated and relatively secondary group in comparison to the gentry, who were still bent on protecting their traditional prerogatives and interests.

In most of China the merchants and entrepreneurs took no initiatives, contenting themselves with reacting as best they could to local political situations created by other groups. At the end of 1911 and the beginning of 1912, the vacuum left by the disappearance of the central power and the disintegration of the local officials prompted them to take the administration of their own cities in hand. Gentry and merchants worked together to maintain social order. Moved by a Confucian sense of local civic responsibility, and on the strength of the experience they had acquired over the past decade, they strove to serve the immediate interests of the local population. In this united front presented by the elite groups, on the whole nothing – except possibly their level of energy – distinguished the merchants from their allies. The chambers of commerce and the guilds ran financial affairs, bought off the bandits and mediated between rival generals.[19]

Despite the fact that throughout China generally the merchants intervened in this fashion to run public affairs, their action was of limited political importance. It took place within the framework of a long-established system, tending simply to improve the way that it functioned. In most cases, the merchants did no more than negotiate with the authorities available, whether these were mandarins who had remained at their posts or revolutionary generals and activists whom the insurrection had carried to power. Their indirect method of control was a risky business, for many local potentates turned against the merchants, whom they proceeded to tax heavily, threaten or remove. In these cases, the merchants became the first victims of the authorities whose establishment they had favoured.

In the general crisis that shook the political system the intervention on the part of the merchants represented no more than a short-term expedient of limited impact. Only the elite groups of Shanghai, who were more powerful and better organised, seized the opportunity presented by the revolutionary upheaval to further their own local and national political ambitions.

From Shanghai to Nanking: the political temptations and frustrations of the emergent bourgeoisie

On 6 November, following the defeat of the imperial garrison, Chen Qimei organised a provisional military government in Shanghai. Alongside activists of the Revolutionary Alliance, it included a number of local elite figures. Li Pingshu as Minister of Civil Affairs, Shen Manyun as Minister of Finance and Wang Yiting as Minister of Communications. In less important posts we also find the former president of the Chamber of Commerce, Zhu Baosan, the compradores Yu Xiaqing and Yu Pinghan and the grain wholesaler, Gu Xingyi.[20]

Within its own particular environment – that of coastal, cosmopolitan and modernised China – the bourgeoisie made itself felt as a powerful political force. If the treaty ports had truly been the enclaves completely, or almost completely, cut off from the interior that some authors describe, the Shanghai merchants might have refused to take action in a national context. But, in truth, the economy of the coastal fringe was oriented just as much towards the hinterland as towards the ocean and their economic links with inland China reinforced the merchants' need and desire for national unity. The elite groups of Shanghai thus supported the republican and national programme of Sun Yat-sen. Within the framework of the apparatus of the Revolutionary Alliance and oriented by its programme of unification, the experience of Shanghai provided a model for the founding of a Chinese Republic in Nanking on 1 January 1912. This provisional national government under Sun Yat-sen[21] was set up with the aid of the elite groups of Shanghai, who advanced it loans estimated at 7 million taels. The programme of the new government paid attention to the grievances of the emergent bourgeoisie. In his manifesto of 5 January 1912 Sun drew up a list of recriminations against the obscurantist Manchu Empire: 'They created privileges and monopolies ... they subjected us to illegal taxes ... they limited the development of external trade to the treaty ports, they imposed *lijin* dues on the circulation of merchandise and paralysed internal trade.' And Sun Yat-sen went on to promise: 'We will revise ... our commercial and mining legislation and abolish the restrictions that are impeding trade'.[22] Under directives from Zhang Jian who had become the Minister of Industry in the Nanking government, offices of industry were set up to relay central government action to the provinces and to coordinate operations.[23]

The three-month period of power of the Nanking government did not allow it to proceed any further. Perhaps it would have been incapable of doing so anyway. A few weeks after Sun Yat-sen assumed the presidency, 'bankers, wealthy wholesalers and compradores were all beginning to feel that the regime was a heavy burden to bear'.[24] In Shanghai itself, relations deteriorated between business circles and Chen Qimei, who was increasingly often resorting to heavy-handed methods to extort the funds that he needed.[25] The Shanghai elite groups had probably hoped that the Nanking government, established thanks to their aid, would soon be in a position to broaden its bases and find other sources of financial support in the country. They were soon disillusioned. The provisional republican government not only lacked adequate social bases but could not even count on an effective party apparatus. By the beginning of 1912, the Revolutionary Alliance, always a very loosely structured organisation, could muster no more than the immediate entourage of Sun Yat-sen. He was consequently forced to stand down and on February 1912 relinquished the presidency of the Republic to Yuan Shikai.

The bourgeoisie's first political venture thus collapsed in failure in the spring of 1912. It had not managed to set up the political structures indispensable for its success. The Shanghai businessmen had not been able to carry the full weight of a national government on their own. They had not been able to extend the benefits of the innovations that the foreign presence had introduced into the treaty ports to the rural and bureaucratic society of China as a whole. The disappointments of this first revolutionary venture and the attraction of a regime bent upon order, together with the hopes raised by economic expansion, explain how it was that the bourgeoisie rallied to Yuan Shikai. When the revolutionary tide ebbed in 1913, it left behind it a military and bureaucratic regime with modernising tendencies and a bourgeoisie that had lost its motivating force, absorbed as it was in the preservation of its own immediate interests and in the tasks of a promising-looking programme of economic development.

2   An unsuccessful Meiji: the failure of Yuan Shikai (1912–16)

When Yuan Shikai came to power, he reactivated the policies that he had played a major part in shaping during the last years of the Empire. On the one hand, he tried to consolidate the central power – his own, in this instance – soliciting the support of the army and the bureaucracy to establish his dictatorship. On the other, he was concerned to introduce a number of changes and in particular to encourage economic development. Like all authoritarian modernisers, his determination to encourage progress stood in striking contrast to his refusal to relinquish the slightest measure of power to the agents of that progress – the merchants, industrialists and bankers. Authoritarianism and modernism were simply two aspects of a single policy aimed at reinforcing the power of the State, which was considered to be the basis of national unity and prosperity.

The conditions now prevailing seemed to favour such a policy much more than before. Now that the 1911 revolution had ousted the foreign dynasty and removed the obstacle to progress that the Manchus had constituted, the central government could claim a new national and legitimate mandate. Furthermore, Yuan Shikai had the advantage of a remarkable team of administrators whose presence at his side underlined the continuity between the reformist policies of before and those of after the 1911 revolution. Most of these men had already played their part in the early attempts at modernisation undertaken by Yuan when he had been governor of Shandong province and then governor general of Zhili. These talented administrators believed that China's progress depended upon the action of the elite bureaucracy that they flattered themselves to be. In truth, they did constitute the best brains trust that a Chinese leader could have hoped for at the beginning of the twentieth century.

After 1912, Tang Shaoyi (1860–1938), a nephew of the famous comprador Tong King Sing, who for the past 25 years had been Yuan Shikai's collaborator in all his diplomatic, financial and railway ventures, moved away from the dictator. But the talented young team that he had recruited and trained remained in Yuan's service. It included Liang Shiyi (1869–1933), a specialist in railway and banking affairs, and Zhou Ziqi (1871–1923), a former diplomat who had played an active part in reforms initiated under the *ancien régime*. Known as the Communications Clique (Jiaotongxi), this bureaucratic partnership trained and controlled by Liang and Zhou brought together a solid team of officials, almost all of Cantonese origin. Yuan could also count on the more remote support of Xu Shichang, one of the principal architects of the administrative reorganisation attempted by the Manchus, and on the collaboration of two great mandarin entrepreneurs – Zhou Xuexi and Zhang Jian – to whom he several times entrusted ministries with economic responsibilities.[26]

The social conservatism of such a team was of a kind to reassure the urban elites rather than alienate them. Furthermore, the group of modern entrepreneurs that was beginning to emerge from the local elites needed public order, national independence and legislative and institutional reforms if they were to make headway. There seemed to be a much closer rapport now, between Yuan's programme and the ambitions of the new bourgeoisie, than there had been a few years earlier between the reformist inclinations of the despised, divided imperial power and the aspirations of the urban elite groups that were closely connected with the local bureaucracy.

Yuan was equally hostile to the parliamentary system, to private autonomy and to freedom of speech. In November 1913, on the strength of his military victory, he ordered the dissolution of the principal opposition party, the Guomindang; in December of the same year, he dissolved parliament. He then moved against all the representative organisations set up, to the benefit of local elite groups, just before and immediately after the revolution. On 4 February 1914, he abolished the local and provincial assemblies that had been returned during the 1912–13 winter on the basis of a greatly expanded electorate (25% of the adult male population) and which, since the revolution, had usurped many of the representative, fiscal and military functions that normally fell to the State bureaucracy.

Meanwhile, Yuan was also strengthening procedures for controlling the appointment of officials, reintroducing the rule that prohibited mandarins from exercising public functions in their own native provinces and embarking upon a veritable administrative reconquest of the country. To free the government from foreign financial domination he tried to make the provinces revert to paying part of their revenues over to Peking and he imposed strict budgets upon his ministers. He reduced the size of the army and also the power of generals in the provinces, where civilian governors now resumed their former pre-eminent positions.[27]

The presidency of Yuan Shikai (1912–13), followed by his dictatorship (1913–16), nevertheless cannot be reduced to a simple restoration attempt. Although Yuan Shikai was hostile to the sharing of political power and to pluralism, he nevertheless recognised the need for changes, which it was his intention both to initiate and to control. He thus proceeded to introduce a series of educational reforms – particularly in the area of primary schooling – as well as economic ones. In the latter sphere, he tried to stimulate growth by passing further legislation and encouraging private enterprise. Zhang Jian, Minister of Agriculture and Trade from October 1913 to December 1915, introduced laws on the registration of commercial firms and companies and ones affecting joint-stock companies. He set up model institutions for the cultivation of cotton and sugar cane; he also drew up a plan for standardising the system of weights and measures. In February 1914, Liang Shiyi was instrumental in establishing the Yuan Shikai dollar as a first step in the direction of monetary unification (still a long way off).[28]

Faced with policies such as these – at once repressive yet stimulatory – business communities responded with a measure of withdrawal. It took the form of giving quasi-absolute priority to objectives of an economic nature. The merchants and businessmen were particularly affected by the suppression of the local assemblies. These had done far more than simply take over a number of administrative functions. They had also provided a forum and a means of communication for the new associations of industrialists, educationists and craftsmen which the revolution had encouraged to multiply. They had constituted a key piece in the society that was beginning to take shape. Through them, groups hitherto excluded or ignored by the mandarins had been beginning to take part in political life. They represented what is, in the Chinese tradition, the closest approximation to liberalism, namely the defence of local interests.[29]

For the Shanghai merchants, the suppression of these assemblies marked the end of an exceptional experiment. In the municipality of the Chinese City, the urban gentry of the *shenshang* had been given a chance to demonstrate its managerial abilities, its aptitude for modernisation, its understanding of democratic procedures, and also its interest in more far-reaching problems of national concern. The Shanghai business world was never again to enjoy such local administrative and political autonomy. The Bureau of Public Works, Policing and Taxation (Gongxunjuan ju), which Yuan set up in place of the former municipality, remained strictly under the thumb of the local bureaucracy. The merchants were deprived of their last means of political expression by the law of 1914 which strengthened government control over the chambers of commerce.[30]

There is no need to repeat my earlier remarks (see Chapter 1) about the prosperity of the modern sector at the time of the First World War. Although the direct stimulus that projected the bourgeoisie into its golden age was provided by the changed international situation during the war, even as early as 1912–13 the modern sector had been experiencing a rapid expansion thanks to good harvests, the rise of silver on the world market, booming external trade, and a certain optimism born of revolutionary hopes (more than of revolutionary experience).

In these circumstances, a return to political and military unrest was what the business world dreaded more than anything. However, the prosperous situation, which neutralised possible reactions in the face of Yuan Shikai's tactics of force, was not enough to get the merchants and businessmen to rally positively around the government. Why was it that Yuan's reformatory dictatorship found no more support among the emergent bourgeoisie than the imperial regime had in the years of its decline? The reason lies not so much in the authoritarianism, arbitrariness and conservatism of the government, but rather in its weakness. Despite Yuan Shikai's reign of terror, he was not the 'strong man' that his contemporaries so often claimed him to be. When under foreign pressure, his government was disarmed as quickly as that of the Manchus had been. His capitulation in May 1915 when presented with the Japanese Twenty-one Demands was probably not so much betrayal as resignation in the face of the inevitable. But the fact remains that Yuan was incapable of providing the emergent bourgeoisie with the nationalistic satisfactions with which Bismarck and the Meiji emperor bought the docility of their new elite groups. Yuan's regime was equally weak on the internal front. His attempts to impose administrative centralisation did not go far enough to destroy the influence of the local elite groups, even if their institutional power was diminished. The militarisation of society was not checked. Despite the reforms that he introduced in the army, Yuan Shikai still did not manage to turn it into an instrument of the nation or to bring it under the control of the central power. The generals, even those in Yuan's own entourage, paid less and less heed to the orders of Peking and seized local power for themselves. By the director's death, the age of the warlords had already arrived.

What kind of support could a government such as this provide for the emergent bourgeoisie? Laws and programmes for the most part remained dead letters. The stimulus for growth did not come from above but resulted from a combination of local initiatives (over a dozen societies for the promotion of industry were created during 1912 alone)[31] and external factors. What is more, finding itself short of financial resources, the government adopted a policy of intensive taxation, the major brunt of which was borne by the merchants. The Shanghai Chamber of Commerce echoed their dissatisfaction: 'If the authorities, as it is avowed, can vary the rates of taxation at will, then the nation cannot be a nation governed by law . . . the hard-earned gold taken from the people is being squandered like so much dirt . . . the mouths of the merchants may be forcibly gagged, but their hearts cannot be forcibly prevented from becoming cold.'[32]

In 1915, Yuan Shikai was nursing a plan to restore the monarchy that is now generally considered as an aberrant manifestation of his personal ambitions. But perhaps it should also be regarded as an attempt to mobilise popular support in the face of the reticence and resistance of the local elites – the expression of a populist strategy designed to reconstruct a nation united around the central power and to strengthen the legitimacy of that power. But here too Yuan failed.

Yuan Shikai thus failed to unite the various power groups present. With no legitimate mandate and threatened by the hostility of the local elites, who distrusted his centralising policies, Yuan Shikai furthermore failed to win support from the new social forces. The little group of modern entrepreneurs preserved its links with the local elites from which it had emerged and continued to identify with their ideas and interests.

All the same, the economic ambitions of these entrepreneurs did call for reforms – monetary unification, fiscal reorganisation and a return to autonomy for the customs offices – and that fact forced them to consider the problem of the nature and role of government and to call the semi-colonial status of China into question. The need for progress led the young bourgeoisie into struggles of a more far-reaching nature and pushed it into seeking from the revolutionary movement the support that had not been forthcoming from this government whose tyranny did not so much demonstrate its strength as mask its weakness. But on the eve of the 1911 revolution and in its aftermath, the emergent Chinese bourgeoisie was placed at a disadvantage in that there existed no State power worthy of the name with which it could enter into partnership. That lack was to cause it to steer its destiny into the tumultuous rapids of revolution.

3   The May Fourth Movement (1919): the bourgeois revolution at last?

The Chinese bourgeoisie's participation in the May Fourth Movement, its commitment alongside students and workers to the anti-government and anti-imperialist struggle, marked a decisive turning point in the history of urban society in China. The political disappointments of the past two decades might well have caused the bourgeoisie to return to corporatism and to the social isolationism traditional in the merchant class. Instead, the urgent need for particularly rapid growth forced it to initiate more and more moves and to intervene increasingly in public life. Now that the bourgeoisie could no longer operate through their defunct institutions, their actions took on a more radical slant. For a while, the bourgeoisie became the most influential group in an alliance between all the urban classes, based upon a common desire for national independence, openness towards the West, individual liberty and economic and social progress.

Although the idea of a bourgeois revolution does not greatly help to illuminate the events of 1911–13, it could be reintroduced at this point, in the context of a longer-term analysis. The notion of a revolutionary break with the past might then be replaced by that of a transition. All the transformations of the past, rooted in the continuing evolution of traditional structures ever since the nineteenth century, eventually led to economic modernisation and social and political revolution in the twentieth. Far from being limited to the revolution itself, the transformations were connected with the expansion of Chinese capitalism, the emergence of a new generation of entrepreneurs, and the business world's growing participation in the political life of the country. All these were phenomena which had a strong impact upon the May Fourth Movement and the surrounding period.

Towards a deeper political consciousness

Following the failure of the reformist policies and the death of Yuan Shikai in 1916, the entrepreneurs turned away from the discredited central government, which could neither repair the division that had developed between North and South nor prevent the rising tide of civil wars. In December 1917, the representatives of the Shanghai General Chamber of Commerce were invited to Peking by the Minister of

Agriculture and Trade to discuss problems of development. However, they declined his offer: 'In view of the disturbed state of the country and the disorganisation of our economies and trade, the merchants consider that they have no spare time to do such things as the government has proposed'.[33]

Some discouraged entrepreneurs turned their backs on politics altogether and returned to philanthropy. They dreamed of creating islands of security and prosperity within Chinese society. They planned model communities; sometimes they even tried to give these concrete form. Zhang Jian turned Nantong into a model town and Zhu Baosan bought 1,000 *mu* in the Shanghai suburbs in order to set up a pilot show city.[34]

But the rapid development of the modern sector called for radical changes in the international status of China (in particular in its customs system), in its political institutions and in its social organisations. And more and more entrepreneurs were coming to realise that in the long term only these changes could ensure the continuation and intensification of a growth initially stimulated by a combination of extremely favourable external circumstances. Their own fate and that of their businesses were increasingly clearly seen to be part and parcel of the general evolution of society and the State: 'Men cannot leave society and live by themselves; we cannot cut ourselves off from the existing chaotic and disorganised Chinese society in order to set up on our own.'[35]

At the annual conference of the Federation of Chambers of Commerce in 1921, Tang Fufu made an impassioned plea for political commitment. It was no longer a question of simply supporting such and such a party or of depending on such and such a strong man; they could trust no one, look to no saviour; the chambers of commerce would have to shoulder direct responsibilities: 'It is now the time for the merchants to renounce a time-worn tradition of not participating in politics ... We refused to become involved in what we called "dirty politics". If politics are dirty, it is because we have permitted them to become so ... Are we slaves and traitors? I say no! The merchants of China will save this country ... Chambers of commerce have always prided themselves that they are non-political organisations. That is now our shame.'[36]

In a less fiery manner, Mu Ouchu took up the same theme: 'The old idea that we have held that businessmen should only care for business is today useful no more. It is the duty of our businessmen to get together and devise every way and means to force our government to improve our internal affairs. We believe that only by so doing can we find hope in the recovery of the business of our country, and that our failure to take such steps will result in the complete failure of all business, the impossibility for our people to make their livings, and finally the destruction of our nation.'[37]

An expansionist philosophy

The arousal of the political consciousness of the bourgeoisie was in part a consequence of the institutional obstacles blocking economic development and was encouraged by the intellectual ferment which characterised the May Fourth period. In the course of the May Fourth Movement, China experienced what it is fair to describe as a veritable cultural revolution. The aim of the intellectuals and students was to sweep away the old values that stood in the way of progress and to replace them with new ideals borrowed from the West. They were willing to reject their cultural heritage to save the nation, sacrifice the past to safeguard the future. For these iconoclasts were ardent nationalists. The movement which was born in 1915 and continued until 1920 took its name from a demonstration organised in Peking on 4 May 1919 to protest against the transfer to Japan of German rights over Shandong decided by the negotiators of the Treaty of Versailles, and to denounce the pro-Japanese ministers who, though members of the Chinese government, were betraying the interests of their country. That demonstration was followed by a series of others throughout the country. The movement for intellectual and moral renewal turned into a vast nationalistic protest in which merchants and workers all supported the action of the intelligentsia.

The May Fourth Movement was the source from which sprang the principal ideological currents that gave direction to the history of contemporary China – liberalism, nationalism and communism. Its legacy was as complex as it was rich. The discovery and immediate adoption of Western theories of the most diverse kinds and the groping progress of political thinking that was still seeking its way led to a seething cauldron that accommodated a mixture of the most contradictory ideas. But the starting point was the realisation of one fact: China was poor and backward. For this there could be only one remedy – industrial development – and one recommendation – that China should learn from the experiences of Europe and the United States and avoid the development of a conflict between capital and labour. These were the major themes in *The International Development of China*, a work that Sun Yat-sen began to write immediately after the 1918 Armistice, in a style that owes something to the industrial lyricism of Saint-Simon. Similar ideas were expressed by John Dewey in the many lectures that he delivered in Chinese universities between 1919 and 1921 and, under his influence, they were taken up by the liberal intelligentsia (Zhang Dongsun and Hu Shi, for example) and also from time to time by the future founder of the Communist Party, Chen Duxiu (1879–1942).[38]

The ideological leaders of the May Fourth Movement envisaged development partially controlled by the State and made possible by the rise of a class of producers that would include both the bourgeoisie and the working class. In this 1919–20 period, the emphasis was laid not on the class struggle but on the deep solidarity of the Chinese people confronted with the problem of development: 'The primary force of human evolution is cooperation and not struggle.'[39] Up until 1921–22, when the conflict between liberals and radicals broke out, the need for economic development made for a measure of agreement over priorities: these were to be nationalism, industrial growth and social harmony. In very classic fashion, contemporary Chinese political thought embarked upon its apprenticeship with utopian ideals.

These theories, which allotted to the bourgeoisie a role of the first importance in the development of the national economy and hence in the destiny of China, found a number of supporters in the business world. John Dewey and Bertrand Russell were invited to visit the Shanghai General Chamber of Commerce. In his newspaper, *Time* (*Shishi xinbao*), Zhang Dongsun seems to have adopted a line much in sympathy with the young entrepreneurs of Shanghai, supporting their actions in the Chamber of Commerce. Sun Yat-sen's prestige in business circles was so high that in 1921 a group of merchants decided to put his theories into practice by presenting Shanghai with a Chinese outer port, as described in *The International Development of China*.[40]

On the whole, however, the ideas of the bourgeoisie stemmed more from their practical business experience than from theoretical speculation. For them, the crucial experience of the war years and the post-war years had been that of economic prosperity in the midst of political chaos. The bourgeoisie seems at this point to have been more sensitive to the advantages of the former than to the disadvantages of the latter. Present euphoria, born of a virtually total ignorance of modern economic cycles, submerged anxiety over the future. The bourgeoisie's optimism matched the theorists' utopias. Illusions engendered by a one-sided experience were added to those encouraged by fumbling political thinking.

The ideas of the bourgeoisie as expressed in the announcements of the chambers of commerce, in the articles of the specialised press and in the declarations made by individual merchants and industrialists revolved around a number of dominant yet antinomic themes, such as nationalism along with international cooperation, and industrial revolution combined with social peace.

The Chinese bourgeoisie joined its voice to all the others demanding that wrongs be put right, the Twenty-one Demands be abolished, extraterritorial concessions be suppressed and a return to autonomy for the customs. None of these themes was particular to the bourgeoisie. Bourgeois nationalism, to which we shall be returning in the next chapter, seems to have been largely engendered by the current of feeling that was making urban society resentful of foreign encroachments. But business circles, more than others, were conscious of the need for foreign involvement if the modern sector was to develop. They broke with the Confucian tradition which knew nothing of reciprocity in relations between different nations and, at the same time, rejected the imperialist policies of gun-boat diplomacy and foreign concessions. Their plea was for cooperation in an atmosphere of respect for national independence.

On the level of internal politics, the theme of international cooperation was matched by that of social harmony in the service of industrial revolution. The concern that the bourgeoisie was now showing for the working class perhaps reflected the preoccupations of a number of Christian employers – Nie Yuntai, Ou Ben (the co-founder of the Nanyang Brothers' Tobacco Company) and the banker Xu Enyuan. It certainly coincided with the campaign launched in 1920 under the aegis of the Young Men's Christian Association (YMCA) and figures such as C. F. Remer and Sherwood Eddy. These influences, combined with the traditional community spirit of the guilds, gave rise to a paternalistic ideology that sought to reconcile the well-being of the workers with the interests of the employers. The *Journal of Friendship between Workers and Merchants (Gongshang zhi you)*, created in 1920, advocated shorter working hours, higher wages and workers' profit-sharing.[41] The need for social progress was seen as an aspect of efficiency. At the inauguration of one of his new cotton mills in 1920, Mu Ouchu declared: 'The modern capitalist values highly the energy of his employees because it is the unseen capital of industry ... It should not be wasted.'[42] As it faced the huge task of development, the bourgeoisie believed in its solidarity with the working class: 'The new industrial system will practice mutual aid between employers and workers'; it was an idea to some extent echoed in working-class circles.[43] The sense of a common threat – that of foreign competition against national industries – strengthened the spirit of solidarity. Progress for the working class was not to be the fruit of conflicts that would be harmful to all parties; it was not to be accomplished in opposition to the bougeoisie but with its aid and at its instigation: 'Pending the formation of a sufficiently intelligent and effective public opinion and the establishment of efficient organs of legislation, the only solution for the labor problem in China can come from voluntary undertakings on the part of more enlightened employers, like Messrs Nieh [Nie Yuntai] and Moh [Mu Ouchu], to better the conditions of their employees.'[44]

The Chinese press took up this theme of a bourgeoisie at once intelligent (*congming*) and farsighted (*yuanjian*). It emphasised the need for an 'awakening of consciousness' (*zibenjiade jiaowu*) and worked to achieve it: the major liberal paper, the *Shanghai Journal (Shenbao)*, pressed for higher wages and explained that these would not have to be paid at the expense of shareholders.

The propaganda put out by industrial circles in favour of education for the populace carried on this theme of social solidarity. The immediate objective was clearly to provide industry with the management and skilled labour that it needed. But the magazine *Education and Industry (Jiaoyu yu zhiye)*, founded in 1917, argued that improving the living conditions of the masses involved a coordinated development of industry and teaching: 'Employers and schools cooperate, work and education progress together.'[45]

Chinese bourgeois philosophy in 1919 was a philosophy of expansion. The resemblances between it and certain aspects of French socialism (Saint-Simonism in particular) and Anglo-American liberalism are not just a matter of intellectual history. *Mutatis mutandis* they result from a similar experience, that of growth. That is why the utopia of the bourgeoisie of the golden age holds a particularly interesting place in the evolution of modern Chinese economic thought. It is free from the interventionism, isolationism and 'voluntarism' that, to varying degrees, have marked most economic thinking from the 'Western Affairs' Movement at the end of the nineteenth century right up to the first Five-Year Plan or the Great Leap Forward. It was, instead, a reflection of the fleeting reality of its own day – the economic miracle engendered by the First World War.

The activation of the bourgeoisie

In the course of 1919, business circles took positive action in a number of ways. At the beginning of June, they organised a strike to show solidarity with the nationalist students who had been arrested by the Peking government for demonstrating their hostility to the Shandong resolution of the Versailles Peace Conference. Simultaneously, they organised a massive boycott movement directed against the Japanese, whom they suspected of aiming to colonise China. Between July 1919 and April 1920, they launched several campaigns in the International Settlement of Shanghai, rejecting taxation and aiming to secure representation for Chinese ratepayers on the municipal council of the Settlement.

We shall be returning to the nationalistic preoccupations that prompted these activities. What we should examine at this point are the modalities through which the bourgeois groups were moved to take such steps, namely (a) the part played by professional organisations in bringing about this transition from action of a hitherto essentially corporatist and local nature to political commitment and activism, and (b) the accession to maturity of an autonomous society that had been left to its own devices by the collapse of State power and now discovered within itself prodigious powers of adaptation and initiative.

The vigour with which the bourgeoisie participated in the May Fourth Movement can be explained by the fact that there arose on the fringes of the merchant class a group of younger, more innovative entrepreneurs of radical inclination. They were excluded from the Shanghai General Chamber of Commerce (which they attempted, unsuccessfully, to win over and reform in 1919–20), but these radicals did manage to establish their influence in some of the regional guilds (particularly those of Canton) and in the new bodies that had materialised in the context of the national crisis and that were soon rivalling the authority of the establishment bourgeois organisations. The political positions adopted by the merchant class became increasingly diverse as its representative structures grew more complex.

The Shanghai Commercial Federation (Shanghai shangye gongtuan lianhehui) was set up on 3 March 1919. At that date it comprised about forty institutions, but a few weeks later the number had risen to over sixty. Its structure was not very different from that of the chambers of commerce, in that its membership was made up of professional corporations and regional guilds. However, the arrangements concerning the life of the Federation (subscriptions, admission of new members, decisions of common interest) were more liberal. Once set up, the Federation took over the very same objectives that the chambers of commerce had always proclaimed – the protection of merchants' interests and the promotion of business. But right from the start there was also a political dimension to its actions, the Federation advocating the institution of a truly democratic administration, the enforced licensing of warlords and their troops, and the promulgation of a constitution.[46]

The street associations (*malu lianhehui*) were more modest in their objectives but their activism was just as hard-hitting. In a typically Chinese fashion these brought together merchants from the major commercial streets in the big cities on the basis of neighbourly relationships and common interests. The largest of the street associations was that of Nanjinglu in Shanghai, which mustered 183 delegates. The 52 street associations of Shanghai had sprung, in August 1919, from a spontaneous movement of resistance to rising municipal taxation, and it was not long before they organised themselves into a federation (Shanghai gemalu shangjie lianhehui) and broadened the base of their militancy, agitating for the revision of the 'Land Regulations' that governed the administration of the International Settlement and for the admission of Chinese to its municipal council.[47]

The new organisations quickly extended their influence, somewhat undermining the Shanghai General Chamber of Commerce. By the spring of 1920, the president of the Shanghai Municipal Council was deploring this turn of events: 'We want to be in a position to feel the pulse of the Chinese feeling ... There was a time when we could look to the Chinese General Chamber of Commerce to help us very greatly but, alas, the Chamber no longer has the same standing as it had. It is no longer so representative of the Chinese community as it was of yore; other rival institutions have challenged its supremacy.'[48]

It was these new organisations that got business circles to become involved in the strike which the students engineered at the beginning of June and in which the workers were already taking part. For instance, on 10 May 1919, the Shanghai Commercial Federation launched a violent attack on the temporising position adopted by the General Chamber of Commerce (which was refusing to condemn the Japanese claims to Shandong) and forced it to take a lead. Once the business strike had started, it was the regional guilds of Guangdong and Shandong that prevented that same General Chamber from bringing it to a premature end.[49]

What was the source of this activist minority's strength, and how did it manage to get its way? One source of the dynamism of the radical wing of the bourgeoisie was clearly the violent nationalist reaction that was currently rocking the whole of urban society. The representatives of the student organisations that had launched the strike kept on pressing the major merchants to cooperate with them. The radicals could also count on pressure coming from the basic strata of small shopkeepers and employees who were always prepared to resort to direct action to get their voices heard. On 4 June, the Chamber of Commerce of the Chinese City of Shanghai was invaded by merchants who took it upon themselves to intervene in its deliberations and pressed it to approve the plan for the strike.[50]

But the influence of the young avant-garde radical and modernist bourgeoisie did not depend solely upon its links with the mass movement. It must also – and above all – be explained by the close connections that this avant-garde preserved with the reformist elite of the *ancien régime*, from which most of its members had emerged. It was thanks to the more or less willing support of these elite groups that the new ideas and experiments won over people from much further afield than the circles in which they had originated.

Despite the unificatory and centralist reaction of Yuan Shikai and the rival ambitions of the militarists, the power of the urban elite groups had increased after the 1911 revolution. Their influence over the bureaucracy for the most part recruited locally had never been stronger. They represented a strong and stable force within Chinese society, even if merchants, landowners and graduates from the modern schools now outnumbered the scholars among them. They dominated local assemblies and organisations and, as the central government's authority waned, their own became an increasingly crucial factor.

These elite groups practised a kind of Confucian democracy, founded upon a general consensus, negotiation and compromise. Thus the leaders of the Shanghai General Chamber of Commerce, who were anxious to preserve the unity of the merchant class, came to stomach a number of decisions which they did not approve of but had failed to avert. For example, on the occasion of the 1919–20 conflict between the Chinese residents of the International Settlement and its municipal council, the General Chamber of Commerce, despite misgivings, supported the fiscal strike decreed by the shopkeepers of the street association.[51] The radical and modernising fringe, for its part, continued to look to the old guard for leadership, out of both their respect for tradition and their need for social prestige. Thus even after their protest against the attitude of the Chamber of Commerce, which 'claimed to represent the Chinese ratepayers but had never won their approval', the International Settlement's shopkeepers and residents, who had formed an Association of Chinese Ratepayers (Shanghai gonggong zujienceide nashui Huaren), elected to the consultative committee which was to represent them on the Shanghai Municipal Council Mu Ouchu, Song Hanzhang and Chen Guangfu, all three directors of that very Chamber of Commerce![52]

So it would be misleading to set up too categorical an opposition between the old guard and the radicals. Just as class structures did not emerge clearly within the complex network of family and geographical ties, so the political positions of these groups remained confused and contradictory. The very same figures were often to be found at the head of both activist and conservative organisations: Zhu Baosan, the president of the General Chamber of Commerce, and Yu Xiaqing, one of its leading directors, were simultaneously two of the most influential of the leaders of the Shanghai Commercial Federation. Gu Xingyi, the president of the relatively progressive Chamber of Commerce of the Chinese City, was at the same time a member of the old guard in the General Chamber. Attitudes were in flux and seemingly incoherent. At the end of May 1919, in the General Chamber of Commerce, Yu Xiaqing, who supported the reformist clan, joined the campaign for the return of Zhu Baosan, who had been dropped as chairman of the

Chamber on account of his pro-Japanese attitude. Meanwhile, one of the founders of the Shanghai Commercial Federation, the Cantonese comprador and industrialist Chen Bingqian, was also to be found at the head of the more conservative faction.[53]

The constantly overlapping aims and the many compromises, the confusion of attitudes and all the interactions between the different factions lead us a long way away from any Marxist analysis that would interpret the involvement of the merchant class in 1919 as a triumph for the lower bourgeoisie and as the starting point of a national and democratic revolution. Yet interpretations such as these, repeated and magnified after the founding of the Chinese Communist Party, were in 1923 used to justify the adoption of a united front policy, to seal an alliance between bourgeois and proletarian forces and between their supposed representatives, the Guomindang and the Communist Parties. We must beware of substituting what was said *about* the bourgeoisie for what the bourgeoisie itself declared. After May 1919, opposition began to develop between the radical wing of the movement, increasingly attracted to Marxism, and its moderate wing, represented by Hu Shi and the liberal theorists grouped around him; the institutions and individuals representative of the bourgeoisie were to be found in the latter camp. The bourgeois involvement of 1919 did not lead to a revolutionary struggle but to an amazing bid for liberalism.

4   The bid for liberalism (1920–3)

It was an amazing bid, for in the absence of a true State power, it was brought about by unilateral action taken by several different social groups – intellectuals, officials and merchant entrepreneurs. But it is not possible to understand the political gamble attempted and lost by the bourgeoisie at this juncture without a detailed look at the context in which it was made. The formation of political consciousness in classes that are excluded from power is necessarily conditioned by the nature of the regime currently established. Having attained a certain social and economic maturity, the Chinese bourgeoisie was called upon to assume its responsibilities in a world that the decline of the Confucian ideology and of the elite groups that represented it had stripped of its traditional forms without, however, giving rise to new liberties. Despotism in the shape of the Empire or the military dictatorship of

Yuan Shikai had disappeared, but it lived on, embodied now in local potentates of whom there were so many that the partial defeats that they suffered at the hands of their adversaries made no significant impact on the general situation. If the involvement of the bourgeoisie often seems ambiguous, disordered and ineffective, that is in part due to the nature of the very political situation that prompted it, little by little, to define itelf.

The age of the warlords was a period of general insecurity and exploitation. All social groups were affected. In the foreign concessions, the bourgeoisie of the treaty ports were spared the looting and extortions by which the merchants of inland China were plagued. But to the extent that its economic activity was pursued within an inter-regional framework, even this bourgeoisie was damaged by the decline of business connections and the disorganisation of the transport and monetary systems. The extent to which militarism hit the society of semi-self-sufficient agricultural producers was relatively random. One village would be ravaged as armies passed through it; another, a little further off, would be spared. Although the spread of civil disorder could inflict disaster upon vast regions, the phenomenon remained essentially local and fragmentary; it was an accumulation of individual disasters. The merchants suffered just as others did from all these harmful hazards: their shops were looted, their warehouses burnt down. But they were also hit by the disturbances taking place *elsewhere*, in some cases very far away indeed. The wars in Sichuan did not threaten the peasants of Jiangsu but they did deprive the Shanghai cotton mill owners of one of their principal markets. In the early 1920s, the business bourgeoisie was the only class whose progress and prosperity was *immediately* dependent upon both internal peace and national unity. On that account, it may be considered as the principal victim of all this militarism, which was a negation of both.

The political thinking of the bourgeoisie at this period – as it emerges from the motions adopted by the chambers of commerce and the banking associations and from the editorials of business journals – coincides on many points with the views that Hu Shi and his collaborators put forward in their new weekly, *Endeavour* (*Nuli zhoubao*). Both groups called for active commitment on the part of the elites (*haoren*), both advocated the use of professional skills to resolve specific problems (*wenti*) and both pressed for good government (*hao zhengfu*) – that is, public government (*gongkaide zhengfu*) which would give a financial account of itself to the nation – and for planning (*jihua*) of such a kind as to introduce order into the successive phases of development yet at the same time encourage individual initiative.[54]

The entrepreneurs can certainly not be regarded as disciples of Hu Shi. Most of them had evolved their political ideas through their understanding of the obstacles that stood in the way of their own economic development. As they saw it, these were militarism, financial disorder and arbitrary bureaucratic intervention. Nor can there be any question of presenting Hu Shi as the spokesman of the Chinese bourgeoisie; the predominance of foreign influences on his political thought runs counter to such an interpretation. All the same, the two currents of thought – one intellectual, the other bourgeois – were very close, and the commitment of the bourgeoisie to Chinese liberalism, often considered as a somewhat aberrant episode in Chinese intellectual history, makes it significant politically as well as socially.

Although the attitudes of the philosophers of *Endeavour* and those of the members of the chambers of commerce often seem identical, active liberalism incorporated a number of inevitable distortions – or rather, necessary adaptations. The most striking feature of this 'sinisation of liberalism' is that it was concerned above all to defend local liberties, rather than individual ones. Influenced by Western theories, Hu Shi and his friends defended human rights. In contrast, the businessmen, who were conditioned by their traditional associations and links of solidarity, were above all concerned to defend their communities against the corrupt maladministration of power (or powers). However, having learned the lesson of the 1911 revolution, the bourgeoisie tried to associate its own aspirations for autonomy with a more general system of organisation, sensing that this alone could bring about the realisation of its dreams. The bourgeoisie thus moved on from the traditional slogan of autonomy (*zizhi*) to press for a provincial federation (*liansheng zizhi*). The decline of central government provided the bourgeoisie with an opportunity to redefine its relations with the State. By devising new State structures, it tried to break out of the vicious circle which for centuries had associated, on the one hand, free enterprise with civil disorder and, on the other, political order with economic exploitation (or repression): for a while, autonomy and federalism became the instruments of its liberal policy and class ambitions.

From 1920 onwards, the autonomist movement seems, on the basis of a fundamental misunderstanding, to have rallied support from all sides: it came from both the conservative elites and the more enlightened or ambitious militarists, and likewise from both the revolutionary intelligentsia and the chambers of commerce. The bourgeoisie made use of this movement to try to further its own contradictory aspirations for both liberty and order. By encouraging the drawing-up of provincial constitutions and the reactivation of the organs of local government, the merchants hoped to consolidate their power in opposition to interventions on the part of the civil or military bureaucracy. Among the local elite groups who were supposed to benefit most from the movement, the merchant class was playing an increasingly predominant role, as can be seen not only from the power acquired by the chambers of commerce in the administration of municipal affairs but also from the ever-increasing number of its representatives to be found in provincial and district assemblies and the entourages of provincial governors.

A provincial or local framework seemed particularly suited to the application of 'professionalism' (*zhiye zhuyi*), which was then being advocated by members of the liberal intelligentsia such as Ding Wenjiang (1887–1936).[55] Professionalism, which was partly inspired by the 'guild socialism' preached by John Dewey, advocated handing public responsibilities over to professional people: 'Up with government by artisans, government by farmers, government by merchants, by teachers, by scholars. Up with government of those who have work to do ... Oppose government by those who have nothing to do.'[56] Taken over in an overtly polemical style by the *Shanghai General Chamber of Commerce Monthly Review*, the theme turned into that of government by professional people (*zhiye zhengzhi*); those without any profession (*wuzhiyezhe*), that is 'nobles, militarists, bureaucrats and politicians', would forfeit their civic rights.[57]

Without going so far as that, most of the plans put forward for provincial constitutions singled out professional interests for particularly full representation and gave local authorities sweeping economic powers – the administration of the railways, telephones and telegraphs, the creation of issuing houses and so on.

Through autonomy, the bourgeoisie was seeking not only to emancipate itself from the bureaucracy, but also to establish an effective system of social control that would operate to its advantage. Recent studies have underlined the coincidence between the development of organs of self-government and that of taxation systems of the *lijia* type and insurance organisations of the *baojia* kind.[58] The proliferation of merchant militia during the early 1920s also testifies to the business circles' desire to take over the maintenance of order. In 1916, the organisation of these militia had been made subject to strict regulations. These measures had followed hard upon Yuan Shikai's dissolution of the local assemblies in 1914 and they had marked a return to the offensive on the part of the bureaucracy. As the movement for autonomy grew, the merchants demanded the liberalisation of these regulations; 'We are asking the government to allow all chambers of commerce to train their own militia so that they can safeguard their defence.'[59] Evoking the precedent of the Hanseatic League, the Hankou Chamber of Commerce went so far as to press for the creation of a veritable league of towns: 'If the towns manage to establish real union throughout the country, our strength will be enormous.'[60]

But even while it favoured autonomist tendencies, the decline of the authority of Peking was considered by the merchants to have negative aspects: no decision-taking could now be expected to preserve social order or to provide guidelines for economic modernisation, which had by now speeded up so much that structures to organise the unification of monetary and customs procedures needed to be set up. The bourgeoisie's nostalgic hankering after an effective State is reflected in many of the motions passed in the chambers of commerce, which continued to press the 'centre' (*zhongyang*) to issue directives and prohibitions and to step in to rectify abuses and so on. The merchants bewailed the impotence of the State even as they continued to fear its arbitrary power. Although they were pressing for autonomy, they could not bring themselves to give up the advantages of centralised order.

In an attempt to get their voices heard through official channels that would operate both flexibly and effectively, business circles set about, on the one hand, trying to establish control over the government, the better to regenerate it, and, on the other, investigating various means of restructuring the State.

During the 'golden age' years, the time-honoured pragmatism of the Chinese merchants took on a new significance: as well as defending the interests of their own particular group, they were now concerned to further progress more generally through a policy that aimed to solve specific problems as they presented themselves (*wenti*). This was the method, advocated by Hu Shi, that the bankers adopted in their relations with the weakened central government, which they were trying to impose their own views on: 'In a situation in which progress is impossible, we must nevertheless make progress.'[61]

Ever since the First World War, Chinese bankers had found themselves in a position of strength on account of the financial difficulties of the central government and the unwillingness of foreign backers to advance loans (for since 1920, these foreign financiers had been bound by the agreements of the New Consortium).[62] The modern Chinese banks were excluded from the financing of external trade by the foreign banks, and from the circuits of internal trade by the *qianzhuang*, so now they seized the opportunity to advance a large number of loans to the government. These investments were often more profitable than might be supposed from the state of public finances. Interest on the loans was generally paid on the nominal value of loan certificates that were usually acquired at much less than cost price. Profits were proportional to the hazards involved: both were extremely high, for the unpredictability and chaos of Chinese political life made speculation on the issuing and sale of loan certificates a very risky business.

Most of the banks involved either had some kind of official status or special connections with government circles. Nearly all were located in Peking or Tianjin and their directors and fund providers included many former and future ministers such as Liang Shiyi, Zhou Ziqi, Wang Kemin and Cao Rulin. The osmosis that operated between the banking and political circles of Peking is illustrated by the combined activities of the Communications Bank and its Clique. This immediately suggests that we might interpret the clashes between bankers and ministers from 1920 onwards as stemming from factional rivalries within the ruling politico-military bureaucracy. But this analysis, though pertinent, would be reductionist, for it takes no account of the links of solidarity between bankers that developed in the face of the failings and mistakes of the government.

The Peking Bankers' Association embodied the unity and power of the local banking community. The influence that it wielded in the National Federation of Bankers' Associations balanced that of the Shanghai banks. In 1920, when the imminence of governmental bankruptcy provoked their intervention at a political level, the Peking bankers, particularly the younger of them (Chang Kia-ngau, Zhou Zuomin (1884–1956) and Wu Dingchang), acted as spokesmen for all their colleagues. Like them, they were determined to 'clean up Chinese public finance'.[63] On the occasion of its first congress, held in Shanghai on 6 December 1920, the National Federation of Bankers' Associations warned the government that if it wanted funds from them it would have to cut down its military expenditure, readjust internal loans and reform the monetary system. As Chang Kia-ngau put it, the intransigence of the bankers was simply an 'expression of their patriotism': 'We will support most heartily any public loan that really aims at the benefit of the country.'[64] The formation of a Chinese Consortium in January 1921 came in response to their willingness to help the government provided it would agree to work for the common weal. The Rolling Stock Loan, the Shanghai Mint Loan and the Peking Octroi Loan which the Consortium agreed to advance a short time later, were all hedged by strict controlling clauses and demands for monetary reform and the reorganisation of the internal debt. The government came to heel: it set up a Commission for Monetary Reform and published its plan for paying off long-term loans.

The banking circles which were such vigilant critics of the Peking government at this time appear to have been speaking for the higher interests of the country as a whole. Their action 'bears a portent deeper than its influence in financial affairs. It is the assertion of a part of the populace – which, perforce must begin with a part – towards its rulers which spells democracy.[65] But the margin dividing control established in the general interest from control established in private interests and between democracy and plutocracy is dangerously narrow. The pragmatic course of action adopted by the bankers did not prove effective enough to regenerate the government or even to defend banking interests. By January 1922, the bankers had given up the idea of controlling the government, preferring to revert to putting themselves at its service and to speculate upon its fate. The bankers' associations of Peking and Shanghai continued to shower it with advice and criticism but gave up all attempts at coercion. By continuing to lend money to the Chinese government without insisting that, in exchange, it should apply the reforms ever promised and ever put off, the bankers were simply prolonging the life of a regime that they condemned.

The limits and failures of pragmatism led business circles to favour a complete recasting of the State system. After a decade of usurpation and military coups, to resuscitate the republican legality that had been instituted by the provisional constitution of 1912 seemed a virtual impossibility. So while the various intellectual groups showed off their constitutional erudition, comparing the respective advantages of Swiss federalism with those of the American brand, the Federation of Chambers of Commerce, as its meeting in October 1921, approved the idea of a National Convention (Guomin huiyi). Provincial assemblies and professional and educational associations would all be represented at this Convention, whose brief would be to decide upon a political regime, to reunite the country, to license troops and to reorganise financial affairs. A permanent executive committee drawn from the chambers of commerce federations and the educational societies was detailed to organise the convocation of this Convention in Shanghai.[66]

But when it eventually met – from March to September 1922 – the Convention did no more than put forward a few constitutional proposals. Meanwhile, the hopes of the liberals and the bourgeoisie came to focus on the warlord Wu Peifu (1874–1939), who for the time being judged it politic to play the card of republican legality. However, the political springtime that he ushered in, in Peking, was too short (lasting no more than a few months) to bring about the constitutional renewal desired by business circles. A military coup by Cao Kun, which ejected the President of the Republic in June 1923, announced the final crisis in which the republican legality that the constitution was supposed to restore foundered for ever.

Now faced with a political vacuum, the Shanghai business circles made an astonishing move: they decided to replace the crumbling State with a 'merchant power' the prompt débâcle of which provided a half-comic half-tragic illustration of the limits that geo-political necessities imposed upon the role of the bourgeoisie and, more generally, on the society of China as a whole.

On 23 June, the General Chamber of Commerce held an assembly in the course of which it declared its independence. Secession, in China a historically classic manifestation of opposition, was usually a course adopted by regional powers and its geographical effect tended to be one of those shifts in the political centre of gravity that are a recurrent feature of troubled times in China. What is surprising in this instance is to find such a strategy applied by a constitutive body – the General Chamber of Commerce – quite without any territorial basis or military force. Abandoning the by now definitively discredited idea of republican legality, the Shanghai businessmen took it upon themselves to ensure a return to 'democracy' by setting up a Committee of the

People's Government (Minzhi weiyuanhui) consisting of 70 members, to which the 35 directors on the board of the General Chamber of Commerce belonged on an *ex officio* basis. Turning its back upon the refuge of provincialism and on alibis of a constitutional nature, merchant power, as such, now laid claim to the leadership of the country.[67]

The audacity of this move provoked ironical sallies from Xu Qian and Yang Quan, both members of the Guomindang; 'Really, it is enough to make you laugh ... The Shanghai Chamber of Commerce wants to organise a government of merchants (*shangren zhengfu*) just as if, apart from the merchants of Shanghai, the people did not exist ... Our merchants are advancing blindly, acting madly and are radically mistaken: the government of the Shanghai merchants is the work of a very tiny group. This type of government is capable of managing only the internal problems of the Chamber of Commerce itself.'[68] Curiously enough, the Chamber's only encouragement came from Mao Zedong, who had been won over by united front policies: 'The Shanghai merchants ... have adopted revolutionary methods; in taking charge of national affairs they show overwhelming courage'.[69]

The mirage of merchant power soon faded away and by August the Shanghai General Chamber of Commerce was busy negotiating the maintenance of local peace with the warlords; the Committee of the People's Government had been replaced by a Militant Association set up to stop the war between the provinces of Zhejiang and Jiangsu!

It was really a problem of the political capacity of a weathercock bourgeoisie which was easily, sometimes quickly, moved but was incapable of tenaciously pursuing whatever course of action it adopted: 'Our chambers of commerce contain plenty of members of the elite ... but what worries me is this: once the meeting is over, the swallows will fly away ... and who will take care of all the unfinished business?.'[70]

But the major explanation for this failure lies in the methods adopted, the goal embraced and the unchanging nature of the Chinese geo-political situation. The methods adopted by the bourgeoisie were those of compromise and negotiation. The merchants relied on their public declarations and their telegrammed circulars to persuade the militarists to lay down their arms. That this was unrealistic was perfectly obvious to some people: 'Negotiating with militarists and politicians on the subject of the licensing of troops ... is like negotiating with a tiger to get its skin.'[71] But was not the very strategy of the bourgeoisie indissolubly linked with the goal for which it was striving? Was it not an integral part of the liberalism that it hoped to bring to triumph? Indeed, was it not the very expression of that liberalism? Yet what chance did liberalism stand in China in 1920? Through a historical tautology that went unrecognised by exporters of the model liberalism, as well as by the Westernised elites keen to find inspiration in it (the American ambassador Jacob Schurman, for example, and Hu Shi, the philosopher), the liberal regime in its elaborated form of self-government within a parliamentary system seemed to be able to function only in liberal societies – stable societies within which a minimal consensus allowed for the clash of different interests without these degenerating into violence and bringing about a definitive split. To say that liberalism was powerless to heal the ills of a China beset by civil war and with its national sovereignty under threat is to put it mildly: the very magnitude of those ills made it impossible for liberalism to gain a footing. The failure of the bourgeoisie between 1920 and 1923 certainly looks like a failure of 'liberalism in an illiberal age'.[72]

Chinese liberalism in the 1920s is more than the avatar of intellectual history it is often reduced to. It coincided with the flowering of urban society in the treaty ports and with the rise of a bourgeoisie whose influence proved all the greater because it remained a part of the class of the elite groups from which it had emerged and with which it remained united. This upsurge of the bourgeoisie during its golden age was the most audacious move made by Chinese autonomous society during the modern period. But what can a society achieve when abandoned to itself? How could its actions possibly be effective at a national level without the intervention of a government capable of converting its many proposals into a plan of more general application? Left without a partner, in the shape of the State, the Chinese bourgeoisie exhausted itself in a sterile monologue; the moves that it initiated collapsed and became bogged down in a narrow corporatism, a corporatism that sought to change the board of directors of the Shanghai Chamber of Commerce into the national government!

The failure of the bid for liberalism prompts one to reflect upon the importance of the State in the development of any society. Since Marx, we have often tended to assume that it is society that produces the State. The sorry history of the Chinese bourgeoisie in the 1920s shows, on the contrary, that the State is indispensable to the constitution of a society and that liberalism itself must be a product of the State. It is hardly surprising that the Chinese bourgeoisie and part of the May Fourth intelligentsia arrived at the conclusion that it was necessary to restore governmental authority and that, despite the fact that it meant giving up the autonomy that they had acquired thanks to economic expansion and the decline of the bureaucratic apparatus over the preceding years, they even worked towards that end.

5   Counter-revolution and the restoration of State power: the bourgeoisie rally to Chiang Kai-shek (1927)

Left isolated by the radicalisation of political life and alarmed by the spread of popular violence, the bourgeoisie ended up by rallying to Chiang Kai-shek and supporting the military coup which carried him to power in April 1927. Was this volte-face inevitable on the part of a class that was basically conservative and whose alliance with the revolution could never have lasted? Was it a case of an authentic bourgeois revolutionary nationalism being crushed by a minority of big compradores and bureaucratic entrepreneurs, and betrayed by them? Trotskyists and Stalinists for a long time wrangled over the interpretation of these events which, through the action of the Comintern, implicated their own political responsibility. That debate, which was really to do with the future of communism in the USSR, in the end had the effect of obscuring the role of the Chinese bourgeoisie which it appeared to be calling attention to. I am therefore deliberately stepping aside from it in order to study the intellectual tendencies, the networks of connections, the local constraints and the factional rivalries which too much attention paid retrospectively to the Chinese and international communist movement has up till now left in obscurity, for all these factors were essential in the political evolution of the bourgeoisie during the 1925–7 crisis.

The re-evaluation of the role of the State

The rallying of the bourgeoisie to Chiang Kai-shek was not just a choice dictated by circumstances and designed to avert the dangers of a revolutionary situation. The path towards it had been paved by a trend of political thought that had been developing for several years, particularly in the intellectual liberal circles that were close to the new bourgeoisie. As early as 1924, Jiang Menglin (1886–1964) was announcing the failure of liberalism and of the new education which had laid emphasis upon the development of the individual.[73] Under the influence of its new director, Chen Qitian, the magazine *The World of Education in China* (*Zhonghua jiaoyujie*) was advocating a nationalist education designed first and foremost to train young citizens who would be of use to the country. A national-state movement (*guojia zhuyi*) associated with Young China and the weekly, *The Awakened Lion* (*Xingshi zhoubao*), was led by Zeng Ji and Li Huang. These two men may have come under the influence of Charles Maurras during a stay in France in the early 1920s. At all events, they exalted the 'external structure' of the country and called for a revolution by the people as a whole (*quanmin geming*), that is an economic, political and cultural retraining that excluded any questioning of the social order.[74]

On certain points, the national-state movement was close to the nineteenth-century ideology of self-strengthening (*ziqiang*) and it arose as a reaction against Marxism and proletarian internationalism. Although it held the seeds of totalitarianism and fascism, initially it did not rule out democratic practices and its elitism was tempered by a measure of populism.

Meanwhile, within the Guomindang itself, conservative Marxists such as Dai Jitao were thinking along relatively parallel lines. From his youthful adhesion to communism Dai Jitao had retained a notion of the class struggle which he now applied to international rivalry, and an appreciation of Leninist techniques of organisation, which he was longing to implement in the service of a national revolution (*guomin geming*) in order to build up an integrated State ruled by an undivided political power.[75]

Even before 1927, these ideas appear to have become widely popular among both the traditional and the modern elite groups. It is hardly surprising that the bourgeoisie rallied to the idea of a strong State guaranteeing national unity and prosperity. And it would be mistaken to interpret its support simply as a reflex action of fear – dictatorship rather than revolution. As we have already seen, Chinese liberalism was perfectly prepared to accommodate a measure of interventionism, and its nostalgic yearning for a strong State dated back to well before the revolutionary explosion. The bourgeoisie had resigned itself to Yuan Shikai purely out of fear and lassitude, but things were different with the advent of Chiang Kai-shek. This it positively desired. The increasing isolation which it found itself confined to by the rise of the revolutionary movement inevitably magnified its need for State support.

The rise of the revolutionary movement and the increasing isolation of the bourgeoisie

From 1923 onwards, Sun Yat-sen's alignment with the communists and the elaboration of a united front policy gave new impetus to the revolutionary movement. Its progress can be charted from the establishment of its base in Canton, through the rise of the workers' trade union movement and the great anti-imperialist Movement of 30 May 1925, to the Northern Expedition (Beifa). In the towns, workers and intellectuals rallied in large numbers to this revolution, but the bourgeoisie – both the *ancien régime* and the new entrepreneurs – progressively disassociated themselves from it. The nationalistic slogans that had provided a unifying focus for the May Fourth Movement could no longer conceal the many social and political antagonisms. A series of clashes developed between the chambers of commerce and Sun Yat-sen, between the Merchants' Corps and the nationalist army cadets, and between the workers' trade unions and the employers' federations.

In the autumn of 1923, the Canton customs' crisis led to a head-on confrontation between Sun Yat-sen and the bourgeoisie of the treaty ports. Towards the end of the war, the increase in customs receipts had made it possible to siphon off a large annual surplus, which the foreign banks then put at the disposal of the central government in Peking. In 1919, the separatist military government of Canton had demanded and obtained that it should be paid a part of this surplus (13.7%). When the Canton government collapsed in March 1920, it had ceased to claim its rights. Sun returned to power in March 1923, following a number of vicissitudes, having been, between 1920 and 1922, first the ally, then the rival, of Chen Jiongming in Canton. Now he demanded that these payments be resumed and also that the arrears be made up. In the meantime, however, a decree issued by the President of the Chinese Republic on 29 July 1922 had allocated all customs surpluses to the fund for the repayment of the accumulated internal debt. Sun Yat-sen threatened to seize the Canton customs receipts by force. In so doing he not only came up against the interests of the foreign powers, but also worried the Chinese bankers and entrepreneurs who held public loan certificates guaranteed by the customs revenues. The various commercial and banking associations of Shanghai and Tianjin begged him not to compromise their interests: 'It was you who founded the Republic ... You have the life of the merchants at heart, we earnestly hope that you will respect the integrity of the customs revenues so that the fund for paying off debts can be kept supplied and the ruination of the merchants be averted.'[76]

Sun Yat-sen's communist allies came to his aid. They defended his policies and tried to shift the debate to a higher level, enlightening the bourgeoisie as to its true interests and contrasting the advantage of immediate profit unfavourably with longer-term prospects of future development; 'Sun's only policy is to restore the sovereignty of the customs ... Not only is this policy not designed to harm the commercial and banking world, but it aims in particular to serve the sovereignty of the State and the interests of the middle classes! Those poor Chinese merchants! Poor bankers! They really lack the most elementary understanding and know nothing about politics.'[77]

The combined pressure of foreign diplomatic bodies and Chinese public opinion forced Sun Yat-sen to give up his plan. But the incident affords one a chance to gauge the hostility that the modern bankers and entrepreneurs of Shanghai and Tianjin were by now feeling towards the revolutionary leader and his policies.

The hostility of the traditional merchants was no less strong. It burst out a few months later on the occasion of the Merchants' Corps incident in Canton. Sun had been ejected from Canton in 1922 but returned early in the following year, thanks to the aid of mercenaries from Yunnan and Guangxi. The military government that he proceeded to set up was always fragile, for it was incapable of controlling the generals, who were his protectors and were constantly demanding further funds. The exploitation and extortion that Sun was now obliged to tolerate caused all the well-to-do of the town to turn against him, together with all the rich Cantonese merchants overseas whose support had been so precious to him at the time of the 1911 revolution.[78] In 1924, the merchants and entrepreneurs refused to accept the paper money issued by the lcoal authorities, organised a series of strikes and called upon the Merchants' Corps to come to their aid. This body had already reached a strength of 13,000 by the end of 1923. Equipment costs were paid by various businesses, some of which maintained 30 or more militiamen. The organisation of these militia spread to a hundred or so towns in Guangdong province. In June 1924, all these volunteer bodies formed a Federated Provincial Corps headed by Chan Lin-pak, a comprador of the Hong Kong and Shanghai Bank and the brother of the president of the Chamber of Commerce. Chan Lin-pak himself described the movement as an organisation for the defence of local interests: 'We are tired of the frequent interruptions of inland traffic, the drop of our trade, the inability of our raw materials to reach their proper market, the loss to our investments . . . The new Merchants' Volunteer Corps of [Guangdong] has no other outside object or purpose than to be a non-partisan military unit for local self-defence'.[79]

The demands of the merchants of Canton in 1924 took up the familiar theme of local autonomy: the guilds should resume responsibility for urban policing and monetary control, and surtax should be abolished. The political ideology and inclinations represented by these merchant militia thus appear to have changed very little, but the extremely rapid radicalisation of Sun's government in 1923 and 1924 brought out their conservative side. Ever since the Guomindang's Reorganisation Congress in January 1924, Sun had been seeking to draw his support from the masses.

The conflict that broke out during the summer of 1924, between the merchants' organisations, on the one hand, and the revolutionary government and workers' unions, on the other, showed up the implicit meanings of all the autonomist slogans. In 1911, the defence of local interests had been assimilated to democracy by reformists and revolutionaries alike. Now it looked more like protection for the elite groups, pure and simple. And the clash of arms with which the conflict ended in October 1924 displayed all the violence of class warfare.

Now that they had lost the popular support that they had hitherto used to protect their own interests, the urban elite groups were obliged to resort to the aid of foreigners. The Cantonese merchants could rely upon a wide network of collusion in the British consulate, the Hong Kong and Shanghai Bank and the customs administration, through which they could order, pay for and import the arms destined to equip their Merchants' Corps. It was in fact a delivery of these armaments that triggered the final confrontation on 15 October 1924. In the course of it, the merchant militia were crushed by government troops and the business district of Xiguan, in western Canton, was burnt to the ground and looted.

In a China where the defence of liberties often became identified with that of local privileges, it is not surprising to find class warfare breaking out over the issue of provincial autonomy. One year later, the problems of the relationship between the bourgeoisie and the revolution was expressed at a national level with the explosion, in the major Chinese towns, of the Movement of 30 May 1925.

The Movement of 30 May 1925

Like the May Fourth Movement, that of 30 May 1925 unfolded in the name of nationalism and anti-imperialism. It was sparked off by a local incident – the death of a striker in a Japanese cotton mill in Shanghai and the subsequent bloody repression of a demonstration organised in the worker's memory. It soon spread to other regions of China, where equally serious incidents flared up in Hankou on 12 June and in Canton on 23 June. The main issue that soon emerged was once again the question of the foreign presence in China and the regime imposed by international treaties. The Thirteen Demands presented by the Shanghai Chamber of Commerce in June 1925 and retained as a basis for negotiations between the commissioners of the Peking government and diplomatic representatives requested that the guilty be punished and that the victims receive compensation. In addition, it made the following proposals: (a) that the Mixed Court of the International Settlement should be returned to the Chinese authorities (article 6); (b) that the Chinese residents should be represented on the Shanghai Municipal Council (article 9); (c) that external roads constructed outside the Settlement should be given back to China (article 10); and (d) that plans for increasing port dues and concerning censorship should be withdrawn (article 11). The means of action had changed hardly at all. The general strike called on 31 May in Shanghai went on until 25 June. And it spread to other towns: in Canton it was to last for 16 months. It was accompanied by a boycott directed initially against Japan, and then against Great Britain.

As in 1919, there were noticeable divergences within the Shanghai bourgeoisie, between the moderates of the General Chamber of Commerce and the more radical members of the street associations, the Commercial Federation and the activists of the Association of

Workers, Merchants and Students (Gongshangxuehui), created on 7 June, to unite the Movement.[80]

What was different in 1925 was the presence, in the large Chinese towns and in particular in Shanghai, of a powerful workers' movement led by a Leninist-type revolutionary party.[81] The General Trades Union, which was created in 1925 in Shanghai and was controlled by the communists, brought together 117 workers' associations with an overall membership of 218,000. This was an autonomous, well-organised force with its own particular objectives. The massive intervention of the working class altered, on the one hand, the conditions of dialogue (or confrontation) between the Chinese and the foreigners and, on the other, the balance of power within the nationalist movement itself.

In 1925, the size of the mass movements frightened the foreign residents, propelling them into negotiations and compromise. In Shanghai, the Chinese side was, as in the past, put by the General Chamber of Commerce, represented by its president Yu Xiaqing and its vice-president Fang Jiaobo. Thanks to the intervention of the working class, the nationalist movement thus acquired new force and the bourgeoisie was on the point of obtaining the reforms for which it had been pressing ever since 1905. The beginning of the crisis offered the commercial organisations a mediating role that they seized to advance their own interests. At this point, they appeared to be close to the trade unions and the strikers. The General Chamber of Commerce set up a Committee for Aid and Peace which collected 2.2 million dollars;[82] it also organised a strike fund.[83]

However, all this was a far cry from the political alliance that has so often been described. Following the conflicts described above and the death, in March 1925, of Sun Yat-sen – the old charismatic leader in whom the merchant communities had so often placed their trust and who, despite the recent disappointments, had continued to inspire them with respect and admiration – the gap between the bourgeoisie and the revolutionary movement grew wider and wider. The representatives of the Shanghai General Chamber of Commerce tended to negotiate with the strikers as they would with any other troublemakers. Like all the elites in provincial towns, they considered themselves responsible for the maintenance of local order and were prepared to make considerable financial sacrifices to ensure 'public peace'. Yu Xiaqing, whose remarkable energy dominated these months of crisis and who was involved in every kind of negotiation, did not act solely in his capacity as president of the General Chamber of Commerce and spokesman for the merchants. As the designated organiser (*huiban*) of a future autonomous municipality, which he had actually negotiated to set up, back in the months of February and March, he was also the official representative of local interests as a whole.[84] Concerned as he was to preserve his popularity, he was most attentive to public opinion: '[He] will heed the smallest criticism from a tiny Chinese organization.'[85] *A fortiori*, he soon gave way when the strikers resorted to violence, as 5,000 dockers did on 13 August. They looted two ships belonging to the Sanbei Company, of which Yu was the proprietor, in a bid to get the Chamber of Commerce to pay them strike compensation.[86] The fact that the Shanghai bourgeoisie agreed to aid the strikers of the summer of 1925 did not only (or even so much) betoken their sympathy for the workers' cause; it was also a consequence of their habitual practice of compromise in the name of the Confucian ideal of social consensus (behaviour which many foreign observers and historians tend to criticise as being two-faced).

Yet amid the patriotic fervour of the summer of 1925, the apparent consensus may be misleading. The authorities of the International Settlement wanted to eject the Chinese bourgeoisie from its position as mediator and arbiter and to force it to abandon the united front of anti-imperialism and concentrate instead on defending the common interests of the employers. To that end, on 6 July 1925, they decided to cut off central electricity supplies: the Chinese factories, which had so far been spared by the strikes, were now obliged to close their doors.

In the months that followed, the representatives of the Chamber of Commerce continued to act as intermediaries, but they had lost the initiative. This had passed, on the one hand, to the foreigners, who pursued a policy of concession alternating with blackmail, and, on the other, to the workers' trade unions.

When the bourgeoisie rallied to the side of Chiang Kai-shek two years later, in April 1927, its choice appeared on the face of it to contradict its earlier commitments. This abrupt volte-face made by an upper bourgeoisie which suddenly took fright at the size of the mass movement has often been condemned. But in truth, beneath all the patriotic ardour of May and June 1925, it is hard to make out any real revolutionary commitment on the part of the bourgeoisie. In these times of crisis, the representatives of the chambers of commerce continued to try to adapt to the situation, as they had always done. They tried to preserve a society which was still in the making and was for that reason all the more vulnerable to revolutionary violence and extremism. From their point of view, it seemed less risky to place their trust in the State than to rush headlong into revolution.

The bourgeoisie rallies to Chiang Kai-shek

The drawing-together of Chiang Kai-shek and the bourgeoisie was encouraged by long standing personal connections, by the political evolution of the Guomindang and also by the weakening of the merchant community of Shanghai. Those personal connections had been forged in Shanghai at the time of the 1911 revolution, in the entourage of the military governor Chen Qimei. After Chen's death, Yu Xiaqing and Zhang Jingjiang (1877–1950), his old collaborators from the Chamber of Commerce and the Zhejiang Clique, promoted the career of his protégé, Chiang Kai-shek. In 1920, when at the request of Sun Yat-sen, who needed funds, Yu Xiaqing set up the Shanghai Stock and Commodity Exchange, he made Chiang Kai-shek a partner in the venture. It brought together a number of figures all of whom were later to play an important role in Chiang's rise to power: Chen Guofu (1892–1951), who was Chen Qimei's nephew; Dai Jitao, one of the Guomindang's most brilliant theorists; and Wen Lanting, who was a friend of Yu Xiaqing and a director of the General Chamber of Commerce.[87]

The relations between the Chinese bourgeoisie and the Guomindang reflect all the political ambiguities of the years 1925–6. When faced with the business community of Canton, badly hit by the repression of 1924, the Guomindang government employed tactics of both seduction – more or less dictated by the doctrine of the united front – and precaution. Its aim was to prevent the rebirth of the bourgeoisie as an autonomous political force. It forbade the reconstitution of the Merchants' Corps, and all activities of a social or philanthropic nature were brought under strict control. At the same time, the government made an effort to get along with such merchants as were prepared to collaborate with it. It encouraged the formation of an Association of Cantonese Merchants, to rival the Chamber of Commerce. It tried to replace the Merchants' Corps by a citizen body to be financed by commercial firms but whose political and military training would fall to the government authorities. Those who refused to cooperate were labelled 'merchants of the comprador type' and were placed under the direct supervision of the Guomindang.[88]

The policy of the Guomindang was not to ruin or destroy the merchant community but to bring it under the supervision of the party and into its service (*danghua*). The base at Canton allowed it to try out what later became the strategies of the Nanking government. The success of its policies in Canton was aided by the defeat and elimination of the town's Merchants' Corps in October 1924, by the flight of the richest merchants, who left to escape from the 'Reds', and also by the relatively old-fashioned character of the Cantonese bourgeoisie, which was still closely linked with the land – a class more elite than entrepreneurial.

The Cantonese bourgeoisie was brought to heel. As for the Shanghai bourgeoisie, it rallied of its own accord. The rallying of the Shanghai bourgeoisie to Chiang Kai-shek has been presented in a number of classic interpretations (for instance, those of Harold Isaacs and André Malraux) as the counter-revolutionary choice made by a bourgeoisie under threat from the insurrectional strikes of November 1926 and January 1927. In reality, it was a triumph for the progressive elements within the merchant community.

Since 1926, following the victorious march of the Northern Expedition (Beifa) and the uprisings that preceded and accompanied it, the mass movements had been putting the whole of the Shanghai bourgeoisie on the defensive. It was not a matter of choosing whether to support the mass movement or resist it, simply of deciding upon the best means of resistance. Some pressed for an alliance with the forces of local militarism which, in Zhejiang province, took the shape of General Sun Chuanfang. Others, who were either more subtle or better informed about the deeper intentions of Chiang Kai-shek, were in favour of placing their trust in the non-communist wing of the Guomindang.

The General Chamber of Commerce elections in June 1926 spotlighted the political divisions within the merchant class. The old pro-Japanese clique, which had been ousted in 1919–20, returned in force with the support of Sun Chuanfang. As a sign of protest against these rigged elections, the outgoing president, Yu Xiaqing, went off on a trip to Japan and 150 members of the Chamber refused to vote. Their abstention facilitated the formation of a board of directors that was undivided but also unrepresentative. The banker Fu Xiao'an had a tough time assuming the presidency: neither his role nor his own personality went unchallenged.[89] Meanwhile, a large fraction of the merchant community went over to Yu Xiaqing and kept up a vociferous campaign of protest throughout the autumn of 1926.

The alliance which helped Chiang Kai-shek to power in Shanghai in late March and early April 1927 was thus formed not with the right wing of the bourgeoisie, by now discredited by its collaboration with Sun Chuanfang, but on the contrary with its most fervently nationalist, modernist and – up to a point – democratic elements. The modern bankers of Shanghai provided Chiang Kai-shek with essential financial assistance. In the autumn of 1926 Chang Kia-ngau, then vice-governor of the Bank of China, arranged for a loan of 500,000 dollars to the Central Bank of Canton, that is to say one-quarter of the sum needed to finance the first phase of the Guomindang troops' Northern Expedition.[90] In January 1926, the Bank of China made another, equally large loan.

When the revolutionary troops arrived in Shanghai, the supply of financial aid from the modern banks to the Guomindang was organised and intensified. Chen Guangfu, the president of the Shanghai Bank of Trade and Savings, met with Chiang Kai-shek several times in late March 1926. Chen agreed to chair a financial commission with the task of raising a loan of 30 million dollars: 2.5% Treasury Bonds were to be guaranteed by the customs surpluses. Chen Guangfu secured the support of the principal financiers of Shanghai. As well as Chiang Kia-ngau, he approached the representatives of both the Shanghai Bankers' Associations and the Native Bankers' Guild. The loan was raised within three months. Meanwhile, Chiang Kai-shek kept pressing for advances of funds to be valorised on the product of the loan. A quarter of a century later, Chen Guangfu explained, in connection with the role that he had played in these events, that his point of view had reflected that of the Shanghai business circles in general: believing that the Guomindang would bring peace and prosperity to the country, his main concern had been to topple the militarists.[91]

As in Canton in 1924, the development of a revolutionary situation in Shanghai, in the spring of 1927, brought about a general realignment of the social forces present. The radical bourgeoisie of the early 1920s continued to fight for Chinese representation on the

Shanghai Municipal Council, for the surrender of the Mixed Court, and against the encroachments of militarism. But its position on the political chessboard had changed completely. Behind the cliché of a national bourgeoisie betraying the revolution under the influence of a clique of compradores, another reality takes shape: here was a bourgeoisie whose radicalism turned into conservatism purely as a result of the general evolution of circumstances which changed its relations to other political forces and protagonists. The bourgeoisie's reversion to conservatism in this instance certainly appears as Karl Mannheim has defined it: it was a dynamic move that essentially represented a conscious rejection of progressivism.[92]

It is an analysis that is confirmed by a study of the reorganisation and mergers that took place in the institutions of the merchant community in the spring of 1927.[93] The General Chamber of Commerce that had emerged from the controversial elections of 1926 now lost its leading role to a Shanghai Federation of Commerce and Industry (Shanghai shangye lianhehui) created and organised by Yu Xiaqing. It was this federation that made contact with Chiang Kai-shek when he arrived in Shanghai on 26 March and immediately offered him a loan of 3 million dollars if only he would re-establish order – in other words break the power of the communist trade unions. The federation was the political mouthpiece for the major commercial organisations of the town which, through their corporative allegiances, were also connected with the Alliance of Shanghai Merchants (Hushang xiehui). Like all the merchant alliances – both official and clandestine – set up since 1926 in China, the Alliance of Shanghai was a Guomindang organisation sprung from the Merchants' Department (Shangminbu) that had been created on the occasion of the Second Party Congress, in January 1926. Very little is known about this Alliance of Shanghai until the point at which it emerged from clandestinity on 20 March 1927. But it appears to have been closely linked with the Federation of Street Associations, whose structures it was to adopt to speed up its own expansion during the month of April 1927. Thus the Federation of Commerce and Industry, created to support the rise of Chiang Kai-shek, merged with the Federation of Street Associations, which many historians consider to have been the organ of the 'lower progressive bourgeoisie' ever since it appeared during the May Fourth Movement.

The bourgeoisie's collaboration with Chiang Kai-shek was positively desired by most of the merchant community and was of great value to Chiang himself. When the merchants refused to sit in the provisional municipal government set up on 29 March under the auspices of the communist trade unions, they effectively paralysed the political initiative of the workers' organisations. The money loaned to Chiang Kai-shek enabled him to recruit and pay strong arm men, most of them members of the Green Gang, and on 12 April at dawn these attacked and disarmed the workers' militia.

Almost immediately, however, the bourgeoisie's relationship of collaboration with the Guomindang turned into one of subordination on one side and exploitation on the other. Having brought off his 12 April coup, Chiang Kai-shek demanded more funds, stepped up extortionate demands and blackmail and subjected the merchants to a veritable reign of terror.[94]

The bankers' enthusiasm cooled. Having overseen the issue of the 30-million-dollar loan stock demanded by Chiang Kai-shek, Chen Guangfu broke off all contact with the nationalist government.[95] As for Chang Kia-ngau, in September 1928 he clashed openly with Chiang Kai-shek, who threatened to throw him into jail.[96] The Chamber of Commerce had lost the political authority it used to wield. Chiang Kai-shek now negotiated with *ad hoc* organisations that could put up no resistance to being sucked into the Guomindang apparatus. Chiang Kai-shek's repression of the bourgeoisie, which began as early as mid-April 1927, looked like a continuation of the factional struggles already taking place within the bourgeoisie. The warrant of arrest put out for Fu Xiao'an, the confiscation of much of his property and the cancellation of his election to the presidency of the General Chamber of Commerce, which was now placed under a supervisory committee, were all measures much to the liking of Yu Xiaqing and his friends. Having been ejected from the board of directors of the Chamber of Commerce in 1926, they regained control of it at the end of April 1927, when three of them (Yu Xiaqing, Wang Yiting and Feng Shaoshan) were requested to sit on a governmental committee set up to supervise its activities. The bourgeoisie was no longer rebelling against abuses of power such as these which, at other times and in other places, it had so vigorously condemned and resisted, for now they were serving the direct interests of the majority faction. The 1927 betrayal was not so much a betrayal of the proletariat by the bourgeoisie as a betrayal of the bourgeoisie by itself. By abdicating its political autonomy, the bourgeoisie laid itself at the mercy of the State power that it had itself helped to restore.

The political rise and fall of the Chinese bourgeoisie began with the revolution which toppled State power in 1911 and ended with the military coup that restored it in 1927. The interval between those two dates saw the emergence of the nearest thing to an autonomous society in Chinese history – an urban society dominated by the united front of business circles, well structured and inspired by a modernist and pro-Western intelligentsia. The experiments and innovations of that golden age still provide terms of reference for our understanding of modern China.

The great interest retrospectively taken in the development of communism, combined with a largely mistaken idea of the period, has led many historians to consider this golden age purely in relation to the later unfolding of the Chinese revolution and to interpret it in a restrictive and teleological fashion, presenting it as a factor of failure in the revolution and obscuring its extraordinary achievements of adaptation and innovation. With that point of view, they have concentrated their attention upon the revolutionary capacity of the Chinese bourgeoisie and upon its 'changes of heart' and 'contradictions'. The analysis of the bourgeoisie and its political role produced by Marxism is a mythical one.

The emergence of an autonomous society tends naturally to limit the interventions of State power, and the defence of individual – or local – liberties encourages a measure of pluralism. But after 1911, the very disintegration of the Chinese State checked the development of an anti-government opposition of the kind that provided the basis for the revolutionary character of the French bourgeoisie at the end of the eighteenth century and of the Russian bourgeoisie a hundred years later. Left to its own devices and absorbed in negotiating with various possible partners and in working for a consensus among the different elite groups, the Chinese bourgeoisie, in contrast, seems to have constituted a factor of stability and moderation in the political life of the 1920s.

All the same, this political life was constantly dominated by opposition to foreign moves of an imperialistic nature. And it is perhaps fair to wonder whether for the Chinese bourgeoisie anti-imperialism did not play the role that opposition to the government played in the history of the European bourgeoisies. Perhaps the nationalism of the Chinese bourgeoisie lends legitimacy to the revolutionary aura with which contemporary historiography is prone to surround it.

6 ⮞ Capitalism, Westernisation and nationalism

When the First World War came to an end, imperialism returned to the offensive in China, aiming to restore rights acquired earlier and reactivate the treaty system. But at the same time, at the Washington Conference (1921–2), modes of domination began to undergo a profound transformation that was eventually to lead to the collapse of the old classic empires and the establishment of United States world hegemony. Seen from China's position, the process of imperialism at this period appeared both complex and contradictory. It combined traditional motives and well-tried techniques of penetration with the more specifically political, ideological and cultural preoccupations which nowadays underpin all plans for general domination over the Third World. American diplomats, for a while supported by the British, came up with the idea of handing over powers to the local bourgeoisies. The latter were thus pushed into assuming a leading political role and taking over from the old colonisers.

Chinese business circles used their new position to attempt to consolidate the bases of a growth that had largely resulted from fortuitous circumstances and to strengthen their own power. Discriminating between 'good' and 'bad' foreigners, they tried to exploit the procedures of American political hegemony – procedures still ill-defined and inclined to be equated with the cosmopolitan opening-up of China – to check manifestations of the classic type of imperialism (particularly on the part of the Japanese, at this juncture), and to establish their own merchant power.

The American efforts, which anticipated the neo-colonialist experiments that were to take place after the Second World War, seem to have been somewhat premature. The United States, not yet recognised as the foremost world power, was unable to develop its strategies freely and was soon forced to abandon the principles proclaimed at the

Washington Conference and revert to the old-fashioned imperialism practised by the Japanese and the British. Besides, the Chinese bourgeoisie was unable to accomplish what was expected of it. The failure of merchant power that we have examined in Chapter 5 was not solely a consequence of the grave difficulties with which China was beset and the intrinsic weaknesses of the bourgeoisie itself. It was also caused by the artificiality of this political experiment to a large extent engineered by the foreigners.

The deterioration of Sino-foreign relations between 1923 and 1927 caused bourgeois nationalism to become much more inward-looking and to revert to tradition. After trying cosmopolitanism and neo-colonialism, it was a matter of a return to basic Chinese principles.

The fact that this deterioration coincided with the switch from prosperity to crisis in no way justifies a determinist interpretation of the period, but it does raise the problem of the relationship between bourgeois nationalism and economic growth, that is the problem of the specific nature and effectiveness of bourgeois nationalism.

1   Bourgeois nationalism and Chinese nationalism

Many Marxist historians of China root the existence of bourgeois nationalism in national capital. According to them, the entrepreneurs who used only Chinese capital were hostile to the foreign presence and foreign competition. Conversely, the compradores were led, through their dependence upon foreign employers and providers of funds, to adopt a policy of compromise if not invariably open collaboration.[1]

It is my belief that an examination of the facts does not confirm such an analysis. For one thing, it is by no means certain that any sizeable modern businesses were founded solely upon Chinese capital. Secondly, even if such national capital did exist, it cannot be considered as the necessary condition of nationalistic commitment. It is true to say that in some cases the benefits that were to be derived from economic collaboration with foreigners made Chinese businessmen more prone to compromise. For instance, the pro-Japanese position adopted by the Shanghai General Chamber of Commerce at the beginning of the May Fourth Movement may in part be explained by the business, financial and commercial links with Japan of the president of the Chamber, Zhu Baosan, and a number of its other principal directors – the Cantonese merchant Gu Xinyi, the comprador Wang Yiting and the coal wholesaler Xie Hengchuang.[2] But at the very same date, the Tianjin Guild of Compradores was energetically supporting the vice-president of the local chamber of commerce, Bian Yinchang, in his campaign for an anti-Japanese boycott.[3]

In reality, bourgeois nationalism in the golden age seems to have stemmed largely from the anti-imperialist feeling that was common to the whole of urban society. No less than the officials, the intellectuals and the lower strata, the merchants and businessmen suffered from Chinese humiliations and rebelled against the injustices heaped upon their country. Every year, they commemorated a National Humiliation Day on 7 May, on the anniversary of the presentation of the Japanese ultimatum of the Twenty-one Demands in 1915. In May 1923, 10,000 Shanghai businessmen joined a huge demonstration. The bourgeoisie added its voice to the rest that were demanding that wrongs be righted, that the Twenty-one Demands be abolished, that extraterritoriality be abolished and that tariff autonomy be restored. It waxed indignant at the scorn that foreign businessmen took no trouble to hide: 'It seems to us that more friendliness and fairer treatment by the several foreign commercial organizations in the Far East toward the Chinese merchants should be emphasized ... Our Chinese merchants suffer much from unfriendliness and unfairness ... Foreign merchants in Shanghai seem to have formed an exclusive set. Individual Chinese merchants or firms have not the privilege of associating with them ... Such an aristocratic manner of living without due regard for their hosts and customers does hurt the feelings of our merchants.'[4]

None of these themes was new, none of this behaviour was peculiar to the bourgeoisie. So perhaps we should ask ourselves what *was* specific about bourgeois nationalism. Indeed, in my view, the question is not only legitimate but necessary. It is certainly legitimate, since economic expansion – whether seen as motivation or strategy – was one of the essential manifestations of modern imperialism. And while that expansion took place to the detriment of the general interests of the dominated country, its most immediate effects were felt in areas such as trade, industry and finance, areas that constituted the peculiar province of the business bourgeoisie. The Chinese merchants were thus bound to be doubly affected by foreign economic intervention: as citizens anxious to 'save the country' (*jiuguo*) and also as entrepreneurs threatened by competition. The fact was – and this is what makes it necessary to ask that question about specificity – that the Chinese merchants themselves recognised that their relations with imperialism worked both ways. In an address to the National Conference of Bankers' Associations, the secretary of the Tianjin Chamber of Commerce had the following comments to make on the plan for a Chinese Banking Consortium designed to undermine the International Consortium: 'The domain that this consortium aims to control falls entirely within your responsibilities ... If you can produce no plan, the foreign consortium will achieve its own aims ... and inevitably you will be blamed ... I sincerely hope that you will consider the development of industry and the management of finance as tasks which, in the interests of the Chinese people, must devolve upon you alone.'[5]

Did the particular responsibility that the bourgeoisie accepted in the area of economic and financial development cause it to adopt a particular position or to analyse the dangers of imperialism in its own specific way?

Bourgeois nationalism and economic exploitation

To establish the existence of a specifically bourgeois nationalism it would be necessary first to show that exploitation beneficial to foreign entrepreneurs and prejudicial to Chinese ones really did take place. That China was politically, economically and financially dependent at this time is well known. But it is much more difficult to determine to what degree that dependence truly did lead to exploitation. Some of the best historians of Chinese economics deny the existence of any such exploitation and regard bourgeois nationalism as a purely political and psychological reaction, the reaction of a class humiliated but not actually damaged.[6]

With the limited information at present at our disposal, we should not engage in a discussion of such a general nature. A number of definite facts certainly show that foreign exploitation both took place and was directly prejudicial to the interests of the Chinese bourgeoisie during the 1920s.[7] But these scattered indications do not allow us to form an overall macro-economic picture. For the Chinese bourgeoisie also stood to gain from a process of development in which the foreigners played an important role: common interests quite often led to reflexes of real solidarity between the two groups. Their ambivalent position did not encourage the Chinese bourgeoisie to regard foreign economic intervention as a break imposed upon national development or even upon its own expansion.

The bourgeoisie's relative indifference to the specifically economic aspects of foreign imperialism can also be explained by the deficiencies of the economic analyses that it produced. These were based on concepts borrowed either from liberalism or from Western socialism, all equally inadequate.

When the leader writer of the *Shanghai General Chamber of Commerce Monthly Review* tried to define the causes for the failure of Chinese industry, he mentioned the scorn that traditional society displayed towards the merchants and craftsmen, the lack of technical training, the indifference shown by public authorities and the deficiencies of commercial legislation and information services, but he made no mention of foreign imperialism. Industrial stagnation was blamed upon the failure of local business circles to adapt and change.[8] In a burst of self-accusation, the General Chamber of Commerce's *Review* accepted the diagnosis produced by the theorists of classic liberal economics. These considered international trade to be the 'driving force of growth' through which economic progress could spread from industrialised countries to less advanced ones. According to them, the persistence of underdevelopment was to be explained by the obstacles with which the political structures and cultural customs of traditional societies blocked these external stimuli.

What seems more surprising in this debate is the limited contribution made by the Marxist–Leninist theories that were now beginning to circulate in China. To be sure, many articles in the communist press decried the economic aspects of imperialist domination. But their analyses reflected the Europe-centred attitudes of the authors they were inspired by. Lenin and his disciples were above all concerned to reveal the economic *motivations* of imperialist expansion, and they concentrated their attention upon ideas that were to do with advanced capitalist countries, for example the hypothesis of underconsumption, and the trend of declining profits. They had reflected hardly at all upon the specifically economic consequences of imperialist expansion in colonial and semi-colonial countries. They concluded that in the long run the expansion of international capitalism would bring about the industrialisation of underdeveloped zones and that competition from these would then threaten the mother countries. They looked forward to the eventual growth in the underdeveloped countries with an optimism that puts one in mind of the liberal theorists. Thus the Chinese communists reproached the foreigners not for undermining their economic development but for furthering that development for their own ends. The 'rape of the Third World' and the 'development of underdevelopment' were not at this date theoretical preoccupations, let alone rallying cries.

Chinese communist writing of the 1920s reflects these limitations. When Zhang Guotao analyses the evils of imperialist domination, he is chiefly concerned with the humiliation involved for the Chinese people. When he ventures onto economic ground, it is to deplore the crisis in the cottage industries, a crisis which – insofar as it existed – testified to changing trends in production but not necessarily to unfavourable ones. Zhang notes some of the aspects to foreign exploitation but only those at governmental level. He condemns the heavy payments imposed upon the Chinese government by way of indemnities or as interest due to the foreigners, but he concentrates chiefly upon the political mechanisms that make such exploitation possible and upon its social consequences. At no point does he attempt to establish any connection between the financial drain, on the one hand, and the difficulties caused by the accumulation of capital and the development of investments, on the other: 'All we know is that one half of the taxes that we pay each year are extorted by foreign governments and bankers ... We have put up with all these sufferings and humiliations for long enough.'[9]

Faced with foreign intervention, the Chinese bourgeoisie does seem to have been aware of the particular responsibilities conferred upon it by the role that it played in the economic development of the nation. But the ambiguity of its own interests and the inadequacy of contemporary thinking in the area of economic theory prevented it from analysing the problem of economic dependence in depth. Its battle against foreign intervention was thus essentially waged on political grounds, as an integral part of the nationalist movement by which the country was currently being shaken. The fact that there were specific interests at stake for the bourgeoisie was not enough to give bourgeois nationalism a truly original character. Nevertheless, it did stamp it with some specific features that marked it out from Chinese nationalism in general.

The moderation of bourgeois nationalism: towards an ideology of cooperation

To the extent that it was oriented essentially towards compromise and not confrontation, bourgeois nationalism was remarkable for its moderation. This was reflected in the relative mildness of its diplomatic claims so far as economic interests were concerned. Besides, a very real sense of its responsibilities distanced the bourgeoisie from the fanatical xenophobia of much of China and caused it to desire true economic cooperation with its foreign partners.

The economic preoccupations of the bourgeoisie marked its nationalism in several ways. In the campaign against the unequal treaties, for example, it is clear that the bourgeoisie did not attach as much importance and urgency to the abolition of extraterritoriality as to the restoration of tariff autonomy.

Immediately after the First World War, Chinese business circles launched a campaign for the restoration of tariff autonomy. In February 1922, when it was announced that the negotiators were planning to make a 5% reduction in the Chinese customs tariff, the Shanghai General Chamber of Commerce set up a special committee with the task of working out how the terms of this revision should be implemented.[10] The countries that were signatories to the Washington agreements also planned to hold a special customs conference to study the abolition of internal customs dues (*lijin*) and, in the longer term, the return of China to complete tariff freedom. The chambers of commerce now set about working out how to apply this programme. In particular, they tried to define the fiscal reforms called for by the abolition of the *lijin* and to modify them to suit commercial and industrial interests.[11] Over and above the immediate measures necessary, they hoped for and demanded a return to complete tariff autonomy. They dreamed of a 'Great Wall designed to protect national produce ... All countries impose heavy taxes on imports of manufactured products ... Our situation is the most unfair in the world ... Today, the Chinese people fervently desires to be delivered from this system, in order to set up Chinese industry.'[12]

Compared with this theme of tariff autonomy, which is constantly reiterated and developed in both political and economic terms, the theme of extraterritoriality seems to have been of minor importance. At the Washington Conference, the merchants certainly chimed in with all the other voices that were demanding the abolition of extraterritoriality but, practically speaking, 'they abstain from taking sides ... The chambers of commerce maintain a prudent reserve ... The merchants, who are practical people, have appreciated the advantages of foreign protection in the big ports and the alacrity with which they hasten to shelter under the foreign umbrella in the foreign concessions testifies in no mean fashion to the favour with which they regard this system.'[13]

Those views, voiced by a French resident, may be complacent but they were not unfounded. After the sacking of the town of Yichang (Hunan) in 1921, the foreign merchants there demanded that an International Settlement be set up in the port. The Hankou General Chamber of Commerce protested against the idea, but the Chinese merchants of Yichang itself supported it.[14] In the business circles of Shanghai, the violent campaign then being organised against the authorities of the International Settlement did not aim to abolish the Settlement but simply to get the municipal authorities to allow Chinese residents a hand in its administration.

The Chinese bourgeoisie was very conscious of its own interests and that may have imposed some limitations upon its nationalistic fervour. But those limitations were also born of its sense of responsibility and its desire to be reasonable. The bourgeoisie was not prepared to consider imperialism as the root of all evils: 'I say that for years our political situation has not been determined by external setbacks but by internal ones ... to speak of the international situation without taking into account our internal difficulties is to behave like a blind man who holds forth about seeing or a deaf one who speaks of music.'[15]

Even if China had managed to improve its international situation, its internal problems would not thereby have been resolved: 'At the present time, with a government such as ours and a country in the state that ours is in, it goes without saying that there is no hope of international success. And even if, by some extraordinary chance, the Twenty-one Demands were completely abolished, Shandong and Jiaozhou were unconditionally returned to us and the problems of the zones of influence, the concessions and the unilateral fixing of customs tariffs were resolved as we would wish, I ask you – would all that make the Chinese Republic a solid and independent State? The first thing to do is to find the right way to resolve internal problems.'[16]

An echo of Hu Shi's analyses seems detectable here: 'Internal reform is a pre-condition for resistance to imperialism.'[17]

It was in vain that communist leaders repeated their warnings: 'International imperialism is the number one enemy of the Chinese people, an enemy we cannot coexist with.'[18] While the bourgeoisie did not embrace the confident cosmopolitanism of a Hu Shi, it did believe that a measure of cooperation with the foreigners ought to be possible. It realised that economic development, the benefits of which it would have liked to control, depended upon foreign input: 'If we wish to give new impetus to our industries, we must first adopt an Open Door policy, make use of foreign capital and introduce mechanical power into our country ... If the country decided to develop its industries on its own, it would never achieve its goal.'[19]

Chinese businessmen were thus depending upon foreign support: 'We expect you to make use of every chance to render assistance to our commercial and industrial enterprises.'[20] But acceptance of that aid was hedged with definite conditions: 'cooperation must in no way interfere with our national finances or undermine our development'. There was to be no question of foreign control, rather 'intelligent action of mutual benefit'. In order to establish what Henri Madier, the president of the French Chamber of Commerce in China, appositely called 'the economic *entente cordiale*', the Chinese bourgeoisie appealed to the intelligence and good will of the foreigners, hoping that 'the saner elements in the allied and friendly nations would be able to persuade their governments to abolish or revise the treaties that are so harmful to a spirit of cooperation'.[21]

This lack of independent means and the inevitable need to resort to the goodwill of others may give a utopian air to what was in reality an effort at original and forward-looking thinking. As early as 1919–20, the Chinese bourgeoisie was already confronting a matter which has been growing in importance ever since, the problems of foreign aid to underdeveloped countries. It set out the desirable solution, as it saw it, quite clearly: there should be economic cooperation in a spirit of respect for national independence and to the mutual benefit of all powers concerned. Even if seldom applied this idea has become a truism, but at the time it was revolutionary. On the one hand, it was opposed to concepts of international diplomacy attached, ever since the nineteenth century, to the acquisition of privileges and zones of influence. On the other, it broke with the Confucian tradition, which regarded China as the centre of the world and had no concept at all of reciprocity in international relations.

With its moderation and its reservations, bourgeois nationalism seemed to accept the realities of an age in which China would continue for a long time to be dominated by the foreign presence. Less utopian than the nationalism of the radical intelligentsia and more open-minded than that of the conservative bureaucracy, bourgeois nationalism might have expected its pragmatic nature to make it particularly effective. The aims of the Chinese bourgeoisie were to foster the benefits afforded by expansion and to keep that expansion going. Its chances of success depended, on the one hand, on the strength of the pressures that it, the Chinese bourgeoisie, could bring to bear and, on the other, on the willingness of its foreign partners to make concessions. Thus, to evaluate the role of bourgeois nationalism, we must find out how these two factors evolved, by studying the various diplomatic, political and economic developments whose rapid succession marked this period of crisis.

2 Nationalist activism: the practice and ideology of boycotting

Economic boycotting was, *par excellence*, the bourgeois mode of nationalist activism. Amid the nationalistic fervour created by the May Fourth Movement, from 1919 on boycotts seemed a semi-permanent fixture. The boycotting movement of 1919–21 led into that of 1923, which in its turn continued into 1924, becoming general in 1925–6 and, as such, integrated into the revolutionary struggle.[22] During this period, the bourgeoisie used boycotting in a bid to gain domination over the national market and to establish a new industrial society.

Between 1919 and 1923, the boycotting movements were directed exclusively against Japan. They were a reaction against the heavy Japanese intervention in the Chinese market place both during and immediately following the war. Japanese competition seemed to the Chinese entrepreneurs all the more threatening in that, not content to exploit the privileges inherent in the treaty system, Japan was also pressing for new political and territorial concessions.

The anti-Japanese boycotts of 1919–23

In May 1919, the Japanese press had given the announcement of a boycott an ironical reception: it would be a quick flare-up that would be over in 'five minutes'. A few weeks later, the *China Weekly Review* was remarking that those 'five minutes' looked like lasting a long time and inflicting considerable damage upon Japanese interests.[23] Unlike the movements of 1908 and 1915, the 1919 boycott was strictly organised and prolonged. The Japanese suffered from it and were alarmed. On several occasions, Japanese residents and diplomats reacted with a violence and an insensitivity that created 'incidents' the consequence of which was simply to reinforce the opposition that they were endeavouring to overcome. One such incident was the 'Funatsu affair', which broke out in Tianjin, in November 1919, just after Bian Yinchang had been elected president of the city's chamber of commerce. As has been mentioned, Bian was a fervent partisan of the boycotting movement. His election made prospects of the compromise desired by the Japanese merchants and diplomats in Tianjin recede. The Japanese consul, Funatsu Tutsuichiro, thereupon proceeded to press first the Commissioner for Foreign Affairs, then the governor of Zhili province and finally the Minister of Agriculture and Trade to persuade the Chinese authorities to annul Bian's election.[24] When the provincial assembly learned of this undiplomatic behaviour, it protested in the strongest terms. At an emergency meeting, the Chamber of Commerce alerted every patriotic union and chamber of commerce in the country. Protests were soon repressed by the Peking authorities, but the affair aroused indignant public feeling and caused the boycott to spread still further in northern China.

Meanwhile, another incident had incensed public feeling in southern China. In the course of disturbances directed against Japanese merchants in Fuzhou, in November 1919, several Chinese had been killed. These deaths, together with the arrival of Japanese gunboats in Fuzhou, caused a frenzy of patriotic indignation. In a letter to the Japanese consul, H. Mori Kaku, the secretary of the Fuzhou students' union, declared: 'I tell you, Mr Mori, our organisation is extremely powerful for, in the first place, we have most of the Fuzhou businessmen with us ... We also have plenty of money, for the businessmen of Fuzhou have given us finance to further our action. We shall continue our efforts until China has regained its sovereignty ... Today we have yet again spat on the portrait of your emperor and on the Japanese flag. That's how much we loathe you, you dirty Japanese dogs.'[25]

The merchants expressed themselves with more moderation, but were equally determined. A tract signed by the Patriotic Friends of the

Commercial World (Shangjie aiguo tongren) included a map of China showing the locations of all the Japanese incursions and bearing the legend, 'To see this is enough to break one's heart'. The accompanying text explained: 'It is only by fighting as hard as we can against enemy merchandise that we shall ever arrest our decline.'[26]

Boycotting activities reached the peak of their intensity all over central and southern China in the spring and early summer of 1920. In the second half of the year, they began to peter out. By refusing to ratify the Versailles Treaty, on 19 March 1920, the American Senate had introduced a new dimension into the Sino–Japanese conflict. It now became part of a whole collection of problems that were eventually to be put before world opinion and resolved a year and a half later, at the Washington Conference. Boycotting was still vigorous in the upper Yangzi region in 1921 but it died out in 1922, after the Washington agreements had sanctioned the return of Shandong to China. In 1923, however, it started up again in even more violent fashion when Chinese and Japanese diplomats clashed, this time over the issue of Liaodong.

Unlike the previous waves of boycotting, the 1923 movement was not sparked off by a particular incident. No acts of aggression or clashes had aroused public passions. This time the movement was part of a vaster campaign organised between March and December on the basis of what were essentially political and diplomatic issues. The objective was to thwart Japan's claims, considered illegitimate, to Port Arthur and Dairen and to get these ports restored to China immediately. The boycotting was deliberately planned, as part of a more organised national campaign.

Admittedly, a number of disturbances did break out in the course of the boycotting, for example at Shaxi (Hubei), where several people were injured on 14 May and, more seriously, in Changsha (Hunan), where three Chinese were killed on 1 June. Such incidents obviously tended to stir up passions and create a climate of hatred. The unremitting concern of the organisers to play down the more dramatic aspects of the affair and restore the movement to a purely rational footing is, in the circumstances, all the more remarkable: 'The Japanese allowed their soldiers to land and to wound and kill many people. They show the utmost scorn for our country and our people ... We must get the government to make the most urgent diplomatic protests ... It is imperative to prevent the masses from again becoming involved in violent demonstrations.'[27]

These leaders appealing for moderation were businessmen. They took charge of the situation right from the start. In earlier days the lead had often come not from them but from the students, but in 1923 it seems to have been the other way about. In the larger cities – Shanghai, Tianjin and Hangzhou – it was now the chambers of commerce and the guilds that were calling for boycotts, organising associations for the salvation of the nation and committees for diplomatic relations and spelling out the objectives and methods of the movement: 'We must first set up an enquiry into Japanese merchandise and its market outlets . . . If, for example, we could track down all the Japanese brands held by the cloth merchants of Jiangsu, we could draw up a list to circulate throughout the country . . . As for enquiries into market outlets, these could be left to the professional guilds. We would then list those outlets . . . and prepare to resist . . . If a merchant is discovered to have bought Japanese merchandise during the boycott, he should be severely punished, but business circles will themselves issue the prohibitions and undertake surveillance. The students should not become involved.'[28]

This programme appears to have been scrupulously applied. The street associations made enquiries regarding the goods that merchants stocked. The merchants themselves imposed the controls. Every conceivable effort was made to prevent losses. In taking the place of the students, the merchants were not solely out to preserve particular interests of their own. They were also pursuing the much more far-reaching policy of reforming the objectives and methods of boycotting.

Towards a new conception of boycotting

The anti-American and anti-Japanese boycotts of 1905 and 1908 had been impassioned reactions tinged with xenophobia. For Chinese merchants whose businesses depended upon the import–export trade, boycotting constituted a double-edged weapon. If external trade was paralysed their own interests were bound to suffer soon, hence the relative brevity of those early boycotts.

From 1919 on, in contrast, the expansion of national industry made it possible for some Chinese entrepreneurs to turn the economic conditions created by the boycotts to their own advantage. The movement of economic protest was now underpinned by a constructive economic plan. Both were inspired by the same ideology of national salvation (*jiuguo*). The 1919 anti-Japanese boycott was accompanied by a sweeping campaign to promote national products, now referred to as 'patriotic products' (*aiguohuo*). Business leaders deliberately attempted to exploit the public's growing repugnance for all things Japanese. Appealing to patriotism was one of the most effective means of winning a response from Chinese financial backers. It was also effective salesmanship. The expression *aiguo* (love of one's country) was one of the terms most commonly used in the advertising campaigns which many new Chinese companies were now launching for their products. The Nanyang Brothers' Tobacco Company advertisements praised in a single breath the intrinsic quality of its cigarettes and their desirability as a national product.[29] Some towns mounted exhibitions (*guohuo chenliesuo*) designed to make Chinese products more widely known.[30] Many tracts and pamphlets were circulated drawing the public's attention to its overriding duty to 'buy Chinese'. One of these pamphlets, preserved in the Japanese archives, spotlights the positive aspects of boycotting. It begins with the announcement that it 'absolutely must be read by all patriots' and in the very first lines defines boycotting as 'a plan of ambitious scope' and 'the principle of a permanent organisation'. 'Patriotic friends' are told that the only hope of salvation lies in their own efforts. The author explains that China has plenty of capital and experts at its disposal; now it must forge ahead and create its own industries: 'When voices are heard on all sides exclaiming: "Long live the industrial joint-stock companies created by the people of the great Chinese nation, long live the people of the great Chinese nation, long live the great Chinese nation" – only then will the objectives of this long-term plan, this permanent organisation of boycotting aimed against the merchandise of a certain nation, be achieved.'[31]

On the other hand, for the students who predominated as organisers of the protest movements (including the boycotting movement) during the May Fourth period, this constructive economic plan was of secondary importance compared to the political and diplomatic struggle. It was no more than the other side of a coin that they preferred not to turn over.

The political and diplomatic effectiveness of the 1919 boycotting remains a matter of uncertainty. No doubt the movement prevented direct negotiations between Tokyo and Peking from taking place in

1920. But it was at the Washington Conference, in 1921–2, that the railways and the German concessions in Shandong were returned to China. And it would be inaccurate to give the boycotting movement the credit for forcing a decision that in fact emerged from the framework of a series of far-reaching international diplomatic manoeuvres designed to put the break on Japanese expansionism.

The economic achievements of the 1919 boycotting movement are even more indefinite. The decline of Japanese exports to China (424 million yen in 1921 as opposed to 656 million in 1919) coincided with the reconversion crisis that first hit Japan in March 1921 and from which the country continued to suffer. As for the stimulating effects of the boycotts upon the development of modern and artisan industries in China, they are certainly noted by contemporary observers. It was claimed that in Hangzhou the 1919 boycotting proved 'a good friend' to the Dingxin Cotton Mill (Dingxin shachang); in Tianjin one direct consequence of the boycotting was the creation of the Beiyan Cotton Mills (Beiyang shangye diyi shachang); and in Canton the anti-Japanese boycotts had greatly helped the hat factories.[32] But the extremely favourable situation generally in 1919, which has already been described, certainly had a more important effect on the Chinese economy than the boycotting did. In fact, C. F. Remer is of the opinion that it was from these peculiarly favourable circumstances that the boycotting drew its strength.

By 1923, the economic miracle was fading fast. And thinking on the subject of boycotting and its long-term usefulness in economic construction began to develop along new lines, placing different emphases.

The merchants attributed the failure of earlier movements to their ephemeral nature and their radical orientation: 'Every time our country runs into diplomatic difficulties, people start talking about promoting national merchandise and boycotting Japanese products. A deafening clamour breaks out and then, when the affair is over, all is forgotten.' So long as the crisis lasted, though, 'the whole country seems to have gone mad. There is no reason to be had anywhere.' On earlier occasions, industrial machinery and semi-finished products had been banned as strictly as consumer goods. As a result, the boycotting 'which seemed to offer us, the industrialists, an excellent chance to develop our own industries', had the opposite effect of closing factories down because of the lack of supplies. So the organisers were hardly to be congratulated: 'Alas! their intentions are excellent, but their stupidity is beyond belief.'[33] This analysis from the *Hunan Industrial Review* (*Hunan shiye zazhi*) was reproduced in a toned-down format by the *Shanghai General Chamber of Commerce Monthly Review*.[34] It was going to be necessary to reconsider the concept of boycotting.

Boycotting was no longer to be a 'passive reaction to a particular situation. It would no longer be a weapon to be brandished at such or such an adversary, depending on the international rivalries of the moment. Even the changing vocabulary was significant. The term 'boycotting' (*paichi*), which implied a violent exclusion, was replaced by the phrase 'breaking off economic relations' (*jingji juejiao*). This more neutral formula suggested not so much an aggressive riposte directed against the foreigners, but rather a refusal to consider their very existence. The focus was shifting from others to China itself and the Chinese people.

In this area, the Chinese were exhorted to follow the example of the foreign powers: 'restrictions on their imports are not aimed against any enemy'; 'the interests of the national economy' were the only consideration. Feelings of resentment should be replaced by statesmanship. Boycotting should now be 'a constant preoccupation' and it was necessary to work out 'a vast, long-term plan'. If machinery and semi-finished products were excepted from the boycotts, it would be possible to keep going for a very long time and to deal mortal blows to the enemies of China while at the same time safeguarding Chinese interests. Boycotting would no longer be a 'suicidal policy'. The key to success lay in improving national production, for 'in the business world, material interests are more important than speeches and propaganda'. In this way, boycotting would be closely associated with the construction of the national economy: 'It is an end, not a means.'[35]

The reference here by Nie Yuntai, the cotton mill owner, to Gandhi testifies to the attention that some of the Chinese bourgeoisie were now paying to the political and economic evolution of India. Some of the Shanghai industrialists had been following the *khaddi* (hand spinning and weaving) campaign, which was at its height in 1921 and in the course of which many foreign fabrics were destroyed. Gandhi's idea was that the *khaddi* movement would lead to the restoration of national independence (*swaraj*) and that was no doubt also the hope of the big cotton mill owners of Ahmedabad, who were financing him. It is impossible not to be struck by the similarity of the preoccupations of

India and China. At a time when no-one was yet speaking of the Third World, both countries were facing problems of underdevelopment and national humiliation. At this period, Gandhi's influence in Chinese business circles was matched by the vogue for Rabindranath Tagore in intellectual ones. Gandhi and Tagore, the one a partisan of non-cooperation, the other of union between East and West, seem to symbolise the two paths between which the Chinese bourgeoisie was torn, as are elite groups in all dependent countries.

The new style of boycotting does not appear to have been much more effective than the earlier kinds, and it came to just as abrupt an end in the autumn of 1923. The temporary drop in trade, particularly noticeable in the Yangzi Valley, made no lasting difference to the situation. This virtually instantaneous failure called into question the methods that had been applied. Unlike its Indian counterpart, the Chinese bourgeoisie either did not think of mobilising the masses in its plan of non-cooperation, or were incapable of doing so. It is, moreover, questionable whether the deliberate isolation of the Chinese market would have led to a more rapid and balanced expansion of the national economy. (The results of the Maoist experiment of self-sufficiency of 1960–70 would seem to suggest not.) Finally, it is important to realise that by no means all the Chinese bourgeoisie were in favour of the ideology of non-cooperation. Although it was quick to take action in the face of the Japanese threat, it was slower to perceive the dangers of American penetration, claimed to be purely cultural and economic in character. The Chinese bourgeoisie deluded itself with the optimism born of the Washington Conference, hoping to become the recipient of disinterested aid from a 'friendly power', and it allowed itself to be seduced by the vision of powers handed over that the new imperialist strategy was dangling before it.

3   The mirages of neo-colonialism

The First World War struck a definitive blow at the diplomacy of imperialism, practised ever since the late nineteenth century by the foreign powers, who were joining forces to facilitate their expansion in China. The decline of the European influence and the rapid expansion of Japan upset the old balance. The united front of the great European powers had been shattered by the Russian revolution and Germany's defeat. The system of unequal treaties was overridden: defeated

Germany and her allies were no longer to benefit from them, and the very principle of the system was repudiated by Soviet Russia. In the aftermath of the war, the Western powers were thus feeling their way towards a new diplomacy.

The initiative came from the American government, which, with renewed vigour, again took up the Open Door idea, urging all powers to renounce military and political expansion in China and calling for international cooperation to guarantee the country the financial and economic aid that was indispensable to it. Not content simply to press for equal opportunities for rival powers, American diplomacy also aimed to set up a new relationship between China and the rest of the world. The powers gathered at the Washington Conference (November 1921 to February 1922) reaffirmed the principles of China's sovereignty and independence and also of its territorial and administrative integrity. They went on to adopt a number of resolutions designed to prepare for the implementation of these principles.

The elimination of the 'diplomacy of imperialism' certainly did not put an end to foreign domination in China, but it did tend to introduce new and hitherto unknown forms of domination. The constitution of the New Consortium in October 1920 was in line with the policies of what Kautsky called 'ultra-imperialism', policies that 'introduce the joint exploitation of the world by internationally united finance capital in place of the mutual rivalries of national finance capitals'.[36] To put that more simply, the Chinese at this period spoke of the foreigners' 'common management' of their country (gongtong guanli). The elimination of separate foreign zones of influence was supposed to render multiple bilateral agreements unnecessary. The military and political apparatus set up by the unequal treaties no longer seemed essential to the development of foreign businesses. It was possible for the domination of international capital to coexist with the presence of an independent and sovereign Chinese government. What the 'old China hands' called Washington's 'absurd generosity' in reality constituted a new type of imperialist expansion. The term 'neo-colonialism' did not appear until after the Second World War in the West. But in China, a few Chinese were condemning 'the new methods of foreign imperialism' (waiguo diguozhuyide xinfangfa) as early as 1923.[37]

The new moves of American diplomacy aroused considerable ill-feeling and scepticism from several governments and also from foreign commercial groups already established in China. The show of harmony in Washington did not stop Japan and Great Britain from embarking upon a veritable commercial war in China, nor the United States from keeping an anxious eye on the progress of Japanese expansion that the return of Shandong to China had done nothing to discourage. As for the 'old China hands', they never stopped bewailing 'the Washington tragedy'.[38]

The contradictions that beset the 'imperialist camp' gave its actions a confused air. The moves of residents in China, those of their governments and those of the diplomats and military supposed to represent these governments were frequently out of step. In the midst of the dangers that threatened – such as military intervention or partition – at least two mirages appeared: the mirage of constructive cooperation equally advantageous to all parties concerned, and the mirage of 'good' and 'bad' foreigners.

The rejection of ultra-imperialism: the Chinese bourgeoisie and the failure of the New International Consortium

The agreement proposed by the Americans and signed on 20 October 1920 by American, English and French banking groups and approved by their respective governments envisaged a New International Consortium to finance all the public loans obtained abroad by the Chinese central or provincial authorities and guaranteed by them. The loans were to be accompanied by conditions that guaranteed the use and repayment of the funds advanced. It was possible that at some point the International Consortium might control the various revenues and funds guaranteed following a mutual agreement and might consider nominating foreign advisers in the context of certain loan agreements.[39] As the International Consortium specifically assumed the task of developing communications, these powers might extend to the revenue and running of the railways or even, as a repeatedly denied rumour asserted, control over the real estate tax. The statutes of the new Consortium briefly noted that 'cooperation from Chinese capital would be welcome'. However, when the Chinese bankers' associations held their first national conference, in December 1920 in Shanghai, they decided not to request admission to the Consortium but instead to take up the foreign challenge and create their own consortium: 'The International Consortium has repeatedly declared its intention to help China ... and we feel grateful. But the fundamental reform of the administrative affairs of this country lies with the Chinese.'[40]

In a series of hard-hitting leading articles, the *Shanghai General Chamber of Commerce Monthly Review* attacked the hidden ambitions of the foreign powers, exposing the 'mechanisms of economic dismemberment' (*jingji guafen*) which China was in danger of being subjected to: 'They want us to mistake a deer for a horse ... In the past, special privileges were conceded to particular powers; now these powers are to enjoy those privileges all together.'[41]

The cooperation that the New Consortium had grudgingly offered to Chinese capital did not involve a partnership of equality. Some Chinese bankers thought that if they were admitted as members of the Consortium, they would benefit from the advantages enjoyed by the foreign bankers; they believed that they would be in a better position to control the moves of the foreign bankers from the inside; and they also thought that they would be able to safeguard their own interests. But they were deluding themselves. Even if the Chinese banking group entered the Consortium, it would never be on the same footing as the other groups. The latter represented their governments and could count on official and diplomatic support. What support could the Chinese group expect from the Peking government, which would be the Consortium's debtor? As for controlling the activities of the foreign groups, nothing could be more uncertain: 'They are powerful and we are weak ... They are rich and we are poor ... They are the masters and we are the invited guests ... They are four and we stand alone'.[42]

The unremitting hostility of Chinese financial and official circles was eventually to prevent the New Consortium from making their investments as planned. This constituted a political victory for the bourgeoisie. Over the preceding years it had been trying, not without success, to take the place of the foreigners in the field of economic modernisation. It was now in a position to supplant them in their role of providers of government funds and controllers of public revenue. By underestimating the strength and determination of the Chinese bankers, the foreign powers had made a mistake that the Washington Conference gave them a chance to repair. American, followed by British, diplomacy now played the card of the Chinese bourgeoisie in an attempt to get power handed over to local elite groups, particularly business circles.

The Washington Conference (1921–2) and the attempt to transfer powers

As soon as the Conference was announced, public opinion in China was mobilised in a great campaign for 'people's diplomacy' (*guomin waijiao*) in which the chambers of commerce and the bankers' associations took the lead. This 'people's diplomacy' looks something of a last resort for a nation that no longer had a unified government and the representativeness of whose official negotiators (*zhengfu daibiao*) was disputed. Between 12 and 17 October 1921, the delegates of the education societies and the chambers of commerce assembled at a conference in Shanghai. They mandated Jiang Menglin and Yu Rizhang (1882–1936) to go to Washington to report the 'will of the people' (*minyi*).[43] The two men, known as the 'people's delegates' to distinguish them from the official Chinese delegation, were first and foremost educationists. But neither was unfamiliar with the business world. Jiang Menglin was the grandson of a banker and his family still held shares in the Shanghai *quianzhuang*. He himself took an interest in economic problems and in 1918 had collaborated with Sun Yat-sen in the publication of *The International Development of China*. As secretary-general of the YMCA, Yu Rizhang, for his part, had many contacts with businessmen and, as a member of the Chinese Consultative Committee (which represented the interests of the Chinese residents on the Shanghai Municipal Council), he was brought into contact with the bankers Song Hangzhang and Chen Guangfu as well as the cotton mill owner Mu Ouchu, who all served alongside him on the same committee.[44]

As the official representatives mandated by the conference of educationists and merchants, these delegates truly were the spokesmen of Chinese public opinion. The conference that brought the educationists and merchants together in this way constituted the starting point for a great popular diplomatic alliance, to which Cai Yuanpei gave his support. Its purpose was to set up a pan-Chinese federation capable of channelling the various currents of public opinion that were provoked by the announcement of the Washington Conference and that had no hope of being expressed by the increasingly illusory manoeuvres of official governmental institutions. If one is prepared, at this point, to reduce the notion of 'the people' to the elite groups not in the government's employ, Jiang Menglin and Yu Rizhang incontestably did represent 'the people'.

The attempt to establish people's diplomacy took place in the context of a liberal and bourgeois current of opinion that stressed the importance of mobilising the energies and abilities of individuals and placed more trust in the social elite than in political institutions. But the audacity of this move prompted misgivings among not only foreign but also Chinese observers: 'If the people itself sets about talking of diplomacy, it means that the government no longer exists. And if the government no longer exists, there is no State. How can hair grow where there is no skin? And where there is no State, where can diplomacy spring from?'[45]

The rise of people's diplomacy in many respects puts one in mind of the exact contemporary plan for a National Convention. Both testify to a deliberate abandonment of procedures that had become totally ineffective, a similar historical impatience, and a similar desire for new initiatives. For a while, these trends were encouraged by the connivance of a number of foreign interests.

In Washington, the people's delegates played an indirect but active role, chiefly devoted to defending Chinese rights to Shandong and China's return to a status of total international equality, for which the bankers' associations and the chambers of commerce, in particular, were agitating. The Washington Conference fulfilled many of the hopes placed in it by the Chinese nationalists. But the unpredictabilities of world diplomatic strategy probably contributed more to that success than did the mobilisation of Chinese people's diplomacy. As one British journalist remarked: 'When a blind cat catches a dead rat it is a case of pure luck.'[46] Even so, to do that the cat must bare its claws. Acting through its organisations, the Chinese bourgeoisie did make its presence and its aspirations felt. And that is what induced Anglo-American diplomacy to take a chance on it.

Would the Chinese bourgeoisie be capable of consolidating the victory handed to it? Could it be the special partner that the United States hoped for? Would it be capable of using the 'friendship' of this powerful ally without becoming subservient to it? And could it rid China of the evils of the old colonialism while averting the perils of neo-colonialism? We have already examined the ideology of merchant power in the context of internal politics. But we also need to approach it from the angle of the new diplomacy. The political ambitions manifested by the business bourgeoisie at this juncture were not simply a reflection of the inherent vitality of this class; they were also a response to foreign encouragement.

Many appeals were made to the Chinese bourgeoisie following the Washington Conference. They came from diplomats as well as from foreign business circles. On his arrival in China, the new British ambassador, Sir Ronald Macleay, stated that 'it was the duty of those who represented China's economic life to take a direct part in her political reorganization'.[47] The president of the Hong Kong and Shanghai Bank, A. O. Lang, also declared his confidence in the political destiny of the Chinese bourgeoisie.[48] E. F. Mackay, the director of the Butterfield and Swire Company and president of the China Association of British Residents, was more circumspect but did wonder whether 'the Chinese merchant class ... cannot combine to oust the present corrupt officials and set up a government on clean, progressive lines by men drawn from their own chambers of commerce'.[49]

These appeals to the Chinese bourgeoisie were based on the proclaimed identity of the interests of *all* merchants in the treaty ports. It was said that the Chinese and the foreigners stood to benefit equally if an end were put to all the disturbances that were paralysing economic development. It was up to the Chinese merchants to agitate for, and bring about, the reform of their own institutions – a reform that the foreigners wholeheartedly desired. The initiative for such reform must come 'from the inside' but it could rely on support 'from the outside'. The foreigners' exhortations to the Chinese merchants were accompanied by various offers of aid. The leaderwriter of the big Shanghai daily, the *North China Daily News*, suggested that, with the help of the merchant class, a well-qualified foreign adviser might quickly reorganise public finances to help along a government that was honest.[50] And E. F. Mackay, flinging oratorical caution to the winds, predicted that, once the corrupt mandarins had been ejected, 'the merchant class ... could assume office, with foreign advisers if necessary, until they felt their own feet and could govern efficiently without such help'.[51]

The foreigners were discreetly attempting to organise a political movement and were impatient to make use of its latent force. The initiative seems to have come from Hankou where, in November 1922, a Foreigners' Association was formed. This forthwith made contact with the delegates of the Chinese chambers of commerce then meeting at their federation's fourth annual conference. Agreement was reached on a programme that included the licensing of troops, the establishment of a constitutional regime and financial reorganisation. The programme was presented as that of the chambers of commerce – and there can be no doubt that it *partly* was – and it received wide publicity in the foreign press in China.[52] To promote the movement and coordinate action, several delegates from the Foreigners' Association were sent to Shanghai. One was W. P. Mills, the very energetic secretary of the Hankou YMCA. His presence made it easier to establish contact with Shanghai business circles: Yu Rizhang, the national secretary of the YMCA and also one of the 'people's delegates' at the Washington Conference, met with them, along with the industrialist Nie Yuntai.[53] A few weeks later, their efforts resulted in the launching of a widespread campaign for demobilisation and for a constitution. The foreigners' encouragement was becoming more and more pressing. The American ambassador to China, Jacob Schurman, addressed the Shanghai General Chamber of Commerce in person and the American consul, Edward S. Cunningham, noted that the Chamber's astonishing 'declaration of independence' and the formation of a merchant government on 23 June 1923 were probably simply applications of the plan that Schurman had suggested in his speech.[54]

Beyond the conservative circles of the chambers of commerce, the idea of political cooperation between the bourgeoisie and the foreigners even appears to have interested some of the Guomindang leaders. As early as 26 January 1923, Sun Yat-sen published a 'Declaration on the peaceful unification of China', in which he urged the principal military leaders to band together and ask 'a friendly power to help them to find the right methods to define and put into practice a policy for the licensing of troops'. He suggested that they might obtain a 'demobilisation loan, the use of which would be supervised by a foreign expert'.[55]

Sun Yat-sen's attitude and the popularity of the campaign for cooperation among business circles during the first half of 1923 were acutely worrying to the Communist Party, which now tried to implement the policy of a united front, as recommended by the Comintern. The communist press attacked the machiavellism of the English and the Americans, who were trying to establish in China 'a feudal bourgeois regime under their own domination'. It declared that 'the middle classes' had been misled by 'the deceptive methods of the foreigners' and should now get a grip on themselves and 'renew their national spirit'. They should 'neither renounce their ancestors nor depend upon foreign forces'. 'Capitalists of Shanghai', this article went on, 'you, whose lips still pronounce the words "sovereign rights" (*zhuquan*) and "spontaneous mobilisation" (*zidong*), will you now follow the foreign capitalists or will you flock together to the embrace of the national revolutionary party?'[56]

And while the British *North China Herald* urged Sun Yat-sen to shake off 'doctrinaire' influences and appeal to the middle classes and the businessmen,[57] the comintern delegate to China, Maring (H. Sneevliet) was exasperated by Sun's persistence in seeking Anglo-American aid: 'Even if Sun Yat-sen manages, thanks to foreign aid, to become President of the Republic, will he be a single step closer to self-determination and independence? Absolutely not! He will simply have contrived to lose his reputation as a sincere nationalist.'[58]

It was not the opposition of the communists that caused the plan for the transfer of powers to fail, however, but the intrinsic weakness of the bourgeoisie itself and its rapidly deteriorating relations with the foreigners, as imperialism of the most traditional type returned to the offensive.

4   Towards a national revolution

Imperialism's return to the offensive and the failure of cooperation

We will not return to the subject of the abortive attempt to establish merchant power, nor to that of the political role of the Chinese businessmen, who were accused by their foreign critics of being 'too timid and self effacing, paying tribute in cold cash to the overbearing and dominant militarists rather than [assuming] the responsibility for a movement to bring order out of chaos'.[59] Such judgements are so hypocritical that we should temper their severity. The fact is that the foreigners who thus condemned the weakness of the Chinese bourgeoisie were to a large extent responsible for that weakness. The imperialism through which the model of liberalism had been introduced into China still constituted one of the major obstacles to its application.

Cooperation had proved difficult enough even when it was a matter of sharing in the benefits of growth. Once the crisis developed, cooperation gave way to ferocious rivalry. Although unable to eradicate the foreign businesses, the Chinese merchants managed to wage a war of attrition in daily business life, undermining the actions of their rivals. The violence of this economic rivalry brought about a deterioration in Chinese relations with even the 'good' foreigners. By the summer of 1923, the English and American diplomats had more or less lost hope in the idea of political intervention on the part of the Chinese bourgeoisie, while the Chinese bourgeoisie, for its part, was becoming increasingly doubtful about the nature of the aid offered by the 'friendly powers'.

During the cotton mills' crisis, the foreign powers found it expedient to reaffirm their solidarity with Japan and to underwrite its expansionist policies in China. In the name of the treaties, they supported Japan's protest against the Chinese embargo tactics designed to prohibit exports of raw cotton and, in May 1923, they forced the Peking government to abrogate the prohibition order.[60]

At the same time, the Lincheng incident[61] was regarded as the last straw by the exasperated foreign residents. They demanded a return to a policy of armed intervention and pressed their respective governments to exploit the situation to wrench new concessions from China; it was an opportunity not to be wasted. The president of the Hong Kong and Shanghai Bank urged the foreign powers 'to wake up and throw away their dreams of a regenerated China'. The British and American residents' organisations demanded the suspension of all advantages granted to China at the Washington Conference.[62] In response to this campaign, the foreign powers adopted a harder line with the Peking government. A note from their diplomatic corps, dated 10 August 1923, demanded not only compensation for the victims and punishment for the guilty but also that a special police force be created for the railways, headed by foreign officers.[63] It was a return to the most classic practices of imperialism. The Lincheng affair fitted into the pattern of a whole string of incidents – missionaries murdered and merchants kidnapped – which had usually been exploited, during the second half of the nineteenth century, to justify the military and diplomatic reprisals taken by the foreign powers.

Somewhat naively, the foreign residents were hoping that this return to traditional methods would 'meet with the approval of substantial Chinese business and banking interests who deprecate chaotic conditions in China but who will not act for fear of persecution at the hands of the present regime'.[64] But the Shanghai guilds and the General Chamber of Commerce reacted spiritedly against the offensive return of the old imperialism. They accused the 'friendly powers ... of supplying the authorities with funds and arms used to prolong the civil war' and they condemned the way in which the Lincheng incident had been exploited politically and diplomatically. In a circular to all the chambers of commerce, they furthermore announced their opposition to the plan for international control over the railways.[65]

So the dream of an economic *entente cordiale* and for cooperation founded on 'intelligence' and good will aimed at 'benefits for all' faded away. As disappointed Pygmalions, the foreign mentors deplored the fecklessness of a bourgeoisie for whom they had in vain striven to engineer a political destiny. They did not see that the powerful support that they had brought to bourgeois nationalism had thrown its development out of balance, fostering unrealistic ambitions and effectively isolating and weakening it.

Jibbing at the collaboration that its foreign partners no longer even bothered to disguise as cooperation, the bourgeoisie saw the path to revolution opening up before it. The communist press was urging it to tread that path: 'Comrades of the commercial world! Do you want to submit willingly to foreign oppression, to this great injustice, this great insult, without striking back?'[66]

But its deteriorating relations with Sun Yat-sen and the Guomindang, together with the experiences and failures of recent years, drove the bourgoisie to resort to a quite different choice.

The return to national values

As we have glimpsed in Chapter 5, in the case of certain liberals – both intellectuals and businessmen – the re-evaluation of the role of the State was accompanied by an attempt to rehabilitate the national past. Immediately after the war, Liang Qichao and the partisans of the 'national essence' (*guocui*) had rejected Western civilisation, deemed inferior, and glorified Chinese tradition instead. Now the mood had changed and it was rather a matter of making use of certain aspects of that tradition to help China to take its place in the modern world while at the same time preserving its cultural identity. Hu Shi and those influenced by him or in the entourage of Gu Jiegang, who were organising a school of 'New History', thus broke with the iconoclasm of 1919: now they no longer rejected the past *en bloc*.[67]

The thinking of some of the entrepreneurs ran along very similar lines. Their objectives – national independence coupled with economic modernisation – remained unchanged. But the achievement of these objectives was not to be dependent upon total openness towards the West and upon Sino-foreign cooperation; it was to rely on the rebirth of national and cultural traditions.

China did not possess the military means to fight its enemies. The imbalance of external trade condemned its economy to dependence. According to the cotton mill owner, Nie Yuntai, the last remaining hope was passive resistance. The Chinese must return to 'a primitive frugality' and practise 'limiting their desires and restricting expenditure'. The urbanised elite groups 'whose lips hymn love of their country but whose bodies reject patriotism' must learn to accept 'daily sacrifices and economies on even the smallest spending'. If 'the country was not to be discarded like a pair of old spats', it was necessary to restore to the Chinese people a sense of its greatness, its history and its dignity. The urbanised elite groups must follow the example set by the peasants and workers, who were working hard to produce more and who spent a minimum of money to benefit the foreigners: it was they who were 'the real patriots'.[68]

On the face of it, the fact that a leading industrialist, one of the most enlightened moreover, should be resorting to this kind of conservative austerity seems paradoxical. His idea was that, in default of customs barriers, the country would be shielded by a wall of resentful non-cooperation and that industrialisation would be based on the policy of a return to the frugality of times past, rejecting the corruptions of urban civilisation and cutting down on the kind of international trading that created inequalities and dependence.

In the short space of the few years between prosperity and crisis, the thinking of the Chinese businessmen thus explored both poles of the ideology of underdevelopment and its remedies: on the one hand, the plan of international cooperation, on the other the promotion of a relative self-sufficiency. As the speedy failure of the new-style 1923 boycotting showed, the adoption of a strategy of self-sufficiency was fraught with insurmountable obstacles just as the strategy of cooperation was. A return to patriotism on the part of a weathercock elite was not enough to protect the Chinese markets – or the Chinese entrepreneurs, for that matter.

Although it took part in the Movement of 30 May 1925, the bourgeoisie did not commit itself to the path of revolutionary nationalism, for that looked too threatening to its immediate interests. The Chinese bourgeoisie was the product of economic growth combined with a state of dependence and it found it impossible to shake off these essential contradictions. It probably hoped that Chiang Kai-shek would free it from its own contradictions and that, through him, capitalism and nationalism would be reconciled. If the bourgeoisie abandoned the merchant class traditions of self-sufficiency and switched to favour the establishment of a strong power, it was not solely in order to protect itself in the face of workers' demands and revolutionary upheaval. It was also because, in the end, only a powerful State seemed to it to have a chance of winning back national independence and holding on to it. Chiang Kai-shek's policies were soon to disappoint these hopes. But the brand of nationalism, at once conservative *and* modernising, adopted by the bourgeoisie as early as the mid-1920s was at least partially reflected in the neo-traditionalist ideology of the Guomindang, with its mixture of Confucian precepts and recommendations for tackling the modern world successfully that the Movement for a New Life began advocating in about 1934.

Bourgeois nationalism, which was both less specific and less revo-lutionary than it is often made out to have been, was prompted and also limited by the position of dependence in which the Chinese entrepreneurs found themselves. The different phases through which the economic cycle passed reveal different aspects to this nationalism. The plan for cooperation, which was inspired by prosperity, receded before a desire for protection in times of crisis. But the entrepreneurs were always conscious of the need for modernisation and this preven-ted their reversion to Chinese cultural traditions from turning into a retrograde reaction of xenophobia. Boycotting, control over sizeable financial resources and social prestige, together with all the chances for negotiation (or blackmail) that the latter entailed, were so many means of action that the bourgeoisie employed to further its nationalist ambitions. But how far these means were effective remains a matter of doubt. The successes scored by the bourgeoisie must for the most part be ascribed to the mass movements that it sometimes managed to control to its own advantage. From 1925 on, however, the advancing tide of revolution made such a strategy increasingly difficult and dangerous. Falling back on the State now seemed to offer the only chance of preserving a measure of openness, essential to economic progress, while at the same time winning back and holding on to the national independence towards which they aspired both as citizens and as entrepreneurs.

If bourgeois nationalism was relatively effective, it was because it rallied together an urban society that, class for class, was ardently patriotic. Yet its very circumspection and moderation doomed it, like liberalism, to failure. The tactical use that the Communist Party made of it from time to time (particularly during the Movement of 30 May 1925) was not enough to turn it into revolutionary nationalism. Essentially conservative, as it was, bourgeois nationalism turned to a strong power in the hope that it would transcend its contradictions and find fulfilment in a national revolution.

Epilogue

1 After 1927: the bureaucracy's return in force and the decline of the bourgeoisie

For many years the Nanking decade (1927–37) was regarded as coinciding with the peak of the upsurge of the bourgeoisie. This thesis, vouched for by the observers and journalists of the 1930s, has been repeated by most of the Western historians who have studied the period. Even in 1975, Jean Chesneaux was still declaring that Chiang Kai-shek's regime was 'founded upon a coalition between the conservative ruling classes ... and the pro-Western business circles'.[1] According to this interpretation, the business bourgeoisie and, more particularly, the Shanghai capitalists, together with the landowners, constituted the principal supporters and beneficiaries of the regime.

Over the past ten years, the main lines of this thesis have been upheld in Soviet works. Having for a long time oscillated between a number of views that reflected current political directives and the vagaries of economic circumstances, Soviet historiography now regards the economic policies of the Guomindang as expressing a true State capitalism.[2] Through its planning efforts, its credit regulations and its development of public investments, the Nanking government is presented as having successfully stimulated national economic growth and created favourable conditions for the expansion of Chinese private enterprise. In this interpretation, the entrepreneurs may no longer be the principal agents of expansion, but they nevertheless remained its principal beneficiaries.

The most circumspect interpretation – in respect of the Nanking regime's bourgeois character (or character favourable to bourgeois interests) – is that of official Chinese historiography itself.[3] Many Chinese historians prefer the term 'bureaucratic capitalism' to that of 'state capitalism' to refer to a system that they condem as 'feudal' and 'comprador'. The economic policies of the Guomindang are not considered to express a true government plan: they simply reflect the ambition and greed of a small handful of highly placed officials symbolically described as belonging to the 'four great families' (*si dajiazu*).[4] These families managed to lay their hands on the State and Party apparatus and used their power to appropriate both private capital and public funds. To win foreign support in their operations of self-aggrandisement, these families were quite prepared to sell off Chinese rights and interests. The expansion of the bourgeoisie, subjected to the oppression of this reactionary and colonialist regime, was blocked.

This analysis, which condemns the compromises of the compradores and bureaucratic capitalists the better to preserve the possibility of cooperation between the communist regime and particular business leaders, rests upon the distinction drawn between the national bourgeoisie, on the one hand, and the compradores and bureaucratic entrepreneurs, on the other. I have several times commented on the artificial nature of such a distinction: it emerges all the more clearly here, for it now becomes apparent that the *a posteriori* condemnation of certain entrepreneurs is based upon the fact that they rallied to Chiang Kai-shek's regime and cooperated with its representatives. Meanwhile, what became of the 'national' bourgeoisie (strangely absent from this picture) after 1927 is not made clear. The truth is that official Chinese historiography does not demolish the thesis of a bourgeois Guomindang regime: it simply turns it into a debased bourgeois regime.

In these works devoted to the history of the Nanking decade, the relations between the Guomindang and the bourgeoisie thus remain a central issue. However, recent Western studies have begun to re-examine the problems of these relations.[5] As expressed most radically, this revisionist thesis maintains that the bourgeoisie 'did not control or significantly influence the Nanking regime' and that Chiang Kai-shek's government was concerned solely to 'emasculate the urban elite politically and to milk the modern sector of the economy'.[6]

If, as I believe, the revisionist thesis is to a large extent well-founded, why has the idea that the Guomindang regime was bourgeois or was well-disposed towards the bourgeoisie persisted for so long, and why does it to a large extent still persist today? Some uncertainties of interpretation clearly stem from the very real ambiguities of this regime, which is so difficult to analyse and define: in a moment of discouragement, one historian has even wondered whether it might not be a regime with no social basis at all.[7] But the misunderstandings also seem to have been deliberately fostered by the Chinese themselves – by communist theorists anxious to make developments in China conform with Marxist schemata, who have sought to establish the existence of a bourgeois phase, never mind whether it was comprador, bureaucratic or feudal, and above all by the government of Chiang Kai-shek, which was skilled at presenting the image of itself that most favoured its interests, the image most likely to win sympathy and financial aid from the West. Just as Mao Zedong's China was able to dangle before the eyes of the leftists and radicals of a Western world in a state of crisis the image of a society still pure, frugal and fraternal, Chiang Kai-Shek's China tried to convince and win over the democrats of Europe and America by exaggerating its bourgeois character. In both cases, the success achieved by these manipulations gives some idea of the degree of our own ignorance as far as China is concerned.

With only limited means of appraising what is really happening in China, foreigners usually turn for their understanding to an intermediary, an interpeter upon whom they are utterly dependent. In the case of China under the Guomindang, the principal intermediary was T. V. Soong (1894-1971), who held the post of Minister of Finance from 1928 to 1933. T. V. Soong, who was educated at Harvard University and spoke English perfectly, held press conferences and received foreign businessmen and advisers. Jean Monnet recorded: 'it was easy for me to deal with T. V. Soong, whose culture was European'.[8] It was no doubt much harder for him, as for others like him, to see that T. V. Soong's concern for the Chinese capitalists was not shared by the Nanking government. Behind the myth created by T. V. Soong for the benefit of his foreign interlocutors, it is today possible to make out a quite different reality – a bourgeoisie subordinated to, and integrated into, the State apparatus, a bureaucracy in a state of flux, uncertain of both its aims and its methods, and a modern economic sector still dominated by the hazards of international circumstances.

The offensive of the Guomindang regime against the bourgeoisie

Once it had been re-established with all its prerogatives and authority, in 1927, the central government stripped the bourgeoisie of the political initiative that it had possessed since the 1911 revolution and,

even more, since the May Fourth Movement of 1919. The Guomindang bureaucracy, much more ambitious in its objectives than that of
the Empire, even managed to deprive the bourgeoisie of some of the
social autonomy that the merchant class had enjoyed in the preceding
century. The refuge that the foreign concessions provided against these
encroachments by the Chinese public authorities was becoming
increasingly fragile and illusory. The bourgeoisie had no choice but to
allow itself, more or less willingly, to be absorbed into the State
apparatus.

The subordination of the bourgeois organisations to the Guomindang regime

Between 1927 and 1932, the Nanking government waged an offensive
designed to subordinate the merchant organisations. It employed
diverse yet complementary strategies, setting up parallel structures,
reorganising or eliminating old institutions and progressively reducing
the field of the bourgoisie's political and social activity. It is in
Shanghai, the stronghold of capitalism and also the headquarters of
the Guomindang, that it is easiest to follow the course and victory of
this offensive.

In the first phase, the Alliance of Shanghai Merchants, set up on
March 1927, developed a multitude of subsidiary organisations (*fen
hui*); to some extent, traditional corporatist structures were thereby
brought under the control of a single body.The guilds, each of which
represented related types of professional activity – silk manufacturing
and the cultivation of cocoons, for example, or the bean and rice trades
– were requested to regroup. The adoption of strongly unificatory
structures coincided with a thorough reorganisation of the leadership
of the professional organisations. Those formerly in command, now
discredited by accusations of elitism or compradorism, were obliged to
make way for successors whose main recommendation was that they
were compliant to the Guomindang. The new regime completed its
takeover of these basic organisations in November 1929, when it
dissolved the Federation of Street Associations, which, as the mouthpiece for certain merchant interests, had been playing an important
role in local politics ever since 1919.

Next, the authorities tackled the chambers of commerce, even
(unsuccessfully) calling for their suppression at the Third National
Congress of the Guomindang, held in March 1929. In April, the

Shanghai Party organisation, working through the Merchants' Alliance, provoked some violent incidents on the premises of the General Chamber of Commerce, which was then forced to close down. The government entrusted the task of reorganising the Chamber to a committee chaired by Yu Xiaqing. The Nanking directives were spelled out in no uncertain fashion: the new chamber would have to 'obey the directives and orders of the Guomindang and would be placed under the authority of the local administration'. On the pretext of unifying the representation of commercial interests, the General Chamber was merged with the chambers of the Chinese City and Zhabei and one-third of the seats were reserved for delegates from the Merchants' Alliance. In this way the major elite groups of the International Settlement, those very men who had built up the Chamber into a respected and influential institution during the 1920s, lost their majority.[9]

Although alive to the danger, the elite groups could do nothing to avert it. A few years later, the president of the Canton Guild, Feng Shaoshan, who had been an active leader of the Chamber since the early 1920s, made a bid to restore its former independence. Making the most of a passing weakness of the regime during the autumn of 1931, he placed himself at the head of a Committee for the Merchants' Movement in the Special Municipality of Shanghai (Shanghai tebieshi shangren yundong weiyuanhui). He laid claim to the entrepreneurs' right to manage their own institutions and, on 18 December 1931, he even tried to storm the Chamber's premises, at the head of a few supporters. But the attempt was unsuccessful.[10] The new Chamber of Commerce of the Municipality of Greater Shanghai henceforth remained under the control of the lesser entrepreneurs of the Chinese City and the Merchants' Alliance, who neither could nor desired to come into conflict with the regime in power; it was now no more than a cog in the machinery of local government.

The bourgeois organisations are stripped of their municipal responsibilites

The trends which, since the nineteenth century, had been encouraging commercial organisations to take over the administration of urban communities were abruptly reversed from 1927 on. The ruling of July 1927 on the Special Municipality of Shanghai and the organic laws of July 1928 and May 1930 transferred to the Municipal Government of

Greater Shanghai (whose authority extended over all the Chinese sectors of the town) responsibilities and powers that had hitherto belonged solely to the chambers of commerce and the guilds. The municipality – directly dependent upon the central government, which kept it under close surveillance through its various bureaux, in particular the Bureau of Social Affairs – was given the task of supervising the professional organisations, settling conflicts, collecting economic statistics, running social and philanthropic works, maintaining hygiene and security and organising town planning. The local elites were thereby deprived of several of their principal areas of activity.

Nevertheless, some continued to act in association with the local authorities either as members of the provisional municipal councils of 1927 or 1932 or as technical advisers to the municipal commissions set up in 1929 to prepare for the fiscal reforms and to plan local investments. But the circle of elite members thus associated with the municipal administration was extremely small and seems to have continued to shrink as time passed. The representatives of the old guard (the merchants Feng Shaoshan and Gu Xingyi and the banker Lin Kanghou) served on the council of 1927 but lost their places on that of 1932. The advisers to the municipal government were recruited from a small group of bankers and entrepreneurs (Chen Guangfu, Yu Xiaqing and Wang Yiting) who, out of conviction, opportunism or expediency, seem to have become unconditional partners of the new regime.[11]

The bourgeoisie was thus stripped of its autonomous representative institutions, eased out of local administration and challenged in the most traditional of its activities. It also lost control of the kind of anti-foreigner movements that it had been organising for the past twenty years, frequently very much to its own advantage.

The institutionalisation of boycotting

When the new regime took over the organisation and control of boycotting, it converted this manifestation of autonomous social resistance into a double-edged weapon that could be directed against both imperialism and the bourgeoisie itself.

The students, like the merchants, lost the initiative in the Boycott of June 1927 that had been triggered by the landing of Japanese troops in Shandong. It was now in the Shanghai headquarters of the Guomindang that the mass organisations met, that regulations were drawn up and that sanctions against contraveners were decreed. Even if the cages designed for the confinement of cheating merchants do not appear to have come in for much use, boycotting nonetheless gave the authorities the means to tighten their control over the business community.

The institutionalisation of boycotting took on more definite shape in the course of the developments that followed. The Boycott of 1928, organised in protest against a second landing of Japanese troops in Shandong, was right from the start controlled and directed by the government. In early May, the headlines of the *Central Daily* (*Zhongyang ribao*) exclaimed: 'General fury against the landing of Japanese troops! Let us all rally behind the Party!'[12] At the end of July, a national anti-Japanese conference laid down the procedures to be followed by all boycotting organisations in China and this time, in Hankou at least, the cages were not left empty![13]

The Boycott of 1931–2 marked the completion of the government takeover. The boycotting was sparked off by the Mukden incident and Japanese aggression in Manchuria in September 1931 and the movement was swiftly taken in hand by the Guomindang apparatus. In Shanghai, the Association for the Salvation of the Nation (literally, the Association of Anti-Japanese Resistance for the Salvation of the Nation (Fanri jiuguo lianhehui)), organised to implement the boycotting, was directed by an executive committee dominated by members of the central and local Party apparatus. Representatives of the business circles were reduced to impotence and in December 1931 they decided to withdraw from the committee altogether. With the backing of the trade unions and school and educational organisations, the Guomindang used the Association for the Salvation of the Nation to radicalise its campaign for popular support. And it was not without evidence that Japan came before the League of Nations to accuse the Chinese authorities of having organised the boycotting themselves. The evidence produced took the form of a circular dated 25 September 1931, from the Yuan executive to provincial and municipal authorities, and entitled 'Plan of action against Japan'. It was quite explicit: all Party committees were to organise 'popular committees of resistance to Japan and for the salvation of the nation'.

C. F. Remer presented world opinion with a defence of the Chinese claim of spontaneous and autonomous action in which the public authorities took no part. But even he was forced to admit that this boycotting was much better coordinated than all previous movements.[14] The strategy of controlled–spontaneous mass movements was invented well before the Cultural Revolution!

The bourgeoisie, dispossessed of all powers of initiative, found that the weapon it had long been using 'for the salvation of the country' was now turned against it. From 1932 on, the punishments for real or supposed disobedience to the boycott took an a new character. It was no longer, as it used to be, a matter of putting the offenders' names on the index, fining them or destroying their stocks. Instead, veritable terrorist attacks were mounted against the delinquent merchants by clandestine groups whose names speak for themselves – 'The blood brigades for the extermination of traitors', 'The brigades of iron and blood', and so on. In the hands of the officials, the Guomindang activists and the gangsters under their protection, boycotting became an instrument of terror, another means of subjecting the bourgeoisie to the power of the State.

The threatened sanctuary of the concessions

Since the nineteenth century, the expansion of the Chinese bourgeoisie had benefited from the existence of the concessions, those foreign enclaves where the merchants installed themselves to escape from the arbitrary interference and exactions of the Chinese authorities. From 1927 on, the concession system came increasingly under threat, both in legal terms and in practice, as a result of the nationalist restoration that the bourgeoisie had actively desired but one of whose first victims it was soon to become.

Following the example of Great Britain, which decided against taking back the concessions of Hankou and Jiujiang after they had been occupied by nationalist and communist forces in the spring of 1927, the great powers opted for a policy of compromise. Out of 33 concessions 20 were returned to the government of Nanking. To be sure, the largest concessions remained in their hands, in particular those of Shanghai. But the foreigners had to agree to return the Mixed Court to China and, in 1930, this was replaced by a district tribunal and a provincial court of appeal, free from all foreign interference. The Chinese residents of the International Settlement at last won the right to be represented on the Municipal Council, first by three delegates, and then, in May 1930, by five. Meanwhile the Municipality of Greater Shanghai was waging a veritable war of attrition against the foreigners, time and again creating incidents and difficulties, and pressing for an even more restrictive interpretation of the treaties or even, sometimes, quite simply ignoring them. The foreigners judged it prudent to avoid a showdown. But as one compromise led to another their privileges were whittled away and the Chinese authorities acquired what amounted to overseeing rights over the Settlement's affairs.[15]

In particular, they managed to extend their control over public opinion, or at least over its formation and expression both in schools and in the press. They successfully enforced the requirements that first all teaching establishments, and later all newspapers, should be registered. Having regained judiciary power over the Chinese residents, they also made the foreign community feel the weight of their administrative power.

The alliance that the Guomindang had established with the Shanghai gangsters in April 1927 also helped it to strengthen its control over the concessions. Unlike policemen and inspectors, thugs and gangsters were not checked by administrative frontiers. Under the leadership of Du Yuesheng (1888–1951), Huang Jinrong and Zhang Xiaolin, the members of the Green Gang (20,000 or maybe even 100,000 strong) were turned into so many agents of the Guomindang, prepared not only to track down trade union leaders and communists but also to kidnap and execute rich merchants who refused to provide funds for the government. Between May and August 1927, a veritable wave of terror crashed upon the merchant community, which was compelled to finance the nationalist troops' march to the northern provinces.

The concessions were increasingly open to the legal or illegal influences of the Guomindang and no longer provided anything more than an illusory refuge for Chinese nationals. Like the merchants of the nineteenth century, the latter now found themselves with nowhere to turn as they faced the growing pressures of the bureaucratic apparatus.

Was the bourgeoisie impotent or did it collude?

The capitalists protested against the exploitation and provocations they were subjected to. In the summer of 1928, when the Northern Expedition had reached its goal and Chiang Kai-shek had reconquered the territory, they made the most of a period of relative political detente and the protection that T. V. Soong, then Minister of Finance, was affording them, to present their grievances and demands at the National Conferences on the Economy (June 1928) and Finance (July 1928). The National Chambers of Commerce Federation which met in October 1928 demanded five seats for its own representatives in the Yuan legislature. The merchants even threatened to discontinue their loans to the government if they did not obtain satisfaction.[16]

The Third Guomindang Congress (March 1929), closely followed by the reorganisation of the Shanghai General Chamber of Commerce, put a stop to these demonstrations of independence. After Feng Shaoshan's unsuccessful attempt to regain control of the Chamber in December 1931, the bourgeoisie seems to have given up all attempts at resistance. Are the many pressures exerted upon it by the Guomindang enough to account for its passivity? Without going so far as to resuscitate the theory of a bourgeois-based regime, it is perhaps legitimate to suggest that the Nanking regime brought to capitalists – some of them, at least – enough advantages to persuade them to rally to it.[17]

The entrepreneurs whose personal careers and financial interests stood to gain most from the regime were the bankers. Under the Republic, the Peking bankers, closely linked with political and administrative circles, built up their fortunes on public loans. From 1927 on, the Shanghai bankers, who had hitherto jealously guarded their independence, in their turn became the principal providers of public funds, thereby linking their fortunes to those of Chiang Kai-shek. Between 1927 and 1931, they underwrote most internal loans (50–75%) to the tune of 1,000 million dollars. The bonds, which the government sold for much less than their nominal value, brought in to the banks real interest of about 20%, considerably more than the official rate of 8.6%. For the banking sector, the early years of the regime were years of prosperity. But during the 1931–2 crisis, market saturation, the invasion of Manchuria and political instability caused the value of loan stocks to plunge. Later, in 1936, the government imposed an obligatory reduction in repayment values. And in the meantime, monetary reform and the banking coup of 1935 afforded it control of the principal credit houses, which were now put under bureaucratic management.

With their prerogatives impaired and definitely stripped of their powers of initiative, some bankers at this point elected to enter the upper echelons of the administration. One was Wu Dingchang, who had embarked upon his career in the Bank of China in 1912, when he engineered a reform that favoured private shareholders; in 1923, inspired by the American model, he had reorganised private banks, collecting all their resources in a common Treasury and Savings Fund; then in 1935, he severed all his connections with free enterprise and became, first, Minister of Industry and then, in 1937, governor of Guizhou province.[18] Chang Kia-ngau was another who, while at the Bank of China, had always, both in Shanghai and in Peking, upheld a liberal concept of banking activities. He had played an active role in setting up the Shanghai Bankers' Association and in launching the *Bankers' Weekly*. At the head of the Chinese Consortium, he had attempted, in 1921, to force the Peking government to impose strict financial controls and adopt budgetary reforms. Ejected from the Bank of China by the 1935 coup, Chang became director of the Ministry of Railways, and then in 1942 was sent on an official mission to the United States to study problems of economic reconstruction.[19]

Qian Yongming opted for a political and administrative career as early as 1927. From 1922 to 1925, he had fiercely defended the Communications Bank against official interference and had served as president of the Shanghai Bankers Association at a time (1920–22) when it was asserting itself as a powerful and autonomous political force. Yet he immediately rallied to Chiang Kai-shek, accepting first the post of Vice-Minister of Finance and in the next year that of Commissioner of Finances for Zhejiang province.[20]

Other bankers were prepared to work as officials in establishments that they had formerly run as entrepreneurs. One was the former director-general of the Bank of China, Song Hangzhang, who after the 1935 reform became chairman of the bank's board of directors, under the control of T.V. Soong. Song Hangzhang, who in 1915–16 had done his utmost to dissociate the Bank of China from the political activities of Yuan Shikai, now put his services at the disposal of the Nanking government. Other bankers, who did not go so far as to become officials nevertheless found themselves pursuing their activities under the more or less direct control of the government authorities and rerouting their careers as they took on the official missions offered them. For example, Chen Guangfu up until 1937 continued to manage his private bank, the Shanghai Bank of Trade and Savings, which he had founded in 1915. His friendship with H.H.Kung (1881–1967), his former colleague in the United States and – it was rumoured – his blood brother, perhaps made it easier for him to accept the control that the latter, as Minister of Finance, exercised over his banking activities. It certainly furthered Chen's public career, for he was sent to the United States to negotiate the conversion of the stock of Chinese silver with a view to monetary reform. After 1937, Chen devoted himself exclusively to his official functions. He directed China's borrowing policies in the United States and, from 1938 to 1941, acted as chairman of the Commission of External Trade for the Ministry of Finance.[21]

Without changing quite so dramatically, the career of Li Ming, the promoter of the Zhejiang Industrial Bank, also took on a more official character. In 1927, he became chairman of the Commission for the Consolidation of internal borrowing, thereby strengthening the government's credit. After 1935, the government gave him the task of reorganising the banking sector.[22]

The financial advantages that the new regime's borrowing policies afforded the bankers between 1927 and 1931, and the prospect of official or semi-official careers that opened up before them, encouraged the bankers to rally to the regime and speeded up the process of converting these entrepreneurs into officials or quasi-officials. Besides, the 1935 banking coup, whereby the government imposed its control over 66–70% of the banking sector, left them with scarcely any other option. On the other hand, the industrialists and traders had been coerced rather than won over. Their fortunes were eroded by increasingly heavy taxation that included consolidated taxes on production in 1928, and revised customs dues in 1928, 1929 and 1933. When the great cotton and flour mill owner Rong Zongjing was made bankrupt in 1935, he reminded the government, from which he was requesting assistance, that over the past three years, his taxes had risen to a total of 10 million dollars.[23] With the exception of a few special cases, such as that of Mu Ouchu, who, having lost control of his cotton mills in the 1923 crisis, in 1929 accepted the post of Vice-Minister of Finance, the industrialists and merchants do not appear to have switched to bureaucratic careers in such striking numbers as the bankers. Clearly, the industrialists and wholesalers were not in a position to finance the government deficit as the bankers did. Consequently, they could not expect such favourable treatment. Besides, up until 1935, they still enjoyed a certain autonomy of action. During the years that followed, when the government, with the backing of the powerful network of official banks, set about extending its control over the industrial and commercial sector, now weakened by the world economic crisis, the entrepreneurs were not invited to offer their services to the State: most were supplanted by officials who had already been appointed in this area.

The process of integrating the bourgeoisie into the State apparatus was thus carried out by dispensing a mixture of force and privileges. The force for the most part struck the entrepreneurs, while most of the privileges went the way of the bankers. The regime's need for money explains the favourable treatment meted out to the bankers. Furthermore, no doubt the practices of modern banking, founded almost entirely upon the financing of public expenditure, made the bankers better prepared to reconvert to the bureaucratic system than the Chinese merchants conditioned as the latter were by their corporatist and autonomous traditions. Thus alienated, the bourgeoisie was no longer its own master. Its fate now depended upon the government which had placed it under its supervision. It depended upon the actions of that government but also, at a deeper level, upon its very nature and the idea that it had elaborated of its role. Our study of the bourgeoisie thus calls for some definition of the Nanking regime.

2   State capitalism, bureaucratic capitalism and the professionalisation of the bureaucracy under the Nanking government (1927–37)

The subordination of the bourgeoisie to the State suggests that, in one of those cyclical movements so well described by E. Balazs,[24] the triumphant bureaucratic apparatus was about to stifle the spirit of enterprise once again. It is natural enough that the symbiosis that operated during the 1930s between the Guomindang officials and a bourgeoisie obedient to government directives should bring to mind the bureaucratic capitalism of the declining years of the imperial regime. Under the Guomindang, as under the Qing, the government was trying to use modern business enterprise to strengthen its own authority, and high-ranking officials were seeking to profit personally from the material and human resources mobilised in the name of economic development. But the role played by the notion of modernisation in the Guomindang ideology and the paramount importance of the resources of the treaty ports to its finances make it impossible to equate the Nanking government with the old Confucian and rural Empire.

In the light of the institutional reforms undertaken by the Guomindang regime, perhaps we should regard the symbiosis between bureaucracy and bourgeoisie as a temporary stage, a means for the State to assist and develop a still weak class of entrepreneurs and to prepare for an eventual flowering of Chinese capitalism. Alternatively, perhaps we should not consider State intervention as providing an initial impulse to private enterprise at all, but rather as the first step in a veritable takeover of development by the public powers. In this case, the partial absorption of the bourgeoisie by the bureaucracy would coincide with the formation of a technostructure operating within the State and Party apparatus. In contrast to the old-style official capitalism of the Qing, characterised by the bureaucratisation of business, this new State capitalism would be based upon the professionalisation of the bureaucracy.

The capitalism and ideology of the Guomindang

Within the Guomindang itself, the ideological trends seem to have been sufficiently contradictory for there to be grounds for upholding each of these two opposing theses. In support of that of a modernising bureaucracy, eager to enter into dialogue with the entrepreneurs and anxious to help them and have them participate in government, we may again refer to the career of T. V. Soong. As we have seen, his first efforts to cooperate with the bourgeoisie dated back to the National Conference on the Economy, which he organised in June 1928. In 1932, anxious to win the support of the business community, in his opposition to Chiang Kai-shek's policies of military spending, which he judged to be excessive, T. V. Soong organised a Conference against the Civil War at the Shanghai General Chamber of Commerce; it was probably the last important political appearance of the bourgeoisie as such. In the following year, T. V. Soong tried to get some of the Shanghai capitalists included among the directors of the National Economic Council (Quanguo jingji weiyuanhui), a government body set up to develop and administer financial and technological aid from Western countries to China. His departure from the government in 1933 brought this collaboration to an end and deprived the business circles of their principal spokesman.

The regime was, in truth, dominated by an anti-capitalist ideology borrowed from the doctrines of Sun Yat-sen and strengthened by the experience of the world crisis. At its Third Congress in March 1929, the Guomindang vigorously repeated its condemnation of private capitalism. In Shanghai itself, many activists from the local Party apparatus, urged on by young leaders mostly from teaching circles and burning with ideological zeal, repeatedly demonstrated their hostility against the bourgeoisie and its representative organisations. In 1929, one of these young activists Chen Dezheng demanded the suppression of the General Chamber of Commerce and the Merchants' Corps. It was also these local Party groups which, beyond the control of the municipal government, in 1931-2 radicalised the boycotting movement, turning it into a campaign of terror against the merchants.[25]

From 1932 on, this 'leftist' attack on Chinese capitalism petered out. The central government and also the officials that it had placed at the head of the Shanghai municipal government seem to have arrived at a compromise with a minority of the elite leaders, who pronounced themselves ready to collaborate with the regime in day-to-day administration. But during the 1930s the leftist anti-capitalism of the Guomindang was replaced by a rightist anti-capitalism overlaid with Confucian precepts and fascist slogans. Although it sought to justify itself by claiming a revolutionary past, this anti-capitalist feeling in many cases arose from traditional attitudes hostile to mercantilism. They found expression in, for example, the behaviour of one such as Han Fuqu, governor of Shandong from 1930 to 1936. He was concerned to improve administration in the countryside and was distrustful of over-rapid industrialisation and urbanisation.[26] As for the modernisers, they found their models in the Italian or German dictatorships and, in the name of efficiency, pressed for economic development planned and coordinated by the State. This was the position adopted by, among others, Liu Jianqun, the theorist of Chinese fascism and the inspiration behind the Blue Shirts. The disciplinary code of this secret organisation classed the 'merchant traitors' among the 'rotten elements' to be eliminated from society and demanded direct State management for heavy industry, mines, transport and external trade.[27] Economic development was desired as a manifestation of national grandeur and power, but in itself it did not represent a priority.

Many other forces were also at work under the cover of these ideologies – greed, nepotism and cliquishness, for example. Economic construction was regarded simply as an opportunity to get rich by many high-ranking officials and by even more of their wives.

The reform of economic institutions and its perverse effects

Uncertainty over objectives gave rise to a wide range of policies. The restoration of internal peace and security – particularly in the middle and lower Yangzi basin – and the repression of workers' strikes and the trade union movement encouraged the activities of the entrepreneurs. More specifically, moreover, the government introduced a series of institutional reforms long desired by the chambers of commerce and the banking and employers' associations. In 1931, the *lijin* was abolished. China recovered its tariff autonomy: dues on imports rose from 4% in 1929 to 10% in 1930, reaching 25% in 1934. A modern Mint was established in Shanghai to prepare the way for the abolition of the tael, decreed in March 1933. The disappearance of this old currency unit simplified the monetary system, which was now based solely upon the silver dollar. Monetary unification was completed in November 1935, when the worldwide rise in the price of silver forced China to adopt a legal (*fabi*) currency to be minted exclusively by four great government banks under the control of a Monetary Reserve Fund.[28]

In 1928, a Central Bank of China was established. It brought under its authority the old semi-official Communications Bank and Bank of China, together with the more recently created Farmers' Bank of China (Zhongguo nongming yinhang). The effect of this was to restructure the modern banking sector. The Central Bank of China took over responsibility for customs receipts from the foreign establishments and the increasing flow of these dues went to swell its treasury. In 1933, the Shanghai Chamber of Compensation took over the task of supervising inter-bank accounts from the Hong Kong and Shanghai Bank.

Ever since 1911, heavy *lijin* dues, the absence of tariff autonomy and the chaotic monetary and banking system had been criticised, rightly enough, as so many obstacles to the development of the modern sector and the expansion of the bourgeoisie. The Nanking government's reforms swept those obstacles away, but immediately set in their place others, equally great. In the zones under government control, the *lijin* was abolished only to be replaced by a host of taxes on production: on cigarettes and flour (1928), cotton yarns, matches and alcohol (1931), mineral ores (1933), and so on. The regained tariff autonomy served not so much to protect national industries as to fill the State coffers: import dues were also levied on raw materials, machinery and equipment and manufactured products. The rationalisation and centralisation of banking structures led on to the 'coup' of November 1935, which amounted to nationalisation. Meanwhile, the introduction of paper money made it possible for the government itself to finance its deficit by frequent issues of new notes, thereby opening up the way to chronic inflation.

All the reforms that the bourgeoisie had longed for thus seemed to rebound against them. Despite a number of superficial similarities, the policies of Nanking do not stand comparison with those of the Japanese leaders of the Meiji era. Although the reforms of the Guomindang government sometimes encouraged the activities of the bourgeoisie, its essential aim certainly was not to create an institutional framework favourable to private enterprise. Indeed, it provided many demonstrations of its unconcern, the most striking probably being the total lack of any aid forthcoming during the early years of the commercial and industrial depression of 1932–5.

Towards State capitalism?

So do the Nanking government's policies indicate a move towards State capitalism? The quasi-nationalisation of the banks in November 1935 did not, in itself, represent a takeover of the principal economic activities since, in China, the expansion of the modern banking sector rested upon the financing of public expenditure much more than upon productive investment. All the same, this nationalisation gave the government many opportunities to intervene in the industrial and commercial sectors, and, following the crisis, members of the business community, with their backs to the wall, were themselves requesting such interventions. At first these took the form of credit: 20 million *yuan* were dispensed to support industrial and commercial enterprises by a Commission for Loans set up, somewhat late in the day, in June 1935 and placed under the control of Du Yuesheng.[29] Later the Bank of China, steered by its new director T. V. Soong, took over control of about fifteen cotton mills (comprising about 13% of all Chinese spindles) and extended its interventions to many sectors of light industry – tobacco, flour, and the processing and selling of rice.

Comparatively speaking, the Central Bank of China, controlled by H. H. Kung, was rather less active. But as far as both these banks were concerned, the interrelations of public and private interests were extremely complex. For example, H. H. Kung and T. V. Soong were the principal shareholders in a private concern, the China Development Finance Corporation (set up in 1934 for the purpose of attracting foreign capital to Chinese businesses), whose main role after 1935 consisted in mediating between the government banks and public agencies – the Ministry of Finance and the National Economic Council, for example – whose responsibility it was to launch major development plans. It sometimes also happened that these influential figures and their families made private investments. H. H. Kung, in partnership with Du Yuesheng, set up the Qixing Company (Qixing gongsi), which speculated on loan certificates, gold, cotton and flour. Then there were the many mixed businesses. Some emerged from the takeover of struggling private concerns such as, for example, the Nanyang Brothers' Tobacco Company, in which T. V. Soong became the major shareholder in 1937. Many of these – the Chinese Refinery of Vegetable Oils (Zhongguo zhiwu youliaochang gufen youxian gongsi), the Chinese Tea Company (Zhongguo chaye gufen Youxian gongsi) and the Shanghai Central Fish Market (Shanghai yushichang gufen youxian gongsi) – were directly organised by Wu Dingchang, the Minister of Industry from 1936 to 1937, with the collaboration of provincial governments and the financial support of private capitalists, mostly from government circles. Most of these companies received aid and enjoyed monopolies and privileges and so had no trouble in crushing private competition.[30]

Only the Natural Resources Commission (Ziyuan weiyuanhui), which came under the direct control of Chiang Kai-shek, and the National Military Council, pursued a policy of confiscation, the consequence of which was to bring most heavy industry and mining concerns under government control. The purpose of this commission, which was the most important of the government economic agencies and which had introduced a Five-Year Investment Plan for 270 million dollars, was to set up a number of industrial bases in the provinces of Hunan, Hubei, Shaanxi and Sichuan, with foreign aid, to provide for the needs of national defence.[31] Inspired by the ideas of Sun

Yat-sen, this plan was supposed to represent the first step towards the establishment of a controlled economy (*tongzhi jingji*). Having studied the German and Soviet experiments, the directors of the commission came to the conclusion that this was the only possible means of development for countries that were latecomers to modernisation. They aimed to create large-scale projects using high concentrations of capital. These were to be partly financed by foreign credit and controlled by the State; it was a strategy that was later adopted for the first Chinese Five-Year Plan (1953–7). Efforts were made to replace the coastal modern and cosmopolitan sector, founded on the expansion of light industry and private capitalism, by a nationalised sector situated within convenient reach of the various natural resources in the inland provinces and oriented towards the production of machinery, in particular military equipment.

After half a century and all kinds of experiments, China has still not made its choice between the alternatives presented at that point. But in 1937, the State sector was still weak. The achievements of the Natural Resources Commission were limited and government industry represented no more than about 11% of (modern) Chinese industrial capital. However, that does not mean that all the industrial concerns outside the public sector belonged to the private sector. The role played in them by high-ranking officials of the regime, in various capacities, conferred on these businesses an ambiguous status, altogether characteristic of bureaucratic capitalism.

The symbiosis between the bourgeoisie and the administration: the emergence of a 'technical intelligentsia'

The corruption that was rife and the confusion of State interests with those of its adminstrators are condemned by most historians. But the system as a whole cannot be defined by these aspects alone. Comparison with businesses placed under bureaucratic supervision and merchant management in the nineteenth century is useful only up to a point. The bureaucrats of 1930 had little in common with the mandarins of 1880. Although promoters such as Wu Dingchang sometimes looked to provincial governors for support, the impulse for development essentially came from a few high-ranking officials working for the central government. The most active among them had studied abroad and they were far better adapted to the modern world and its industrial and financial techniques than their predecessors of the Qing era had ever been.

Many of them had emerged from liberal circles and had pursued a university or technical career before being employed by the regime. Despite their involvement in the administrative and/or political arena, they continued to regard themselves as experts. One example is provided by the most illustrious of them, Weng Wenhao (1889–?). He had trained as a geologist in Belgium and later became director of the Institute of Geological Exploration and also taught at the Qinghua University of Peking. Then he was appointed head of the Natural Resources Commission, over which he presided without interruption from 1935 to 1947. In this post, which at the outbreak of war he combined with the important job of Minister of the Economy, with responsibility for controlling the entire field of industrial, mining, commercial and agricultural activities, Weng surrounded himself with aides who enjoyed a reputation for their skills, honesty and 'professionalism'. At first, Weng Wenhao was close to Hu Shi, collaborating with him to produce the *Independent Criticism* magazine (*Duli pinglun*), which came out in Peking from 1932 on. A few years later, when he had become a supporter of State capitalism and planned development, Weng resolutely took his stand with the regime, without, however, abandoning a certain freedom of thought and action in the areas in which he was qualified to operate.[32]

At a relatively more modest level, the personnel recruited to run the (Chinese) municipality of Shanghai provides another example of the rise of this technical and modernising elite in the administration. The forty or so leaders who between 1927 and 1937 successively served as mayors or heads of the main municipal services constituted a group of young men (40 years old on average) who had all been educated up to university level and over half of whom had gone on to acquire specialised skills abroad. In general, they appear to have been well qualified for their jobs and, given the difficult circumstances in which they laboured, they made a by no means negligible impact.[33]

By admitting technicians and banking and economic experts, the Chinese bureaucracy speeded up its own transformation – at least as regards the upper echelons of the administration. There these experts tended to form a group relatively independent from the central power, a 'technostructure' which collaborated with the political system but did not identify with it. The 'technical intelligentsia', as it is known in the USSR, where, as a group, it occupies a very important place in society, exercised its skills and fulfilled its responsibilities within the system yet retained a relatively critical attitude towards the political power.[34] The ambiguity of the relations between the Guomindang regime and those who managed the economy was to come to the surface in the post-war years (1945–9), when even Weng Wenhao ended up, in 1948, by abandoning the cause of the nationalist government.

This bureaucratic bourgeoisie, in many respects closer to the new class of present-day socialist systems than to the liberal bourgeoisies of the West, should really not be judged either on the basis of its relations with private enterprise or on the grounds of corruption (common, to varying degrees, to all the 'new classes'), but on its ability to further the economic development of the country.

Was it responsible for the stagnation condemned by Douglas S. Paauw and Lloyd E. Eastman?[35] Or should it, on the contrary, be congratulated for the expansion described by Ramon Myers and Thomas G. Rawsky?[36] The uncertain economic record of the Nanking decade does not make it easy to decide. But this uncertainty essentially concerns the evolution of the rural world, for historians are in general agreement as to the progress made in the small modern sector. The index of industrial production, established by J. K. Chang, shows that, with an annual growth rate of 8–9%, the Nanking decade equalled the development that obtained through most of the republican era (1912–37). Moreover, Rawsky draws attention to the qualitative progress achieved by the industries in the process of modernisation.

But beneath this generally expansionist tendency, a cycle similar enough to that of the 1920s can be glimpsed. Following the economic miracle of the post-war years, interrupted by the crisis of 1923–4, which was then prolonged by three years of revolution and civil war, the modern sector, from 1928 on, enjoyed a new period of prosperity which lasted up until the crisis of 1932. By 1935, a quarter of Chinese factories had closed down. Business was just picking up again when, in 1937, the Sino-Japanese War broke out.

In the 1930s, as in the previous decade, these economic fluctuations were determined essentially by external factors. The formidable depreciation of silver, which dropped over half its value on the international market between 1928 and 1931 and which coincided with the world crisis, had the effect of a devaluation for China. Its stimulatory action compensated, as far as exports were concerned, for the effects of the Western crisis and, by putting the break on certain imports, made up for the customs tariffs that were too low to protect national industries. When the pound sterling was devalued in 1931, followed by the American dollar in 1934, the value of silver rose sharply and the effect of falling prices was immediately felt by Chinese producers, while in the treaty ports efforts were made to keep imports at the same prices as over the preceding period. The buying power of silver consequently did not increase as rapidly in China as on foreign markets and this disparity provoked a massive run on silver and violent deflation. These waves of inflation and deflation, combined with the effects of Japanese aggression in Manchuria and in Shanghai, contributed more than any other factor to undermine the economy of the treaty ports during the 1930s.[37]

Compared with China's permanent dependence upon the world market, the bureaucracy's return in force and the decline of the business bourgeoisie were of no more than secondary importance. It was not bureaucratisation that checked the progress of the modern sector and hence that of the business bourgeoisie too, but the intrinsic weakness of China as a nation.

3   Communists and capitalists

The 1949 revolution seemed to offer China another chance to break the vicious circle of underdevelopment and at last to become the 'rich and powerful' nation the nineteenth-century reformers had dreamed of. As they faced the task of modernisation that their predecessors had failed to accomplish, the new leaders held one or two trump cards: not so much the liberation of the social forces to which the Party rhetoric constantly referred, but rather the rebirth of a full and complete State power. The restoration of the State made it possible for China to regain the internal peace and national independence and sovereignty that it had lacked for over a century. The Peking government was able to implement the development strategy that its Nanking predecessor had merely gestured towards. In the first five-year period (1953–7), the priorities for official investment were heavy industry and the inland provinces; foreign intervention took the form of Soviet aid negotiated and controlled entirely by the government, and the problem of relations between the State and business was settled to the benefit of the former, by extending the mixed and public sector and adopting centralised planning.

Despite a few spectacular successes, the strategy of the first Five-Year Plan itself created new imbalances and blockages to which Mao Zedong was drawing attention as early as 1956. All the controversy surrounding the abondonment of the Soviet model, the adoption of a 'Chinese way', the opposition between radicals and pragmatists and even the application of today's policies of readjustment and reform have constantly highlighted the permanence or recurrence of the same problems that had already been present in the pre-revolutionary years.

Central to these problems are the relations between the State and the elite groups – the bureaucrats and the social agents (i.e. those whose strength stems from their wealth or their social position rather than from power delegated by the State) – whose collaboration is indispensable if the State is to get economic development off the ground. In 1949 the new regime's modernising impetus was checked by the incompetence of its own cadres, most of whom had emerged from rural guerilla groups. It thus found itself forced to adopt a relatively conciliatory policy towards the entrepreneurs. Mao Zedong praised 'the positive qualities of urban capitalism' and Liu Shaoqi criticised 'Comrades who, despite common sense, persist in attacking the bourgeoisie'.[38] The compromise that the regime now reached with the capitalists was by no means unfavourable to the latter – quite the reverse. Three years after the communist victory, these capitalists felt strong enough to organise a counterattack against the power that was encroaching on the areas in which they had traditionally exercised their skills. Their action took a number of indirect forms that included sabotage, evasion and disregard of official orders. But it nonetheless constituted a threat to State power. The Party reacted in shattering fashion and the bourgeoisie emerged physically broken from the 'Five Antis' (Wufan) Campaign, which in 1952 brought to an end the dominant economic role that it had played in the modern sector for half a century. It also forfeited all its social prestige and all its political influence.

Four years later, in 1956, the nationalisation of commercial and industrial businesses set the seal on the elimination of the bourgeoisie as an autonomous social force. The government entrusted business management to its own cadres. In so doing, it speeded up the institutionalisation of a bureaucratic elite whose power was based on the takeover of all sorts of apparatuses (such as the army, the police, State administration and the Chinese Communist Party) and which made the most of its prerogatives to control the means of production. But since it was more interested in protecting its own status than in modernising the economy, this elite tended to behave more as a parasite than as an agent of State capitalism.

The phenomenon is a common one and 'the new class' had already been criticised by Milovan Djilas when, in 1962, Mao called upon the Party and the masses to fight against the danger of a 'capitalist restoration'. But why did Mao continue to speak of the bourgeoisie when he was really attacking the new bureaucratic elites? Why did he mask the new realities of the situation under old concepts? The mismatch between the facts and the words applied to them betrayed Mao's constant desire to make a show of his respect for Marxist orthodoxy, even as he stepped aside from the paths that Marx and Lenin had mapped out. He depended heavily upon the vocabulary of the class struggle as used by Marx in his analysis of capitalist society to illuminate contradictions in socialist society that Marx had not foreseen. With the vocabulary unchanged, it was possible to deny that any ideological innovation was involved and to forestall accusations of deviationism. The homogeneity of historical time could thus be confirmed as could that of the categories by which it was structured.

However, none of this could resuscitate the bourgeoisie. And over and above all the verbal subtleties, the events of the Cultural Revolution showed clearly that the true target of the mass movements unleashed by the 'Great Helmsman' was the State and Party bureaucracy.

Mao's death in 1976 removed the obstacles that he had tried to erect to prevent the bureaucratic elite groups from becoming a ruling class. Nothing now stood in the way of the institutionalisation of their power and their metamorphosis into a State bourgeoisie, except, to a certain extent, the ever more pressing needs of modernisation.

It was these that prompted Deng Xiaoping to appeal once again to private initiative and the entrepreneurs – not in order to revive capitalism, but to rationalise the structures of the Chinese economy and improve its management and performance. However, associating the survivors of the old bourgeoisie with the setting-up of the modernisation programme did not mean offering them control of it. Besides, the old bourgeois elite groups were now much weakened. The structures that had welded them into a class had been destroyed, and the remaining informal networks based on kinship or common geographical origins were, on their own, not enough to replace them. Faced with the power represented by State and Party, the survivors of the bourgeoisie were no longer in a position to present a threat comparable to that which had so alarmed the 1951–2 leaders. The specific qualities that were still theirs and that rendered them valuable to the present leaders in no way constituted an obstacle to their integration into the official apparatus. The gap separating these survivors from the new ruling caste, which seemed at last to have set its power on a stable footing, now seemed virtually closed. The privileges, mores and interests of the two groups coincided closely. All the same, the process of amalgamating the new and the old elites was not entirely smooth or trouble-free. Many of the new managers, who felt less well equipped to exploit the advantages of the open policy than the former capitalists, tried to stand in the way of their rivals by opposing the new economic strategy. But it was no longer a matter of principle with them, just competitive rivalry.

The process currently under way may be regarded as illustrating Robert Michels' prophetic analysis according to which 'the class struggle will always lead to the creation of new oligarchies which will fuse with the old'. As is well known, Michels regarded the inevitable resurgence of social oligarchies as an effect of the organisational principle and an expression of 'necessities of a tactical and technical order which stem from the consolidation of any disciplined political aggregate'.[39]

By reason of the great expanse and diversity of its territory and population, China is probably one of the countries on whose political life such constraints weigh most heavily. However, here the amalgamation of elite groups has not been a matter of 'the older groups positively attracting, absorbing and assimilating . . . the new ones' in the manner described by Michels.[40] Instead, what has happened is that part of the old bourgeoisie has been integrated into the communist bureaucracy. It was clearly the break that the revolution constituted that explains why this sort of process took place. But another factor to be remembered is the force of the centralising tradition that the communist bureaucracy inherited. In the name of national unity, this tradition legitimised the existence of a strong government imposing its authority through a dominant caste. Seen from this point of view, the integration of the old bourgeoisie into the communist bureaucracy seems above all a reflection of the policical traditions of the Chinese nation.

Many thinkers have been intrigued by the predominance of the bureaucratic apparatus in both the imperial mandarin system and the communist system of cadres. But the elimination of the bourgeoisie as a dominant force in urban society, combined with its retention or return in the management of national development is just as remarkable. The existence of a business bourgeoisie made the modernisation of the Chinese bureaucracy possible, if not easy, and that modernisation was necessary if this vast rural country was to achieve a technological and economic breakthrough. In its golden age, the bourgeoisie had learned that without a State apparatus capable of maintaining (or restoring) national unity and independence, such a breakthrough was impossible. To the extent that the Chinese historical tradition excluded the coexistence of a strong (or relatively strong) State together with autonomous groups within a pluralist society, symbiosis between the bureaucracy and the bourgeoisie may thus appear as the latter's only possible means of survival.

Obscured but not destroyed, the influence of the bourgeoisie might thus continue to make itself felt within the system through the pockets of autonomy inevitably created by even a partial professionalisation of the bureaucratic leadership. It is even conceivable that, if circumstances happened to change – as a result either of continuing political crises or else of an economic breakthrough – the business bourgeoisie might one day recover its true social identity.

Notes

The following abbreviations are used in the notes and bibliography.
BCEO   *Bulletin commercial d'Extrême-Orient*
CEB   *Chinese Economic Bulletin*
CWR   *China Weekly Review*
LSYJ   *Lishi yanjiu*
MGRWZ Li Xin et Sun sibai (eds.) *Minguo renwuzhuan*
NCH   *North China Herald*
NLZB   *Nuli zhoubao*
TR   *China, Inspectorate General of Customs, Returns of Trade and Trade Reports*
SQSL   *Shanghai qianzhuang shiliao*
WSQJ   *Wusi shiqi qikan jieshao*
WWC 1925   China Weekly Review (ed.) *Who's Who in China, 1925*
WWC 1931   China Weekly Review (ed.) *Who's Who in China, 1931*
WSYD   *Wusi yundong zai Shanghai shiliao xuanji*
XHZS   *Xinhaigeming zai Shanghai shiliao xuanji*
YHYK   *Yinhang yuekan*
YHZB   *Yinhang zhoubao*
ZSHYB *Shanghai zongshanghui yuebao*
ZBJDMR *Zhongguo jindaimingren tujian*

Prologue

1 *Far Eastern Economic Review*, 1 June 1979, p. 27. *Time Magazine*, 17 March 1980, p. 17.
2 See the report of the Ministry of Trade broadcast by the New China Agency, 27 November 1982 (BBC, *Summary of World Broadcasts*, part 3, *The Far East*, Daily, 7194/B II 9). See also *International Herald Tribune*, 1 June 1983. By way of comparison, it is interesting to note that following the nationalisation programme carried out in 1956, 15 million of these small private businesses still survived in China (*Beijing Review*, Peking, 19 January 1983, p. 17)
3 *Far Eastern Economic Review*, 1 June 1979, pp. 24–6.
4 Marie-Claire Bergère, 'Les problèmes du développement et la rôle de la bourgeoisie chinoise: la crise économique de 1920–1923' thesis for a *doctorat d'Etat*, prepared under the supervision of Jean Chesneaux and presented to the University of Paris VII, June 1975.
5 Jean Chesneaux, *Le Mouvement ouvrier chinois de 1919 à 1927*, Paris–The Hague, Mouton, 1962.
6 Lucien Bianco, 'Les paysans et la Révolution', *Politique étrangère*, no. 1 (1968), pp. 117–41; Lucien Bianco, 'Les paysans dans la Révolution', in C. Aubert *et al.*, *Regards froids sur la Chine*, Paris, Le Seuil, 1976, pp. 283–308.

Tradition, opening-up and modernity

1 Mark Elvin, *The Pattern of the Chinese Past*, Stanford, Stanford University Press, 1973; Ramon H. Myers, *The Chinese Peasant Economy: Agricultural Development in Hopei and Shantung, 1890–1949*, Cambridge, Mass., Harvard University Press, 1970; H. Ramon Myers, *The Chinese*

Economy: Past and Present, Belmont, California, Wadsworth, 1980; Dwight H. Perkins, *Agricultural Development in China, 1368–1968*, Chicago, Aldine, 1969; Dwight H. Perkins (ed.), *China's Modern Economy in Historical Perspective*, Stanford, Stanford University Press, 1975; William G. Skinner (ed.), *The City in Late Imperial China*, Stanford, Stanford University Press, 1977; William E. Willmott (ed.), *Economic Organization in Chinese Society*, Stanford, Stanford University Press, 1972.

2 Max Weber, *Gesammelte Aufsätze zur Religionensoziologie*, vol. 1 *Die Wirtschaftsethik der Weltreligionen, 1. Konfuzianismus und Taoismus*, Tübingen, J. C. R. Mohr, 1922, repr. Paul Sibeck, 1963–72, 3 vols. Max Weber's theses have been adopted by most Western sociologists and political historians interested in China, such as Marion J. Levy and Shih Kuo-heng, *The Rise of the Modern Chinese Business Class: Two Introductory Essays*, New York, IPR, 1949; Lucian W. Pye, *The Spirit of Chinese Politics*, Cambridge, Mass., MIT Press, 1968; and Richard Solomon, *Mao's Revolution and the Chinese Political Culture*, Berkeley, University of California Press, 1971. They have also been adopted by Chinese historians such as Li Yiyuan and Yang Guoshu, *Zhongguorende xingge: keji conghexingde taolun* (The Character of the Chinese: An Interdisciplinary Discussion), Nankang, Taibei, Institute of Ethnology, Academia Sinica, 1972 (Monograph Series B, no. 4). On the thesis of an economic failure under the Ming and Qing dynasties and an account of the relevant historical literature, see Thomas A. Metzger, *Escape from Predicament: Neo-Confucianism and China's Evolving Political Culture*, New York, Columbia University Press, 1977, pp. 3–5, 237–9; and Thomas A. Metzger, 'On the Historical Roots of Economic Modernization in China: The Increasing Differentiation of the Economy from the Policy during the late Ming and Early Ch'ing Times', in *Conference on Modern Chinese Economic History*, Taibei, The Institute of Economics, Academia Sinica, 1977, pp. 38–45.

3 Perkins, *Agricultural Development*, p. 240.

4 Perkins, *Agricultural Development*, pp. 16–17. In the seventeenth and eighteenth centuries, most European peasants harvested little more than four times the seed sown. Only in a few favoured zones – the Netherlands and England – did they manage to produce six to ten times the seed sown.

5 Elvin, *The Pattern of the Chinese Past*, p. 268.

6 William G. Skinner, 'Marketing and Social Structure in Rural China', *Journal of Asian Studies*, vol. 24, nos. 1–3 (November 1964, February 1965, May 1965), pp. 3–43, pp. 195–228, pp. 363–99. See in particular vol. 24, no. 2 (February 1965), p. 227.

7 That is to say, 20 million people. See Skinner (ed.), *The City in Late Imperial China*, pp. 211–20.

8 Susan M. Jones, 'Finance in Ningpo, 1750–1850', in Willmott (ed.), *Economic Organization*, pp. 47–8. See also Andrea L. Mac Elderry, *Shanghai Old-Style Banks (Ch'ien-chuang), 1880–1935: A Traditional Institution in a Changing Society*, Ann Arbor, Michigan, 1976 (Michigan Papers in Chinese Studies, no. 25). The rise of the houses known as Shanxi banks (after the native province of their proprietors) came earlier than that of the *qianzhuang* banks. But the main business of the Shanxi banks was transferring the public funds that were deposited with them.

9 For a detailed discussion of the works that blame Confucianism for the Chinese failure to modernise (such as those by Joseph R. Levenson and Benjamin I. Schwartz), see Ramon H. Myers and Thomas A. Metzger, 'Sinological Shadows. The State of Modern China Studies in the United States', *Washington Review*, spring 1980.

10 Etienne Balazs, 'Les villes chinoises. Histoire des institutions administratives et judiciaires', *Recueils de la société Jean Bodin*, no. 6 (1954), pp. 225–39.

11 Albert Feuerwerker, *China's Early Industrialization: Sheng Hsuan-huai (1844–1916) and Mandarin Enterprise*, Cambridge, Mass., Harvard University Press, 1973.

12 Metzger, *Escape from Predicament*, pp. 14–19.

13 Thomas A. Metzger, *The Internal Organization of Ch'ing Bureaucracy*, Cambridge, Mass., Harvard University Press.

14 Thomas A. Metzger, 'The Organizational Capabilities of the Ch'ing State in the Field of Commerce: The Liang-huai Monopoly 1740–1840', in Willmott (ed.), *Economic Organization*, p. 16. Many examples of efficient cooperation between the imperial bureaucracy and private entrepreneurs during the nineteenth century may be found in the remarkable work by

William T. Rowe, *Hankow, Commerce and Society in a Chinese City, 1796–1889*, Stanford, Stanford University Press, 1984.

15 Myers, *The Chinese Economy: Past and Present*, p. 75.

16 Metzger, 'On the Historical Roots of Economic Modernization in China'.

17 According to Evelyn Rawsky, *Education and Popular Literacy in Ch'ing China*, Ann Arbor, University of Michigan Press, 1979, p. 23. In the eighteenth and nineteenth centuries, 30–45% of the male population understood enough characters to use written documents, generally of a specific nature and pertaining to particular professional activities: sale agreements, farm leases, accounts, and so on. If we accept Rawksy's criteria of literacy (familiarity with a limited number of characters related to particular activities), the level of literacy appears to have been higher in China than in France in the sixteenth century.

18 Perkins, *Agricultural Development*, p. 115, calculates that in the 1930s, 20–30% of the harvest was sold on the spot, 10% was sold in distant parts of China and 3% was exported. A hundred years earlier, less of it was put on the market, but the proportion sold on the spot was at least as high.

19 William G. Skinner, 'Cities and the Hierarchy of Local Systems', in Skinner (ed.), *The City in Late Imperial China*, pp. 275–351.

20 Karl Polanyi, *The Great Transformation*, Boston, Beacon Press, repr. 1957, chapter 5, 'Evolution of the Market Pattern'; Simon Kuznets, *Modern Economic Growth Rate, Structure and Spread*, New Haven, Yale University Press, 1966, p. 9.

21 Mark Elvin, 'The High Level Equilibrium Trap: the Causes of the Decline of Invention in the Traditional Chinese Textile Industries', in Willmott (ed.), *Economic Organization*, pp. 137–72.

22 For a general view of the problems of proto-industrialisation, see Franklin Mendels, 'Proto-Industrialization: The First Phase of the Process of Industrialization', *Journal of Economic History*, vol. 32 (1972), pp. 241–61. See also Pierre Deyon and Franklin Mendels (eds.), *La Protoindustrialisation: Théorie et réalité*, 2 vols., Lille, Université des arts, lettres et sciences humaines, 1982. Instances of correlation between proto-industrialisation, demographic growth and rural pauperisation have been studied in detail by H. Medick, in P. Kriedte, P. Medick and J. Schlumbohm, *Industrialisierung vor der Industrialisierung. Gewerbliche Warenproduktion auf dem Land in der Formationsperiode des Kapitalismus*, Göttingen, Vanderhoeck and Ruprecht, 1977. Pierre Jeannin provides an analysis and a perceptive critique of Medick's thesis in 'La proto-industrialisation: développement ou impasse?', *Annales. Economies, Sociétés, Civilisations*, no. 1 (January–February 1980), pp. 52–65.

23 Yü Ying-shih, *Trade and Expansion in Han China: A Study in the Structure of Sino-Barbarian Economic Relations*, Berkeley and Los Angeles, University of California Press, 1967.

24 William G. Skinner, 'Regional Urbanization in Nineteenth Century China', in Skinner (ed.), *The City in Late Imperial China*, pp. 211–53; Gilbert Rozman, *Urban Network in Ch'ing China and Tokugawa Japan*, Princeton, New Jersey, Princeton University Press, 1973, pp. 6, 88.

25 Chang Chung-li, *The Chinese Gentry: Studies on their Role in Nineteenth Century Chinese Society*, Seattle, University of Washington Press, 2nd edn, 1970 (1st edn 1956), pp. 116–19, 137.

26 He Bingdi (Ho Ping-ti), *Zhongguo huiguan shilun* (History of the *Landmannschaft* in China), Taibei, Xuesheng shuju, 1966; Chang Perry (Chang P'eng), 'The Distribution and Relative Strength of the Provincial Merchants Groups in China, 1842–1911', doctoral dissertation, University of Washington, 1958.

27 Wellington Chan, 'Merchant Organizations in Late Imperial China: Patterns of Change and Development', *Journal of the Royal Asiatic Society*, Hong Kong, vol. 15 (1975), pp. 28–42.

28 See, among others, Balazs, 'Les villes chinoises'.

29 Skinner, 'Cities and the Hierarchy of Local Systems'.

30 Etienne Balazs, *La Bureaucratie céleste. Recherches sur l'économie et la société de la Chine traditionelle*, Paris, Gallimard, 1968. See also Levy and Shih Kuo-heng, *The Rise of the Modern Chinese Business Class*.

31 Ho Ping-ti, 'The Salt Merchants of Yang-chou. A Study of Commercial Capitalism in Eighteenth Century China', *Harvard Journal of Asiatic Studies*, vol. 17 (1954), pp. 130–68. Other examples of a diversification of careers within great families such as these are provided by the same author in *The Ladder of Success in Imperial China. Aspects of Social Mobility, 1368–1911*, New York, Columbia University Press, 1962, chapter 2; by James H. Cole, 'Shaohsing: Studies in Ch'ing Social History', Ph.D. dissertation, Stanford University, 1975, chapter 3,

'Gentry or Merchant?'; and by Susan Jones, 'Rural–Urban Continuities. Leading Families of two Chekiang Market Towns', *Ch'ing-shih wen-t'i* (Historical Questions Relating to the Qing), vol. 3, no. 7 (November 1977), pp. 67–104.

32 Frederick W. Mote, 'The Transformation of Nanking, 1350–1400', in Skinner (ed.), *The City in Late Imperial China*, pp. 101–54.

33 Fernand Braudel, *Civilisation matérielle, économie et capitalisme, XVe–XVIIIe siècle*, vol. 3, *Le Temps du monde*, Paris, Armand Colin, 1979, chapter 1, 'Les divisions de l'espace et du temps en Europe'; Immanuel Wallerstein, *The Modern World System: Capitalist Agriculture and the Origins of the European World-Economy in the Sixteenth Century*, New York, Academic Press, 1974.

34 For a general critical study of Wallerstein's views on the evolution of peripheral countries, see Theda Skocpol, 'Wallerstein's World Capitalist System: A Theoretical and Historical Critique', *American Journal of Sociology*, vol. 82, no. 5 (March 1977), pp. 1075–90. The application of the theory of the 'development of underdevelopment' to the Chinese case is presented and discussed in Philip C. C. Huang (ed.), *The Development of Underdevelopment in China: A Symposium*, White Plains, M. E. Sharpe, 1980. According to Robert F. Denberger, 'The Role of the Foreigner in China's Economic Development 1840–1949', in Perkins (ed.), *China's Modern Economy in Historical Perspective*, pp. 19–48, the destructive effects of foreign aggression on the Chinese economy have been exaggerated by some historians.

35 John K. Fairbank, 'The Creation of the Treaty System', in John K. Fairbank, *The Cambridge History of China*, vol. 10, *Late Ch'ing, 1800–1911*, part 1, Cambridge, Cambridge University Press, 1978, pp. 213–63.

36 See Albert Feuerwerker, *The Chinese Economy ca. 1870–1911*, Ann Arbor, Michigan, 1969 (Michigan Papers in Chinese Studies, no. 5); and Albert Feuerwerker, *The Foreign Establishment in the Early Twentieth Century*, Ann Arbor, Michigan, 1976 (Michigan Papers in Chinese Studies, no. 29).

37 Paul A. Varg, 'The Myth of the China Market 1890–1914', *American Historical Review*, February 1968, pp. 742–57. On a number of disappointments arising from foreign investments, see Hou Chi-ming, *Foreign Investment and Economic Development in China, 1840–1937*, Cambridge, Mass., Harvard University Press, 1965.

38 The imperial bureaucracy prevented the Germans from exploiting some of the concessions and advantages that they had obtained in Shandong in 1898. See John Schrecker, *Imperialism and Chinese Nationalism: Germany in Shantung*, Cambridge, Mass., Harvard University Press, 1971.

39 Feuerwerker, *The Chinese Economy ca. 1870–1911*, p. 59. On the same subject, see Thomas G. Rawsky, 'Chinese Dominance of Treaty Port Commerce and its Implication, 1860–1875', *Explorations in Economic History*, vol. 7, no. 4 (1970), pp. 451–73.

40 John E. Wills Jr, 'Maritime China from Wang Chih to Shih Lang. Themes in Peripheral History', in Jonathan Spence and John E. Wills Jr (eds.), *From Ming to Ch'ing: Conquest, Region and Continuity in Seventeenth Century China*, New Haven, Yale University Press, 1979, pp. 201–38.

41 Marie-Claire Bergère, ' "The other China": Shanghai from 1919 to 1949', in Christopher Howe (ed.), *Shanghai, Revolution and Development in an Asian Metropolis*, Cambridge, Cambridge University Press, 1981, pp. 1–34.

42 This is the thesis developed by Rhoads Murphey in his two books, *The Treaty Ports and China's Modernization: What Went Wrong?*, Ann Arbor, Michigan, 1970 (Michigan Papers in Chinese Studies, no. 7) and *The Outsiders: The Western Experience in India and China*, Ann Arbor, University of Michigan Press, 1977.

43 H. D. Fong, *The Growth and Decline of Rural Industrial Enterprise in North China*, Tientsin, Chihli Press, 1936, pp. 8–28.

44 Skinner, 'Marketing and Social Structure in Rural China'.

45 Alexander Gerschenkron, *Economic Backwardness in Historical Perspective*, Cambridge, Mass., Harvard University Press, 1962.

46 See the critical assessment of Gerschenkron's theses by Myers and Metzger, 'Sinological Shadows: The State of Modern China Studies'.

47 Martin Malia, *Comprendre la révolution russe*, Paris, Le Seuil, 1980, pp. 36–41, 81.

48 Wallerstein, *The Modern World-System*, chapter 3. Wallerstein ascribes the strength of States in the core to the size of the surpluses (liable to taxation) that this zone comes to possess, and also

302   Notes to pages 32–52

to the support forthcoming from their dominant capitalist classes, which require the government to reciprocate by protecting their industries and helping them to maintain their control over international trade. Conversely, he claims, the weakness of the periphery is due to the small profit that the State derives from world trade and to the fact that, since it is profitable for their dominant capitalist classes to deal directly with the entrepreneurs of the core, they tend not to concentrate on furthering a policy of national development.

49 For example Yung Wing (Rong Hong), 1828–1912, who graduated from the University of Yale in 1854; the first Chinese barristers, Wu Tingfang (1842–1922) and Ho Kai (Hi Qi, 1859–1914); the compradores Tong King-sing (Tan Jingxing, 1832–92) and Zheng Guangying (1842–1923); the journalist Wang Tao (1828–97); Ma Jianzhong (1844–1900), the first Chinese to obtain a French *baccalauréat*, in 1878, and his brother Ma Liang (Ma Xiangbo, 1840–1939), one of the founders of the Aurora University in Shanghai.

50 Paul A. Cohen, *Between Tradition and Modernity: Wang T'ao and Reform in Late Ch'ing China*, Cambridge, Mass., Harvard University Press, 1974, chapter 6, 'Pioneer Reformers and the Littoral'.

51 Wellington Chan, *Merchants, Mandarins and Modern Enterprise in Late Ch'ing China*, Cambridge, Mass., Harvard University Press, 1977, pp. 213–34.

52 Skinner, 'Regional Urbanization', pp. 205–9.

53 Hao Yen-p'ing, *The Comprador in Nineteenth Century China: Bridge between East and West*, Cambridge, Mass., Harvard University Press, 1970, Chapter 5, 'The Comprador as a Nouveau Rich'. See also Marianne Bastid, *L'Evolution de la société chinoise à la fin de la dynastie des Qing*, Paris, EHESS, 1979 (Cahiers du Centre Chine, no. 1).

54 Kojima Yoshio, 'Shinghai kakumei ni okeru Shanhai dokuritsu to shōshinsō' (The Gentry, the Merchant Class and the Independence Movement in Shanghai during the 1911 Revolution), *Tōyō shigaku ronshū* (Collection of Oriental History), Tokyo, no. 6 (August 1960), pp. 113–34.

55 Hao Yen-p'ing, *The Comprador*, p. 102.

56 Susan Jones, 'The Ningpo Gang and Financial Power in Shanghai', in Mark Elvin and William G. Skinner (eds.), *The Chinese City between Two Worlds*, Stanford, Stanford University Press, 1974, pp. 73–96; Susan Jones, 'Finance in Ningpo', pp. 75–7; Mac Elderry, *Shanghai Old-Style Banks*, chapter 3, 'Ch'en-chuang: 1800–1870'.

57 Chan, *Merchants, Mandarins and Modern Enterprise*, pp. 146–7.

58 Michael R. Godley, *The Mandarin-Capitalists from Nanyang: Overseas Chinese Enterprise in the Modernization of China 1893–1911*, Cambridge, Cambridge University Press, 1981, chapter 4, 'The Recruitment of Chang Pi-shih', and chapter 7, 'South China's Railroad Offensive'.

59 *Maoxin Fuxin Shenxin xitong: Rongjia qiye shiliao, 1896–1937* (The Maoxin–Fuxin–Shenxin Group: Material for a History of the Business Concerns of the Rong Family, 1896–1937) (herafter *Rongjia qiye shiliao*), Shanghai, Shanghai shehui kexueyuan Jingji Yanjiusuo (Institute of Economics of the Shanghai Academy of Social Sciences), Shanghai renmin chubanshe (1st edn 1962), repr. 1980, 2 vols.; Chan, *Merchants, Mandarins and Modern Enterprise*, pp. 39–147; Fuo Feng, 'Baihuoye dawang: Yong'an guojia' (The Department Store Kings: the Guo Family of the Yong'an Company), *Nanbeiji* (North Pole, South Pole), Hong Kong, no. 120 (16 May 1980).

60 Chan, *Merchants, Mandarins and Modern Enterprise*, pp. 89–92.

61 The analysis by Maurice Dobb, *Studies on the Development of Capitalism*, London, Routledge and Kegan Paul, revised edn, 1967, p. 121, is extremely pertinent: 'It [merchant capital] continued to exist in the pores of society ... to acquire political privileges was their first ambition. Since they were essentially parasites on the old economic order, their fortune was, in the last analysis, associated with their host.'

62 Hao Yen-p'ing, *The Comprador*, pp. 180–206.

63 Marie-Claire Bergère, *Une crise financière à Shanghai à la fin de l'Ancien Régime*, Paris–The Hague, Mouton, 1964.

64 Carl F. Remer, *A Study of Chinese Boycotts*, Baltimore, The Johns Hopkins Press, 1933; Kikuchi Takaharu, *Chūgoku minzoku undō no kihon kōzō: taigai boikotto no kenkyū* (The Basic Structure of Nationalist Movements in China: The Anti-foreigner Boycotts), Tokyo, Daian, 1966.

65 Philip A. Kuhn, 'Local Self-Government under the Republic. Problems of Control, Auton-

omy and Mobilization', in Frederic Wakeman and Carolyn Grant (eds.), *Conflict and Control in Late Imperial China*, Berkeley, University of California Press, 1975, pp. 257–98.

66 On the disintegration of the traditional gentry and the urbanisation of the elite groups, see Philip A. Kuhn, *Rebellion and its enemies in Late Imperial China: Militarization and Social Structure*, Cambridge, Mass. Harvard University Press, 1970, pp. 223–5; Joseph W. Esherick, *Reform and Revolution in China: The 1911 Revolution in Hunan and Hubei*, Berkeley, University of California Press, 1976, chapter 3, 'The Urban Reformist Elite'; and William T. Rowe, 'Urban Control in Late Imperial China. The Pao-chia System in Hankou', in Joshua A. Fogel and William T. Rowe (eds.), *Perspectives on a Changing China*, Boulder, Westview Press, 1979, pp. 89–112.

67 See above, p. 21.

68 Marianne Bastid, *Aspects de la réforme de l'enseignement en Chine au début du XXe siècle d'après les écrits de Zhang Jian*, Paris–The Hague, Mouton, 1971, pp. 46–53, 65, 71–3.

69 Mark Elvin, 'The Gentry Democracy in Shanghai', Ph.D. dissertation, Cambridge University, 1968, pp. 42–3, 48–52, 58, 89.

70 Huang Yanpei was an active member of the Jiangsu education society. After the 1911 revolution, he became one of those principally responsible for Chinese educational policies. He was, himself, an ardent partisan of professional training and worked in liaison with industrial circles to promote it. After 1949, his career continued under the new regime, which appointed him to a number of mainly honorific posts.

   Ma Liang (Xiangbo), brought up as a Catholic, helped the Jesuit missionaries to set up the Aurora University (Zhendan xueyuan) in Shanghai in 1903. Two years later, Ma Liang withdrew from this establishment and, with the support of the gentry, created the rival Fudan University (Fudan gongxue). Luo Zhen-yu, who was strongly influenced by the Japanese model, took an active part in the reformist movement, but after the 1911 revolution, he adopted a reactionary political attitude and thereafter devoted himself essentially to scholarly pursuits.

   Xu Dinglin, who held a number of mandarin qualifications, himself set up factories and schools and was a keen promoter of industry and education at a provincial level.

71 H. S. Brunnert and V. V. Hagelstrom, *Present Day Political Organization of China* (translated from the Russian) (1st edn 1910) repr. Taibei, Book World Company, no date, pp. 184, 358–63, 408–9.

72 Chan, *Merchants, Mandarins and Modern Enterprise*, p. 226.

73 Bastid, *Aspects de la réforme de l'enseignement*, pp. 71–2.

74 In the classic handbook of Chinese institutions, *Present Day Political Organization of China*, by the two Russian sinologists, Brunnert and Hagelstrom (1910), it is interesting to find the term *zemstvos* (p. 180) used to refer to local and provincial assemblies. In China, as in Tsarist Russia, the importance of the political role played by these assemblies stood in sharp contrast to the confining legal limitations that the State power attempted to impose upon their activities.

75 Bastid, *Aspects de la réforme de l'enseignement*, pp. 73–4.

76 John Fincher, 'Political Provincialism and the National Revolution', in Mary Clabaugh Wright (ed.), *China in Revolution: The First Phase, 1900–1913*, New Haven, London, Yale University Press, 1968, p. 215; Escherick, *Reform and Revolution in China*, pp. 91–6.

77 Chang P'eng-yuan, 'The Constitutionalists', in Wright (ed.), *China in Revolution*, p. 149.

78 Chang P'eng-yuan, 'The Constitutionalists', p. 161.

79 François Furet, *Interpreting the French Revolution*, Cambridge, Cambridge University Press, 1981.

The economic miracle

1 Yan Zhongping *et al.*, *Zhongguo jindai jingjishi tongji ziliao xuanji* (Selection of Statistical Material on the Economic History of Modern China) (hereafter *Tongji ziliao*), Peking, Kexue chubanshe, 1955, p. 153.

2 Charles F. Remer, *The Foreign Trade of China*, Shanghai, Commercial Press, 1926, p. 196; Yan Zhongpin, *Zhongguo mianfangzhi shigao* (History of the Cotton Industry in China), Peking, Kexue chubanshe, 3rd edn 1963, pp. 81, 151–2.

3 *Chinese Economic Journal*, vol. 12, no. 1 (January 1933).
4 *La Politique de Pékin*, 14 May 1916, p. 4; Cheng Yu-kwei, *Foreign Trade and the Development of China: An Historical and Integrated Analysis through 1948*, Washington DC, University Press of Washington, 1956, p. 262; Alfred Pinnick, *Silver and China: An Investigation of the Monetary Principles Governing China's Trade and Prosperity*, Shanghai, Kelly and Walsh, 1930, p. 11.
5 A. W. Ferrin, *Chinese Currency and Finance*, Washington DC, US Department of Commerce, 1919 (Special Agent Series, no. 186).
6 Remer, *The Foreign Trade*, p. 184.
7 China, Inspectorate General of Customs, *Returns of Trade and Trade Reports*, Shanghai, annual (hereafter *TR*), 1915, 'Report from Shanghai', p. 729.
8 *China Weekly Review* (hearafter *CWR*), Shanghai, weekly, 4 January 1919, p. 189.
9 *CWR*, 11 January 1919; Yan Zhongping, *Tongji ziliao*, pp. 66–7.
10 Zhou Xiuluan, *Di yici shijiedazhan shiqi Zhongguo minzugongyede fazhan* (The Development of Chinese National Industries during the First World War) (hereafter *Zhongguo minzugongyede fazhan*), Shanghai renmin chubanshe, 1958.
11 Yan Zhongping, *Zhongguo mianfangzhi shigao*, p. 163.
12 Yan Zhongping, *Tongji ziliao*, p. 65.
13 *TR*, 1919, Reports from various ports.
14 *TR*, 1919, 'Report from Shanghai', p. 705; *CWR*, 19 July 1919, p. 507.
15 *CWR*, 25 December 1920, p. 326.
16 John K. Chang, *Industrial Development in pre-Communist China: A Quantitative Analysis*, Edinburgh, The University Press, 1969.
17 *CWR*, 25 October 1919, p. 326.
18 *CWR*, 1 November 1919, p. 376.
19 *Rongjia qiye shiliao*, pp. 39–117; Wan Lin, 'Zhongguode "miansha dawang" "mianfen dawang" Wuxi Rongshi jiazu baofashi' (History of the Irresistible Rise of the Rong Family from Wuxi, the 'Cotton and Flour Kings'), *Jingji daobao zhoukan* (Economic Bulletin), Peking, weekly, no. 50 (14 December 1947).
20 Yan Zhongping, *Zhongguo mianfangzhi shigao*, p. 175.
21 *TR*, 1916, 'Report from Hankow', p. 538.
22 *CWR*, 22 March 1919, p. 146.
23 *Nanyang xiongdi yancao gongsi shiliao* (Material for the History of the Nanyang Brothers' Tobacco Company), Zhongguo kexueyuan Shanghai jingji yanjiusuo (Institute of Economics of the Shanghai Academy of Sciences of China), Shanghai renmin chubanshe, 1958.
24 *CWR*, 23 April 1921; 13 August 1921; Chen zhen *et al.*, *Zhongguo jindai gongyeshi ziliao* (Material for the History of Modern Industry in China) (hereafter *Gongyeshi ziliao*), 4 vols., Peking, Sanlian shudian, 1957–61, vol. 1, pp. 502–9.
25 *Beijing gongye shiliao* (Material for the History of Industries in Peking), Peking, Zhongguo renmin daxue gongyejingjixi (Department of Industrial Economy of the People's University), 1960, p. 2.
26 Yan Zhongping, *Tongji ziliao*, p. 102; Zhou Xiuluan, *Zhongguo minzugongyede fazhan*, pp. 52–7.
27 *Shanghai minzu jiqigongye* (The National Mechanical Engineering Industries of Shanghai), Peking, Zhongguo shehui kexueyuan Jingji yanjiusuo (Institute of Economics of the Academy of Social Sciences of China), Zhonghua shuju (1st edn 1966), 2nd edn 1979, 2 vols. (Zhongguo zibenzhuyi gongshangye shiliao congkan (Collection of Material on the History of Capitalist Industry and Trade in China)), vol. 1, pp. 210–30.
28 Zhou Xiuluan, *Zhongguo minzugongyede fazhan*, chapter 2.
29 Remer, *The Foreign Trade*, p. 193; *TR*, 1915, 1916, 'Reports from Changsa, from Nanning'.
30 Yan Zhongping, *Tongji ziliao*, pp. 72–3.
31 *Shanghai qianzhuang shiliao* (Material for the History of the *qianzhuang* Banks of Shanghai) (hereafter *SQSL*), Shanghai, Zhongguo renmin yinhang Shanghaishi fenhang (People's Bank of China, Shanghai branch), Shanghai renmin chubanshe, 1960, pp. 98, 105–8.
32 *SQSL*, pp. 840–2.
33 *SQSL*, pp. 634–7.
34 The information provided by the Institute of Economics of the Nakai University of Tianjin

(*1913 nian– 1952 nian Nankai zhishu ziliao huibian* (Collection of Material on the Nankai Indexes, 1913–1952), Peking, Tongji chubanshe, repr. 1958, pp. 2–7) is based upon weekly records of Tianjin prices. These records relate to 78 products in 1913, 83 products in 1919, 100 products in 1926 and 127 products in 1949. The percentage of manufactured gooods involved (50.38%) is higher than that of agricultural products and raw materials (49.62%) and this does not accurately reflect the structures of the Chinese economy.

The general index of the Shanghai Market bureau is based upon records of the prices of 147 products and is calculated on the basis of five basic criteria: the prices of grain, food products, textiles, metals and a variety of other products. Some products assume an undeserved importance – metals, for example, compared to textiles. See *Chinese Economic Bulletin* (hereafter *CEB*), Peking, weekly, 21 June 1924, 'Methods of Price Investigation'.

35 Yan Zhongping, *Tongji ziliao*, table 61, p. 165.
36 *SQSL*, p. 202.
37 Chesneaux, *Le Mouvement ouvrier chinois de 1919 à 1927*, p. 197; *Shanghai zongshanghui yuebao* (The Shanghai General Chamber of Commerce Monthly Review) (hereafter *ZSHYB*), vol. 4, no. 4 (April 1924), pp. 35–5.
38 Marie-Claire Bergère, 'Une crise de subsistance en Chine, 1920–1922', *Annales, Economies, Sociétés, Civilisations*, no. 6 (November–December 1973), pp. 1361–1402.
39 *CWR*, 2 October 1920, pp. 217ff; Bulletin commercial d'Extrême-Orient (hereafter *BCEO*), Shanghai, monthly, Weekly financial reports, 1920, 1921.
40 *CWR*, 12 March 1921, p. 73.
41 Tsing Tung-chun, *De la production et du commerce de la soie en Chine*, Paris, Geuthner, 1928, p. 138.
42 *Bulletin des soies et des soiries et moniteur des soies*, Lyons, weekly prices, 1919, 1920.
43 *CWR*, 27 November 1920, p. 726; 18 December 1920, pp. 154–5; 11 February 1922, p. 462.
44 *CWR*, 16 October 1920, p. 330.
45 *BCEO*, July 1921; *CEB*, 1 July 1922, p. 3.
46 *CWR*, 16 October 1920, p. 331.
47 *BCEO*, January 1922, pp. 35–6.
48 *CWR*, 4 June 1921, p. 14, 'The Trade of China, 1920'.
49 See Table 2.8.
50 *BCEO*, September 1921, p. 41.
51 *BCEO*, October 1921 (readers' letters).
52 *CWR*, 9 April 1921, p. 292.
53 For example, in Tianjin, where Chinese merchants refused to take delivery of the cotton fabrics that they had ordered. See 'Tianjin huobang yu waiguo yanghang zhengchi buxia qingxing zhi yangjuiu' (Investigation into the Circumstances of the Unresolved Conflict between [Chinese] Wholesalers and Foreign Firms in Tianjin), *Yinhang zhoubao* (Bankers' Weekly) (hereafter *YHZB*), Shanghai, vol. 5, no. 12 (5 April 1921).
54 *North China Herald* (hereafter *NCH*), supplement to the *North China Daily News*, Shanghai, weekly, 27 November 1920, p. 611.
55 See above, p. 80.
56 *CWR*, 2 July 1921, p. 250; 23 July 1921, p. 386; 3 September 1921, p. 38; *NCH*, 2 July 1921, p. 11; 30 July 1921, p. 338; 13 August 1921, p. 475; 10 December 1921, p. 178; *SQSL*, pp. 117, 585, 634–40.
57 *CEB*, 25 March 1922, pp. 3–4.
58 *CEB*, 18 December 1920, p. 164; 18 March 1922, p. 11; *CWR*, 11 December 1920, p. 108.
59 The information given in this section is taken from Marie-Claire Bergère, *Capitalisme national et impérialisme. La crise des filatures chinoises en 1923*, Paris, EHESS, 1980 (Cahiers du Centre Chine, no. 2).
60 See below, p. 259.

The new entrepreneurs in the city

1 This is, in my view, true of Jean Chesneaux, in *Le Mouvement ouvrier chinois de 1919 à 1927*.
2 Luo Zhiru, *Tongjibiaozhong zhi Shanghai* (Shanghai in Statistical Tables) (hereafter *Tongjibiao*),

Nanjing guoli zhongyang yanjiuyuan Shekhuikexue yanjiusuo jikan (Quarterly Review of the Institute of Social Sciences of the Academia Sinica, Nanking), 1932, no. 4, p. 21, table 29.

3 Zou Yiren, *Jiu Shanghai renkou bianqian* (Evolution of the Population of Old Shanghai) (hereafter *Shanghai renkou*), Shanghai renmin chubanshe, 1980, p. 11; Luo Zhiru, *Tongjibiao*, p. 27, table 41.

4 Luo Zhiru, *Tongjibiao*, p. 15, table 18; Zou Yiren, *Shanghai renkou*, p. 90, table 1.

5 Luo Zhiru, *Tongjibiao*, p. 16, table 20.

6 Luo Zhiru, *Tongjibiao*, p. 16, table 21.

7 Luo Zhiru, *Tongjibiao*, p. 17, table 22; Richard Feetham, *Report of the Hon. Richard Feetham: The Shanghai Municipal Council*, 2 vols., Shanghai, North China Daily News and Herald, 1931, vol. 1, p. 347.

8 Luo Zhiru, *Tongjibiao*, p. 63, table 130.

9 Zou Yiren, *Shanghai renkou*, pp. 7, 9.

10 *Shanghai chunqiu* (Shanghai Annals), Hong Kong, Zhongguo tushubianyiguan, 1967, part 1, pp. 58–9.

11 According to *Shanghai chunqiu*, part 2, p. 80, over eighty of these organisations were listed in 1912.

12 For a list of the various financial establishments in Shanghai, see *Shanghai zhinan* (Guide to Shanghai: A Chinese Directory to the Port), Shanghai shangwu yinshuguan, 10th edn, 1919, *quan* 6, pp. 32b–34.

13 For the service industries, see *Shanghai zhinan*, *quan*, 6, pp.34–45.

14 See *Shanghai zhinan*, *quan* 6, pp. 6–32b.

15 See *Shanghai zhinan*, *quan* 6, pp. 1–6. For the chinese cotton mills, see also the *ZSHYB* enquiry, vol. 1, no. 4 (July 1921).

16 *Shanghai minzu jiqigongye*, vol. 1, pp. 288–9; Hao (*The Comprador*, p. 135) puts the industrial investments of Zhu Zhiyao between 1897 and 1910 at 365 million dollars.

17 Wang Jingyu, *Zhongguo jindai gongyeshi ziliao, dier ji, 1895–1914 nian* (Material for the History of Modern Industry in China, 2nd series, 1895–1914) (hereafter *Jindai gongyeshi*), 2 vols., Peking, Zhongguo kexueyuan Jingji yanjiusuo (Institute of Economics of the Academy of Sciences of China), Kexue chubanshe, 1957, vol. 2, pp. 881, 956–7.

18 Li Xin and Sun Sibai (eds.), *Minguo renwuzhuan* (Biographies of Figures of the Republican Period) (hereafter *MGRWZ*), 3 vols., Peking, Zhongguo shehui kexueyuan Jindaishi yanjiusuo (Institute of Modern History of the Academy of Social Sciences of China), Zhonghua shuju, 1978–1981 (Zhonghua minguoshi ziliao conggao (Project for a Collection of Material on the History of the Chinese Republic)), vol. 1, pp. 298–303.

19 China Weekly Review (ed.), *Who's Who in China*, 4th edn (hereafter: *WWC 1931*), Shanghai, 1931, p. 20.

20 *MGRWZ*, vol. 2, pp. 249–55; *Zhongguo jindaimingren tujian* (Illustrated Record of Famous Chinese of the Modern Period) (hereafter *ZGJDMR*), Taibei, Tianyi chubanshe, 1977 (repr. 1st edn, Shanghai, 1925), p. 249.

21 *Shanghai minzu jiqigongye*, vol. 1, pp. 288–9.

22 *Shanghai Yong'an gongside chansheng fazhan he gaizao* (Creation, Development and Transformation of the Yong'an (Wing On) Company of Shanghai), Shanghai shehui kexueyuan Jingji yanjiusuo (Institute of Economics of the Shanghai Academy of Social Sciences), Shanghai renmin chubanshe, 1981, p. 62, table 10.

23 Guo Feng, 'Baihuoye dawang: Yong'an guojia'.

24 Robert Keith Schoppa, *Chinese Elites and Political Change: Zhejiang Province in the Early Twentieth Century*, Cambridge, Mass., Harvard University Press, 1982, p. 160, table 17.

25 David D. Buck, *Urban Change in China: Politics and Development in Tsinan, Shantung, 1890–1949*, Madison, University of Wisconsin Press, 1978, pp. 147–8.

26 Samuel C. Chu, *Reformer in Modern China: Chang chien, 1853–1926*, New York, Columbia University Press, 1965, p. 33.

27 Fang Teng, 'Yu Xiaqing lun' (On the Subject of Yu Xiaqing), *Zazhi yuekan* (Monthly Miscellany), Shanghai, irregular monthly, vol. 12, no. 2 (November 1943), pp. 46–51; vol. 12, no. 3 (December 1943), pp. 62–7; vol. 12, no. 4 (January 1944), pp. 59–64.

28 Barry, Keenan, *The Dewey Experiment in China: Educational Reform and Political Power in the Early Republic*, Cambridge, Mass., Harvard University Press, 1977, pp. 56–73.

29 The anti-Christian persecutions of the eighteenth century ejected the European missionaries from China. However, small local Catholic communities continued to exist here and there, practising their religion in a more or less clandestine fashion. The Shanghai and lower Yangzi community included several important families such as the Wu (whose conversion dated back to Ricci's arrival in China, in the early seventeenth century), the Ma and the Zhu families.

30 *Shanghai minzu jiqigongye*, vol. 1, pp. 139–64, 281–302.

31 *ZGJDMR*, pp. 469–71.

32 *MGRWZ*, vol. 1, pp. 278–84.

33 Howard L. Boorman and Richard Howard (eds.), *Biographical Dictionary of Republican China*, 4 vols., New York, Columbia University Press, 1967–71, vol. 3, pp. 452–3; *MGRWZ*, vol. 1, pp. 270–3.

34 *ZGJDMR*, pp. 469–71.

35 *WWC 1931*, pp. 38–9; *ZGJDMR*, pp. 277–9, 345–7; Boorman and Howard, *Biographical Dictionary*, vol. 2, pp. 316–19; *MGRWZ*, vol. 2, pp. 316–19; *MGRWZ*, vol. 2, pp. 265–70.

36 The honours awarded are given in a number of biographical articles in *WWC 1931* and *ZGJDMR*.

37 Boorman and Howard, *Biographical Dictionary*, vol. 3, pp. 195–7; vol. 1, pp. 26–30.

38 Boorman and Howard, *Biographical Dictionary*, vol. 2, pp. 316–19; *MGRWZ*, vol. 2, pp. 271–5.

39 William Yinson Lee (ed.), *World Chinese Biographies* (bilingual English-Chinese edn), Shanghai, Globe Publishing Company, 1944, p. 7.

40 *MGRWZ*, vol. 2, pp. 265–70.

41 China Weekly Review (ed.), *Who's Who in China*, 3rd edn (hereafter *WWC 1925*), Shanghai, 1925, p. 690.

42 Xu Cangshui, *Shanghai yinhanggonghui shiyeshi* (History of the Achievements of the Association of Modern Banks of Shanghai) (hereafter *Yinhanggonghui*), brochure published to celebrate the appearance of no. 400 of the *Bankers' Weekly* (*Yinhang zhoubao*), Shanghai, Yinhang zhoubaoshe, 26 May 1925 (supplement), pp. 11–12.

43 Xu Cangshui, *Yinhanggonghui*, pp. 12–13.

44 *MGRWZ*, vol. 3, p. 238; Boorman and Howard, *Biographical Dictionary*, vol. 1, pp. 26–30.

45 *ZGJDMR*, pp. 239–95.

46 *Shina keizai tsūsetsu* (General Handbook of Chinese Economics), Tokyo, Yamagushi kōtō shōgo gakkō, Tōa keizai kenkyūkai (Advanced School of Commerce of Yamaguchi, Research Seminar on Far-Eastern Economics), 1928, p. 321.

47 *Yinhang yuekan* (Monthly Banking Review) (hereafter *YHYK*), Peking, monthly, no. 1 (January 1921). On the creation of banking associations, see *CWR*, 10 February 1921, p. 649.

48 *ZGJDMR*, pp. 345–7; *WWC 1925*, p. 690.

49 James C. Sandford, 'Chinese Commercial Organization and Behavior in Shanghai of the Late Nineteenth Century and Early Twentieth Century', Ph.D. dissertation, Harvard University, 1976, 440ff, chapter 5, 'The Shanghai Chinese Chamber of Commerce'. On the composition of the board of directors of the General Chamber of Commerce in 1911, see Kojima Yoshio, 'Shingai kakumei ni okeru Shanghai dokuritsu to shōshinsō', pp. 113–14. A list of the directors elected in 1918 may be found in *Shibao* (Time), Shanghai, daily, 14 October 1918.

50 Wang Jingyu, *Jindai gongyeshi*, vol. 2, pp. 907–9.

51 Wang Jingyu, *Jindai gongyeshi*, vol. 2, pp. 907, 909.

52 For a list of the directors elected in 1920, see *ZSHYB*, vol. 1, no. 1 (July 1921).

53 *ZGJDMR*, p. 337; *WWC 1931*, p. 358.

54 *Haishang mingrenzhuan* (Biographies of Shanghai Celebrities), Shanghai, Wenming shuju, no date, p. 5.

55 *ZGJDMR*, p. 310.

56 See, for example, the article by Feng Shaoshan, 'Jinri zhi san dawenti' (The Three Great Problems of Today), *ZSHYB*, vol. 3, no. 1 (January 1923), in which the author puts forward a strong defence of the position adopted by progressive business circles in Shanghai in relation to the main problems of the day.

57 For a list of directors elected in 1922, see *ZSHYB*, vol. 2, no. 8 (August 1922).

58 *Shanghai zongshanghui huiyuanlu* (Record of the Members of the Shanghai General Chamber of Commerce), brochure published by the Chamber of Commerce, Shanghai, April 1928, pp. 60ff.

The social structures of the new bourgeoisie

1 See, for example, the classic work by Levy and Shih Kuo-heng, *The Rise of the Modern Chinese Business Class.*

2 Louis Bergeron, *Banquiers, négociants et manufacturiers parisiens du directoire à l'Empire*, Paris, Mouton, 1978.

3 On Yu Xiaqing, see Fang Ten, 'Yu Xiaqing lun'. See also Liu Taotian, 'Hangyejia Yu Xiaqing xiansheng zhuanlüe' (Brief Biography of the Shipbuilder Yu Xiaqing), *Jiaoyu yu zhiye* (Education and Profession), Shanghai, irregular monthly, no. 183 (1 March 1937), pp. 233–41; Wang Beiping and Zeng Daci (eds.), *Yu Xiaqing xiansheng* (Mr Yu Xiaqing), Shanghai, Ningbo wenxueshe, 1946. This last work, published immediately after Yu Xiaqing's death, is mainly hagiographical. It is surprising that no historical study has been devoted to this figure who played a role of capital importance in the economic and political life of Shanghai for over half a century, except for the recent article by Ding Richu *et al.*, 'Yu Xiaqing jianlun' (On the Subject of Yu Xiaqing), *Lishi yanjiu* (Historical Research) (hereafter *LSYJ*), Peking, 1981, no. 3, pp. 145–66. See also Chen Laixin, *Yu xiaqing ni tsuite* (On the Subject of Yu Xiaqing), Kyōto daigaku jimbum kagaku kenkyūjo (Institute for Research on the Human Sciences of the University of Kyoto), kyō dō kenkyū hōkoku (research reports), 'Gōshi undō no kenkyū' (Research on the May Fourth Movement), series 2, no. 5, 1983.

4 On Zheng Bozhao, see Cheng Renjie, 'Yingmei yan'gongsi maiban Zheng Bozhao' (The Comprador of the British American Tobacco Company, Zheng Bozhao), *Wenshi ziliao xuanji* (Selection of Material Relating to Culture and History), ed. Zhongguo renmin zhengzhixieshang huiyi (Consultative Political Conference of the Chinese People), Shanghai renmin chubanshe, 1978, no. 1, pp. 130–54.

5 He Bingdi, *Zhongguo huigan shilun*; Negishi Tadashi, *Shanghai no girudo* (The Shanghai Guilds), Tokyo, Nippon Hyōronsha, 1951; Negishi Tadashi, *Chūgoku no girudo* (The Guilds in China), Tokyo, Nippon Hyoron Shinsha, 1953; on the complexity of the organisation of the Ningbo Guild and its evolution, see Sanford, 'Chinese Commercial Organization', pp. 216–47.

6 *SQSL*, pp. 730–3; Zheng Yifang, *Shanghai qianzhuang 1843–1947. Zhongguo zhuantong jinrongyede tuibian* (The *qianzhuang* Banks of Shanghai, 1843–1947. The Evolution of Traditional Chinese Finance), Taibei, Institute of the Three Principles of the People, Academia Sinica, 1981, pp. 31–8.

7 *SQSL*, pp. 770–1; Mac Elderry, *Shanghai Old-Style Banks*, p. 52.

8 Wu Peichu, 'Jiu Shanghai waishang yinhang maiban' (The Compradores of the Foreign Banks of Old Shanghai), *Wenshi ziliao xuanji*, Shanghai renmin chubanshe, 1980, no. 1, pp. 155–7; *SQSL*, pp. 743–4; Mac Elderry, *Shanghai Old-Style Banks*, p. 50; Zhang Guohui, 'Shijiu shiqi houbanqi Zhongguo qianzhuangde maibanhua' (The transformation of the Chinese *qianzhuang* Banks into Comprador Enterprises during the Second Half of the Nineteenth Century), *LSYJ*, 1963, no. 6, pp. 85–98.

9 Mac Elderry, *Shanghai Old-Style Banks*, p. 134; *SQSL*, pp. 210, 769.

10 Boorman and Howard, *Biographical Dictionary*, vol. 2, pp. 316–19; *MGRWZ*, vol. 2, p. 271.

11 Hao Yen-p'ing, *The Comprador*, p. 53; *Shanghai minzu jiqigongye*, vol. 1, p. 460.

12 *ZGJDMR*, pp. 273–6; Wang Jingyu, *Jindai gongyeshi*, vol. 2, pp. 954–6.

13 *Liu Hongsheng qiye shiliao* (Material for a History of the Business Concerns of Liu Hongsheng), 3 vols., Shanghai shehui kexueyuan Jingjiyanjiusuo (Institute of Economics of the Shanghai Academy of Social Sciences), Shanghai renmin chubanshe, 1981, vol. 1, pp. 3–4

14 Sanford, 'Chinese Commercial Organization', pp. 238–40, 277.

15 Negishi Tadashi, *Chūgoku no girudo*, p. 38; Tōa Dōbunkai (ed.), *Shina keisai zensho* (Complete Handbook of Chinese Economics), 12 vols., Ōsaka, Tokyo, Maruzen, Tōa Dōbunkai, 1907–8, vol. 2, pp. 74–85.

16 Negishi Tadashi, *Baiben seido no kenkyū* (Research into the Comprador System); Tokyo, Nihon Tosho, 1948, pp. 234–41.

17 Cheng Renjie, 'Yingmei yan'gongsi maiban Zheng Bozhao'.
18 *MGRWZ*, vol. 1, pp. 298–303; *Nanyang xiongdi yancao gongsi shiliao*, pp. 134–8.
19 *ZGJDMR*, pp. 261–5.
20 *Nanyang xiongdi yancao gongsi shiliao*, pp. 2, 138.
21 *MGRWZ*, vol. 1, pp. 298–303.
22 *MGRWZ*, vol. 1, pp. 285–90.
23 *ZGJDMR*, pp. 528–31.
24 Negishi Tadashi, *Chūgoku no girudo*, p. 203; Tōa Dōbunkai, *Shina keisai zensho*, vol. 2, pp. 74–85.
25 Wu Peichu, 'Jiu Shanghai waishang yinhang maiban'.
26 Richard C. Bush, *The Politics of Cotton Textiles in Kuomintang China*, New York, Garland, 1982, pp. 58–66.
27 MGRWZ , vol. 1, pp. 274–7; *Jiaoyu yu zhiye*, no. 163, 1 March 1935, pp. 101–8.
28 Cheng Renjie, 'Yingmei yan'gongsi maiban Zheng Bozhao'.
29 *Rongjia qiye shiliao*, vol. 1, p. 289.
30 *Shanghai Yong'an gongsi*, pp. 1–11.
31 *Rongjia qiye shiliao*, vol. 1, pp. 54–6; Bush, *The Politics of Cotton Textiles*, pp. 59–60.
32 *Shanghai Yong'an gongsi*, pp. 11–13.
33 *MGRWZ*, vol. 2, pp. 249–55; *ZGJDMR*, p. 249; *WWC 1925*, p. 612. Chen Zhen, *Gongyeshi ziliao*, vol. 1, pp. 397–401; Yan Zhongping, *Zhongguo mianfangzhi shigao*, p. 328.
34 *MGRWZ*, vol. 1, p. 278; *Rongjia qiye shiliao*, pp. 3–20.
35 *MGRWZ*, vol. 1, p. 309.
36 Qi Yisheng, 'Yong'an jituande chuanshiren' (The Founders of the Yong'an [Wing On] Group), *Nanbeiji* (North Pole, South Pole), Hong Kong, monthly, no. 12 (16 May 1980), pp. 8–10.
37 Bush, *The Politics of Cotton Textiles*, pp. 46–7.
38 Mu Ouchu, *Ouchu wushi zishu* (Autobiography of [Mu] Ouchu at Fifty), Shanghai, Commercial Press, 1926; *MGRWZ*, vol. 1, pp. 270–3; *WWC 1925*, p. 610; *ZGJDMR*, p. 245; Boorman and Howard, *Biographical Dictionary*, vol. 3, pp. 38–40.
39 *Rongjia qiye shiliao*, vol. 1, pp. 287–88.
40 *Shanghai Yong'an gongsi*, p. 12.
41 *MGRWZ*, vol. 1, pp. 304–8; *Shanghai minzu jiqigongye*, vol. 1, p. 460; *Dalong jiqichangde fasheng fazhan yu gaizao* (Creation, Development and Transformation of the Dalong Mechanical Engineering Works), Shanghai, Zhongguo kexueyuan Shanghai jingji yanjiusuo (Shanghai Institute of Economics of the Academy of Sciences of China), Shanghai renmin chubanshe, 1958, pp. 2–3.
42 Bush, *The Politics of Cotton Textiles*, p. 62; Qi Yizheng, 'Yong'an jituande chuanshiren', pp. 8–10; *Yong'an fangzhiyinran gongsi* (The Yong'an [Wing On] Spinning, Weaving, Dyeing and Printing Company), Peking, Zhongguo kexueyuan Jinji yanjiusuo (Institute of Economics of the Academy of Social Sciences of China) *et al.*, Zhonghua shuju, 1964 (Zhongguo zibenzbhuyi gongshangye shiliao congkan (Series of Material on the History of Capitalist Industry and Trade in China)), pp. 55–7.
43 Shanghai Yong'an gongsi, p. 6; Chen Zhen, *Gongyeshi ziliao*, vol. 1, pp. 450–2; Bush, *The Politics of Cotton Textiles*, p. 61.
44 *MGRWZ*, vol. 1, pp. 309–13.
45 *Shanghai Yong'an gongsi*, p. 80.
46 *MGRWZ*, vol. 1, pp. 304–8.
47 *MGRWZ*, vol. 2, pp. 249–55; *Hengfeng shachangde fasheng fazhan yu gaizao* (The Creation, Development and Evolution of the Hengfeng Cotton Mills), Shanghai, Zhongguo kexueyuan Jingji yanjiusuo (Institute of Economics of the Academy of Sciences of China) *et al.*, Shanghai renmin chubanshe, 1958, pp. 3–5, 34–7, 43–4.
48 *MGRWZ*, vol. 2, p. 249–55.
49 The disadvantages of nepotism seem to have been more keenly experienced in bureaucratic or semi-bureaucratic capitalist businesses of the type set up in the late nineteenth century, which, in partially renovated forms, continued to operate even during the golden age in the northern provinces of China. For example, in 1920, the military governor of Anhui province, Ni Sichong, felt no qualms about entrusting the management of the Dafeng Mills in Tianjin,

in which he had invested 200,000 dollars, to his eldest son, who had no business experience and who rapidly brought the enterprise to the brink of ruin (see Zhu Chunfu, 'Beiyang junfa dui Tianjin jindaigongyede touzi' (The Investments of the Warlords of the Northern Clique in the Modern Industries of Tianjin), *Tianjin wenshi ziliao xuanji*, no. 4 (October 1979), p. 159).

50 Bergeron, *Banquiers, négociants et manufacturiers*, pp. 65–80.
51 *Shanghai minzu jiqigongye*, vol. 1, chapters 2, 3.
52 *Shanghai minzu jiqigongye*, vol. 1, p. 197.
53 *Shanghai minzu jiqigongye*, vol. 1, pp. 45, 58, 67.
54 *Shanghai minzu jiqigongye*, vol. 1, pp. 111, 127, 169, 196–7, 462.
55 *Shanghai minzu jiqigongye*, vol. 1, pp. 463, 466.
56 *Shanghai minzu jiqigongye*, vol. 1, p. 250.
57 *Shanghai minzu jiqigongye*, vol. 1, pp. 205, 209.
58 *Shanghai minzu jiqigongye*, vol. 1, pp. 209, 229, 247, 254–5, 280.
59 *Shanghai minzu jiqigongye*, vol. 1, pp. 220–1. The presence of large numbers of joiners in the workforces of the early naval yards and mechanical engineering workshops is explained by the continuing importance of woodwork in shipbuilding in the 1850–60 period and by the use of wooden moulds in the manufacture of metallic parts.
60 *Shanghai minzu jiqigongye*, vol. 1, pp. 244–6.
61 *Shanghai minzu jiqigongye*, vol. 1, p. 460.
62 On Zhu Zhiyao, see *Shanghai minzu jiqigongye*, vol. 1, pp. 139–64, 281–302. Some of my information is taken from a manuscript record specially drawn up by research workers of the Shanghai Institute of Economics of the Shanghai Academy of Social Sciences: 'Zhu Zhiyao', Shanghai, September 1981, 15ff. In compiling this record, various sources of evidence were used, such as interviews with relatives of Zhu Zhiyao and documents preserved in the archives of the Commercial and Industrial Federation of the Shanghai Municipal Government (Shanghaishi gongshangye lianhehui dang'an shi).
63 *Shanghai minzu jiqigongye*, vol. 1, pp. 139–41.
64 See above, p. 97.
65 *MGRWZ*, vol. 1, pp. 304–8.
66 *Shanghai minzu jiqigongye*, vol. 1, pp. 273–8.
67 *Shanghai minzu jiqigongye*, vol. 1, p. 263.
68 See 'Zhongguo shachang zhi tiaocha' (Enquiry into the Chinese Cotton Mills), *ZSHYB*, vol. 1, no. 4 (April 1921), *shiye tiaocha* (industrial enquiries) section, pp. 1–9. The enquiry was carried out in 1920, when the cotton mills were enjoying a period of rapid expansion. The statistics relate to the situation in September 1920 and enable us to understand the development of the cotton mills at this date.
69 This category clearly also includes the Guo brothers, founders of the Wing On (Yong'an) Cotton Mills, who began their careers in Shanghai when they set up their department stores there. They are not taken into account in Figure 4.3, since their first cotton mill did not start operation until more than a year after the *Shanghai zongshanghui yuebao* enquiry, on which the figure is based.
70 *MGRWZ*, vol. 1, pp. 285–90.
71 *MGRWZ*, vol. 2, pp. 249–55.
72 *WWC 1931*, p. 344.
73 *MGRWZ*, vol. 1, pp. 270–3.
74 Bush, *The Politics of Cotton Textiles*, pp. 59–60.
75 *WWC 1925*, p. 414; *ZSHYB*, vol. 1, no. 4 (April 1921).
76 *MGRWZ*, vol. 1, pp. 270–3.
77 Zhen Chen, *Gongyeshi ziliao*, vol. 1, no. 4 (April 192?).
78 H. D. Fong, *Reminiscences of a Chinese Economist at 70*, Singapore, South Seas Press, 1975, pp. 8–9.
79 On the development of the cotton industries of Tianjin and the role played by the 'new bureaucracy' in that development see Zhu Chunfu, 'Beiyang junfa dui Tianjin jindaigongyede touzi'.
80 For example, the Hubei warlord, Wang Zhanyuan, invested in the modern Qingfeng Mills in Tianjin, but he spent much greater sums on buying up several thousand buildings in Tianjin, Baoding, Peking and Jinan. See Zhao Shixian, 'Junfa Wang Zhanyuan jingying gongshangye

gaikuang' (The Evolution of Warlord Wang Zhanguan's Industrial and Commercial Enterprises), *Tianjin wenshi ziliao xuanji*, no. 4 (October 1979), pp. 163–71.

81 The Anfu Club emerged out of a series of friendly reunions held in a restaurant in Anfu Alley (Anfu hutong). These were attended by partisans of Duan Qirui and representatives of the warlords who were their allies. After the election of the New Parliament, in the summer of 1918, the Club was organised on bureaucratic lines. By now its membership ran into hundreds. Nevertheless, it did not call itself a 'party' (*dang*) since, following the parliamentary difficulties of 1912–17, that word had acquired a derogatory sense, suggesting factional rivalries. See Andrew J. Nathan, *Peking Politics, 1918–1923: Factionalism and the Failure of Constitutionalism*, Berkeley, University of California Press, 1976 (Michigan Studies on China), pp. 107, 226–32.

82 Wang Jingkang and Zhang Zesheng, 'Yuyuan shachangde xingshuai shilüe' (History of the Rise and Fall of the Yuyuan Cotton Mills), *Tianjin wenshi ziliao xuanji*, no. 4 (October 1979), pp. 172–9.

83 However, family and local links of solidarity did play a relatively important role in the political and business circles of the North. Investors in the Tianjin cotton mills were linked by various family connections: for example, Cao Rui was the brother of Cao Kun, and Xu Shichang was the brother of Xu Shizhang. The interplay of local links of solidarity severely undermined the orderly running of the Huaxin Cotton Mills, for the Wuxi shareholders (grouped around Yang Weiyun) were in constant rivalry with the shareholders who were natives of Anhui – Zhou Xuexi and Sun Duosen. But these traditional links of solidarity appear to have been less important than those upon which the politico-military cliques were based.

84 The Zhili clique, led by one of Yuan Shikai's former officers, Feng Guozhang, was composed of high-ranking civil and military officials such as Cao Kun, the governor of Zhili province, and Zhang Zuolin, the military governor of the Manchurian provinces. Once it had defeated the Anfu Club, in 1920, the Zhili Clique dominated the political life of Peking and northern China up until 1922 (see Nathan, *Peking Politics*, pp. 232–9).

85 Zhou Xuexi's father, Zhou Fu, had collaborated closely with Li Hongzhang and had several times acted in the capacity of provincial governor or viceroy, during the early years of the century. On the career and business activities of Zhou Xeuxi, see Boorman and Howard, *Biographical Dictionary*, vol. 1, pp. 409–13; Albert Feuerwerker, 'Industrial Enterprise in Twentieth Century China: The Chee Hsin Cement Company', in Albert Feuerwerker, Rhoads Murphey and Marcy C. Wright (eds.), *Approaches to Modern China History*, Berkeley, University of California Press, 1967, pp. 304–41.

86 Yang Tongyi, 'Wuxi Yangshi yu Zhongguo mianfangyede guanxi' (The Links between the Yang Family, from Wuxi, and the Chinese Cotton Industry), *Gongshang shiliao* (Material on the History of Industry and Trade), Peking, Wenshi ziliao chubanshe, 1981, vol. 2, pp. 54–70.

87 Wang Jingkang and Zhang Zesheng, 'Yuyuan shachangde xingshuai shilüe'.

88 'Autobiography of Chiang Chia-ao [Chang Kia-ngau]', unpublished manuscript, translated from the Chinese, Oral History Project, Columbia University, c. 1960, 148ff, f.16.

The bourgeoisie, the State and the revolution, 1911–27

1 The role played by the bourgeoisie in the 1911 revolution was once again strongly stressed at the conference held in Wuhan (12–14 October 1981) to commemorate the 70th anniversary of that revolution. Eight of the 81 Chinese lectures delivered at the conference have been translated by Jerome Chen, 'The Role of the Chinese Bourgeoisie in 1911. Essays by Chinese Marxist Historians at the Wuhan Conference on the 1911 Revolution, October 12–14 1981', *Chinese Studies in History*, vol. 17, no. 4 (summer 1984); vol. 18, nos. 3–4 (spring–summer 1985).

   For a critical analysis of Chinese historiography in this field, see Marie-Claire Bergère, 'La révolution de 1911 jugée par les historiens de la République populaire de Chine', *Revue historique*, Paris, quarterly, no. 230 (October–December 1963), pp. 403–36; Winston Hsieh, *Chinese Historiography on the Revolution of 1911: A Critical Survey and a Selected Bibliography*, Stanford, Hoover Institution Press, 1975; Joseph W. Esherick, '1911: A Review', *Modern China*, Beverly Hills, California, quarterly, vol. 2, no. 2 (April 1976), pp. 141–84; Zhang

Kaiyuan, 'Xinhai gemingshi yangjiude sanshinian' (Studies over the Past Thirty Years on the 1911 Revolution), *Jinian xinhai geming qishizhounian xueshu taolunhui lunwenji* (Collection of Papers Presented at the Conference to Commemorate the 70th Anniversary of the 1911 Revolution) (hereafter *Qishizhounian xueshu taolunhui*), 3 vols., Peking, Zhonghua shuju, 1983, vol. 3, pp. 2117–39.

2 Zhang Kaiyuan, 'Xinhai geming yu Jiang-Zhe zichanjieji' (The 1911 Revolution and the bourgeoisies of Jiangsu and Zhejiang), *Qishizhounian xueshu taolunhui*, vol. 1, pp. 281–321, translated in Chen, 'The Role of the Chinese Bourgeoisie in 1911'.

3 Qiu Jie, 'Guangdong shangren yu xinhai geming' (The Merchants of Canton and the 1911 Revolution), *Qishizhounian xueshu taolunhui*, vol. 1, pp. 362–96. See also Edward J. Rhoads, *China's Republican Revolution: The Case of Kwangtung*, Cambridge, Mass., Harvard University Press, 1975.

4 Pi Mingxiu, 'Wuchang shouyizhongde Wuhan shanghui shangtuan' (The Chambers of Commerce and the Merchant Militia of Wuhan during the Wuchang Uprising), *Qishizhounian xueshu taolunhui*, vol. 1, pp. 322–61, translated in Chen, 'The Role of the Chinese Bourgeoisie in 1911'.

5 The traditional and conservative nature of the 1911 uprisings is underlined, in particular, by Ichiko Chūzō, 'The Role of the Gentry: An Hypothesis', in Wright (ed.), *China in Revolution: The First Phase, 1900–1913*, pp. 297–318.

6 Schoppa, *Chinese Elites and Political Change*, in particular chapter 10, 'The 1911 Revolution'.

7 See above, Chapter 3. On the constitutionalist movement, see Zhang Pengyuan (Chang P'eng-yuan), *Lixianpai yu xinhai geming* (The Constitutionalists and the 1911 Revolution), Taibei, Institute of Modern History, Academia Sinica, 1969.

8 Lin Zengping, 'Lüelun minzu zichanjieji shangceng yu Qingwei lixianpai' (Brief Essay on the Greater National Bourgeoisie and the Constitutionalist party at the End of the Qing Dynasty), *Xinhaigeming congkan* (Collection on the History of the 1911 Revolution), Peking, Zhonghua shuju, vol. 2, 1980, pp. 48–62.

9 Ding Richu, 'Shanghai zibenjia jieji yu xinhai geming'.

10 Ding Richu, 'Shanghai zibenjia jieji yu xinhai geming'. On the figures who played a political role in the events in Shanghai in 1911–12, see *Xinhai geming zai Shanghai shiliao xuanji* (Selection of Material on the History of the 1911 Revolution in Shanghai) (hereafter *XHZS*), Shanghai, Shanghai shehui kexueyuan Lishi yanjiusuo (Institute of History of the Shanghai Academy of Social Sciences), Shanghai renmin chubanshe, 1966, part 7, 'Shanghai zhengzhi huodongzhongde zhuyaoren' (Principal Actors in the Political Movement in Shanghai). On the geographical links of solidarity between Chen Qimei and some of the revolutionary entrepreneurs, see *Xinhai geming huiyilu* (Collection of Memoirs on the 1911 Revolution), 5 vols., Peking, Zhongguo renmin zhengzhi xieshanghuiyi quanguo weiyuanhui, Wenshiziliao yanjiu weiyuanhui (National Bureau of the Consultative Political Conference of the Chinese People, Commission for Research on Material concerning Civilisation and History), Zhonghua shuju, 1961–3, vol. 4, pp. 10–11.

11 Apart from the sources cited above, see Wu Qiandui, 'Shanghai guangfu he Hujun dudufu' (The 1911 Revolution and the Military Government of Shanghai), *Qishizhounian xueshu taolunhui*, vol. 1, pp. 815–38.

12 *SQSL*, pp. 734–7.

13 On the careers of the revolutionary elite, see Kojima Yoshio, 'Shingsi kakumei ni okeru Shanhai dokuritsu to shōshinsō'.

14 *XHZS*, p. 982.

15 Marie-Claire Bergère, *La Bourgeoisie chinoise et la révolution de 1911*, Paris–The Hague, Mouton, 1968, pp. 41–2, 125–6.

16 See on this subject Esherick, *Reform and Revolution in China*, pp. 237–50.

17 Bergère, *La Bourgeoisie chinoise et la révolution de 1911*, p. 16.

18 As well as the sources and studies mentioned above, see Yao Quanxing, 'Chen Qimei yu Shanghai guangfu' (Chen Qimei and the 1911 Revolution in Shanghai), *Shehui kexue* (Social Sciences), Shanghai, monthly, 1981, no. 2.

19 Bergère, *La Bourgeoisie chinoise et la révolution de 1911*, pp. 69–80.

20 Wu Qiandui, 'Shanghai guangfu he Hujun dudufu'.

21 *NCH*, 13 July 1912, p. 109; 1 March 1913, p. 650.
22 *Zongli quanji* (Complete Works of the President [Sun Yat-sen]), 5 vols., Shanghai, Minzhi shuju, 1930,. vol. 2, pp. 10–12.
23 *Jindaishi ziliao* (Documents of Modern History), Peking, irregular, special issue 'Xinhai geming ziliao' (Documents on the 1911 Revolution), 1961, no. 1, pp. 58, 201.
24 Shen Yunsun, 'Zhonghua shiyeyinhang shimo' (History of the Chinese Bank for Industry), *Jindaishi ziliao*, 1957, no. 6, pp. 120–39.
25 *Archives du ministère des Affaires étrangères* (Paris), China, internal politics, revolution in China. Reports of the French consul general, Shanghai, 13, 17 and 18 January 1912.
26 Ernest P. Young, *The Presidency of Yuan Shikai, Liberalism and Dictatorship in Early Republican China*, Ann Arbor, University of Michigan Press, 1977, chapter 3, 'The Presidential Team'.
27 Ernest P. Young, 'Politics in the Aftermath of the Revolution: The Era of Yuan Shikai, 1912–1916', in Fairbank (ed.), *The Cambridge History of China*, vol. 12, *Republican China, 1912–1949*, part 1, pp. 208–55.
28 On the economic policies of Yuan Shikai, see Kikuchi, *Chūgoku minzoku undō no kihon kōzō*, pp. 154–78.
29 On the decline of the powers of the government officials to the benefit of local elite groups and the merchants, see Esherick, *Reform and Revolution in China*, pp. 246–55.
30 Mark Elvin, 'The Gentry Democracy in Chinese Shanghai, 1905–1914', in Jack Gray (ed.), *Modern China's Search for a Political Form*, London, Oxford University Press, 1969, pp. 41–65; 'Shanghai shizhi jinhua shilüe' (Brief History of the Progress of the Municipal Government of Shanghai), in Shanghai tongshe (ed.), *Shanghai yanjiu ziliao* (Material for Research on Shanghai), Taibei, China Press, repr. 1973 (1st edn, Shanghai, 1936), pp. 75–8.
31 Wang Jingyu, *Jindai gongyeshi*, p. 860–7.
32 *NCH*, 19 February 1916, p. 467.
33 *NCH*, 22 December 1917, p. 709.
34 *CEB*, 23 December 1922, p. 2.
35 Al Lü, 'Jinrongjie jinhou zhi juewu ruhe?' (What will now be the Attitude of Financial Circles?), *YHYK*, vol. 2, no. 5 (May 1922), *Pingtan* section.
36 *NCH*, 15 October 1921, p. 151.
37 H. Y. Moh [Mu Ouchu], 'Causes for the High Price of Cotton and the Low Price of Yarn', *CWR*, 23 December 1922, pp. 140–1.
38 Robert W. Clopton, and Ou Tsuin-chen (transl. and ed.), *John Dewey: Lectures in China, 1919–1920*, Honolulu, East–West Center, 1973. For a more detailed study of the philosophy of expansion adopted by the bourgeoisie during its golden age, see Marie-Claire Bergère, 'La bourgeoisie chinoise et les problèmes de développement économique', *Revue d'historie moderne et contemporaine*, vol. 16, April–June 1969, pp. 246–67.
39 Sun Yat-sen, *The International Development of China*, 2nd edn, London, Hutchinson, 1928, p. 158.
40 *CWR*, 26 March 1921, p. 176.
41 *Wusi shiqi qikan jieshao* (Introduction to the Periodical Literature of the May Fourth Period) (hereafter WSQJ), 3 vols., Peking, Zhongguo zhongyang Makesi Enkesi Liening Sidalin zhuzuo bianyiju yanjiushi (Research Department of the Bureau for the Translation of the works of Marx, Engels, Lenin and Stalin of the Central Committee of the Chinese Communist Party), Renmin chubanshe, 1958–9, vol. 3, pp. 292–4.
42 *CWR*, 10 July 1920, p. 324.
43 See *Ningbo gongshang zhoukan* (Workshops of Ningbo Weekly), cited in *WSQJ*, vol. 3, p. 289.
44 Hu Shi, *CWR*, 10 July 1920, p. 324.
45 *WSQJ*, vol. 3, p. 303.
46 On the establishment and programme of the Federation, see *Wusi yundong zai Shanghai shiliao xuanji* (Selection of Material for the History of the May Fourth Movement in Shanghai) (hereafter WSYD), Shanghai, Shanghai shehui kexueyuan Lishi yanjiusuo (Institute of History of the Shanghai Academy of Social Sciences), Shanghai renmin chubanshe, 1960, pp. 648–54. Most of the documents presented by *WSYD* are announcements made by the Federation, originally published in the newspaper *Minguo ribao* (The Republic's Daily), an organ of the Guomindang.
47 *NCH*, 27 September 1919, p. 796; 1 November 1919, p. 299.

48 Feetham, *Report of the Hon.*, vol. 1, pp. 126–7.
49 *WSYD*, pp. 172–3, 389.
50 Chow Tse-tsung, *The May Fourth Movement: Intellectual Revolution in Modern China*, Cambridge, Mass., Harvard University Press, 1960, pp. 151–7.
51 *NCH*, 24 April 1920, p. 185.
52 *NCH*, 12 June 1920, p. 660; 11 December 1920, p. 745.
53 Sanford, 'Chinese Commercial Organization', pp. 342, 346.
54 Hu Shi, 'Womende zhengzhi zhuzhang' (Our Political Proposals), *Nuli zhoubao* (Endeavour) (hereafter *NLZB*), Peking, weekly, no. 2, 14 May 1922, English translation in Jerome B. Grieder, *Hu Shih and the Chinese Renaissance: Liberalism in the Chinese Revolution, 1917–1937*, Cambridge, Mass., Harvard University Press, 1970, p. 191.
55 Ding Wenjiang, 'Shaoshurende zeren' (The Responsibilities of a Minority), *NLZB*, no. 67, 26 August 1923; Wu Yugan, 'Liansheng zizhi yu zhiyezhuyi' (Provincial Federalism and Professionalism), *Taipingyang* (The Pacific Ocean), Shanghai, monthly, vol. 3, no. 7 (September 1922).
56 *NCH*, 23 October 1920, p. 223.
57 Zhi Bing, 'Shiju zagan' (Various Impressions of the Existing Situation), *ZSHYB*, vol. 3, no. 2 (February 1923), *Yanlun* section.
58 See Kuhn, 'Local Self-Government under the Republic', pp. 257–98. The *lijia* and *baojia* were organised under a decimal hierarchy and functioned as organs of self-management. But the public authorities also made use of them to channel local business initiatives to their own advantage.
59 ' "Qing hecheng zhengfu texu quanguo shanghui zilian shangtuan an", Sichuan Chengdu zongshanghui daibiao tiyi' (Let Concerted Efforts be Made to Persuade the Government to Give the Chambers of Commerce Special Authorisation to Train their own Merchant Militia. Motion Presented by the General Chamber of Commerce of Chengdu, Sichuan), *ZSHYB*, vol. 3, no. 4 (April 1923).
60 ' "Baohu shangbu anquan yi'an". Hankou zongshanghui tiyi' (Proposal concerning the Protection of Commercial Centres. Motion Presented by the General Chamber of Commerce of Hankou), *ZSHYB*, vol. 3, no. 5 (May 1923).
61 Ai Lü, 'Jingrongjie jinhou zhi guewu ruhe?'
62 The New Consortium, organised immediately after the war and composed of the principal foreign interests in China, aimed to coordinate the financing of Chinese development. But as the Peking government was unable to provide the political and financial guarantees demanded by those advancing funds, the paradoxical consequence of the formation of the consortium was to put a stop to all foreign loans to China.
63 Upton Close (pseud. for J.W. Hall), 'The Chinese Bankers Assert Themselves', *CWR*, 19 February 1921; Upton Close, 'The Turning Point of the Consortium', *CWR*, 15 October 1921; Upton Close, 'Close ups of China's Money Losses', *China Review*, China Trade Bureau, New York, monthly, vol. 2, no. 4 (April 1922).
64 'Formation of a Chinese Banking Consortium', *CWR*, 29 January 1921, pp. 470ff.
65 Close, 'The Chinese Bankers Assert Themselves'.
66 Ru Xuan, 'Guanyu guoshihuiyi zhi pianyan' (Some Notes on the Subject of the Convention of National Affairs), *ZSHYB*, vol. 1, no. 5 (November 1921), *Yanlun* section; Ru Xuan, 'Guoshi yu guoshihuiyi' (The Affairs of the Nation and the Convention of National Affairs), *ZSHYB*, vol. 2, no. 2 (February 1922), *Yanlun* section.
67 *ZSHYB*, vol. 3, no. 7 (July 1923), *Huiwu jizai* section.
68 'Shangren zhengfude piping' (Critique of the Merchants' Government), *Dongfang zazhi* (The Eastern Miscellany), Shanghai, monthly, vol. 20, no. 11 (20 June 1923).
69 [Mao] Zedong, 'Beijing zhengbian yu shangren' (The Peking Coup d'Etat and the Merchants), *Xiangdao zhoubao* (The Guide Weekly), Shanghai, weekly, special issue on the Peking coup d'état, nos. 31–2, 11 July 1923.
70 ' "Qing weizhi quanguoshanghui lianhehui tongguo yi'an lizheng shixing an", Hubei Yidu shanghui tiyi' (Let the Motions Voted by the Conference of the National Federation of Chambers of Commerce be Upheld and Let every Effort be Made to Apply them. Motion Presented by the Chamber of Commerce of Yidu, Hubei), *ZSHYB*, vol. 3, no. 4 (April 1923).

71 Zhi Bing, 'Shiju zagan'. This lack of realism is also underlined vigorously in June 1922 by the 'First Manifesto of the Chinese Communist Party on Current Affairs'.

72 Eugene Lubot, *Liberalism in an Illiberal Age: New Culture Liberals in Republican China, 1919–1937*, Westport, Connecticut, Greenwood Press, 1982.

73 Keenan, *The Dewey Experiment*, p. 119.

74 Nicole Dulioust, 'Quelques aspects de la presse chinoise pendant le Mouvement du 30 Mai 1925', *Chine, Cahiers d'études chinoises de l'INALCO*, Paris, INALCO, no. 1, 1980.

75 Hermann Mast III and William G. Saywell, 'Revolution out of Tradition: The Political Ideology of Tai Chi-t'ao', *Journal of Asian Studies*, vol. 34, no. 1 (November 1974), pp. 73–98.

76 'Yinghangjie qing Sun Wen weichi neizhai jijin' (Banking Circles Beg Sun Yat-sen to Support the Fund for Paying off Internal Debts), *YHYK*, vol. 3, no. 12 (December 1923), *Yinhangjie xiaoxi huiwen* section.

77 [Cai] Hesen, 'Wei shouhui haiguanzhuquan shi gao quanguo guomin' (Declaration to the Chinese People on the Return of Maritime Customs Rights), *Xiangdao zhoubao*, no. 48, 12 December 1923, p. 365.

78 *South China Morning Post*, Hong Kong, daily, 24 July 1923.

79 *CWR*, 21 June 1924, p. 82.

80 Huang Yifeng, 'Wusa yundong zhongde dazibenjieji' (The Greater Bourgeoisie during the Movement of 30 May), *LSYJ*, 1965, no. 3, pp. 11–24.

81 Chesneaux, *Le Mouvement ouvrier chinois de 1919 à 1927*, chapter 11, 'Le Mouvement du 30 mai à Shanghai ...'.

82 *NCH*, 14 November 1925, p. 294.

83 *NCH*, 29 August 1925, p. 251.

84 *NCH*, 21 March, p. 478; 25 April 1925, p. 140; 13 June 1925, p. 440.

85 *CWR*, 24 July 1926, pp. 188–90.

86 *NCH*, 15 August 1925, p. 167.

87 Parks M. Coble Jr, *The Shanghai Capitalists and the Nationalist Government, 1927–1937*, Cambridge, Mass., Harvard University Press, 1980, p. 29.

88 Joseph Fewsmith, *Party, State and Local Elites in Shanghai Republican China: Merchant Organizations and Politics in Shanghai, 1890–1930*, Honolulu, University of Hawaii Press, 1985, pp. 107–10; *CWR*, 7 March 1925, p. 21; 21 November 1925, p. 288; 13 February 1926, p. 316.

89 'Power and Politics of the Chinese Chamber of Commerce', *CWR*, 24 July 1926, p. 190; 17 July 1926, p. 316.

90 'Autobiography of Chang Chia-ao', pp. 53–63.

91 'Reminiscences of Chen Guangfu as told to Julie Lien-yin How, Dec. 6 1960–June 5 1960', unpublished manuscript, Oral History Project, Columbia University, chapter 5, 'The National Revolution of 1925–1927'.

92 Karl Mannheim, *Essays on Sociology and Social Psychology*, London, Oxford University Press, 1953, chapter 2.

93 Fewsmith, *Party, State and Local Elites*, pp. 115–25.

94 Parks M. Coble Jr, 'The Kuomintang Regime and the Shanghai Capitalists, 1927–1929', *China Quarterly*, London, quarterly, no. 77 (March 1979), pp. 1–24.

95 'Reminiscences of Chen Guangfu', pp. 64–5.

96 'Autobiography of Chang Chia-ao', pp. 55–7.

Capitalism, Westernisation and nationalism

1 Chinese historians are now beginning to modify this thesis. Apart from the articles by Ding Richu already cited, see Fan Bochuan, 'Ershiji chuqi Zhongguo zibenzhuyi fazhande qingkuang yu tedian' (General Conditions and Particular Features of the Development of Chinese Capitalism in the Early Twentieth Century), *LSYJ*, 1983, no. 4, pp. 11–24, and in particular the author's remarks about the collaboration between national capital and the foreigners (p. 21).

2 *WSYD*, pp. 243–4.

3 *Peking and Tientsin Times*, Tianjin, daily, 21 November 1919.

4 *CWR*, 16 December 1922, p. 86, quotation of remarks made by M. Samuel V. Zau, one of the Chinese delegates to the Pan Pacific Commercial conference in Honolulu.

5 'Quanguo yinhang gonghui lianhehuiyi ji' (Notes on the Conference of the National Federation of Bankers' Associations), *YHYK*, vol. 1, no. 6 (June 1921).

6 See, for example, Hou Chi-ming, *Foreign Investment and Economic Development in China, 1840–1937*; and Robert F. Denberger, 'The Role of the Foreigner in China's Economic Development, 1840–1949'. Albert Feuerwerker is also at pains to refute the thesis of exploitation.

7 See, for example, the expansion of Japanese cotton mills in China, described above, p. 68.

8 Wang Zhiwei, 'Zhongguo gongshangye shibai zhi yuanyin ji qi bujiu fangfa' (The Failure of Chinese Industry and Trade: The Causes and the Remedies), *ZSHYB*, vol. 3, no. 6 (June 1923), *Yanlun* section. For another example of an analysis that pays most attention to the internal causes of economic failure, see Zhang Hanying, 'Lun woguo waiguo maoyi shibai zhi yuanyin' (The Causes of the Failure of Chinese External Trade), *Shangxue jikan* (Quarterly Review of Commercial Studies), Peking, vol. 1, no. 1 (February 1923).

9 Zhang Guotao (Chang Kuo-t'ao), 'Zhongguo yi tuolile guoji qinlüede weixianma?' (Is China now safe from International Aggression?), *Xiandao zhoubao*, 18 October 1922, no. 6, p. 45.

10 Jiang Hengyuan, *Zhongguo guanshui shiliao* (Material for the History of Customs Tariffs in China), Shanghai, Renwen bianjisuo, 1931, part 14, p. 39.

11 'Guanshui yanjiuhuiyi jilu' (Report of the Study Commission on Customs Tariffs), in Beijing yinhangyuekanshe (ed.), *Zhongguo guanshui wenti* (The Problem of Customs Tariffs in China), Peking, 1923, pp. 34–81.

12 ' "Yuzhou cailijiashuihou yingxing yingge banfa an" ', Shanghai zongshanghui tiyi' (On the Means of Prosperity and Renewal after the Future Reform Abolishing the *lijin* and Raising Customs Tariffs. Motion Presented by the Shanghai General Chamber of Commerce), *ZSHYB*, vol. 3, no. 2 (February 1923).

13 *BCEO*, April 1921.

14 *NCH*, 16 July 1921, p. 172.

15 Ru Xuan, 'Guanyu juoshihuiyi zhi pianyan'.

16 Ru Xuan, 'Duiyu shangjiao lianxihui "duiwai xuanyan" zhi wo jian' (My Point of View on the 'Declaration of Foreign Policy' of the Joint Conference of Merchants and Educationists), *ZSHYB*, vol. 1, no. 4 (October 1921).

17 Hu Shi, 'Guojide Zhongguo' (China in the Concert of Nations), *NLZB*, no. 22 (1 October 1922), French translation in Marie-Claire Bergère and Tchang Fou-jouei, '*Sauvons la patrie!' Le Mouvement du 4 mai 1919 et le nationalisme chinois*, Paris, POF, 1978, pp. 103–14.

18 Zhang Guotao, 'Zhongguo yi tuolile guoji qinlüede weixianma?'

19 Report of the High Commissioner for Industry, Ye Gongchuo, to the Peking Chamber of Commerce, *La Politique de Pékin*, Peking, weekly, special issue, January 1920, pp. 21–2; and 29 January 1920, p. 147.

20 Mu Ouchu, cited by *NCH*, 13 January 1923, p. 95.

21 *La Politique de Pékin*, special issue, January 1920.

22 On the boycotting movements, see Remer, *A Study of Chinese Boycotts*.

23 *CWR*, 2 August 1919, p. 358.

24 *North China Star*, Peking, daily, 20 and 21 November 1919; Japan, Gaimushō (Ministry of Foreign Affairs), *Shina ni oite Nihon shōhin dōmei haiseki ikken, zakken* (The Boycotting of Japanese Merchandise in China, Miscellaneous Business), vol. 7, 1920 (1922–2720), 11 February 1920, items 780 469–77.

25 Japan, Gaimushō (Ministry of Foreign Affairs), *Shina ni oite Nihon shōhin dōmai haiseki ikken, fukumei sho* (The Boycotting of Japanese Merchandise in China, Reports), vol. 1, items 791 043–4.

26 Japan, Gaimushō, *Shina ni oite Nihon shōhin dōmei haiseki ikken, fukumei sho*, vol. 1, item 791 064.

27 Nie Yuntai, 'Wei Ribing qiangsha shimin shi jinggao guomin' (Warning to the Nation concerning the Incident during which Japanese Soldiers Fired on the Crowds), *ZSHYB*, vol. 3, no. 6 (June 1923), *Yanlun* section.

28 Zhi Bing, 'Guoquan huifu yu jingji juejiao' (The Return of Sovereign Rights and the Breaking-off of Economic Relations), *ZSHYB*, vol. 3, no. 4 (April 1923), *Yanlun* section.

29 Japan, Gaimushō, *Shina ni oite Nihon shōhin dōmei haiseki ikken, fukumei sho*, vol. 1, item 791 107.

30 *TR*, 1919, 'Report from Wuchow', p. 1214; 'Report from Hangchow', p. 844.
31 Japan, Gaimushō, *Shina ni oite Nihon shōhin dōmei haiseki ikken* (The Boycotting of Japanese Merchandise in China), P.J. to the consular despatch from Zhifu (Chefoo), 29 August 1919, vol. 6, items 740 856–73.
32 *TR*, 1919, 'Report from Hangchow', p. 846; Report from Tientsin', p. 243; 'Report from Canton', pp. 1022, 1027. For a more detailed study of the stimulatory effects of the boycotting, see Marie-Claire Bergère, 'Le Mouvement du 4 mai 1919 en Chine: la conjoncture économique et le rôle de la bourgeoisie nationale', *Revue historique*, Paris, quarterly, no. 241 (April–June 1969), pp. 309–26.
33 Wen Han, 'You gongye jiandishang lun weichi guohuo dizhi Rihuo' (The Promotion of National Merchandise and the Anti-Japanese Boycott Considered from Industry's Point of View), *Shiye zazhi* (Businessman's Companion), Changsha, monthly, no. 71 (September 1923).
34 'Tichang guohuo zxhi wo jian' (My Point of View on the Promotion of National Merchandise), *ZSHYB*, vol. 4, no. 5 (May 1924), *Yanlun* section.
35 Nie Yuntai, 'Wei Ribing qiangsha shimin shi jinggao guomin'. A study devoted to Indian boycotting appeared in the magazine of the Chinese Cotton Millowners' Association: 'Yindu waiguo mainbu zhi paichi yundong' (The Movement to Boycott Foreign Cotton Textiles in India), *Huashang shachang lianhehui jikan* (Quarterly Review of the Chinese Cotton Millowners' Association, 'The China Cotton Journal'), Shanghai, vol. 3, no. 2 (March 1922), pp. 186ff.
36 Cited in Benjamin J. Cohen, *The Question of Imperialism: The Political Economy of Dominance and Dependence*, New York, Basic Books, 1973, p. 48.
37 [Cai] Hesen, 'Waiguo diguozhuyizhe dui Huade xinjiufa' (Old and New Methods of Foreign Imperialists in Relation to China), *Xiangdao zhoubao*, no. 22 (25 April 1923), pp. 158–60.
38 'The Tragedy of Washington', *NCH*, 14 January 1922, p. 74.
39 Carnegie Endowment for International Peace, Division of International Law (ed.), *The Consortium: The Official Text of the Four Powers Agreement for a Loan to China and Relevant Documents*, Washington, 1921.
40 Chang Kia-ngau, cited in *CWR*, 29 January 1921, pp. 470ff.
41 Ru Xuan, 'Xin yinhangtuan yu jingjiguafen' (The New Consortium and the Economic Dismemberment of China), *ZSHYB*, vol. 1, no. 6 (December 1921), *Yanlun* section.
42 Ru Xuan, Lun wo guo yinghangtuan bu yi jiaru siqiang zuzhi zhi xin yinhangtuan' (The Chinese Consortium must not join the New Consortium Organised by the Four Powers), *ZSHYB*, vol. 2, no. 1 (January 1922).
43 'Quanguo shangjiao lianxihuiyi shimoji' (Notes on the Proceedings of the Joint Conference of the National Federations of Chambers of Commerce and Education Societies), *ZSHYB*, vol. 1, no. 4 (October 1921), *Jishi* section.
44 W. S. A. Pott, 'The People's Delegates to the Pacific Conference', *CWR*, 22 October 1921.
45 Ru Xuan, 'Duiyu shangjiao lianxihui "duiwai xuanyan" zhi wo jian'. The American press considered this move to be an interesting manifestation of 'liberal elements' (*CWR*, 22 October 1921) and was better disposed towards it than the British press (*NCH*, 1 October 1921).
46 *NCH*, 18 February 1922, p. 420.
47 'Sir Ronald Macleay and China's Merchants', *NCH*, 17 February 1923, pp. 446–7.
48 Cited in *NCH*, 10 March 1923, pp. 664–5.
49 *NCH*, 19 May 1923, pp. 471–2. See also *NCH*, 23 June 1923, p. 818.
50 'Plain Words to the Merchants', *NCH*, 14 April 1923, p. 77.
51 *NCH*, 23 June 1923, p. 818.
52 See the *NCH* editorial, 16 December 1922, pp. 711–12.
53 *Shenbao*, Shanghai, daily, 27 November 1922; 5 January 1923.
54 United States National Archives, Dispatch from the Consul General Edward S. Cunningham, Shanghai, 26 June 1923, 893.00/5095.
55 'Heping tongyi xuanyan' (Declaration on Peaceful Unification), in Chang Qiyun *et al.* (eds.), *Guofo quanshu* (Complete Works of the Father of the Country [Sun Yat-sen]), Taibei, Guofeng yanjiuyuan, 1960, p. 755. In his memoirs, the journalist H. E. Abend even suggests that when the American ambassador to China, Jacob G. Schurman, visited Canton in 1923, Sun Yat-sen

seized the opportunity to ask him to organise a foreign expedition and also to send financiers, technicians and administrators to help him to set up a central government. See Hallet Edward Abend, *My Years in China (1928 [i.e. 1926]–1941)*, London, 1944, pp. 24ff. On Sun's attempts to establish closer links with the Western powers in 1923, see Wilbur, *Sun Yat-sen: A Frustrated Patriot*, New York, Columbia University Press, 1976, pp. 141–5, 153–9.

56 [Cai] Hesen, 'Wanguo gongmin dahui yu Shanghaide caibing yundong' (The Foreigners' Association and the Shanghai Movement for the Licensing of Troops), *Xiangdao zhoubao*, no. 14 (30 December 1922), p. 109.

57 *NCH*, 15 March 1923, p. 633.

58 Sun De [Maring], 'Zhongguo gaizao zhi waiguo yuanzhu' (Foreign Aid for the Reconstruction of China), *Xiangdao zhoubao*, no. 29 (June 1923), p. 214.

59 *CWR*, 8 October 1921, editorial, p. 258. See also 'The Present State of China. The Merchant Class', *Peking and Tientsin Times*, 19 April 1923.

60 See above, p. 94.

61 On 6 May, an express train was held up at Lincheng (Shandong) by bandits who took several dozen passengers prisoner, including many foreigners.

62 *NCH*, 19 May 1923, pp. 471–2; 30 June 1923, pp. 883–8.

63 *China Year Book 1924*, Tianjin, annual, pp. 819ff.

64 *CWR*, 7 July 1923, p. 172.

65 'Wei wairen ganyu hulu shi zhi Fu lingxiu gongshi han' (Letter Addressed to Mr Fu [Batalha de Freitas], Doyen of the Diplomatic Corps, on the Subject of Foreign Interference in the Protection of the Railways), *ZSYHB*, vol. 3, no. 9 (September 1923), *Huiwu jizai* section; 'You wei hulu shi zhi ge zongshanghui yizhi fouren han' (Letter addressed to all the General Chambers of Commerce urging them to Protest Unanimously against the Plan for the Protection of the Railways), *ZSHYB*, vol. 3, no. 9 (September 1923), *Huiwu jizai* section.

66 [Cai] Hesen, 'Shangren gangjue dao waiguo diguozhuyi zhuchang Zhongguo neiluande di yi sheng' (The Merchants are Beginning to Realise that Foreign Imperialism Encourages Internal Disturbances), *Xiangdao zhoubao*, no. 44, 27 October 1923, p. 333.

67 See Laurence A. Schneider, *Ku Chieh-kan and China's New History: Nationalism and the Quest for Alternative Traditions*, Berkeley, University of California Press, 1971.

68 Nie Yuntai, 'Wei Ribing qiangsha shimin shi jinggao guomin'.

Epilogue

1 Jean Chesneaux and Françoise Le Barbier, *La Chine*, vol. 3, *La Marche de la révolution, 1921–1949*, Paris, Hatier, 1975, p. 76.

2 On the successive interpretations of the Nanking decade by Soviet historiography, see A. V. Meliksetov, *Bjurokratičeskij kapital v Kitae. Ekonomičeskaja politika gomin'dana i razvitie gosudarstvennogo kaitalizma v 1927–1937 gg* (Bureaucratic Capitalism in China. Economic Policies of the Guomindang and the Development of State Capitalism, 1927–1937), Moscow, Nauka (principal editors of oriental literature), 1972, chapter 9. The thesis of State capitalism is illustrated in more detail in the works of A. V. Meliksetov. Apart from the work cited above, see his 'K voprosu ob istoričeskoi roli bjurokratičeskogo kapitala v gomin'danovskom Kitae' (The Problem of the Historic Role of Bureaucratic Capital in Gudomindang China), *Strany Dal'nego Vostoka (Istorija i ekonomika)* (Far-Eastern Countries, History and Economics), Academy of Sciences of the USSR, Institute of Oriental Studies, Moscow, Nauka, 1971, pp. 147–90; and 'Nekotorye osobennosti kapitalističeskogo razvitiya Kitaya v gody gomin'danovskogo gospodstva (1927–1949)' (Some Particular Features of Capitalist Development in China during the Years of the Guomindang Reign), in A. I. Levkovskiy and U. N. Rosaliev, *Krupnyj kapital i monopolii stran Azii* (Large Capital Resources and Monopolies in Asian Countries), Moscow, Nauka, 1970, pp. 47–74.

3 The most classic illustrations of this historiography are provided by the works of Chen Boda, *Zhongguo si dajiazu* (The Four Great Families of China), Hong Kong, Nanyang shudian, 1947; and *Renmin gongdi Jiang Jieshi* (Chiang Kai-shek, Enemy of the People), Kalgan, Jinchaji xinhua shudian, 1948. See also Xu Dixin, *Guanliao ziben lun* (On the Subject of Bureaucratic Capitalism), Hong Kong, Nanyang shudian, 1947.

4 These 'four families' are those of Chiang Kai-shek, T. V. Soong, H. H. Kung and the brothers Chen Lifu and Chen Guofu.

5 See Lloyd E. Eastman, *The Abortive Revolution: China under Nationalist Rule, 1927–1937*, Cambridge, Mass., Harvard University Press, 1974; Coble, *The Shanghai Capitalists*; Bergère ' "The Other China": Shanghai from 1919 to 1949'

6 Coble, *The Shanghai Capitalists*, p. 3.

7 Lloyd E. Eastman, 'Some Themes on Wartime China', *Chinese Republican Studies Newsletter*, quarterly, vol. 1, no. 1 (October 1975), p. 14.

8 Jean Monnet, *Mémoires*, Paris, Fayard, 1976, p. 134.

9 See Shirley Garrett, 'Chambers of Commerce', in Elvin and Skinner (eds.), *The Chinese City between Two Worlds*, pp. 227–8; Coble, *The Shanghai Capitalists*, pp. 57–65; and Fewsmith, *Party, State and Local Elites*, pp. 156–9. Fewsmith's interpretation of the reorganisation of the General Chamber of Commerce is quite different from the one given here (which is also that given by Coble). In Fewsmith's view, the reorganisation strengthened the power of the businessmen. In truth, only a tiny elite group who were close to the central power, benefited from it.

10 Christian Henriot, 'Le gouvernement municipal de Shanghai, 1927–1937', thesis for a *doctorat de 3ᵉ cycle*, INALCO-Paris III, June 1983, pp. 105–6.

11 Henriot, 'Le gouvernement municipal', pp. 76–91.

12 *Shenbao*, 24 June 1927, p. 13; 30 June 1927, p. 13; 2 July 1927, p. 13.

13 Remer, *A Study of Chinese Boycotts*, pp. 138–40.

14 Remer, *A Study of Chinese Boycotts*, p. 249; Henriot, 'Le gouvernement municipal', pp. 98–101.

15 Bergère, ' "The Other China": Shanghai from 1919 to 1949'.

16 Coble, *The Shanghai Capitalists*, pp. 48–54.

17 This is Fewsmith's thesis, in *Party, State and Local Elites*.

18 Boorman and Howard, *Biographical Dictionary*, vol. 3, p. 452; Y. C. Wang, *Chinese Intellectuals and the West, 1872–1949*, Chapel Hill, University of North Carolina Press, 1966, p. 418.

19 Boorman and Howard, *Biographical Dictionary*, vol. 1, p. 26.

20 Boorman and Howard, vol. 1, p. 379.

21 Boorman and Howard, vol. 1, p.192.

22 Borman and Howard, vol. 1, p. 817.

23 Coble, *The Shanghai Capitalists*, p. 362.

24 Etienne Balazs, *Chinese Civilization and Bureaucracy*, New Haven and London, Yale University Press, 1964, chapter 6, 'Chinese Towns'.

25 Henriot, 'Le gouvernement municipal', pp. 60–2, 98–9.

26 Buck, *Urban Change in China*, p. 167.

27 Eastman, *The Abortive Revolution*, p. 47.

28 The reform of economic institutions under the Guomindang has been studied by Paul T. K. Shih (ed.), *The Strenuous Decade: China's Nation-building Efforts, 1927–1937*, Jamaica, New York, St John University Press, 1970; and by a former American adviser to Chiang Kai-shek's government (see Arthur N. Young, *China's Nation-Building Effort, 1927–1937: The Financial and Economic Record*, Stanford, Hoover Institution Press, 1971).

29 Coble, *The Shanghai Capitalists*, pp. 267–71; Bush, *The Politics of Cotton Textiles in Kuomintang China*, pp. 233–47.

30 Coble, *The Shanghai Capitalists*, pp. 286–301.

31 William C. Kirby, *Germany and Republican China*, Stanford, Stanford University Press, 1984.

32 Boorman and Howard, *Biographical Dictionary*, vol. 4, p. 411. On Weng Wenhao's collaboration with the review *Duli pinglun*, see Lubot, *Liberalism in an Illiberal Age*, pp. 84–5.

33 Henriot, 'Le gouvernement municipal', chapter 5, 'Le personnel municipal'.

34 By way of comparison, see Kendall E. Bailes, *Technology and Society under Lenin and Stalin: Origins of the Soviet Technical Intelligentsia, 1917–1941*, Princeton, New Jersey, Princeton University Press, 1978.

35 Douglas S. Paauw, 'The Kuomintang and Economic Stagnation, 1928–1937', *Journal of Asian Studies*, vol. 14, no. 2 (February 1957), pp. 213–20; Eastman, *The Abortive Revolution*, chapter 5.

36 Myers, *The Chinese Peasant Economy*; Thomas G. Rawsky, 'China's Republican Economy: An Introduction', Joint Centre on Modern East Asia, University of Toronto and York University, Discussion Paper no. 1 (1978).

37 Marie-Claire Bergère, 'Pour une histoire économique de la chine moderne', *Annales. Économies, Sociétés, Civilisations*, no. 4 (July–August 1969), pp. 860–75.
38 Mao and Liu are cited here from John Gardner, 'The *Wu-fan* Campaign in Shanghai. A Study in the Consolidation of Urban Control', in Doak Barnett (ed.), *Chinese Communist Politics in Action*, Seattle, University of Washington Press, 1969, pp. 486ff.
39 Robert Michels, *Les Partis politiques* (transl. from the German by S. Jankelevitch), Paris, Flammarion, 1971, pp. 291–6.
40 Michels, *Les Partis politiques*, p. 280.

Bibliography

Abend, Hallet Edward, *My years in China (1928 [i.e. 1926]–1941)*, London 1944.

Ai Lü, 'Jinrongjie jinhou zhi juewu ruhe?' (What will now be the Attitude of Financial Circles?) *Yinhang yuekan*, vol. 2, no. 5 (May 1922).

Allen, George and Donnithorne, Audrey G., *Western Enterprise in Far Eastern Economic Development, China and Japan*, London, Allen and Unwin, 1954.

Archives du ministère des Affaires étrangères (Paris), Chine, politique intérieure, révolution en Chine.

'Autobiography of Chang Chai-ao [Chang Kia-ngau]', unpublished manuscript (trans. from Chinese), Oral History Project, Columbia University, *c.* 1960.

Bailes, Kendall E., *Technology and Society under Lenin and Stalin: Origins of the Soviet Technical Intelligentsia, 1917–1941*, Princeton, New Jersey, Princeton University Press, 1978.

Balazs, Etienne, *La Bureaucratie céleste. Recherches sur l'économie et la société de la Chine traditionnelle*, Paris, Gallimard, 1968.

Balazs, Etienne, 'Les villes chinoises. Histoire des institutions administratives et judiciaires', *Recueils de la Société Jean Bodin*, no. 6 (1954), pp. 225–39.

'"Baohu shangbu anquan yi'an". Hankou zongshanghui tiyi' (Proposal concerning the Protection of Commercial Centres. Motion Presented by the General Chamber of Commerce of Hankou), *Shanghai zongshanghui yuebuo*, vol. 3, no. 5 (May 1923).

Bastid, Marianne, *Aspects de la réforme de l'enseignement en Chine au début du xxe siècle d'après les écrits de Zhang Jian*, Paris – The Hague, Mouton, 1971.

Bastid, Marianne, *L'Évolution de la société chinoise à la fin de la dynastie des Qing*, Paris, EHESS, 1979 (Cahiers du Centre Chine, no. 1)

Beijing gongye shiliao (Material for the History of Industries in Peking), Peking, Zhongguo renmin daxue gongyejingjixi (Department of Industrial Economy of the People's University), 1960.

'"Beijing guanshui yanjiuhui duiyu cailijiashuihou xin tian yingye suode liangshui wei bian juyi shixing qing taolun an"', Jiangxi Nanchang zongshanghui tiyi' (The Government Commission on Customs Tariffs

Proposes that following Abolition of the *lijin* and an Increase in Customs Dues, Two New Taxes be Introduced, One on Business, the Other on Revenue. It is Requested that Application of these Proposals be Deferred. Motion Presented by the General Chamber of Commerce of Nanchang, Jiangxi), *Shanghai zongshanghui yuebao*, vol. 3, no. 2 (February 1923).

Beijing Review, weekly, Peking.

Bergère, Marie-Claire, *La Bourgeoisie chinoise et la révolution de 1911*, Paris–The Hague, Houton, 1968.

Bergère, Marie-Claire, 'La Bourgeoisie chinoise et les problèmes de développement économique', *Revue d'histoire moderne et contemporaine*, vol. 16, April–June, 1969, pp. 246–67.

Bergère, Marie-Claire, *Capitalisme national et impérialisme, La crise des filatures chinoises en 1923*, Paris, EHESS, 1980 (Cahiers du Centre Chine, no. 2).

Bergère, Marie-Claire, 'Une crise de subsistance en Chine, 1920–22', *Annales. Économies, Sociétés, Civilisations*, no. 6 (28th year), November–December 1973, pp. 1361–1402.

Bergère, Marie-Claire, *Une crise financière à Shanghai à la fin de l'Ancien Régime*, Paris–The Hague, Mouton, 1964.

Bergère, Marie-Claire, 'Pour une histoire économique de la Chine moderne', *Annales, Economies, Sociétés, Civilisations*, no. 4 (24th year) July–August 1969, pp. 860–75.

Bergère, Marie-Claire, 'Le Mouvement du 4 mai 1919 en Chine: la conjoncture économique et le rôle de la bourgeoisie nationale', *Revue historique*, Paris, quarterly, no. 241 (April–June 1969), pp. 309–26.

Bergère, Marie-Claire, 'Les problèmes du développement et le rôle de la bourgeoisie chinoise: la crise économique de 1920–1923', thesis for a *doctorat d'Etat*, supervised by Jean Chesneaux and presented at the University of Paris VII, June 1975, unpublished.

Bergère, Marie-Claire, 'La révolution de 1911 jugée par les historiens de la République populaire de Chine'. *Revue historique*, Paris, quarterly, no. 230 (October–December 1963), pp. 403–36.

Bergère, Marie-Claire, 'Shanghai ou "l'autre Chine", 1919–1949', *Annales. Economies, Sociétés, Civilisations*, no. 5 (34th year), September–October 1979, pp. 1039–68.

Bergère, Marie-Claire and Tchang Fou-jouei, '*Sauvons la patrie!*' Le Mouvement du 4 mai 1919 et le nationalisme chinois*, Paris, POF, 1978.

Bergeron, Louis, *Banquiers, négociants et manufacturiers parisiens du Directoire à l'Empire*, Paris, Mouton, 1978.

Bianco, Lucien, 'Les paysans et la Révolution', *Politique étrangère*, 1968, no. 1, pp. 117–41.

Bianco, Lucien, 'Les paysans dans la Révolution', in Aubert, C. *et al.*, *Regards froids sur la Chine*, Paris, Le Seuil, 1976, pp. 283–308.

Boorman, Howard L. and Howard, Richard C., (eds), *Biographical Dictionary of Republican China*, 4 vols., New York, Columbia University Press, 1967–71.

Braudel, Fernand, *Civilisation matérielle, économie et capitalisme, xve–xviie siècle*, vol. 3, *Le Temps du monde*, Paris, Armand Colin, 1979.

Brunnert, H. S. and Hagelstrom, V. V., *Present Day Political Organization of China*, transl. from Russian (1st edn 1910), repr. Taibei, Book World Company.

Buck, David D., *Urban Change in China, Politics and Development in Tsinan, Shantung, 1890–1949*, Madison, University of Wisconsin Press, 1978.

Bulletin commercial d'Extrême-Orient, Shanghai, Chambre de commerce française en Chine, monthly.

Bulletin des soies et des soieries et moniteur des soies, Lyons, weekly.

Bush, Richard C., *The Politics of Cotton Textiles in Kuomintang China*, New York, Garland, 1982.

[Cai] Hesen, 'Shangren ganjue dao waiguo diguozhuyi zhuchang Zhongguo neiluande di yi sheng' (The Merchants are Beginning to Realise that Foreign Imperialism Encourages Internal Disturbances), *Xiangdao zhoubao*, no. 44, 27 October 1923.

[Cai] Hesen, 'Waiguo diguozhuyizhe dui Huade xinjiufa' (Old and New Methods of Foreign Imperialists in Relation to China), *Xiangdao zhoubao*, no. 22 (25 April 1923), pp. 158–60.

[Cai] Hesen, 'Wanguo gongmin dahui yu Shanghaide caibing yundong' (The Foreigners' Association and the Shanghai Movement for the Licensing of Troops), *Xiangdao zhoubao*, no. 14, 30 December 1922.

[Cai] Hesen, 'Wei shouhui haiguanzhuquan shi gao quanguo guomin', (Declaration to the Chinese People on the Return of Maritime Customs Rights), *Xiangdao zhoubao*, no. 48, 12 December 1923.

Carnegie Endowment for International Peace, Division of International Law, (ed.), *The Consortium: The Official Text of the Four Powers of Agreement for a Loan to China and Relevant Documents*, Washington, 1921.

Cartier, Michel, 'La croissance démographique chinoise du xviiie siècle et l'enregistrement des *pao-chia*', *Annales de démographie historique*, Paris, Mouton, EHESS, 1979, pp. 9–29.

Chan, Wellington, 'Merchant Organizations in Late Imperial China: Patterns of Change and Development', *Journal of the Royal Asiatic Society*, The Hong Kong Branch, vol. 15 (1975), pp. 28–42.

Chan, Wellington, 'Bureaucratic Capital and Chou Hsüeh-hsi in Late Ch'ing China', *Modern Asian Studies*, vol. 11, no. 3 (1977), pp. 435–8.

Chan, Wellington, *'Merchants, Mandarins and Modern Enterprise in Late Ch'ing China*, Cambridge, Mass., Harvard University Press, 1977.

Chang Chung-li, *The Chinese Gentry: Studies on their Role in Nineteenth Century*

Chinese Society, Seattle, University of Washington Press (1st edn, 1956), 2nd paperback edn, 1970.

Chang, John K., *Industrial Development in pre-Communist China: A Quantitative Analysis*, Edinburgh, The University Press, 1969.

Chang Kuo-t'ao, *The Rise of the Chinese Communist Party, 1921–1927: The Autobiography of Chang Kuo-t'ao*, 2 vols., Lawrence, University Press of Kansas, 1971, 1972.

Chang Kuo-t'ao, *see* Zhang Guotao.

Chang P'eng-yuan, 'The Constitutionalists', in Wright (ed.), *China in Revolution: The First Phase, 1900–1913*, pp. 143–83.

Chang P'eng-yuan, *see* Zhang Pengyuan.

Chang Perry (Chang P'eng), 'The Distribution and Relative Strength of the Provincial Merchants Groups in China, 1842–1911', doctoral dissertation, University of Washington, 1958.

Chao Kang, *The Development of Cotton Textile Production in China*, Cambridge, Mass., Harvard University Press, 1977 (Harvard East Asian Monographs, no. 74).

Chen Boda, *Renmin gongdi Jiang Jieshi* (Chiang Kai-shek, Enemy of the People), Kalgan, Jinchaji xinhua shudian, 1948.

Chen Boda, *Zhongguo si dajiazu* (The Four Great Families of China), Hong Kong, Nanyang shudian, 1947.

Chen, Jerome (translated introduction), 'The Role of the Chinese Bourgeoisie in 1911. Essays by Chinese Marxist Historians at the Wuhan Conference on the 1911 Revolution, October 12–14, 1981', *Chinese Studies in History*, vol. 17, no. 4 (summer 1984), vol. 18, nos. 3–4 (spring–summer 1985).

Chen Laixin, *Yu Xiaqing ni tsuite* (On the Subject of Yu Xiaqing), Kyōto daigaku jimbum kagaku kenkyūjo (Institute for Research on the Human Sciences of the University of Kyoto), kyō dō kenkyū hōkoku (research reports), 'Gōshi undō no kenkyū, (Research on the May Fourth Movement), series 2, no. 5, 1983.

Chen Zhen *et al.*, *Zhongguo jindai gongyeshi ziliao* (Material for the History of Modern Industry in China), 4 vols., Peking, Sanlian shudian, 1957–61.

Cheng Renjie, 'Yingmei yan'gongsi maiban Zheng Bozhao' (The Comprador of the British American Tobacco Company, Zheng Bozhao), *Wenshi ziliao xuanji*, Shanghai renmin chubanshe, 1978, no. 1, pp. 130–54.

Cheng Yu-kwei, *Foreign Trade and the Development of China: An Historical and Integrated Analysis through 1948*, Washington DC, University Press of Washington, 1956.

Chesneaux, Jean, *Le Mouvement ouvrier chinois de 1919 à 1927*, Paris–The Hague, Mouton, 1962.

Chesneaux, Jean and Le Barbier, Françoise, *La Chine*, vol. 3, *La Marche de la révolution, 1921–1949*, Paris, Hatier, 1975.

China Quarterly, London, quarterly, 1960–.

China Review, China Trade Bureau, New York, monthly, 1921–4.

China Weekly Review, Shanghai, weekly, 1917–53.

China Weekly Review (ed.), *Who's Who in China*, Shanghai, 1925 (3rd edn) and 1931 (4th edn).

China Year Book (The), 1912–39, ed. Woodhead, H. W. G., London, G. Routledge; 1912–19, New York, E. P. Dutton; 1921–39, Peking and Tientsin, Tientsin Press; annual.

Chine, Cahiers d'Etudes Chinoises, INALCO, Paris, irregular, 1980–.

China, Inspectorate General Customs, *Returns of Trade and Trade Reports*, Shanghai, annual (The Maritime Customs 1, Statistical Series 3–5).

Chinese Economic Bulletin, Chinese Government Bureau of Economic Information, Peking, weekly, 1919–27.

Chinese Economic Journal, Chinese Government Bureau of Economic Information, Peking, then Shanghai, monthly, 1919–27.

Chinese Republican Studies Newsletter, quarterly, 1975–.

Ch'ing-shih wen-t' i (Questions on Qing History), Society for the Ch'ing Studies, New Haven, half yearly, 1965–85.

Chow Tse-Tsung, *The May Fourth Movement: Intellectual Revolution in Modern China*, Cambridge, Mass., Harvard University Press, 1960.

Chu, Samuel C., *Reformer in Modern China: Chang Chien, 1853–1926*, New York, Columbia University Press, 1965.

Clopton, Robert W. and Ou Tsuin-Chen (trans. and ed.), *John Dewey: Lectures in China, 1919–1920*, Honolulu, East–West Center, 1973.

Close, Upton (pseud. of Hall, J. W.), 'The Chinese Bankers Assert Themselves', *China Weekly Review*, 19 February 1921.

Close, Upton, 'The Turning Point of the Consortium', *China Weekly Review*, 15 October 1921.

Close, Upton, 'Close ups of China's Money Losses', *China Review*, China Trade Bureau, New York, monthly, vol. 2, no. 4 (April 1922).

Coble, Parks M. Jr, 'The Kuomintang Regime and the Shanghai Capitalists, 1927–1929', *China Quarterly*, no. 77 (March 1979), pp. 1–24.

Coble, Parks M. Jr, *The Shanghai Capitalists and the Nationalist Government, 1927–1937*, Cambridge, Mass., Harvard University Press, 1980.

Cohen, Benjamin J., *The Question of Imperialism: The Political Economy of Dominance and Dependance*, New York, Basic Books, 1973.

Cohen, Paul A., *Between Tradition and Modernity: Wang T'ao and Reform in Late Ch'ing China*, Cambridge, Mass., Harvard University Press, 1974.

Cole, James H., 'Shaohsing: Studies in Ch'ing Social History', Ph.D. dissertation, Stanford University, 1975.

Conference on Modern Chinese Economic History, Taipei, The Institute of Economics, Academia Sinica, 1977.

Dai Jitao, 'Duo Huzhou houde ganxiang' (Impressions on my Return from Huchow), *Jianshe* (The Construction) Shanghai, monthly, vol. 2, no. 6 (August 1920), pp. 1229–44.

Dalong jiqichangde fasheng fazhan yu gaizao (Creation, Development and Transformation of the Dalong Mechanical Engineering Works), Shanghai, Zhongguo kexueyuan Shanghai jingji yanjiusuo (Shanghai, Institute of Economics of the Academy of Sciences of China), Shanghai renmin chubanshe, 1958.

Denberger, Robert F., 'The Role of the Foreigner in China's Economic Development, 1840–1949', in Perkins (ed.), *China's Modern Economy in Historical Perspective*, pp. 19–48.

Deyon, Pierre and Mendels, Franklin (eds.), *La Proto-Industrialisation: théorie et réalité*, 2 vols., Lille, Université des arts, lettres et sciences humaines, 1982.

Dietrich, Craig, 'Cotton Culture and Manufacture in Early Ch'ing China', in Willmott (ed.), *Economic Organization in Chinese Society*, pp. 109–36.

Ding Richu, 'Shanghai zibenjia jieji yu xinhai geming' (The Shanghai Capitalist Class and the 1911 Revolution), *Jinian xinhai geming qishizhounian xueshu taolunhui lunwenji*, vol. 1, pp. 281–321.

Ding Richu *et al.*, 'Yu Xiaqing jianlun' (On the Subject of Yu Xiaqing), *Lishi yanjiu*, 1981, no. 3, pp. 145–66.

Ding, Wenjiang, 'Shaoshurende zeren' (The Responsibilities of a Minority), *Nuli zhoubao*, no. 67, 26 August 1923.

Dobb, Maurice, *Papers on Capitalism, Development and Planning*, London, 1967.

Dongfang zazhi (The Eastern Miscellany), Shanghai, monthly, 1904–48.

Dulioust, Nicole, 'Quelques aspects de la presse chinoise pendant le Mouvement du 30 mai 1925', *Chine, cahiers d'études chinoises de l'INALCO*, Paris, INALCO, no. 1, 1980.

Eastman, Lloyd E., *The Abortive Revolution: China under Nationalist Rule, 1927–1937*, Cambridge, Mass., Harvard University Press, 1974.

Eastman, Lloyd E., 'Some Themes on Wartime China', *Chinese Republican Studies Newsletter*, vol. 1, no. 1 (October 1975).

Elvin, Mark, 'The Administration of Shanghai 1904–1914', in Elvin and Skinner (eds.), *The Chinese City between Two Worlds*, pp. 239–62.

Elvin, Mark, 'The County of Shanghai', in Skinner (ed.), *The City in Late Imperial China*, pp. 239–62.

Elvin, Mark, 'The Gentry Democracy in Shanghai', PhD. dissertation, Cambridge University, 1968.

Elvin, Mark, 'The Gentry Democracy in Chinese Shanghai, 1905–1914', in Gray, Jack (ed.), *Modern China's Search for a Political Form*, London, Oxford University Press, 1969.

Elvin, Mark, 'The High Level Equilibrium Trap: The Causes of the Decline of Invention in the Traditional Chinese Textile Industries', in Willmott (ed.), *Economic Organization in Chinese Society*, pp. 137–72.

Elvin, Mark, *The Pattern of the Chinese Past*, Stanford, Stanford University Press, 1973.

Elvin, Mark, 'Skills and Resources in Late Traditional China', in Perkins (ed.), *China's Modern Economy in Historical Perspective*, pp. 85–114.

Elvin, Mark and Skinner, William G. (eds.) *The Chinese City between Two Worlds*, Stanford, Stanford University Press, 1974.

Esherick, Joseph W., '1911: A Review', *Modern China*, Beverly Hills, Calif., quarterly, vol. 2, no. 2 (April 1976), pp. 141–84.

Esherick, Joseph W., *Reform and Revolution in China: The 1911 Revolution in Hunan and Hubei*, Berkeley, University of California Press, 1976.

Fairbank, John K., 'The Creation of the Treaty System', in Fairbank, John K. (ed.), *The Cambridge History of China*, vol. 10, *Late Ch'ing 1800–1911*, part 1, pp. 213–63.

Fairbank, John K. *et al.* (eds.), *The Cambridge History of China*, vols. 10–11, *Late Ch'ing 1800–1911*, vol. 12, *Republican China 1912–1949*, part 1, Cambridge, Cambridge University Press, 1978–80 (vols. 10–11), 1983 (vol. 12).

Fairbank, John K. *et al.* (eds.), *East Asia: The Great Transformation*, London, Allen and Unwin, 1965.

Fan Bochuan, 'Ershiji chuqi Zhongguo zibenzhuyi fazhande qingkuang yu tedian' (General Conditions and Particular Features of the Development of Chinese Capitalism in the Early Twentieth Century), *Lishi yanjiu*, 1983, no. 4.

Fang Teng, 'Yu Xiaqing lun' (On the Subject of Yu Xiaqing), *Zazhi yuekan* (Monthly Miscellany), Shanghai, irregular monthly, vol. 12, no. 2 (November 1943), pp. 46–51; vol. 12, no. 3 (December 1943), pp. 62–7; vol. 12, no. 4 (January 1944), pp. 59–64.

Feng Shaoshan, 'Jinri zhi san dawenti' (The Three Great Problems of Today), *Shanghai zongshanghui yuebao*, vol. 3, no. 1 (January 1923).

Feetham, Richard, *Report of the Hon. Richard Feetham: The Shanghai Municipal Council*, 2 vols., Shanghai, North China Daily News and Herald, 1931.

Ferrin, A. W., *Chinese Currency and Finance*, Washington DC, US Department of Commerce, 1919 (Special Agent Series, 186).

Feuerwerker, Albert, *China's Early Industrialization: Sheng Hsuan-huai (1844–1916) and Mandarin Enterprise*, Cambridge, Mass., Harvard University Press, 1958.

Feuerwerker, Albert, 'Industrial Enterprise in Twentieth Century China: The Chee Hsin Cement Company', in Feuerwerker, Albert, Murphey, Rhoads and Wright, Mary C. (eds.), *Approaches to Modern China History*, Berkeley, University of California Press, 1967.

Feuerwerker, Albert, *The Chinese Economy ca. 1870–1911*, Ann Arbor, Michigan, 1969 (Michigan Papers in Chinese Studies, no. 5).

Feuerwerker, Albert, *State and Society in Eighteenth Century China: The Ch'ing Empire in its Glory*, Ann Arbor, University of Michigan, 1976 (Michigan Papers in Chinese Studies, no. 27).

Fewsmith, Joseph, *Party, State, and Local Elites in Republican China; Merchant Organizations and Politics in Shanghai, 1890–1930*, Honolulu, University of Hawaii Press, 1985.

Fincher, John, 'Political Provincialism and the National Revolution', in Wright (ed.), *China in Revolution: The First Phase, 1900–1913*, pp. 185–226.

Fong, H. D., *The Growth and Decline of Rural Industrial Enterprise in North China*, Tientsin, Chihli Press, 1936.

Fong H. D., *Reminiscences of a Chinese Economist at 70*, Singapore, South Seas Press, 1975.

Furet, François, *Interpreting the French Revolution*, Cambridge, Cambridge University Press, 1981.

Gardner, John, 'The *Wu-fan* Campaign in Shanghai. A Study in Consolidation of Urban Control', in Barnett Doak (ed.), *Chinese Communist Politics in Action*, Seattle, University of Washington Press, 1969, pp. 477–539.

Garret, Shirley, 'Chambers of Commerce', in Elvin and Skinner (eds.), *The Chinese City between Two Worlds*, pp. 213–38.

Gerschenkron, Alexander, *Economic Backwardness in Historical Perspective*, Cambridge, Mass., Harvard University Press, 1962.

Gipoulon, Catherine, *Qiu Jin. Femme et révolutionnaire en Chine au xixe siècle*, Paris, Editions des femmes, 1976.

Godley, Michael R., *The Mandarin-Capitalists from Nanyang: Overseas Chinese Enterprise in the Modernisation of China*, Cambridge, Cambridge University Press, 1981.

Gongshang shiliao (Material on the History of Industry and Trade), 2 vols., Peking, Wenshi, ziliao chubanshe, 1981.

Grieder, Jerome B., *Hu Shih and the Chinese Renaissance: Liberalism in the Chinese Revolution 1917–1937*, Cambridge, Mass., Harvard University Press, 1970.

'Guanshui yanjiuhuiyi jilu' (Report of the Study Commission on Customs Tariffs), in Beijing yinhangyuekanshe (ed.), *Zongguo guanshui wenti* (The Problem of Customs Tariffs in China), Peking, 1923.

'"Guanyu cailijiashui zhi Beijing yanjiuhuiyi yu bubian shangqing zhudian qing taolun an"', Hubei quansheng shanghui lianhehui tiyi' (Let there be a Discussion of Certain Points of View of the Government Study Commission on the Abolition of the *lijin* and Tax Increases, Points of View that are Unfavourable to Commercial Interests, Motion Presented by the Provincial Federation of the Chambers of Commere of Hubei), *Shanghai zongshanghui yuebao*, vol. 3, no. 2 (February 1923).

Guo Feng, 'Baihuoye dawang; Yong'an guojia' (The Department Store

Kings: The Guo Family of the Yong'an Company), *Nanbeiji* (North Pole, South Pole), Hong Kong, no. 120, 16 May 1980.

Haishang mingrenzhuan (Biographies of Shanghai Celebrities), Shanghai, Wenming shuju, no date.

Hao Yen-p'ing, *The Comprador in Nineteenth Century China: Bridge between East and West*, Cambridge, Mass., Harvard University Press, 1970.

He Bingdi, *Zhongguo huiguan shilun* (History of the *Landmannschaft* in China), Taibei, Xuesheng shuju. 1966.

He Bingdi, *see* Ho Ping-ti.

Hengfeng shachangde fasheng fazhan yu gaizao (The Creation, Development and Evolution of the Hengfeng Cotton Mills), Shanghai, Zhongguo kexueyuan Jingji yanjiusuo (Institute of Economics of the Academy of Sciences of China) *et al.*, Shanghai renmin chubanshe, 1958.

Henriot, Christian, 'Le gouvernement municipal de Shanghai, 1927–1937', thesis for a *doctorat de 3ᵉ cycle*, INALCO-Paris III, June 1983.

Henriot, Christian, 'Le nouveau journalisme politique chinois (1895–1911): Shanghai–Hong Kong)', *Chine, Cahiers d'études chinoises*, Paris, Centre d'études chinoises de l'INALCO, 1980, pp. 5–80.

'Heping tongyi xuanyuan' (Declaration on Peaceful Unification), in Chang Qiyun *et al.* (eds.), *Guofu quanshu* (Complete Works of the Father of the Country [Sun Yat-sen]), Taibei, Guofeng yanjiuyuan, 1960, p. 755.

Ho Ping-ti, 'The Salt Merchants of Yang-chou. A Study of Commercial Capitalism in Eighteenth Century China', *Harvard Journal of Asiatic Studies*, vol. 17 (1954), pp. 130–68.

Ho Ping-ti, *Studies of the Population of China*, New York, Columbia University Press, 1959.

Ho Ping-ti, *The Ladder of Success in Imperial China: Aspects of Social Mobility 1368–1911*, New York, Columbia University Press, 1962.

Ho Ping-ti, *see* He Bingdi.

Hou Chi-ming, *Foreign Investment and Economic Development in China, 1840–1937*, Cambridge, Mass., Harvard University Press, 1965.

Hsiao Liang-lin, *China's Foreign Trade Statistics, 1864–1949*, Cambridge, Mass., Harvard University Press, 1974.

Hsieh, Winston, *Chinese Historiography on the Revolution of 1911: A Critical Survey and a Selected Bibliography*, Stanford, Hoover Institution Press, 1975.

Hu Shi, 'Guojide Zhongguo' (China in the Concert of Nations), *Nuli zhoubao*, no. 22, 1 October 1922.

Hu Shi, 'Womende zhengzhi zhuzhang' (Our Political Proposals), *Nuli zhoubao*, no. 2, 14 May 1922.

Huang, Philip C. C. (ed.), *The Development of Underdevelopment in China: A Symposium*, White Plains, M. E. Sharpe, 1980.

Huang Yifeng, 'Wusa yundong zhongde dazibenjieji' (The Greater Bourgeoisie during the Movement of 30 May), *Lishi yanjiu*, 1965, no. 3, pp. 11–24.

Ichiko Chūzo, 'The role of the Gentry: An Hypothesis', in Wright (ed.), *China in Revolution: The First Phase 1900–1913*, pp. 297–318.

Japan, Gaimushō (Ministry of Foreign Affairs), *Shina ni oite Nihon shōhin dōmei haiseki ikken* (The Boycotting of Japanese Merchandise in China).

Japan, Gaimushō (Ministry of Foreign Affairs), *Shina ni oite Nihon shōhin dōmei haiseki ikken, fukumei sho* (The Boycotting of Japanese Merchandise in China, Reports).

Jeannin, Pierre, 'La Proto-industrialisation: développement ou impasse?', *Annales. Economies, Sociétés, Civilisations*, no. 1 (35th year), January–February 1980, pp. 52–65.

Jiang Hengyuan, *Zhongguo guanshui shiliao* (Material for the History of Customs Tariffs in China), Shanghai, Renwen bianjisuo, 1931.

Jiaoyu yu zhiye (Education and Profession). Shanghai, then Chongqing, irregular monthly, 1917–49.

Jindaishi ziliao (Documents of Modern History), Peking, irregular, special issue, 'Xinhai geming ziliao' (Documents on the 1911 Revolution), 1961, no. 1.

Jinian xinhai geming qishizhounian xueshu taolunhui lunwenji (Collection of Communications Presented to the Conference to Commemorate the 70th Anniversary of the 1911 Revolution), 3 vols., Peking, Zhonghua shuju, 1983.

Jones, Susan M., 'Finance in Ningpo, 1750–1850', in Willmott (ed.), *Economic Organization in Chinese Society*, pp. 47–78.

Jones, Susan, 'The Ningpo Pang and Financial Power in Shanghai', in Elvin and Skinner (eds.), *The Chinese City between Two Worlds*, p. 73–96.

Jones, Susan, 'Rural–Urban Continuities. Leading Families of two Chekiang Market Towns', *Ch'ing-shih wen't'i*, vol. 3, no. 7 (November 1977), pp. 67–104.

Keenan, Barry, *The Dewey Experiment in China: Educational Reform and Political Power in the Early Republic* (Cambridge, Mass., Harvard University Press, 1977.

Kikuchi Takaharu, *Chūgoku minzoku undō no kihon kōzō: taigai boikotto no kenkyū* (The Basic Structure of Nationalist Movements in China: The Antiforeigner Boycotts), Tokyo, Daian, 1966.

Kirby, William C., *Germany and Republican China*, Stanford, Stanford University Press, 1984.

Kojima Yoshio, 'Shingai kakumei ni okeru Shanhai dokuritsu to shōshinsō' (The Gentry, the Merchant Class and the Independence Movement in Shanghai during the 1911 Revolution), *Tōyō shigaku ronshū* (Collection of Oriental History), Tokyo, no. 6 (August 1960), pp. 113–14.

Kriedte, P., Medick, H. and Schlumbohm, J., *Industrialisierung vor der Industrialisierung. Gewerbliche Warenproduktion auf dem Land in der Formationsperiode des Kapitalismus*, Göttingen, Vanderhoeck u. Ruprecht, 1977.

Kuh, Philip A., *Rebellion and its Enemies in Late Imperial China: Militarization and Social Structure*, Cambridge, Mass., Harvard University Press, 1970.

Kuhn, Philip A., 'Local Self-Government under the Republic. Problems of Control, Authority and Mobilization', in Wakeman, Frederic and Grant, Carolyn (eds.), *Conflict and Control in Late Imperial China*, Berkeley, University of California Press, 1975, pp. 257–98.

Kung, H. D., 'The Growth of Population in Six Chinese Cities', *Chinese Economic Journal and Bulletin*, Shanghai, weekly, vol. 30, no. 3 (March 1937).

Kuznets, Simon, *Modern Economic Growth Rate, Structure and Spread*, New Haven, Yale University Press, 1966.

Lee, William Yinson (ed.), *World Chinese Biographies*, Shanghai Globe Publishing Company (bilingual English–Chinese edn), 1944.

Le Roy Ladurie, Emmanuel, *Les Paysans du Languedoc*, Paris, Sevpen, 1966.

Levy, Marion J. and Shih Kuo-heng, *The Rise of the Modern Chinese Business Class: Two Introductory Essays*, New York, IPR, 1949.

Lishi yanyiu (Historical Studies), Peking.

Lin Xin and Sun Sibai (eds.), *Minguo renwuzhuan* (Biographies of Figures of the Republican Period), 3 vols., Peking, Zhongguo shehui kexueyuan Jindaishi yanjiusuo (Institute of Modern History of the Academy of Social Sciences of China), Zhonghua shuju, 1978–81 (Zhongua minguoshi ziliao conggao (Project for a Collection of Material on the History of the Chinese Republic)).

Li Yiyuan and Yang Guoshu, *Zhongguorende xinggee: keji conghexingde taolun* (The Character of the Chinese; An Interdisciplinary Discussion, Nakang, Taibei, Institute of Ethnology, Academia Sinica, 1972 (Monograph Series B, no. 4).

Lin Zengping, 'Lüelun minzu zichanjieji shangceng yu Qingwei lixianpai' (Brief Essay on the Greater National Bourgeoisie and the Constitutionalist Party at the End of the Qing Dynasty), *Xinhaigeming congkan* (Collection on the History of the 1911 Revolution), Peking, Zhongua shuju, vol. 2, 1980, pp. 48–62.

Liu Hongsheng giye shiliao (Material for a History of the Business Concerns of Liv Hongsheng), 3 vols., Shanghai shehui kexueyuan Jingji yanjiusuo (Institute of Economics of the Shanghai Academy of Social Sciences) Shanghai renmin chubanshe, 1981 (Shanghai zibenzhuyi dianxingqiye shiliao (Material for the History of Typical Capitalist Business Concerns in Shanghai)).

Liu Taotian, 'Hangyejia Yu Xiaqing xiansheng zhuanlüe' (Brief Biography of the Shipbuilder, Yu Xiaqing), *Jiaoyu yu zhiye*, no. 183, 1 March 1937, pp. 233–41.

Lubot, Eugène, *Liberalism in an Illiberal Age: New Culture Liberals in Republican China, 1919–1937*, Westport, Connecticut, Greenwood Press, 1982.

Luo Zhiru, *Tongjibiaozhong zhi Shanghai* (Shanghai in Statistical Tables), Nanjing guoli zhongyang yanjiuyuan Shehuikexue yanjiusuo jikan (Quarterly Review of the Institute of Social Sciences of the Academia Sinica), Nanking, 1932, no. 4.

MacElderry, Andrea L., *Shanghai Old-Style Banks (Ch'ien-chuang), 1880–1935: A Traditional Institution in a Changing Society*, Ann Arbor, University of Michigan, 1976 (Michigan Papers in Chinese Studies, no. 25).

Malia, Martin, *Comprendre la révolution russe*, Paris, Le Seuil, 1980.

Mannheim, Karl, *Essays on Sociology and Social Psychology*, London, Oxford University Press, 1953.

Mao Dun, *Minuit* (French transl.), Peking, Foreign language editions, 1957.

[Mao] Zedong, 'Beijing zhengbian yu shangren' (The Peking Coup d'Etat and the Merchants), *Xiangdao zhoubao*, nos. 31–2, 11 July 1923.

Maoxin Fuxin Shenxin xitong. Rongjia qiye shiliao, 1896–1937 (The Maoxin–Fuxin–Shenxin group. Material for a History of the Business Concerns of the Rong Family, 1896–1937), 2 vols., Shanghai, Shanghai shehui kexueyuan Jingji yanjiusuo (Institute of Economics of the Shanghai Academy of Social Sciences), Shanghai renmin chubanshe (1st edn 1962), repr. 1980.

Maoxin Fuxin Shenxin zonggongsi sazhounian jiniance (Book to Commemorate the 30th Anniversary of the Maoxin–Fuxin–Shenxing General Company), Shanghai, Shijie shuju, 1929.

Mast, Herman III and Saywell, William G., 'Revolution out of Tradition: The Political Ideology of Tai Chi-t'ao', *Journal of Asian Studies*, vol. 34, no. 1 (November 1974), pp. 73–98.

Meliksetov, A. V., 'Nekotorye osobennosti kapitalističeskogo razvitiya Kitaya v gody gomin'danovskogo gospodstva (1927–1949)' (Some Particular Features of Capitalist Development in China during the Years of the Guomindang Reign), in Levkovskiy, A. I. and Rosaliev, U. N., *Krupnyj kapital i monopolii stran Azii* (Large Capital Resources and Monopolies in Asian Countries), Moscow, Nauka (Principal editors of oriental literature), 1970.

Meliksetov, A. V., 'K voprosu ob istoričeskoi roli bjurokratičeskogo kapitala v gomin'danovskom Kitae' (The Problem of the Historic Role of Bureaucratic Capital in Guomindang China), *Strany Dal'nego Vostoka (Istorija i ekonomika)* (Far-Eastern Countries, History and Economics), Academy of Sciences of the USSR, Institute of Oriental Studies, Moscow, Nauka (Principal editors of oriental literature), 1971.

Meliksetov, A. V., *Bjurokratičeskij kapital v Kitae. Ekonomičeskaja politika gomin' dana i razvitie gosudarstvennogo kapitalizma v 1927–1937 gg* (Bureaucratic Capitalism in China, Economic Policies of the Guomindang and the Development of State Capitalism, 1927–1937), Moscow, Nauka (Principal editors of oriental literature), 1972.

Mendels, Franklin, 'Proto-Industrialization: The First Phase of the Process of Industrialization', *Journal of Economic History*, vol. 32 (1972), pp. 241–61.

Metzger, Thomas A., *Escape from Predicament: Neo-confucianism and China's Evolving Political Culture*, New York, Columbia University Press, 1977.

Metzger, Thomas A., *The Internal Organization of Ch'ing Bureaucracy*, Cambridge, Mass., Harvard University Press, 1973.

Metzger, Thomas A., 'On the Historical Roots of Economic Modernization in China: The Increasing Differentiation of the Economy from the Policy during the Late Ming and Early Ch'ing Times', in *Conference on Modern Chinese Economic History*, Taibei, The Institute of Economics, Academia Sinica, 1977, pp. 38–45.

Metzger, Thomas A., 'The Organizational Capabilities of the Ch'ing State in the Field of Commerce: The Liang-huai Monopoly 1740–1840', in Willmott (ed.), *Economic Organization in Chinese Society*, pp. 9–46.

Michels, Robert, *Les Partis politiques* (transl. from German by Jankelevitch, S.), Paris, Flammarion, 1971.

Monnet, Jean, *Mémoires*, Paris, Fayard, 1976.

Mote, Frederick W., 'The Transformation of Nanking, 1350–1400', in Skinner (ed.), *The City in Late Imperial China*, pp. 101–54.

[Mu Ouchu] Moh, H. Y., 'Causes for the High Price of Cotton and the Low Price of Yarn', *China Weekly Review*, 23 December 1922.

Mu Ouchu, *Ouchu wushi zishu* (Autobiography of [Mu] Ouchu at Fifty), Shanghai, Commercial Press, 1926.

Murphey, Rhoads, *The Outsiders: The Western Experience in India and China*, Ann Arbor, University of Michigan Press, 1977.

Murphey, Rhoads, *The Treaty Ports and China's Modernization: What Went Wrong?*, Ann Arbor, Michigan, 1970 (Michigan Papers in Chinese Studies, no. 7).

Myers, Ramon H., *The Chinese Economy: Past and Present*, Belmont, California, Wadsworth, 1980.

Myers, Ramon H., *The Chinese Peasant Economy: Agricultural Development in Hopei and Shantung, 1890–1949*, Cambridge, Mass., Harvard University Press, 1970.

Myers, Ramon H. and Metzger, Thomas A., 'Sinological Shadows. The State of Modern China Studies in the United States', *Washington Review*, spring, 1980.

Nanyang xiongdi yancao gongsi shiliao (Material for the History of the Nanyang Brothers' Tobacco Company), Zhongguo kexueyuan Shanghai jingji yanjiusuo (Institute of Economics of the Shanghai Academy of Sciences of China), Shanghai renmin chubanshe, 1958.

Nathan, Andrew J., *Peking Politics, 1918–1923: Factionalism and Failure of Constitutionalism*, Berkeley, University of California Press, 1976, (Michigan Studies on China).

Needham, Joseph T., *Science and Civilization in China*, vol. 4, part 2, *Mechanical Engineering*, Cambridge, Cambridge University Press, 1965.

Negishi Tadashi, *Baiben seido no kenkyū* (Research into the Comprador System), Tokyo, Nihon Tosho, 1948.

Negishi Tadashi, *Shanhai no girudo* (The Shanghai Guilds), Tokyo, Nippon Hyōronsha, 1951.

Negishi Tadashi, *Chūgoku no girudo* (The Guilds in China), Tokyo, Nippon Hyōron Shinsha, 1953.

Nie Yuntai, 'Wei Ribing qiangsha shimin shi jinggao guomin' (Warning to the Nation concerning the Incident during which Japanese Soldiers Fired on the Crowds), *Shanghai zongshanghui yuebao*, vol. 3, no. 6 (June 1923).

North China Herald, supplement of the *North China Daily News*, Shanghai, weekly.

North China Star, Peking, weekly.

Nuli zhoubao (Endeavour), Peking, weekly, 1922–3.

Paauw, Douglas S., 'The Kuomintang and Economic Stagnation, 1928–1937', *Journal of Asian Studies*, vol. 4, no. 2 (February 1957), pp. 213–20.

Peking and Tientsin Times, Tianjin, daily.

Perkins, Dwight H., *Agricultural Development in China, 1368–1968*, Chicago, Aldine, 1969.

Perkins, Dwight H. (ed.), *China's Modern Economy in Historical Perspective*, Stanford, Stanford University Press, 1975.

Pi Mingxiu, 'Wuchang shouyizhongde Wuhan shanghui shangtuan' (The Chambers of Commerce and the Merchant Militia of Wuhan during the Wuchang Uprising). *Jinian xinhai geming qishizhounian xueshū taolunhui lunwenji*, vol. 1, pp. 322–61.

Pinnick, Alfred, *Silver and China, an Investigation of the Monetary Principles Governing China's Trade and Prosperity*, Shanghai, Kelly and Walsh, 1930.

Polanyi, Karl, *The Great Transformation*, Boston, Beacon Press, 1st paperback edn, 1957.

Politique de Pékin (La), Peking, weekly.

Pott, W. S. A., 'The People's Delegates to the Pacific Conference', *China Weekly Review*, 22 October 1921.

Pye, Lucian W., *The Spirit of Chinese Politics*, Cambridge, Mass., MIT Press, 1968.

Qi Yisheng, 'Yong'an jituande chuanshiren' (The Founders of the Yong'an [Wing On] Group), *Nanbeiji* (North Pole, South Pole), Hong Kong, monthly, no. 12, 16 May 1980, pp. 8–10.

'Qing fencheng ge xunyueshi ge tujun xiheng baomin limo tongyi an' (Let the Marshals and Warlords be Instructed to Stop Fighting, Protect the People and Work as Hard as Possible for Unification), *Shanghai zongshanghui yuebao*, vol. 3, no. 6 (June 1923).

' "Qing hencheng zhengfu texu quanguo shanghui zilian shangtuan an", Sichuan Chengdu zongshanghui daibiao tiyi' (Let Concerted Efforts be Made to Persuade the Government to Give the Chambers of Commerce Special Authorization to Train their own Merchant Militia. Motion presented by the General Chamber of Commerce of Chengdu, Sichuan), *Shanghai zongshanghui yuebao*, vol. 3, no. 4 (April 1923).

' "Qing weizhi quanguoshanghui lianhehui tongguo yi'an lizheng shixing an", Hubei Yidu shanghui tiyi' (Let the Motions Voted by the Conference of the National Federation of Chambers of Commerce be Upheld and let Every Effort be Made to Apply them. Motion Presented by the Chamber of Commerce of Yidu, Hubei), *Shanghai zongshanghui yuebao*, vol. 3, no. 4 (April 1923).

Qishizhounian xueshu taolunhui, see *Jinian xinhai geming qishizhounian xueshu taolunhui lunwenji*.

Qiu Jie, 'Guangdong shangren yu xinhai geming' (The Merchants of Canton and the 1911 Revolution), *Jinian xinhai geming qishizhounian xueshu taolunhui lunwenji*, vol. 1, pp. 362–96.

'Quanguo shangjiao lianxihuiy shimoji' (Notes on the Proceedings of the Common Conference of the National Federations of the Chambers of Commerce and the Education Societies), *Shanghai zongshanghui yuebao*, vol. 1, no. 4 (October 1921).

'Quanguo yinhang gonghui lianhehuiyi ji' (Notes on the Conference of the National Federation of Banking Associations), *Yinhang yuekan*, vol. 1, no. 6 (June 1921).

Rawsky, Evelyn, *Education and Popular Literacy in Ch'ing China*, Ann Arbor, University of Michigan Press, 1979.

Rawsky, Thomas G., 'China's Republican Economy: An Introduction', Joint Centre on Modern East Asia, University of Toronto and York University, Discussion Paper no. 1 (1978).

Rawsky, Thomas G., 'Chinese Dominance of Treaty Port Commerce and its Implication, 1860–1875', *Explorations in Economic History*, vol. 7, no. 4 (1970), pp. 451–73.

Remer, Charles F., *The Foreign Trade of China*, Shanghai, Commercial Press, 1926.

Remer, Carl F., *A Study of Chinese Boycotts*, Baltimore, The Johns Hopkins Press, 1933.

'Reminiscences of Chen Guangfu as Told to Julie Lien-Yin How, Dec. 6

1960–June 5 1961' (unpublished manuscript), Oral History Project, Columbia University.

Rhoads, Edward J., *China's Republican Revolution: The Case of Kwangtung*, Cambridge, Mass., Harvard University Press, 1975.

Rhoads, Edward J., 'Merchants Associations in Canton 1895–1911', in Elvin and Skinner (eds.), *The Chinese City between Two Worlds*, pp. 97–118.

Riskin, Carl, 'Surplus and Stagnation in Modern China', in Perkins (ed.), *China's Modern Economy in Historical Perspective*, pp. 48–84.

Rodes, Jean, *Scènes de la vie révolutionnaire en Chine*, Paris, Plon, Nourrit, 3rd edn, 1917.

Rongjia qiye shiliao, see *Maoxin Fuxin Shenxin xitong.Rongjia giye shiliao*.

Rowe, William T., *Hankow, Commerce and Society in a Chinese City, 1796–1889*, Stanford, Stanford University Press, 1984.

Rowe, William T., 'Urban Control in Late Imperial China. The *Pao-chia* System in Hankow', in Fogel, Joshua A. and Rowe, William T. (eds.), *Perspectives on a Changing China*, Boulder, Westview Press, 1979.

Rozman, Gilbert, *Urban Networks in Ch'ing China and Tokugawa Japan*, Princeton, New Jersey, Princeton University Press, 1973.

Ru Xuan, 'Duiyu shangjiao lianxihui "duiwai xuanyan" zho wo jian' (My Point of View on the 'Declaration of Foreign Policy' of the Joint Conference of Merchants and Educationalists), *Shanghai zongshanghui yuebao*, vol. 1, no. 4 (October 1921).

Ru Xuan, 'Guanyu guoshihuiyi zhi pianyan' (Some Notes on the Subject of the Convention of National Affairs), *Shanghai zongshanghui yuebao*, vol. 1, no. 5 (November 1921).

Ru Xuan, 'Guoshi yu guoshihuiyi' (The Affairs of the Nation and the Convention of National Affairs), *Shanghai zongshanghui yuebao*, vol. 2, no. 2 (February 1922).

Ru Xuan, 'Lun wo guo yinhangtuan bu yi jiaru siqiang zuzhi zhi xin yinhangtuan' (The Chinese Consortium must not Join the New Consortium Organised by the Four Powers), *Shanghai zongshanghui yuebao*, vol. 2, no. 1 (January 1922).

Ru Xuan, 'Xin yinhangtuan yu jingjiguafen' (The New Consortium and the Economic Dismemberment of China), *Shanghai zongshanghui yuebao*, vol. 1, no. 6 (December 1921).

Sanford, James C., 'Chinese Commercial Organization and Behavior in Shanghai of the Late Nineteenth and Early Twentieth Century', Ph. D. dissertation, Harvard University, 1976, 440ff.

Schneider, Laurence A., *Ku Chieh-kang and China's New History: Nationalism and the Quest for Alternative Traditions*, Berkeley, University of California Press, 1971.

Schneider, S. J., 'T'ung-oil 1900–1924. An Export Trade in the Central China Setting', Ph. D. dissertation, Harvard University, 1956.

Schoppa, Keith Robert, *Chinese Elites and Political Change: Zhejiang Province in the Early Twentieth Century*, Cambridge, Mass., Harvard University Press, 1982.

Schrecker, John, *Imperialism and Chinese Nationalism: Germany in Shantung*, Cambridge, Mass., Harvard University Press, 1971.

Shanghai chunqiu (Shanghai Annals), Hong Kong, Zhongguo tushubianyiguan, 1967.

Shanghai minzu jiqigongye (The National Mechanical Engineering Industries of Shanghai), 2 vols., Peking, Zhongguo shehui kexueyuan Jingji yanjiusuo (Institute of Economics of the Academy of Social Sciences of China), Zhonghua shuju (1st edn 1966), 2nd edn 1979 (Zhongguo zibenzhuyi gongshangye shiliao congkan (Collection of Material on the History of Capitalist Industry and Trade in China)).

Shanghai qianzhuang shiliao (Material for the History of the *qianzhuang* Banks of Shanghai), Shanghai, Zhongguo renmin yinhang Shanghaishi fenhang (People's Bank of China, Shanghai branch), Shanghai renmin chubanshe, 1960.

'Shanghai shizhi jinhua shilüe' (Brief History of the Progress of the Municipal Government of Shanghai), in Shanghai tongshe (ed.), *Shanghai yanjiu ziliao* (Material for Research on Shanghai) (1st edn, Shanghai, 1936), Taibei, China Press, repr. 1973.

Shanghai Yong'an gongside chansheng fazhan he gaizao (Creation, Development and Transformation of the Yong'an [Wing On] Company of Shanghai, Shanghai. Shanghai shehui kexueyuan Jingji yanjiusuo (Institute of Economics of the Shanghai Academy of Social Sciences), Shanghai renmin chubanshe, 1981.

Shanghai zhinan (Guide to Shanghai: A Chinese Directory to the Port), Shanghai shangwu yinshuguan, 10th edn, rev. 1919.

Shanghai zongshanghui yuebao (Monthly Review of the Chinese General Chamber of Commerce of Shanghai), Shanghai, monthly.

Shanghai zongshanghui huiyuanlu (Record of the Members of the Shanghai General Chamber of Commerce), brochure published by the Chamber of Commerce, Shanghai (April 1928), 60 pp.

Shang Yue (ed.), *Ming Qing shehui Jingji xingtaide yanjiu* (Study on the Economic Structures of the Ming and Qing Periods, Shanghai, Shanghai renmin chubanshe, 1957.

Shenbao, Shanghai, daily, 1872–1949.

Shen Yunsun, 'Zhonghua shiyeyinhang shimo' (History of the Chinese Bank for Industry), *Jindaishi ziliao*, 1957, no. 6, pp. 120–39.

Shiba Yoshinobu, 'Ningbo and its Hinterland', in Skinner (ed.), *The City in Late Imperial China*, pp. 391–440.

Shih, Paul T. K. (ed.), *The Strenuous Decade: China's Nation-building Efforts,
1927–1937*, Jamaica, New York, St John University Press, 1970.

Shina keizai tsūsetsu (General Handbook of Chinese Economics), Tokyo,
Yamagushi kōtō shōgo gakkō, Tōa keizai kenkyūkai (Advanced School of
Commerce of Yamaguchi, Research Seminar on Far-Eastern Economics),
1928.

Shiye zazhi (Businessman's Companion), Changsha, monthly.

Skinner, William G., 'Cities and the Hierarchy of Local Systems', in Skinner
(ed.), *The City in Late Imperial China*, pp. 275–351.

Skinner, William G. (ed.), *The City in Late Imperial China*, Stanford, Stanford
University Press, 1977.

Skinner, William G., 'Marketing and Social Structure in Rural China',
Journal of Asian Studies, vol. 24, nos. 1–3 (November 1964, February 1965,
May 1965), pp. 3–43, pp. 195–228, pp. 363–99.

Skinner, William G., 'Regional Urbanization in Nineteenth Century China',
in Skinner (ed.), *The City in Late Imperial China*, pp. 211–53.

Skocpol, Theda, 'Wallerstein's World Capitalist System: A Theoretical and
Historical Critique', *American Journal of Sociology*, vol. 82, no. 5 (March
1977), pp. 1075–90.

Solomon, Richard, *Mao's Revolution and the Chinese Political Culture*, Berkeley,
University of California Press, 1971.

South China Morning Post, Hong Kong, daily.

Sun De [Maring], 'Zhongguo gaizao zhi waiguo yuanzhu' (Foreign Aid for
the Reconstruction of China), *Xiangdao zhoubao*, no. 29 (June 1923).

Sun Yat-sen, *The International Development of China*, London, Hutchinson, 2nd
edn, 1928.

[Sun Yat-sen], *Guofu quanshu* (Complete Works of the Father of the Country),
ed. Chang Qiyun *et al.*, Taibei, Guofeng yanjiuyuan, 1960.

[Sun Yat-sen], *Zongli quanji* (Complete Works of the President), 5 vols.,
Shanghai, minzhi shuju, 1930.

'Tianjin huobang yu waiguo yanghang zhengchi buxia qingxing zhi yanjiu'
(Investigation into the Circumstances of the Unresolved Conflict between
[Chinese] Wholesalers, and Foreign Firms in Tianjin), *Yinhang zhoubao*,
vol. 5, no. 12, 5 April 1921.

Tianjin wenshiziliao xuanji, see *Wenshiziliao xuanji*.

'Tichang guohuo zhi wo jian' (My Point of View on the Promotion of
National Merchandise), *Shanghai zongshanghui yuebao*, vol. 4, no. 5 (May
1924).

Tōa Dōbunkai (ed.), *Shina keisai zensho* (Complete Handbook of Chinese
Economics), 12 vols., Ōsaka, Tokyo, Maruzen, Tōa Dōbunkai, 1907–8.

Tōa Dōbunkai (ed.), *Shina shōbetsu zenshi* (Complete List of the Provinces of
China), 18 vols., Tokyo, Tōa Dōbunkai, 1917–20.

Tsing Tung-chun, *De la production et du commerce de la soie en Chine*, Paris, Geuthner, 1928.

Varg, Paul A., 'The Myth of the China Market 1890–1914', *American Historical Review*, February 1968, pp. 742–57.

Wallerstein, Immanuel, *The Modern World-System: Capitalist Agriculture and the Origins of the European World-Economy in the Sixteenth Century*, New York, Academic Press, 1974.

Wan Lin, 'Zhongguode "miansha dawang" "mianfen dawang" Wuxi Rongshi jiazu baofashi' (History of the Irresistible Rise of the Rong Family from Wuxi, 'The Cotton and Flour Kings'), *Jingji daobao zhoukan* (Economic Bulletin), Peking, weekly, no. 50, 14 December 1947.

Wang Beiping and Zheng Daci (eds.), *Yu Xiaqing xiansheng* (Mr Yu Xiaqing), Shanghai, Ningbo wenxueshe, 1946.

Wang Jingkang and Zhang Zesheng, 'Yuyuan shachangde xingshuai shilüe' (History of the Rise and Fall of the Yuyuan Cotton Mills), *Tianjin wenshi ziliao xuanji*, no. 4 (October 1979), pp. 172–9.

Wang Jingliu, 'Shijiu shiji waiguo qin Hua qiyezhongde Huashang fugu huadong' (Investments of Chinese Merchants in the Foreign Businesses which are Invading China in the Twentieth Century), *Lishi yanjiu*, 1965, no. 4, pp. 39–74.

Wang Jingyu, *Zhongguo jindai gongyeshi ziliao, dier ji, 1895–1914 nian* (Material for the History of Modern Industry in China, 2nd series, 1895–1914), 2 vols., Peking, Zhongguo kexueyuan Jingji yanjiusuo (Institute of Economics of the Academy of Sciences of China), Kexue chubanshe, 1957.

Wang, Y. C., *Chinese Intellectuals and the West, 1872–1949*, Chapel Hill, University of North Carolina Press, 1966.

Wang Yeh-chien, 'Evolution of the Chinese Monetary System, 1644–1850', in *Conference on Modern Chinese Economic History*, pp. 469–96.

Wang Yeh-chien, *Land Taxation in Imperial China, 1750–1911*, Cambridge, Mass., Harvard University Press, 1974.

Weng Yeh-chien, 'The Secular Trend of Prices during the Ch'ing Period', *Journal of the Institute of Chinese Studies of the Chinese University of Hong Kong*, vol. 5, no. 2 (1972), pp. 347–68.

Wang Zhiwei, 'Zhongguo gongshangye shibai zhi yuanyin ji qi bujiu fangfa' (The Failure of Chinese Industry and Trade: The Causes and the Remedies), *Shanghai zongshanghui yuebao*, vol. 3, no. 6 (June 1923).

Weber, Max, *Gesammelte Aufsätze zur Religionensoziologie* (Tübingen, J. C. R. Mohr, 1922), repr. Paul Sibeck 1963–72, 3 vols., vol. 1, *Die Wirtschaftsethik der Weltreligionen, 1. Konfuzianismus und Taoismus*.

'Wei wairen ganyu hulu shi zhi Fu lingxiu gongshi han' (Letter Addressed to Mr Fu [Batalha de Freitas], Doyen of the Diplomatic Corps, on the Subject of Foreign Interference in the Protection of the Railways), *Shanghai zongshanghui yuebao*, vol. 3, no. 9 (September 1923).

Wen Han, 'You gongye jiandishang lun weichi guohuo dizhi Rihuo' (The Promotion of National Merchandise and the Anti-Japanese Boycott, considered from Industry's Point of View), *Shiye zazhi* (Businessman's Companion) Changsha, monthly, no. 71 (September 1923).

Whenshi zilao xuanji (Selection of Material concerning Culture and History), ed. Zhongguo renmin zhengzhixieshang huiyi (The Chinese People's Consultative Political Conference), Wenshiziliao gongzuo weiyuanhui (Commission for Material on Culture and History). Irregular places of publication vary with regional editions, separate numeration for the series concerning Shanghai. The material concerning Tianjin is published under the title *Tianjin wenshi ziliao* (Collection for Internal Circulation [neibu]).

Wilbur, Martin C., *Sun Yat-sen, Frustrated Patriot*, New York, Columbia University Press, 1976.

Will, Pierre Étienne, *Bureaucratie et famine en Chine au xviiie siècle*, Paris, Mouton, EHESS, 1980.

Willmott, William E. (ed.), *Economic Organization in Chinese Society*, Stanford, Stanford University Press, 1972.

Wills, John E. Jr, 'Maritime China from Wang Chih to Shih Lang. Themes in Peripheral History', in Spence, Jonathan and Wills, John E. Jr (eds.), *From Ming to Ch'ing: Conquest, Region and Continuity in Seventeenth Century China*, New Haven, Yale University Press, 1979, pp. 201–38.

Wright, Mary Clabaugh (ed.), *China in Revolution: The First Phase, 1900–1913*, New Haven, London, Yale University Press, 1968.

Wu Peichu, 'Jiu Shanghai waishang yinhang maiban' (The Compradores of the Foreign Banks of Old Shanghai), *Wenshi ziliao xuanji*, Shanghai renmin chubanshe, 1980, no. 1, pp. 127–65.

Wu Qiandui, 'Shanghai guangfu he Hujun dudufu' (The 1911 Revolution and the Military Government of Shanghai), *Jinian xinhai geming qishizhounian xueshu taolunhui lunwenji*, vol. 1, pp. 815–38.

Wu Yugan, 'Liansheng zizhi yu zhiyezhuyi' (Provincial Federalism and Professionalism) *Taipingyang* (The Pacific Ocean), Shanghai monthly, vol. 3, no. 7 (September 1922).

Wusu shiqi qikan jieshao (Introduction to the Periodical Literature of the May Fourth period, 3 vols., Peking, Zhonggong zhongyang Makesi Enkesi Liening Sidalin zhuzuo bianyiju yanjiushi (Research Department of the Bureau for the Translation of the Works of Marx, Engels, Lenin and Stalin of the Central Committee of the Chinese Communist Party), Renmin chubanshe, 1958–9.

Wusi yundong zai Shanghai shiliao xuanji (Selection of Material for the History of the May Fourth Movement in Shanghai), Shanghai, Shanghai shehui kexueyuan Lishi yanjiusuo (Institute of History of the Shanghai Academy of Social Sciences), Shanghai renmin chubanshe, 1960.

Xiangdao zhoubao (The Guide Weekly), Shanghai, then Canton, weekly, 1922–7.

Xinhai geming huiylu (Collection of Memoirs on the 1911 Revolution), 5 vols., Peking Zhongguo renmin zhengzhi xieshanghuiyi quanguo weiyuanhui, Wenshiziliao yanjiu weiyuanhui (National Bureau of the Consultative Political Conference of the Chinese People, Commission for Research on Material concerning Civilisation and History), Zhonghua shuju, 1961–3.

Xinhai geming zai Shanghai shiliao xuanji (Selection of Material on the History of the 1911 Revolution in Shanghai), Shanghai, Shanghai shehui kexueyuan Lishi yanjiusuo (Institute of History of the Shanghai Academy of Social Sciences), Shanghai renmin chubanshe (1st edn 1966), 1981.

Xu Cangshui, *Shanghai yinhanggonghui shiyeshi* (History of the Achievements of the Association of Modern Banks of Shanghai), brochure edited to celebrate the appearance of the 400th edition of the *Bankers' Weekly (Yinhang zhoubao)*, Shanghai, Yinhang zhoubaoshe, 26 May 1925.

Xu Dixin, *Guanliao ziben lun* (On the Subject of Bureaucratic Capitalism), Hong Kong, Nanyang shudian, 1947.

Xu Ying, *Dangdai Zhongguo shiyerenwushi* (Biographies of the Industrialists of Contemporary China), Shanghai, Zhonghua shuju, 1948.

Yan Zhongping *et al.*, *Zhongguo jindai jingjishi tongji ziliao xuanji* (Selection of Statistical Material on the Economic History of Modern China), Peking Kexue chubanshe, 1955.

Yan Zhongping, *Zhongguo mianfangzhi shigao* (History of the Cotton Industry in China), Peking, Kexue chubanshe, 3rd edn, 1963.

Yang Tongyi, 'Wuxi Yangshi yu Zhongguo mianfangyede guanxi' (The Links between the Yang Family, from Wuxi, and the Chinese Cotton Industry), *Gongshang shiliao* (Material on the History of Industry and Trade), Peking, Wenshi ziliao chubanshe, vol. 2, 1981, pp. 54–70.

Yao Quanxing, 'Chen Qimei yu Shanghai guangfu' (Chen Qimei and the 1911 Revolution in Shanghai), *Shehui kexue* (Social Sciences), Shanghai, monthly, 1981, no. 2.

1913 nian–1952 nian Nankai zihhu ziliao huibian (Collection of Material on the Indices of Nankai 1913–1952), Peking Tongji chubanshe, repr. 1958.

'Yindu waiguo mianbu zhi paichi yundong' (The Movement to Boycott Foreign Cotton Textiles in India), *Huashang shachang lianhehui jikan* (Quarterly Review of the Chinese Cotton Millowners' Association, 'The China Cotton Journal'), Shanghai, vol. 3, no. 2, 20 March 1922.

'Yinhangije qing Sun Wen weichi neizhai jijn' (Banking Circles Beg Sun Yat-sen to Support the Fund for Paying off Internal Debts), *Yinhang yuekan*, vol. 3, no. 12 (December 1923).

Yinhang yuekan (Monthly Banking Review), Peking, published by Yinhang yuekanshe, 1921–8.

Yinhang zhoubao (The Bankers' Weekly), Shanghai, published by Yinhang zhoubaoshe, 1917–50.

Yong' an fangzhivinran gongsi (The Young'an [Wing on] Spinning, Weaving, Dyeing and Printing Company), Peking, Zhongguo kexueyuan Jingji yanjiusuo (Institute of Economics of the Academy of Social Sciences of China) *et al.*, Zhonghua shuju, 1964 (Zhongguo zibenzhuyi gongshangye shiliao congkan (Series of Material on the History of Capitalist Industry and Trade in China)).

'You wei hulu shi zhi ge zongshanghui yizhi fouren han' (Letter Addressed to all the General Chambers of Commerce Urging them to Protest Unanimously against the Plan for the Protection of the Railways), *Shanghai zongshanghui yuebo*, vol. 3, no. 9 (September 1923).

Young, Arthur N., *China's Nation-building Effort, 1927–1937: The Financial and Economic Record*, Stanford, Hoover Institution Press, 1971.

Young, Ernest P., 'Politics in the Aftermath of Revolution: The Era of Yuan Shih-k'ai, 1912–1916', in Fairbank (ed.), *The Cambridge History of China*, vol. 12, *Republican China 1912–1940*, part 1, pp. 208–55.

Young, Ernest P., *The Presidency of Yuan Shih-k'ai, Liberalism and Dictatorship in Early Republican China*, Ann Arbor, University of Michigan Press, 1977.

Yu Ying-shih, *Trade and Expansion in Han China: A Study in the Structure of Sino-Barbarian Economic Relations*, Berkeley and Los Angeles, University of California Press, 1967.

'"Yuzhou cailijiashuihou yingxing yingge banfa an"', Shanghai zongshanghui tiyi' (On the Means of Prosperity and Renewal after the Future Reform Abolishing the *lijin* and Raising Customs Tariffs. Motion Presented by the Shanghai General Chamber of Commerce), *Shanghai zongshanghui yuebao*, vol. 3, no. 2 (February 1923).

Zen Sun E-tu, 'Sericulture and Silk Textile Production in Ch'ing China', in Willmott (ed.), *Economic Organisation in Chinese Society*, pp. 79–108.

Zhang Guohui, 'Shijiu shiji houbanqi Zhongguo qianzhuangde maibanhua' (The Transformation of the Chinese *qianzhuang* Banks into Comprador Enterprises during the Second Half of the Nineteenth Century), *Lishi yanjiu*, 1963, no. 6. pp. 85–98.

Zhang Guotao, 'Zhongguo yi tuolile guoji qinlüede weixianma?' (Is China now Safe from International Aggression?), *Xiangdao zhoubao*, no. 6, 18 October 1922.

Zhang Guotao, *see* Chang Kuo-t'ao.

Zhang Hanying, 'Lun woguo waiguo maoyi shibai zhi yuanyin' (The Causes of the Failure of Chinese External Trade), *Shangxue jikan* (Quarterly Review of Commercial Studies), Peking, quarterly, vol. 1, no. 1 (February 1923).

Zhang Kaiyuan, 'Xinhai gemingshi yanjiude sanshinian' (Studies over the Past Thirty Years on the 1911 Revolution), *Jinian xinhai geming qishizhounian xueshu taolunhui lunwenji*, vol. 3, pp. 2117–39.

Zhang Kaiyuan, 'Xinhai geming yu Jiang-Zhe zichanjiej' (The 1911 Revolution and the Bourgeoisies of Jiangsu and Zhejiang), *Jinian xinhai geming qishizhounian xueshu taolunhui lunwenji*, vol. 1, pp. 242–80.

Zhang Pengyuan, *Lixianpai yu xinhai geming* (The Constitutionalists and the 1911 Revolution), Taibei, Institute of Modern History, Academia Sinica, 1969.

Zhang Pengyuan, *see* Chang P'eng-yuan.

Zhang Yu-fa (Chang Yü-fa), *Qingjide lixian tuanti* (The Constitutionalist Groups at the End of the Qing), Taibei, Institute of Modern History, Academia Sinica, 1917.

Zhang Yulan, *Zhongguo yinhangye fazhanshi* (History of the Development of Modern banks in China), Shanghai, Shanghai renmin chubanshe, 1957.

Zhao Shixian, 'Junfa Wang Zhanyuan jingying gongshangye gaikuang' (The Evolution of Warlord Wang Zhanyuan's Industrial and Commercial Enterprises), *Tianjin wenshi ziliao xuanji*, no. 4 (October 1979), pp. 163–71.

Zheng Yifang, *Shanghai qianzhuang 1843–1947. Zhongguo zhuantong jinrongyede tuibian* (The Qianzhuang Banks of Shanghai, 1843–1947. The Evolution of Traditional Chinese Finance), Taibei, Institute of the Three Principles of the People, Academia Sinica, 1981.

Zhi Bing, 'Guoquan huifu yu jingji juejiao' (The Return of Sovereign Rights and the Breaking off of Economic Relations), *Shanghai zongshanghui yuebao*, vol. 3, no. 4 (April 1923).

Zhi Bing 'Shiju zagan' (Various Impressions of the Existing Situation), *Shanghai zongshanghui yuebao*, vol. 3, no. 2 (February 1923).

Zhongguo jindaimingren tujian (Illustrated Record of Famous Chinese of the Modern Period), Taibei, tianyi chubanshe, 1977 (1st edn, Shanghai, 1925).

Zhou Xiuluan, *Di yici shijiedazhan shiqi Zhongguo minzugongyede fazhan* (The Development of Chinese National Industries during the First World War), Shanghai renmin chubanshe, 1958.

Zhu Chunfu, 'Beiyang junfa dui Tianjin jindaigongyede touzi' (The Investments of the Warlords of the Northern Clique in the Modern Industries of Tianjin), *Tianjin wenshi ziliao xuanji*, no. 4 (October 1979), pp. 146–62.

Zou Yiren, *Jiu Shanghai renkou bianqian* (Evolution of the Population of Old Shanghai) Shanghai renmin chubanshe, 1980.

Index

356

Other books in the series

Maurice Aymard (ed.): *Dutch capitalism and world capitalism/Capitalisme hollandais et capitalisme mondial*

Ivan T. Berend, György Ránki: *The European periphery and industrialization, 1780–1914*

Pierre Bourdieu: *Algeria 1960*

Ferenc Fehér: *The frozen revolution: an essay on Jacobinism*

Andre Gunder Frank: *Mexican agriculture 1521–1630: transformation of the mode of production*

Georges Haupt: *Aspects of international socialism, 1871–1914*

Caglar Keyder: *The definition of a peripheral economy: Turkey 1923–1929*

Peter Kriedte, Hans Medick, Jürgen Schlumbohm: *Industrialization before industrialization: rural industry in the genesis of capitalism*

Antoni Maczak, Henryk Samsonowicz and Peter Burke (eds.): *East-Central Europe in transition*

Bruce McGowan: *Economic life in Ottoman Europe: taxation, trade and the struggle for the land, 1660–1800*

Ernest Mandel: *Long waves of capitalist development: the Marxist interpretation*

Michel Morineau: *Incroyables gazettes et fabuleux métaux: les retours des trésors américains, d'après les gazettes hollandaises (XVIᵉ–XVIIIᵉ siècles)*

Luisa Passerini: *Fascism and popular memory: the cultural experience of the Turin working class*

Henri H. Stahl: *Traditional Romanian village communities: the transition from the communal to the capitalist mode of production in the Danube region*

Lucette Valensi: *Tunisian peasants in the eighteenth and nineteenth centuries*

Immanuel Wallerstein: *The capitalist world-economy: essays*

Immanuel Wallerstein: *The politics of the world-economy: the states, the movements and the civilizations*